Panoptic Dreams

Sean P. Hier

Panoptic Dreams
Streetscape Video Surveillance in Canada

UBCPress · Vancouver · Toronto

20 19 18 17 16 15 14 13 12 11 10   5 4 3 2 1

Printed in Canada on FSC-certified ancient-forest-free paper (100% post-consumer recycled) that is processed chlorine- and acid-free.

Library and Archives Canada Cataloguing in Publication

Hier, Sean P. (Sean Patrick), 1971-
  Panoptic dreams : streetscape video surveillance in Canada / Sean P. Hier.

Includes bibliographical references and index.
ISBN 978-0-7748-1871-1 (bound); ISBN 978-0-7748-1872-8 (pbk.)

  1. Video surveillance – Canada. 2. Video surveillance – Social aspects – Canada. 3. Privacy, Right of – Canada. I. Title.

| HV8158.H53 2010 | 363.2'32 | C2010-903463-5 |

e-book ISBNs: 978-0-7748-1873-5 (PDF); 978-0-7748-1874-2 (epub)

Canadä

UBC Press gratefully acknowledges the financial support for our publishing program of the Government of Canada (through the Canada Book Fund), the Canada Council for the Arts, and the British Columbia Arts Council.

This book has been published with the help of a grant from the Canadian Federation for the Humanities and Social Sciences, through the Aid to Scholarly Publications Programme, using funds provided by the Social Sciences and Humanities Research Council of Canada.

Printed and bound in Canada by Friesens
Set in Stone by Artegraphica Design Co. Ltd.
Copy editor: Dallas Harrison
Proofreader: Kate Spezowka

UBC Press
The University of British Columbia
2029 West Mall
Vancouver, BC V6T 1Z2
www.ubcpress.ca

For Mary Elizabeth

Contents

Figures and Tables

Preface

In the early twenty-first century, the information and privacy commissioner of Canada, George Radwanski, started to argue that privacy, if not the defining issue of the next decade, is nevertheless an issue whose time for consideration has come (2002a, 2002b, 2002c, 2002d). Commissioner Radwanski's declaration partially captured the state of privacy protection legislation and advocacy work concerning public-area closed-circuit television (CCTV) surveillance in Canada. Throughout the 1990s, privacy advocates and civil libertarians became increasingly interested in developing a privacy protection policy framework for public-area video surveillance. Several legal cases and legislative investigations at the federal and provincial levels occurred from 1991 to 2004; the information and privacy commissioner of Quebec, Jennifer Stoddart, held public hearings on video surveillance in 2003; the Office of the Information and Privacy Commissioner of Canada (OPC), along with provincial Offices of Information and Privacy Commissioners (OIPCs), adopted standardized guidelines or minimal rules to encourage best practices in public-area video surveillance conducted by public bodies and law enforcement agencies by 2006; and Commissioner Radwanski launched a constitutional challenge to general video surveillance practices in public places in 2002.

Judged against the history of privacy protection legislation and advocacy in Canada and elsewhere, the current state of privacy protection concerning public-area video surveillance in Canada is remarkable. In a relatively short span of time, significant advances were made in institutionalizing CCTV surveillance privacy protection measures as information and privacy commissioners across the country struggled to adapt to rapid developments in imaging technologies in particular and the proliferation of new information and communication technologies in general. Although considerable amounts of time and effort were devoted to developing a standardized public-area CCTV surveillance privacy protection framework across the country, the privacy policy sector has been unable to standardize the ways that public-area streetscape CCTV surveillance systems are established (see Chapters 1 and 2 for an explanation of public-area streetscapes).

The privacy policy sector is composed of a group of individuals who are formally or institutionally affiliated with civil liberties organizations and information and privacy protection agencies. The privacy policy sector has enacted a number of laws, codes, guidelines, conventions, tactics, and practices to *regulate* the ways in which personal information is gathered and processed by public and private bodies and law enforcement agencies. In terms of regulating how video surveillance systems are established and administered, the provincial OIPCs constitute the primary institution responsible for ensuring compliance with provincial laws and privacy protection guidelines or minimal rule protocols.

The inability of the privacy policy sector to standardize how public-area streetscape monitoring programs are established – which is reinforced by a pragmatic approach adopted by Canada's privacy policy sector to encouraging voluntary compliance with a general set of privacy protection guidelines – has inadvertently contributed to the consolidation of two patterns or trends: not only has a diverse group of people staged various forms of resistance to monitoring initiatives, but also a range of different monitoring systems has been designed based on several different arguments and tactics. The ways that monitoring systems are designed pose implications for how they are used on a daily basis and whether they will realize their intended goals and objectives. Understanding the complexity of factors that inform how monitoring systems are established, therefore, is an important first step toward developing a comprehensive knowledge about streetscape video surveillance in Canada.

Although the number of streetscape monitoring programs in Canada has continued to grow since the early 1990s, few studies, academic or otherwise, have been presented to explain how monitoring systems are developed and how they are used (or where and why they are used). The dearth of information on streetscape monitoring not only limits academic understandings of policing, surveillance, and crime control strategies in Canada but also limits the extent to which members of the privacy policy sector as well as proponents and opponents of monitoring initiatives in specific Canadian cities can engage in informed dialogue and debate about the merits, limitations, and organizational designs of monitoring systems. With some of Canada's largest cities now running monitoring systems (Toronto, Calgary, Winnipeg, Halifax), empirically informed comparative data are long overdue.

Admittedly, publishing a book about Canadian streetscape CCTV surveillance in 2010 might be perceived by certain observers as a curious investment of time and labour. Compared with some of the cities of other countries, the number of Canadian cities that use CCTV surveillance cameras to survey streetscapes is not large, and CCTV surveillance cameras have proliferated in areas where members of the public frequently interact (grocery stores, gas stations, the workplace, public transit). Even public opinion polls, ranging from polling conducted by regional business improvement associations to academic institutions, consistently reveal a high level of support for camera-based surveillance. Considering the expanding number of privacy protection concerns that appear in most daily newspapers, an in-depth study of a few surveillance cameras on a few city streets in a few Canadian cities might seem decidedly passé.

Yet it is because streetscape CCTV surveillance in Canada is still in its infancy that the information and argumentation informing this book matter. Before his exit from public office, Commissioner Radwanski became fond of arguing that emerging CCTV surveillance initiatives in cities such as Vancouver, Kelowna, Hamilton, and Toronto represent the thin edge of the wedge that will irrevocably change our whole notion of rights and freedoms in Canada (2002a, 2002b, 2002c, 2002d). When Interim Privacy Commissioner Robert Marleau withdrew Commissioner Radwanski's appeal in 2003 (see Chapter 5), existing monitoring programs expanded, and new ones appeared across the country. With no indication in sight that streetscape monitoring programs will decrease in number or size, it is important to introduce comprehensive, empirically informed discussion and debate.

An early qualification is necessary. The intention of this book is neither to discourage nor to encourage streetscape monitoring programs in Canada. Informed by seven years of study, including hundreds of interviews and analyses of thousands of documents, the book explains how streetscape monitoring systems have been developed in Canada. Part of the explanation involves a critique of the privacy protection framework developed by Canada's privacy policy sector. Another part of the explanation involves assessing the governance structures that have inconsistently diffused across Canadian cities to influence the design of specific monitoring programs. A third part of the explanation involves examining claims-making activities and the social construction and contestation of crime, fear of crime, and social problems in various cities. The book offers no single explanation for why streetscape monitoring programs are adopted or rejected, and it offers no single recommendation for how city stakeholders and members of the privacy policy sector should act or respond to streetscape monitoring proposals. Based on the empirical findings of the study, a number of ideal and pragmatic recommendations are presented in Chapter 10, but the interpretation of findings avoids arguments about the inherent evils or the unqualified benefits of streetscape surveillance cameras.

Panoptic Dreams analyzes the main components of the rise of monitoring programs in Canada between 1981 and 2005. There are two main parts to the rise of streetscape monitoring. The first part concerns the grand narrative of establishing monitoring programs across the country. The grand narrative is composed of several individuals, forces, desires, events, dynamics, claims, activities, and interactions, with a particular focus on the emergence and uneven diffusion of governance structures that influence the design and implementation of monitoring systems. Integral to the grand narrative of how monitoring programs have been established is a set of patterns or trends influenced by formal privacy protection policies and informal municipal promotional tactics and designs. The second part concerns the local or regional stories that inform or underscore the grand narrative. The regional stories, which also involve a dynamic set of individuals and activities, begin in Drummondville, Quebec (see Chapter 3), and end in Thunder Bay, Ontario (see Chapter 9). Taken together, regional developments between 1981 and 2005 contributed to increasing standardization of the ways that monitoring programs were implemented across the country, and they continue to influence how programs are implemented today.

Given that the aim of the book is to document empirically and assess analytically the rise and diffusion of streetscape monitoring programs in the context of emerging governance structures formed within and beyond the privacy policy sector, an equal amount of analytical attention is not granted to every city discussed in the book. Rather, the aim is to account for the main developments in designing and implementing monitoring programs as they relate to the formation of privacy policy and organizational protocols. Design and implementation processes in some cities, consequently, are presented in their own chapters; processes in other cities are presented together in a single chapter.

Who should read *Panoptic Dreams*? The information presented throughout the book will appeal to anyone interested in surveillance, crime control, and the social construction of social problems, but the arguments were prepared with three audiences in mind: academics, privacy advocates, and citizens and stakeholders in cities running a surveillance program or thinking about introducing one. The material presented in the following pages is important, first, for academic and professional researchers because of the theoretical, conceptual, empirical, and policy insights developed in Chapters 1, 2, and 10 and illustrated in Chapters 3 to 9. However, the book is especially relevant for criminologists and sociologists, not least because a considerable amount of discussion is currently taking place about the professional status and public influence of criminological and sociological research activities. The debate is robust in the criminology literature. The growing consensus seems to be that criminologists and, necessarily, professional criminological knowledge exercise an insufficient degree of influence on public policy debates about crime and social disorder. The irony of the decline of practically useful criminological knowledge is that criminologists are experiencing difficulty communicating with policy makers at the very moment that everyday life is saturated with "crime talk" (Chancer and McLaughlin 2007; see also Simon 2007).

At least two reasons have been offered to explain the decline of publicly influential criminology. The first reason is the alleged absence of convincing, scientifically informed evidence. Austin (2003, 558) wastes no time sugar-coating what he sees as the problem: "Despite the annual publication of hundreds of peer-refereed articles and text books ... most studies being produced by criminologists are so flawed that they are essentially useless." While I am not ready to endorse wholeheartedly Austin's methodological remedy for this state of affairs – that is, to embrace an unadulterated conception of science and the experimental design – his wider point is a good one: there is something decidedly troubling about the difficulties that criminologists experience in disseminating criminological research findings to policy makers, police, politicians, and the public (see, too, Haggerty 2004 and Mathews 2009).

The second reason offered to explain the dearth of evidence that can be translated into policy discussion and planning is a perceived ideological bias in criminological research. According to this argument, a large number of criminologists has narrowed their specializations and oriented their arguments toward likeminded criminologists. It is more common to find ideologically charged debates and disagreements among criminologists, so the argument goes, than it is to find practically applicable research findings. The consequence has been a growing tendency among academic criminologists to maintain the intellectual boundaries of criminology at the expense of producing politically influential research.

Luckily for me, I am not a criminologist (at least not by formal training)! But the debates being staged among criminologists about the applicability of scholarly research activities are mirrored in the global debate about public sociology (see Burawoy 2004). Without wishing to delve into a long and nuanced analysis of disciplinary utility, I will say simply that academic researchers, be they sociologists, criminologists, or practitioners of some other disciplinary persuasion, are recognizing the limitations of abstract and inward-focused argumentation and analysis. This book was prepared with the intention of developing a relevant set of analyses that will satisfy academic curiosity and contribute to policy discussions and operational design protocols nationally, provincially, and regionally. In other words, the book is not only for academic researchers but also for members of the privacy policy sector and concerned citizens/stakeholders – be they advocates or opponents of monitoring initiatives – in specific Canadian cities.

The second audience of the book, then, is composed of policy makers, privacy advocates, and civil libertarians. The book is an explicit study of neither activism nor public policy, yet privacy protection advocacy and CCTV policy figure prominently in the analyses. Some of the interviews informing the findings were conducted with members of the privacy policy sector; it is clear that there is limited knowledge among members of the privacy policy sector about the empirical scope of monitoring practices and the nuances of how monitoring systems are designed and maintained. A brief overview of the scope of Canadian streetscape monitoring programs (other than the ones analyzed in the book) is presented in Appendix A, and detailed analyses of the dynamics of establishing specific monitoring initiatives are presented in Chapters 3 to 9. In addition to the rich empirical data presented throughout the book, Chapter 10 provides certain insights into some of the challenges facing privacy protection in the context of an institutionalized pragmatic policy orientation to public-area video surveillance.

The third audience for the book is composed of the general public, especially stakeholders and concerned citizens in cities running or considering a monitoring program. A characteristic shared by interviewees in the study – ranging from civil libertarians to concerned citizens – is a lack of understanding about the scope, structure, and utility of streetscape CCTV surveillance systems. The book is written in an accessible style to appeal to readers beyond a narrow academic audience, and it offers a candid examination of how streetscape video surveillance systems have been established in Canada. The research findings are important for cities and communities considering streetscape systems because, under certain conditions, CCTV surveillance programs might be able to contribute to the reduction of crime and other activities deemed undesirable by city representatives. Too often, however, unfounded or dubious claims about CCTV surveillance are made in the process of developing and promoting systems (e.g., that CCTV systems are always abused by people in positions of power, that such systems always reduce crime rates, that other cities have realized indisputable successes with CCTV systems). The book provides a set of empirical and comparative findings that proponents and opponents of streetscape CCTV surveillance alike can draw on to develop a more complete understanding of relevant issues and concerns.

Finally, an explanation of the title of the book is necessary. A considerable amount of surveillance theory generally, and theory about CCTV surveillance particularly, has reproduced some variation on the exercise of panoptic power (see Hier, Walby, and Greenberg 2006). Briefly, the panopticon is an eighteenth-century organizational design composed of a centralized inspection lodge that enables inspectors to watch over workers, prisoners, patients, and other persons of interest. The idea is that, because the people who are placed under surveillance cannot verify when they are being watched (the inspection lodge is protected by blinds and lighting), they develop strategies of self-discipline and control. That is, equipped with the knowledge that we could be under surveillance at any time, we regulate our own actions and behaviors to accord with the normative expectations of inspectors. As Foucault (1979) explained, the power of the panoptic function is such that inspectors do not even need to be in the tower: the physical/architectural design as a visible expression of power ensures the disciplinary effect.

The book is presented under the title *Panoptic Dreams* because, although advocates of streetscape monitoring programs across the country share the dream of a panoptic system of surveillance and disciplinary social control, the reality is that streetscape monitoring does not always produce its desired effects. The title is not intended to be a form of academic rhetoric or subtle political gerrymandering; rather, it is meant to signify the large gap that exists between claims making and promotional rhetoric, on the one hand, and the reality of what CCTV systems can do, on the other. The book focuses on the former rather than on the latter, with a special interest in documenting the shifting rationalizations for maintaining systems once in place and the implications that organizational design processes pose for applications and uses. Most proponents of streetscape monitoring systems are initially motivated by the dream of panoptic disciplinary power, and they aspire to develop surveillance systems to prevent crime and social disorder. Yet in city after city, the initial dream of enacting a preventative system of discipline and social control quickly gives way to shifting rationalizations for CCTV surveillance as a policing mechanism to detect criminal activity after the fact and to make people feel safer on city streets.

Beyond matters pertaining to the disciplinary potential of CCTV surveillance systems, the panoptic metaphor – alongside its popular cousin, Big Brother – also tends to suggest consensual efforts among powerful societal interests to establish mechanisms of surveillance. Rather than a seamless process of coalition building and structural collaboration among powerful societal interests, however, the story of streetscape monitoring programs in Canada is filled with conflict, negotiation, compromise, and adjustment. To be blunt, there is no homogeneous "them" that surveys, or aspires to watch over, a homogeneous "us." The mythical Big Brother figure that saturates political commentary on public-area CCTV surveillance is in actuality composed of a group of concerned citizens, politicians, police officers, and businesspeople who devote large amounts of their time to addressing crime, fear of crime, vandalism, and violence. Proponents of streetscape monitoring programs are not, of course, all the same: some have personal interests that are motivated by consumer interests, profitability, and the possibility of lower insurance premiums, but many more are motivated by a different set of interests that is less inwardly focused. Throughout the book, it becomes clear that there is no singular interest that propels monitoring initiatives, nor is there a linear path that CCTV advocates follow to design and introduce monitoring programs.

The book is presented in three parts spanning ten chapters. Part 1 is composed of two chapters that introduce the arguments and explain the methods used to enact the history of streetscape monitoring in Canada (Chapter 1); and that conceptualize public-area streetscape CCTV surveillance (Chapter 2). Part 2 presents four chapters that examine streetscape monitoring practices and privacy protection protocols in the province of Quebec and the rise of streetscape monitoring in four French and three Anglo-Canadian cities with the intention of illustrating the ways that monitoring programs have diffused based on formal and informal policy influences. The three substantive chapters comprising the majority of Part 3 examine successful and unsuccessful monitoring initiatives. The final chapter in Part 3 revisits some of the empirical, theoretical, conceptual, and political findings and presents a set of ideal and pragmatic regulatory recommendations oriented toward maximizing progressive trends in the diffusion process. The final chapter also presents responses to five critical public interest questions based on recurrent issues and dilemmas that emerged in interviews over the course of the investigation.

Acknowledgments

The data informing this book were collected in the period spanning April 2002 to July 2009. Along the way, several research assistants contributed to my wider project on surveillance practices and social problems. I foremost wish to thank Dan Lett, who worked on the project since 2005. Dan endured thousands of miles of travel, dozens of hours of negotiating interviews and entry, the nearly unbearable Ontario summer heat, and a good dose of administrative bullying to bring the project to fruition. I also wish to thank Kevin Walby, Grace Chung, Kate Hughes, J.P. Sapinski, Kara Taylor, Scott Thompson, and Beth Collins for research assistance.

I would like to thank Josh Greenberg for his collaboration on the project. Josh was a co-investigator on the main grant that made this book possible. I benefited from our many hours of discussion, and I thank Josh for participating in the data-gathering process.

I owe a special debt of gratitude to the hundreds of people who gave their time to speak with members of the research team, to search for documents, and to answer questions and clarify misunderstandings. Their ongoing support is appreciated.

I would also like to thank my editor at UBC Press, Randy Schmidt, for putting the book together. Finally, I thank the anonymous reviewers who vetted the manuscript. Each reviewer carefully assessed the first draft and offered many helpful suggestions to strengthen the final version. I appreciate the kind remarks and supportive comments offered on the initial draft.

The book is dedicated to Mary Elizabeth Leighton, who attended to childcare demands (with only mild protest and resistance) while the data for this book were collected, analyzed, organized, and presented.

Acronyms

7/7	7 July 2005 bus and subway bombings in London, England
9/11	11 September 2001 attacks in New York and Washington
Access Act	Act Respecting Access to Documents Held by Public Bodies and the Protection of Personal Information (Quebec)
APEC	Asia-Pacific Economic Cooperation
BCCLA	British Columbia Civil Liberties Association
BIA(s)	business improvement association(s)
BMOB	Bank of Montreal Building (Sudbury, Ontario)
CACP	Canadian Association of Chiefs of Police
CAI	Commission d'accès à l'information
CAU	Crime Analysis Unit (London, Ontario, Police Service)
CAUSE	Citizens' Advisory Committee for Urban Safety Enhancement (Vancouver)
CCAPS	Community, Contract and Aboriginal Policing Services
CCBA	City Centre Business Association (Windsor, Ontario)
CCCS	Coordinating Committee for Community Safety (London, Ontario)
CCRTF	City Centre Revitalization Task Force (Windsor, Ontario)
CCSERT	City Centre Security Enhancement Resource Team (Windsor, Ontario)
CCTV	closed-circuit television
CEDCSC	City's Economic Development and Community Services Committee (Brockville, Ontario)
C.O.P.P.	*Challenging Our Patrol Priorities* (Hamilton Police Service)
CP Rail	Canadian Pacific Rail
CPSC	Community and Protective Services Committee (London, Ontario)
CPTED	crime prevention through environmental design
CSA	Canadian Standards Association

DERA	Downtown Eastside Residents Association (Vancouver, British Columbia)
DKA	Downtown Kelowna Association
DSCAC	Downtown Surveillance Camera Advisory Committee (London, Ontario)
DSSC	Downtown Safety and Security Committee (Metro Centre, Sudbury, Ontario)
DTES	Downtown Eastside (Vancouver, British Columbia)
ETSSC	Eye on the Street Steering Committee (Thunder Bay, Ontario)
FASE	Friends Against Senseless Endings (London, Ontario)
FIPPA	Freedom of Information and Protection of Privacy Act
FOI	freedom of information
HDBIA	Hamilton Downtown Business Improvement Association
HPS	Hamilton Police Service
HWPSB	Hamilton-Wentworth Police Services Board
IVBIA	International Village Business Improvement Association (Hamilton, Ontario)
LDBA	London Downtown Business Association
LPS	London Police Service (Ontario)
LPSB	London Police Service Board (Ontario)
LVMAC	Lions Video Monitoring Advisory Committee (Sudbury, Ontario)
MADD	Mothers Against Drunk Driving
MFIPPA	Municipal Freedom of Information and Protection of Privacy Act
NCPB	National Contract Policing Branch
NSWP	Neighbourhood Safety Watch Program (Vancouver)
NW	Neighbourhood Watch (London, Ontario)
OIPC(s)	Offices of the Information and Privacy Commissioner(s) (provincial)
OPC	Office of the Information and Privacy Commissioner of Canada
OPP	Ontario Provincial Police
PDBIA	Peterborough Downtown Business Improvement Association (Ontario)
PIPEDA	Personal Information Protection and Electronic Documents Act
PMO	Prime Minister's Office
QANGO	quasi-autonomous non-governmental organization
QMI	Quality Management Institute
Quebec Act	Act Respecting Access to Public Documents and the Protection of Personal Privacy

RCMP	Royal Canadian Mounted Police
SARA	Scanning, Analysis, Research, and Action (committee in Windsor, Ontario)
SCAN	Surveillance Camera Awareness Network
SCC	Safe Community Coalition (Brockville, Ontario)
SQ	Sureté du Québec
SSHRC	Social Sciences and Humanities Research Council of Canada
STCC	Stop the Cameras Coalition (Peterborough, Ontario)
SPVM	Service de police de la Ville de Montréal
TAVIS	Toronto Anti-Violence Intervention Strategy
V2010-ISU	Vancouver 2010 Integrated Security Unit
VPB	Vancouver Police Board (British Columbia)
VPD	Vancouver Police Department (British Columbia)
VMAC	Video Monitoring Advisory Committee (Sudbury, Ontario)
WPS	Windsor Police Service (Ontario)

Part 1
Streetscape Monitoring Programs in Canada

1
Introduction

Since the 1960s, public-area CCTV surveillance monitoring systems have been used around the world to address crime, fear of crime, and perceptions of social disorder. Interest in CCTV surveillance cameras to monitor city streets and public transit has been especially strong in the aftermath of the 9/11 terrorist attacks on Washington and New York and the 7/7 bus and subway bombings in London. Drawing support from broader trends in the intensification of surveillance in everyday life (see, e.g., Ball and Webster 2003), the international proliferation of claims about the global terrorist threat not only brought into clear view the extent to which routine public activities were monitored by CCTV surveillance cameras before 9/11 but also provided a set of political opportunities for those wishing to expand the scope of CCTV surveillance in public areas after 9/11.

As international awareness of, and support for, CCTV surveillance increased after 9/11, software and hardware developers boosted their efforts to improve the quality and capabilities of video surveillance camera networks. The combination of technological advancement, declining costs, changing perceptions of policing and public space, and the heightened global security environment provided proponents of CCTV surveillance with a greater number of resources in promoting the utility of video surveillance systems and in downplaying (or in some cases trivializing) the importance of civil liberties and personal privacy. This was true for proponents of CCTV surveillance in large urban centres and in small rural communities alike. The 7/7 attacks further increased international interest in public-area CCTV surveillance, based on the indispensable role attributed to CCTV surveillance cameras in identifying the bombers. After 7/7, the international press consistently reported on Britain as the CCTV surveillance capital of the world. It is important to recognize, however, that public-area CCTV surveillance systems have also been established in cities across Europe and in the United States, South Africa, China, Japan, the Middle East, India, Pakistan, Australia,

New Zealand, and Brazil (Norris, McCahill, and Wood 2004; see also Kana-shiro 2008).

Canadian cities have not been impervious to global trends in establishing public-area CCTV surveillance systems. Over the past thirty years, proponents of CCTV surveillance in several Canadian cities have introduced monitoring programs to survey public areas such as city streets, municipal parks, pedestrian tunnel passages, and public transit. This book focuses on processes involved in establishing public-area streetscape CCTV surveillance monitoring programs in Canada, including the governance structures and privacy protection policy frameworks that accompanied the expansion of monitoring initiatives, between 1981 and 2005.

Public-area streetscapes encompass the entire area between buildings located on opposing sides of city streets. Elements of the streetscape include sidewalks, landscapes, utilities, roads, businesses, residential properties, rest areas, bus stops, vehicles, vendors, pedestrians, and cyclists. There are currently at least twenty-two Canadian cities running CCTV monitoring programs designed to survey public-area streetscapes. Most of the programs are located in the provinces of Ontario, British Columbia, and Quebec (see Appendix A). Compared to some other countries, the number of Canadian cities where CCTV surveillance cameras are used to monitor streetscapes is small. Canada is notable, however, for the number of cities where proposals for streetscape CCTV surveillance systems have been rejected – whether based on public and government discussion and debate, the mobilization of formal protest groups, informal networks of community resistance, short- and long-term funding concerns, or the enactment and execution of privacy laws and policy frameworks.[1] The events of 9/11 and 7/7 continue to influence dialogue and debate about, and justification for, the continuation and expansion of CCTV surveillance systems across the country. But efforts to develop monitoring programs have hitherto demonstrated that neither increasingly available monitoring technologies nor claims about the global terrorist threat guarantee the success of promotional efforts.

Several sociological and criminological investigations of CCTV surveillance in public areas were published in the past fifteen years. The majority of studies investigated CCTV monitoring programs in the United Kingdom (e.g., Webster 2009, 2004; Fussey 2007; Waples and Gill 2006; Gill and Spriggs 2005; Goold 2004; McCahill 2002; Coleman and Sim 2000; Norris and Armstrong 1999; Ditton and Short 1999; Fyfe and Bannister 1998, 1996). Research studies from the United Kingdom yield important insights into the promotion, implementation, applications, and effects of CCTV surveillance, but surveillance systems, and the responses that they elicit, occur differently across sociopolitical and cultural contexts (Hier et al. 2007).

Unlike the United Kingdom, for example, where the Home Office's City Challenge Competitions (1994-99), Crime Reduction Partnership CCTV

Initiative (1999-2003), and crime reduction funding programs entailed investing several billion pounds to support well over 100,000 public-area CCTV surveillance systems (Norris, McCahill, and Wood 2004; Mackay 2003), neither the federal nor the provincial governments in Canada have developed comparable initiatives for establishing public-area monitoring systems generally and streetscape monitoring systems particularly.[2] The absence of a government policy initiative to encourage monitoring programs in Canadian cities, combined with a set of structural, legislative, pragmatic, and historical challenges encountered by federal and provincial information and privacy commissioners (Bennett 2003), distinguishes Canadian monitoring programs in several respects. In contrast to the United Kingdom, where the central government's CCTV surveillance policy initiative entailed joint-funding schemes between the Home Office and community safety partnership networks (i.e., businesspeople, city councillors, police officers, media personnel) that contributed to the standardization of promotional, planning, and implementation processes (Coleman 2006; Coleman and Sim 2000; see also Webster 2004), Canadian systems have exhibited greater variation. Community partnership networks have been instrumental in setting up several Canadian programs, particularly concerning aspects of funding and the acquisition of monitoring equipment. But grassroots citizen groups, community organizations, and ordinary citizens have also played important roles in mobilizing public and government support for streetscape systems.

The Office of the Information and Privacy Commissioner of Canada (OPC) and the provincial Offices of the Information and Privacy Commissioner (OIPCs) offer a basic set of standardized quasi-legal guidelines for the use of public-area video surveillance. The guidelines consist of principles or key issues to assist federal, provincial, and municipal institutions and law enforcement agencies in deciding whether the collection of personal information by means of video surveillance is justified and, if so, how to build privacy protection into monitoring programs. The OPC's *Guidelines for the Use of Video Surveillance of Public Places by Police and Law Enforcement Agencies*[3] is a synthesis of OIPC's guidelines that were adopted early in the twenty-first century; it applies to public and private organizations and police and law enforcement agencies (e.g., the Royal Canadian Mounted Police [RCMP]) under federal jurisdiction. The guideline protocols offered by the OIPCs apply to legal institutions (e.g., police, city administration) governed by provincial and municipal privacy protection legislation; their primary purpose is to ensure compliance with standard provincial and municipal legislation.[4] The principles informing the federal and provincial guidelines include provisions for determining the necessity of video surveillance as a last resort and the importance of conducting privacy impact assessments prior to commencing monitoring activities; public consultations and the legality of monitoring practices; collection of personal information, the formation of surveillance policies, and design and implementation concerns; and matters pertaining to the access, use, disclosure, auditing, and disposal of surveillance records.[5]

The harmonization of a Canada-wide privacy protection framework on the use of video surveillance by public and private bodies and law enforcement agencies can be traced to privacy protection advocacy work that began in Quebec in 1991. In concert with the Ligue des droits et libertés, the Commission d'accès à l'information (CAI) ruled on the legality of the Sherbrooke Police Service (i.e., a public body) using video surveillance cameras to collect personal information about private citizens in Sherbrooke (see Chapter 3). Within a decade, the CAI's continuing initiative to promote best practices in the design and deployment of public-area CCTV systems, combined with an emergent "privacy pragmatism"[6] policy orientation promoted by the OIPCs of Ontario (Cavoukian 1998) and British Columbia (Flaherty 1998) in the late 1990s,[7] contributed to the formal adoption of guidelines applying to the use of surveillance cameras by provincial/municipal institutions in British Columbia (2000), Alberta (2001), Ontario (2001), and Quebec (2002).

Although the privacy protection guidelines have been addressed to some extent in most cities that developed streetscape monitoring programs between 2001 and 2005 (and to an extent in cities that established systems prior to 2001), the design and implementation process remains inconsistent. Canadian streetscape initiatives exhibit considerable variation in terms of the value placed on public consultation and how public consultation is defined; the role of city council endorsement, which is commonly linked to the creation of an auditing or oversight committee, to data-sharing agreements, and to multilateral decision making and responsibility-sharing arrangements; privacy impact assessments and what they entail; the importance attributed to signage; regularity and consistency in monitoring practices and information handling and disposal; and the type of information that informs needs assessment.

One reason why the design of monitoring programs remains inconsistent in the context of a Canada-wide privacy protection framework is that the principles informing the guidelines are neither as clear nor as comprehensive as they could be, leaving them open to multiple interpretations and adaptations. They are vague because OIPCs developed a pragmatic set of principles to be used in diverse communities facing different challenges and concerns. A second reason why the process is inconsistent is that compliance with both the content and the spirit of the guidelines is more voluntary than compulsory. A third, historical reason has to do with the ways that OIPCs have responded to specific monitoring initiatives, to the outcome of and public understanding pertaining to the OPC's effort to challenge the constitutional standing of public-area video surveillance in 2002-3 (see Chapter 5), and to the failure to foster or reinforce a cumulative, empirically informed policy framework capable of standardizing processes of establishing systems across Canadian cities. Finally, a fourth, supplementary reason concerns the legislative role of information and privacy commissioners in the country more generally. Canadian privacy legislation does not clearly specify the multiple regulatory, advisory, and educational roles that information and privacy commissioners play in privacy protection. In practice, privacy protection agencies as quasi-autonomous non-governmental organizations (QANGOs) tend to be proactive rather than reactive and strive to educate rather than regulate (Bennett 2003). Combined with the proliferation of privacy concerns in the twenty-first century (e.g., database security, no-fly lists, identity theft), and the competing demands placed on time and resources, information and privacy commissioners' harmonized privacy protection framework has hitherto failed to standardize how streetscape CCTV surveillance programs are established.

The pragmatic policy framework pertaining to public-area CCTV surveillance in Canada has exercised two discernible influences on the process of establishing streetscape programs in specific cities. First, it has partially enabled people from diverse social locations to stage various forms of resistance to monitoring initiatives. In some cities, people occupying positions of power (e.g., city councillors) have used particular interpretations of privacy protection guidelines and associated legislation to encourage the pragmatic formation of auditing systems, oversight committees, operational manuals, codes of practice, data-sharing agreements, and funding formulas; different interpretations by people in positions of power have been articulated to encourage city officials to opt out of administrative, oversight, and funding responsibilities. In other cities, privacy protection organizations and protest coalitions have directly challenged proposals to install surveillance cameras on city streets. Instances of resistance to streetscape monitoring initiatives, inside and outside city administrations, are significant because they call into question the efficiency, or at least the cultural specificity, that is typically attributed to community safety partnership networks in the promotion and implementation of monitoring programs (see Chapter 2).

The second influence concerns the way that the Canada-wide pragmatic privacy protection policy orientation, in conjunction with a wide range of situational factors at the regional, national, and global levels, has partially enabled proponents of streetscape systems to adopt several approaches to establishing monitoring programs. Despite idiosyncratic variability across Canadian cities (see Chapters 3-9), there has been a general diffusion of streetscape systems (Walby 2006). This diffusion entails the transmission of information about monitoring programs (e.g., funding, ownership, benefits, and effectiveness) through sources such as media reporting, CCTV promotional materials, police statistics, and program spokespersons to CCTV advocates in cities that potentially emulate part or all of existing systems.

Although the diffusion of streetscape monitoring programs has taken place regionally, provincially, nationally, and globally, the diffusion process is neither singular nor consistent. At least three key dimensions in the diffusion of streetscape monitoring programs can be identified. First, there is an ideational diffusion of monitoring programs that usually entails the dissemination of claims about the importance, effectiveness, and benefits of streetscape video surveillance. The ideational diffusion often takes place through news media reporting, but it also takes place through national and regional business improvement association meetings, local and international police association meetings, word of mouth, and, in the case of CCTV advocacy in Sudbury, concerted efforts to promote streetscape monitoring by distributing a range of promotional materials (see Chapter 4).

Second, there is an administrative diffusion that entails the transmission of operational protocols such as data-handling rules and codes of practice and organizational design structures such as oversight committees and auditing committees. The administrative diffusion does not easily graft onto the ideational diffusion of monitoring initiatives, and the data presented throughout the book demonstrate that the administrative design of monitoring systems has been influenced as much by the organizational structures of existing monitoring programs, not all of which were informed by formal policy provisions, as it has by formal privacy protection advocacy and legislation. This is to suggest not that formal policy protection measures are inconsequential for how monitoring systems are planned and promoted, but that they have not been the sole or even the primary influence on system design.

Third, there is a diffusion of the privacy policy framework that was enacted by the privacy policy sector. Formal privacy protection policy was itself a product of diffusion among privacy protection agencies at the federal and provincial levels, and it has diffused inconsistently with administrative structures to influence how systems are designed, for better and for worse. In some cities, the content and the spirit of the recommendations forwarded by the OIPCs have been used to refine operational protocol and organizational design by building privacy protection measures into monitoring systems. The latter refinements usually happen when city administrators become involved in multilateral decision-making and responsibility-sharing models introduced into planning processes. In other cities, however, the recommendations have been selectively used to reinforce operational protocol and organizational design already in place.

Hence, the uneven ideational and administrative diffusion of streetscape monitoring programs has intersected with the uneven policy diffusion to foster progressive and negative trends in how monitoring programs are established in Canada. On the one hand, certain progressive trends in establishing systems have emerged, whereby increased importance has been granted to consulting members of the public, submitting formal proposals to city councillors, and developing operational guidelines and codes of practice/terms of reference based on municipal and provincial legislation. On the other hand, however, certain negative trends have emerged, whereby proponents have selectively and uncritically drawn from privacy protection measures and existing governance structures in other cities to promote monitoring initiatives and appease OIPCs and dissenters (they also sometimes ignore developments in other monitoring systems altogether). The progressive and negative trends in the diffusion of monitoring systems across the country are not mutually exclusive, and they have been predominantly retroactive rather than proactive: proponents of monitoring programs have not always been ideationally inspired by existing Canadian systems (thereby encouraging a more consistent and cumulative administrative diffusion of monitoring systems); rather, efforts to establish monitoring programs have often entailed seeking out existing systems either to bolster rhetorical promotional support or to respond to various forms of resistance. In other words, what appears to be the ideational and administrative diffusion of streetscape monitoring programs across Canadian cities sometimes has more to do with efforts to consolidate already-existing promotional processes that diffused ideationally from non-Canadian regions (see Chapter 10 for a fuller discussion of the diffusion process).

The flexibility characterizing design and implementation processes matters. A small but growing body of international research examines how effective camera systems are at reducing crime rates, but more fundamental factors such as resource allocation, planning, composition of stakeholders, initial and ongoing funding, and system management also influence the degree to which expectations of monitoring systems will ultimately be realized. Proponents of Canadian streetscape CCTV systems enjoy considerable freedom in determining how monitoring programs are formed as well as the kinds of systems that are adopted and the specific administrative characteristics. This flexibility enables diverse and, at times, unpredictable reactions to monitoring initiatives, inside and outside local governments/city administrations, and it fosters opportunities for journalists, government representatives, businesspeople, privacy advocates, and other Canadians to adopt many influential positions on streetscape CCTV surveillance initiatives.

Beyond the general observation that Canadian monitoring initiatives have diffused from national and global sources, therefore, it is necessary to examine the nuances of how diffusion takes place, what exactly diffuses, inconsistencies in the diffusion process, and how privacy protection policies interact with the governance structures of specific programs. It is also necessary to examine how the organizational and operational structures of existing monitoring programs intersect with a range of local or regional factors (e.g., claims-making activities, funding availability, local personalities, revitaliza- tion activities, policing budgets, crime publicity, protest groups, media coverage, city involvement, CCTV effectiveness studies, the extent to which privacy commissioners and civil libertarians become involved) to articulate the importance and the dangers of streetscape video surveillance.

The aim of this book is threefold. Based on a Canada-wide investigation of public-area streetscape monitoring programs, its first aim is empirical: to understand the processes involved in designing, planning, and implementing streetscape CCTV surveillance programs in Canadian cities. By examining information on cities that have either implemented systems or attempted to implement them, the book provides analyses of the dynamics involved in establishing monitoring programs in Canadian cities of varying sizes and demographic characteristics, city- and coalition-based resistance to initiatives to establish monitoring programs, and the factors involved in rejecting or defeating proposals to install surveillance cameras to monitor city street- scapes. A comparison of thirteen cities with different histories and experi- ences enables a description of the complexity of relations involved in planning, promoting, and introducing monitoring programs.

The second aim of the book is to contribute a theoretical understanding of establishing streetscape CCTV surveillance programs. Over the past decade, a standard set of arguments has emerged to explain how public-area CCTV surveillance systems generally are developed. Indicative of so-called late- modern crime control strategies (Garland 2001), the basic argument is that international trends toward preventative crime control strategies have tran- spired, whereby older patterns of addressing the social dimensions of crime (e.g., poverty) have given way to situational controls and risk-based strategies to reduce opportunities for crime to happen. The intensification of surveil- lance in everyday life after 9/11 and 7/7 surely supports these general argu- ments. What is potentially problematic about this framework, however, is that it has been explained in the context of neoliberal managerial forces, prioritizing cost-effective, prudent business and community partnership networks in the *consensual* promotion and implementation of streetscape CCTV surveillance practices. Shared material interests, so the argument goes, bring together businesspeople, politicians, police, and journalists, who col- lectively lay claim to risks and dangers of public areas and city streetscapes and who, without difficulty, convince members of the public and other stakeholders that surveillance cameras are vital to ensuring public security and personal safety (see Chapter 2).

There is no reason to deny that material interests figure strongly in the process of establishing Canadian monitoring programs. The information presented in this book indicates, however, that a less essentialist and more comprehensive framework needs to be formulated to explain the diversity of interests in, and the inconsistent outcomes of, efforts to establish monitoring systems. By relying on managerial strategies as a point to begin analysis, regardless of how accurately the managerial framework explains CCTV surveillance programs in certain cities inside and outside Canada, we run the risk of overlooking the diversity of responses to streetscape CCTV surveillance initiatives in Canadian cities.

The third aim of the book is to develop a stronger set of resources capable of informing how monitoring initiatives are designed. Based on systematic and comparative empirical analyses, the findings are used to reflect critically on CCTV surveillance policy and design structure and to explore a number of arguments that will help academics, privacy advocates, and community-based interests to assess the strengths and weaknesses of establishing streetscape monitoring systems (see Chapter 10). The overall purpose of the book is not to encourage an either/or position on streetscape CCTV surveillance – that is, city representatives either should or should not establish monitoring programs – but to examine the different aspects of establishing monitoring systems that may be seen as progressive or negative, depending on where individuals are situated in the debate. The primary aim of strengthening understanding of streetscape monitoring programs is to foster a well-informed dialogue about the implications of, and different dimensions involved in, introducing monitoring programs to survey city streetscapes and to identify aspects of good practice in streetscape CCTV surveillance planning, promotion, design, and implementation.

The Study
Data for this study were gathered during a six-year investigation of how Canadian streetscape CCTV surveillance programs have been established (2003-9).[8] The process of establishing streetscape CCTV surveillance programs is conceptualized in two interrelated ways: first, in terms of the multidimensional decision-making and planning processes involved in efforts to develop specific monitoring programs, regardless of whether or not they are implemented; second, in terms of the general policy, promotional, and governance dynamics observed across Canada between 1981 and 2005. In certain cities where programs were introduced prior to 2005, operational issues as they pertain to design processes are also addressed.

The study was serendipitously set in motion when the Hamilton Police Service announced its intention to develop a CCTV surveillance system to monitor downtown streetscapes in Hamilton, Ontario. Early in 2002, the *Hamilton Spectator* reported that the Hamilton Police Service intended to install five CCTV surveillance cameras to survey downtown streetscapes. The initiative emerged in the context of a downtown revitalization campaign that played out in the local press as well as a publicized robbery involving an athlete competing in the Canadian Figure Skating Championships (see

Chapter 7). In April 2002, members of the Hamilton Police Service initiated a series of public forums to gather feedback on what they described as a CCTV surveillance proposal. Incidentally, the consultations took place after five cameras and eight monitors had already been acquired. I attended several of the forums and soon developed an interest in monitoring programs and practices.

The study began with two simple research questions: Where are public-area streetscape CCTV surveillance monitoring programs located in Canada? How are public-area streetscape CCTV surveillance monitoring programs developed? These initial questions were posed because, after consulting the international research literature, I discovered that the rapid expansion of video surveillance in some other countries was not taking place in Canada. It also seemed likely that community partnership initiatives to install surveillance cameras on city streets – in the absence of standardized state funding and legitimization – would attract considerable public outcry. It followed that there must be certain promotional dynamics involved in convincing members of the Canadian public (including police officers, politicians, businesspeople, and community representatives) that installing surveillance cameras to survey city streetscapes is a legitimate and necessary crime control measure.

After a cursory investigation of Canadian cities that were running monitoring programs, it became apparent that streetscape CCTV initiatives were neither always driven by police and government nor always met with public approval. Members of the research team[9] came across the case of London, Ontario, for example, where a citizens' group formed in response to the murder of a young person and lent symbolic support for the establishment of London's Downtown Camera Project (see Chapter 6). We also became aware of the streetscape CCTV system in Sudbury, Ontario, where surveillance cameras were installed to survey city streets without clear evidence of public consultation or engagement (see Chapter 4). We learned that a streetscape CCTV surveillance proposal was rejected in Brockville, Ontario, after a critical editorial campaign staged by local journalists helped to articulate a short-lived episode of civic resistance (see Chapter 8). And we discovered that a group called Stop the Cameras Coalition was instrumental in resisting plans to install streetscape cameras in downtown Peterborough, Ontario (see Chapter 8). Clearly, the unproblematic community partnership relationships theorized among police, politicians, members of the public, and the press in the CCTV literature did not uniformly apply to streetscape CCTV surveillance programs in Canada.

Prior to investigating the complexity of responses to streetscape CCTV surveillance initiatives, our first task was primarily empirical and demographic: to find out where streetscape surveillance programs were running in Canada, where they were being considered, and where proposals had been defeated or rejected. The scope of streetscape CCTV surveillance pro-grams was initially determined through comprehensive print media searches, Internet searches, and a questionnaire distributed to some Canadian police forces.[10] When members of the research team entered the field and began to conduct interviews (see below), streetscape initiatives were also discovered through a snowballing effect, whereby the existence of programs was con-veyed through word of mouth. The study revealed at least twenty-two Can-adian cities where streetscape CCTV monitoring programs were operating and dozens of cities where proponents of monitoring programs had either started to develop plans for public-area streetscape CCTV surveillance or, in some instances, where proposals to install surveillance cameras on city streets were rejected.

The primary data-gathering method involved semi-structured interviews in cities where streetscape CCTV proposals or programs had been initiated. Interviewees were initially identified through available documents as well as contacts made via telephone with police, representatives at city halls, and members of community organizations. The purpose of the interviews was to create a social history of how streetscape CCTV surveillance programs in Canada are established. Because no study of the development of Canadian monitoring programs existed, an oral history of monitoring systems was developed to supplement the limited number of documents that could be obtained via the Internet. The interviewing process, in turn, contributed to the collection of a large set of reports, proposals, organizational communica-tions, and operating guidelines.

In each city investigated, as many people as possible were interviewed to develop the most reliable set of findings as well as to produce a set of find-ings that would enable cross-checks and verification of claims and evidence. In practice, this meant seeking out interviews with representatives of com-munity organizations, shelters, police, politicians, mayors, program man-agers, businesspeople, lawyers, and privacy advocates. Flexibility in the interview selection process proved valuable: although almost all interviewees identified crime reduction as the main reason for supporting streetscape CCTV surveillance initiatives, there is considerable diversity in patterns of identifying which social problems require attention and what proponents of monitoring systems expect of CCTV surveillance.

Police, for example, primarily but not exclusively promote or endorse CCTV as a tool to assist in detection and investigation after a crime has oc-curred (and to provide evidence for court proceedings), although they often speak publicly about CCTV as a crime prevention tool. Conversely, members of business communities tend to support CCTV surveillance systems for purposes of crime prevention, as they are generally more interested in pre-venting damage to property than they are in policing damage to property after it has occurred (although, in discussions with business representatives, there was often a conflation between understandings of crime prevention and prosecution). And city councillors generally tend to support CCTV surveillance as a means to enhance the quality of downtown areas, which often means seeking to regulate panhandling, vagrancy, loitering, youth, nuisance, and potential vandals. While typical police, business, and council interests overlap in several respects (and intersect with industry interests), the general differences are important to keep in mind because they figure into processes of planning and funding monitoring systems.

The interviews, which numbered more than 300 and spanned more than forty cities, involved a combination of telephone and in-person semi-structured sessions.[11] Interviews ranged from fifteen minutes to three hours. All interviews were recorded, and key interviews were transcribed. The study began with the assumption that in-person interviews would be the most effective way to generate data, and we decided to visit every city running a monitoring program. We also reasoned that on-site visits would facilitate a familiarity with communities, streetscapes, local cultures, cameras, monitoring stations, and interviewees that could not be realized over the telephone. In the process of setting up in-person interviews, however, we discovered that several people were willing and eager to talk on the spot. We also discovered that telephone interviews revealed information about the history of monitoring initiatives that was equally as useful as information from in-person meetings and that they helped us to focus our time and efforts better by strengthening our understanding of key actors, events, factors, and interests prior to travelling to cities. In some instances, initial telephone interviews were sufficient to develop the social history of monitoring initiatives, while others required follow-up and in-person meetings with members of the research team.

Interviews were conducted using a semi-structured interview schedule. A standard set of questions pertaining to the origin of efforts to install monitoring programs, details of proposed or actual systems, privacy concerns, operational guidelines, regulation, and funding was used. The physical sites where in-person interviews were held ranged from alleyways in the Downtown Eastside of Vancouver to boardrooms, pubs, personal residences, and, in more than one instance, "on the go," talking while walking down city streets (and under surveillance cameras). Telephone interviews were conducted with people in their homes, in their offices, and, in more than one instance, in their automobiles.

In addition to interviews and analyses of available documents, we conducted analyses of the Canadian print media, the partial results of which appear in Greenberg and Hier (2009). And a large amount of material was gathered through freedom of information (FOI) requests directed at a number of agencies and organizations: the Office of the Information and Privacy Commissioner of Canada, the Department of Justice, Transport Canada,

Public Safety and Emergency Preparedness, the RCMP, and several municipal police forces and city administrations. The FOI requests produced thousands of pages of documents, ranging from municipal operational protocols to internal memoranda in federal government agencies.

The initial intention of the study was to present findings on every Canadian city that initiated efforts to develop streetscape CCTV surveillance monitoring programs. By the end of the primary data-gathering stage, however, it became clear that an empirically based, comprehensive portrait would be overwhelming to readers. Rather than sacrificing depth for breadth, the book examines the foundations of establishing CCTV surveillance programs in Canada. That is, it presents information to explain the main developments in establishing streetscape monitoring that form not only the bases for the ideational and administrative diffusion of monitoring programs across the country but also the privacy protection policy framework that developed in response to monitoring systems.

Most researchers are aware that the decision to leave the field and start preparing results is never easy. After years of intensive but partitioned interviewing, as well as full print media analyses and primary and secondary data collection and analyses, a sufficient amount of information had been collected to offer a useful and original assessment of establishing monitoring systems across the country. What follows is a set of findings that comprise the first comprehensive effort to understand and explain Canadian public-area streetscape CCTV surveillance monitoring programs.

2
Establishing Streetscape Monitoring Programs

Over the past decade, a small group of sociologists and criminologists started to examine the dynamics involved in promoting public-area CCTV surveillance systems. Investigations into what is commonly referred to as open-street, high-street, city-centre, and urban video surveillance systems led to many progressive insights that supplemented earlier investigations into the applications and effects of CCTV surveillance monitoring practices. What has been missing from the literature on the ways that monitoring programs are established, however, is a clear conceptual explanation for what public-area, and specifically public-area streetscape, CCTV surveillance systems actually are.

The first portion of this chapter explains CCTV surveillance and conceptualizes public-area CCTV surveillance systems. To provide some context for the empirical analyses presented in Chapters 3 to 9, special, albeit brief, attention is also granted to the use of video surveillance cameras by Canadian police forces in the 1970s and 1980s. Next, public-area CCTV surveillance and private-area CCTV surveillance are differentiated, and public-area streetscape CCTV surveillance monitoring programs are conceptualized. The focus is on monitoring programs designed to survey public-area streetscapes to differentiate formal streetscape monitoring programs, regardless of who operates or assumes ownership of them, from private applications of CCTV surveillance in public places. Examples of the latter include owners of private businesses who focus their cameras on public-area streetscapes, private citizens who use cell-phone cameras to capture images of public-area streetscapes, and security personnel working for private security firms who use surveillance technologies (e.g., camera phones) to record public-area streetscape activities.

The second portion of the chapter reviews the main explanatory frameworks that have been developed to account for how public-area streetscape CCTV monitoring programs are established. Reminiscent of trends in the surveillance literature generally (see Haggerty 2006), the most influential explanations for public-area CCTV surveillance have reproduced variations on the logic of panoptical power. That is, analysts have reproduced variations on the argument that CCTV surveillance monitoring programs represent an asymmetrical power relationship, whereby privileged members of society impose systems of surveillance on the general population for purposes of furthering their own material agendas and interests. There is some empirical justification for this argument, but a less essentialist framework that can account for the complexity of interests and relations involved in establishing Canadian streetscape monitoring programs is developed.

Conceptualizing CCTV Surveillance

CCTV surveillance refers to the use of closed-circuit television systems for the purpose of surveying a wide range of human and non-human phenomena. Since the 9/11 terrorist attacks in the United States, CCTV surveillance has been primarily associated with crime control in popular discourse. The applications of CCTV surveillance, however, range from wildlife research to surgery.

Technologically, CCTV systems differ from broadcast video, whereby video images and audio tracks are converted into signals and transmitted on an open-circuit system (e.g., traditional television). In CCTV systems, signals from a video source – a camera – are transmitted by direct connection through coaxial or fibre optic cables to receiving equipment (e.g., recorders, television screens, computer monitors) to create a closed circuit that is not easily accessible from outside the system (Matchett 2003). More recently, point-to-point wireless links have granted outside users easier access to monitoring networks. Although encrypted wireless systems are not theoretically closed-circuit systems, neither are they readily accessible to any interested party.

Surveillance by means of analogue and, to a lesser extent, digital CCTV was widespread in a variety of social locations by the close of the twentieth century. Yet it was not until the 1960s that images from a camera could be captured without requiring chemical processing. As early as 1956, Ampex introduced the Ampex VRX-1000, the first commercially available videotape recorder. It was priced at approximately $50,000 US, which effectively restricted its use to mass-media institutions. Close to a decade later, Sony produced more affordable reel-to-reel home technologies, and in the 1970s Sony's Betamax squared off against JVC's Video Home System (VHS) in the so-called format wars. As the 1970s came to a close, home videotape recorders gained mass-market appeal, and in the early 1980s digital video appeared on the market. Technological advancement, in other words, combined with growing market demand, facilitated the expanding applications of imaging technologies.

The potential benefits of newly emerging video surveillance technologies were not lost on Canadian police forces. Caught up in the intensification of policing technologies and bureaucratic expansion throughout the 1960s and 1970s, police across the country utilized video technologies. In 1973, for example, police officers in London, Ontario, used a CCTV camera to monitor a hotel room believed to be a common gaming house. In the late 1970s, Vancouver police started to videotape impaired drivers taking sobriety tests – based on earlier practices in Vernon, British Columbia. In 1980, the police in Calgary used a video camera to record an accused murderer's re-enactment of a crime scene (Metheson 1986). Beginning in 1983, the police in Ontario used video surveillance equipment in public washrooms to apprehend gay men cruising in so-called tearooms (Walby 2009). Cameras were used for general crowd surveillance by police forces in the late 1980s. And as video surveillance became increasingly popular, Canadian police forces used video cameras for a growing number of reasons, including lineups, eyewitness testimony, witness interviews, crime scenes, confessions, and cell-block surveillance (Metheson 1986).

What is notable about instances of police applications of video surveillance technologies throughout the 1970s and 1980s is that they entailed targeted, non-continuous surveillance practices. Whether overt or covert in nature, monitoring practices were temporary, event-specific, and primarily conducted in private (hotels) or semi-private (police headquarters) spaces. As technological developments enabled more effective surveillance practices in the 1980s, and as costs associated with monitoring equipment declined and the video surveillance industry expanded, the role of CCTV surveillance systems in policing practices changed. Caught up in wider transformations in policing that took place with advances in, and the incorporation of, information and communication technologies generally (see Haggerty and Ericson 1997), police use of video surveillance technologies quickly became routine rather than atypical (e.g., traffic lights, photo radar, patrol cars, interrogation rooms). Nevertheless, the culture of policing influences police applications of surveillance technologies as much as surveillance technologies influence the culture of policing (Manning 1992), and there is no reason to believe that police will adopt CCTV surveillance systems simply because monitoring technologies are available.

By the early 1990s, the use of camera-based surveillance technologies extended far beyond the institution of policing. Reminiscent of international trends in the use of visual surveillance technologies in public and private spaces, Canadians arguably normalized the ubiquitous gaze of CCTV cameras with the proliferation of camera technologies in airports, hospitals, shopping malls, corner stores, grocery stores, schools, government buildings, and, more recently, buses and trains. Of course, current camera-based surveillance practices are not limited to public and commercial spaces, and their applications are far greater than policing and security. Cell-phone cameras, spy cameras, wireless baby cameras, and Internet cameras are among the expanding variety of technologies available for use by ordinary citizens in the course of their daily affairs. Rear-view car cameras, residential home cameras, miniature covert cameras, and even personal mobile wearable computer cameras are growing in popularity. While surveillance camera technologies are still used primarily in the private commercial sector (Goold 2004), accompanying growing trends in private-sector, personal, and police camera surveillance use have been public-area CCTV surveillance networks.

Public-Area CCTV Surveillance

What is public-area CCTV surveillance? Although the terms "public" and "private" are widely and uncritically used in common parlance and academic research, their meanings are neither given nor static. Because the meanings of, and the boundaries drawn between, public and private change across time and space, it is necessary to understand the general notions of publicity and privacy as multi-faceted, protean, and variable.

In a generic sense, the term "public area" denotes open democratic spaces where people, irrespective of their identities or ascribed characteristics, are able to come together to meet, interact, associate, organize, or be left alone to pursue their individual or collective interests in a manner that is relatively unregulated or unrestricted. Public areas are relatively unregulated or unrestricted because most Canadians, for example, have come to rely on their constitutional rights to be able to gather, associate, interact, or otherwise enter into publicly designated areas independent of excessive intrusion by state agents, private interests, or other citizens, but they do not extend this expectation to unlimited freedoms to act or present themselves in any manner that they wish (e.g., nude sunbathing on a public sidewalk). In one sense, then, public areas are determined by the degree to which a person is able to gain access to certain spatial zones in the relative absence of interference by individuals or groups seeking to lay a proprietary claim to public space.

Although public areas are physical places – and most sociologists and criminologists refer to the physical dimension when they discuss public-area surveillance – that is not all they are. Public areas are also symbolically meaningful democratic spaces, domains, or spheres where associational life and sociability happen. In a world where public spaces (in the physical sense) are increasingly being replaced with publicly and privately funded roadways, shopping malls, and housing projects, and where the colonization of public space by private interests (e.g., the proliferation of billboards) has become commonplace, the symbolic value and emotive significance of public areas as physical meeting places and locations of democratic inter-activity have heightened. When government agencies, for example, act in the collective, public interest to preserve the physical and socio-symbolic dimensions of publicly designated areas, and when activists lobby the government to protect public spaces, a third – political – dimension of public areas is invoked. Here the government is understood to act on behalf of the public good, holding back private economic interests and market forces (some of which might be state driven). The preservation of the public interest as a political entity is, in this regard, oriented toward utilitarian ends that are spatial and symbolic in character.

It follows that the meaning of public areas is influenced by interrelated assumptions about physical, symbolic, and politically contestable space. This tripartite notion of public areas is presupposed by an understanding of, or implies a concomitant set of contrasting notions about, private areas. Like public areas, private areas are composed of physical locations, symbolically meaningful spaces of interaction (some of which relate to hermeneutic personal space around the body), and political struggles. In contrast to public areas, which are defined by normative ideals of democratic interaction and relative openness, private areas are characterized by normative restrictions and limited access, and they are conditioned by proprietary rights and claims to ownership. Whether by virtue of ownership or standards that are mutually (and symbolically) recognized and respected, private areas are relatively restricted spaces to which only a certain number of people are generally permitted access (and for which only a certain number of people set the rules of access). Private areas are relatively regulated in that they are based on standards of exclusion, but people are not entirely free to do what they wish in private areas (e.g., when development projects on private property contravene public zoning bylaws).

What becomes clear from the conceptual distinction between public and private areas is that the notions of public and private, although often understood in terms of idealized or fixed spaces of physicality, sociability, and politicization, blur into one another and intersect in multiple and sometimes conflicting ways. Not only are the meanings of public and private areas contextual, then, but they are also interactive and mutually constitutive. For example, members of the Canadian public regularly enter and use public parks, yet they expect to enjoy a certain degree of personal privacy in these public areas. It is not unreasonable to speculate that young lovers enjoying a picnic in a public park would feel that their privacy was compromised if a stranger sat a few yards away from their blanket and stared at them or took their picture.

To offer a more contextual example, residents in cities across Canada often support private businesses who fund CCTV surveillance cameras to monitor publicly designated areas from remote public or private locations (and, more often than not, monitoring stations in Canada are not accessible to members of the public). Sometimes, privately funded cameras purchased with the intention to monitor publicly designated areas are mounted on buildings owned by private businesses (spaces, moreover, that are sometimes rented with public funds). Interestingly, the common explanation for why citizens support privately funded cameras to monitor public areas is to protect their right to move in public spaces without excessive intrusion on their personal privacy and their right to be left alone in public (e.g., by excessive and, perhaps, aggressive panhandlers). To extend the example further, privately funded cameras on public streets sometimes have the technological capability to gaze into private residences and public offices – that is, into public and private spaces where it is conceivable that internal public or private cameras watch over employees and clients. The latter applications of CCTV surveillance could be understood as an affront to one's personal expectations of privacy or public interest, depending on the context and scale of surveillance.

Suffice it to say that common-sense understandings of public and private areas, while seemingly straightforward, are complicated. We live in a world of hybridized public and private areas and associations whose substance and meaning are constantly changing (Sheller and Urry 2003). The hybridity of public-private space makes it difficult to define in absolute or fixed terms what public areas are. On a theoretical level, one of the most fundamental distinctions that can be made between public and private conditions pertains to one's inner self/body versus the outer bodily space of the social and physical world (Madanipour 2003). On a practical level, however, assumptions about social, spatial, and symbolic fixity that are required to maintain an absolute distinction between public and private areas fail to recognize fully that the private citizen, her images, and her information enter public and private areas in complex and multi-faceted ways. Such assumptions also fail to recognize fully that intersections of what is normatively understood by public and private areas manifest in multi-faceted symbolic and material ways and that they pose implications for expectations pertaining to individuals' rights to be left alone physically, socially, symbolically, and informationally.

Given the explanatory difficulties associated with adopting an absolute position on conditions of privacy, their protective measures, and their concomitant states of publicity, a useful starting point to conceptualize public-area CCTV surveillance programs is to examine the articulated intentions of monitoring practices and systems rather than their specific applications to supposedly static public domains. Examining articulated intentions implies the need to develop an understanding of the various interpretations, claims, and values attributed to public areas and how they figure into planning, designing, and deciding whether or not to implement a CCTV surveillance system to monitor certain spatial locations. Most proponents of public-area CCTV monitoring programs agree on the physical or spatial parameters to be surveyed. What they fail to agree on is the degree of privacy that should be afforded in public spaces, how best to maximize citizens' democratic freedom to interact in a relatively unrestricted manner, the extent to which problems exist in these spaces, and the degree to which surveillance cameras will reduce alleged problems.

We are left, therefore, with two primary dimensions informing popular understandings of public areas – the spatial and the symbolic – and it is at the intersection of these normative dimensions that public areas become politically contestable. It is also at the political intersection of the spatial and symbolic dimensions of public areas where the analyses of establishing public-area streetscape CCTV surveillance programs commence. Because the significance of public-area streetscapes is not simply logically given on the basis of demarcating parameters of physical space, but also symbolically negotiated through shared meanings, it is important to understand how public-area streetscapes, their characteristics, and their supposed dangers are constructed or defined prior to being recognized as spatial locations that require the implementation of a CCTV surveillance monitoring program. Youth vagrancy, panhandling, and what are commonly identified as anti-social behaviours, for example, do not become problematic phenomena linked to certain physical spaces on the basis of their inherently defiant character. Rather, certain activities, their perpetrators, and the geographies where they transpire acquire particular meanings and, in the case of public areas, reputations through sociocultural processes of claims making, typification, and definitional struggle. As the information presented in this book demonstrates, a considerable amount of public-area streetscape CCTV surveillance promotional and decision-making activity in Canada involves normatively and ideologically charged claims about the problematic status of youth, homeless people, and public intoxication in certain spatial zones as well as the utility of video surveillance camera networks, practices, and images to deal with them.

By focusing the analyses on CCTV surveillance programs that survey, or articulate the primary intention of surveying, public-area streetscapes, monitoring of other public areas such as parks, parking lots, and public buildings where citizens commonly interact under the gaze of surveillance cameras is placed in the background of analysis. There are several reasons why the focus is on public-area streetscape CCTV surveillance programs. First, there are simply far too many CCTV surveillance practices in public areas (e.g., parks, schools, government buildings, municipal parking garages) to analyze and present in a coherent, concise, and sociologically convincing manner. Second, public-area streetscapes and their immediate surroundings are commonly attributed with diverse meanings and significance. Public-area streetscapes can be spaces of democratic interaction, and this possibility makes efforts to regulate certain forms of sociability (loitering), while encouraging others (shopping), significant. Public-area streetscapes also serve as people's homes and, in some instances, places of refuge. Third, public-area streetscapes are often necessary arteries of movement to gain access to essential services such as health care, banking, groceries, and education. In other words, a person can often avoid a public park or a public parking lot, but it is more difficult to avoid certain city streetscapes where essential services are offered. And fourth, by foregrounding streetscapes as public areas targeted for CCTV surveillance, insights can be gleaned into the ways that different spatial locations are imbued with normative meanings, reified in local policy, operational, or community discourse, and acted on through techniques of spatial regulation. That is, how public spaces in the physical sense take on symbolic meanings as dangerous locations through politicized claims-making activities can be explained. The analyses also show how proponents of CCTV surveillance seek to act on certain physical spaces and some of the people who use them, partially based on symbolically constructed images or moral geographies that emerge in the decision-making and planning stages.

Establishing Streetscape Monitoring Programs[1]

Three general approaches characterize research on public-area streetscape CCTV surveillance. The most common approach seeks to understand the application and effects of camera monitoring practices. Whereas a relatively small set of researchers measures the effects of camera monitoring practices on crime rates and the displacement of crime (e.g., Waples and Gill 2006; Gill and Spriggs 2005; Welsh and Farrington 2005, 2004a, 2004b, 2003; Gill 2003), a larger set of researchers theorizes CCTV surveillance as a means to extend disciplinary forms of crime prevention and social control (e.g., Ditton and Short 1999; Fyfe and Bannister 1998, 1996; Davis 1990; see also Garland 2001 and Reeve 1998).

As Hier et al. (2007) (see also Hier, Walby, and Greenberg 2006 and Hier 2004) explain, the metaphor of the panopticon has been especially appealing to researchers interested in the disciplinary effects of public-area streetscape CCTV surveillance. The panopticon is an architectural design proposed by Jeremy Bentham in the late eighteenth century to facilitate the supervision of prisoners from a central location. The idea of the panoptic prison consisted of an inspection tower surrounded by a semi-circular structure that housed inmates in separate cells. Each cell was to be made available to the unidirectional gaze of the inspectors, and the utility of panoptic supervision was based on assumptions of uncertainty. Prisoners would not be aware of when inspectors were watching, and a state of uncertainty induced by the visible and unverifiable expression of power ensured the normalization of discipline and self-control. The panopticon, in other words, was an expression of power that simultaneously totalized and individualized the population.

The physical character of public-area streetscape CCTV surveillance understandably invites comparisons to panoptic supervision. CCTV surveillance is regularly understood to involve a small group of people whose presence is inferred but unverifiable by those under the gaze of surveillance cameras.

A small group of inspectors, so the argument goes, watch over a larger group of people in an asymmetrical relation of power and social control. One of the most prominent arguments against the use of the panoptic metaphor, however, is that streetscape CCTV surveillance does not function as a mechanism to maintain a state of complete societal visualization. Investigations of daily CCTV control-room applications in the United Kingdom, for example, have concluded that CCTV surveillance operators tend to focus attention on certain individuals and groups (youth, homeless persons, black men) by using visual cues (clothing) to infer a person's moral character and whether his presence in a particular public place (a shopping area) is normatively appropriate (Goold 2004; Norris and Armstrong 1999; see also McCahill 2002 and Williams and Johnstone 2000). Whether moralized targeting practices are a feature of streetscape monitoring activities in Canadian cities is an empirical question necessitating detailed ethnographic analyses of control-room activities and organizational structures. Suffice it to say, however, that streetscape CCTV surveillance promotional efforts in Canada have tended to single out specific populations as problematic.

Whereas ethnographic research has documented some of the routine daily *applications* and *effects* of CCTV monitoring programs, a second line of inquiry has sought to understand and explain the processes involved in *establishing* streetscape CCTV monitoring systems (e.g., Hier et al. 2007; Hier, Walby, and Greenberg 2006; Goold 2004; Hier 2004). One of the most influential arguments pertaining to establishment processes was developed by Coleman and Sim (2000), who argue that the promotion of streetscape CCTV in Liverpool involved the social construction of moral visions oriented toward recasting and promoting the city as a safe place to do business (see also Coleman 2006, 2005, 2003a, 2003b). Drawing on media coverage and interviews with local business and government officials, Coleman and Sim explain how the establishment of Liverpool's CCTV network involved members of the City Centre Business Partnership constructing and promoting definitions of urban risk that would resonate with the public and reverberate in new crime control policies.

Coleman and Sim (2000, 626) conceptualize Liverpool's CCTV surveillance program in terms of neoliberal patterns of consumption and leisure to argue that the city's monitoring program was predicated on business interests of "attracting capital and people of the right sort." This sequence of processes, they continue, functioned as social-ordering strategies that sorted responsibilized and prudent individual consumers from undesirable outsiders, the latter necessitating containment, control, and ultimately symbolic expurgation from the imaginary boundaries of the city. They maintain that local elites, acting in unison, capitalized on effective coalition building and a priori privileged media access. This enabled the elites, say Coleman and Sim, to construct visions of urban renewal involving the marginalization of undesirable individuals whose images and identities could not be reconciled with the new, consumer-friendly, post-industrial Liverpool. Coleman and Sim conclude that a "consensual world-view" (636) pertaining to the implementation of Liverpool's CCTV program was consolidated on the basis of what amounted to structural-cultural advantage in the primary definition or preferred framing of urban risk and moral turpitude. Coleman and Sim's (2000) analysis offers an important step forward in the CCTV surveillance literature for at least two reasons. First, it effectively displaces the panoptic paradigm by exploring the discursive processes through which streetscape CCTV initiatives are consolidated. They provide a valuable case study concerned with the material and ideological dimensions of establishing streetscape CCTV programs, and they shift analytical attention away from the technological effects or applications of CCTV surveillance to prioritize the human interactions involved in establishing monitoring programs. Second, their interview data illustrate that business/elite interests occupy an important position in establishing and maintaining CCTV surveillance programs. Not only does this address consumerism as a significant dimension of streetscape camera surveillance systems, but it also suggests that monitoring programs are often tied to material relations and interests.

Notwithstanding these important and progressive insights, however, Coleman and Sim's (2000) framework is also problematic for at least three interrelated empirical, theoretical, and political reasons. First, by focusing attention on how local elite partnerships are constructed on the basis of ideological and material interests, they neglect the identities and possible roles played by people who do not occupy so-called elite social positions in CCTV surveillance promotion. Following Norris and Armstrong (1999), they contend that CCTV surveillance entails the exercise of power with "a number of dimensions" (624). Yet on the basis of their methodological strategies (interviews with official sources exclusively), they attend overwhelmingly to how the new business elite collaborate with police and political officials to further their material interests at the expense of undesirable others. The promotion of streetscape CCTV programs, however, sometimes involves the participation of ordinary people (e.g., members of citizens' initiative groups) whose interests and goals may or may not be consistent with the interests and goals of official institutional actors.

Second, on a theoretical level, the validity of Coleman and Sim's (2000) analysis remains contingent on a leap of faith concerning the extent to which a single (consumer) subject position was constituted in light of what may conceivably have been perceived by members of the public as the erosion of personal privacy and an infringement on the right to enjoy the unobstructed use of public space (Hier 2004). By relying on the explanatory purchase of the claims-making activities of primary definers, they invest power in the specific ideological contents of elite/media discourses. Not only does this reproduce the same kind of subject determinism found in asymmetrical conceptions of the exercise of panoptic power, but it also ignores the significance of possible counter-discourses, acts of resistance, and ultimately the potential failure of responsibilization strategies to consolidate and maintain high levels of public consent.

And third, politically, Coleman and Sim pursue a line of inquiry that essentially limits neoliberalism to an instrumental, materialist project devoted to the expansion of capitalist relations through the promotion of consumerist ideology. As they argue,

> The cameras were therefore crucial to ... the "social construction of suspicion" – a process that was increasingly left to emergent "primary definers" from the private sector. This involved an instrumental drive that *prioritized profit and loss* underpinned by the construction of a preferred and particular moral order built on the politics of inclusionary respectability and exclusionary otherness. (Coleman and Sim 2000, 629; emphasis added)

> Agents and agencies of the neo-liberal state are constructing the boundaries and possibilities of the new urban frontier while simultaneously engaging in a project of social control that will have far-reaching consequences for how we understand the meanings of public space, social justice, and the parameters of state power. (Coleman 2003a, 12; emphasis added)

While they acknowledge that the production of moral visions is central to neoliberal projects, the moral dimensions of neoliberalism are reduced to epiphenomena of private capital. In contrast to more complex formulations that conceptualize neoliberalism as entailing ongoing processes with contingent outcomes (e.g., Hall 1988), Coleman and Sim conceptualize neoliberalism generally, and CCTV surveillance specifically, as part of a coherent state strategy aimed at re-establishing (or consolidating) the conditions for sustained capitalist accumulation.

The Problematics of Establishing Streetscape Monitoring Programs

Similar to many other public policy issues, streetscape CCTV surveillance becomes invested with social meaning and significance through the many ways that social problems and their perceived surveillance solutions are constructed, understood, contested, and modified through claims and counter-claims. The role of mainstream news and popular media is of marked importance. Media outlets construct and purvey the images that embody and represent perceived social problems (e.g., crime, anti-social behaviour, nuisance, terrorism), and images of social problems signify social disorder or threat through the constitution of certain subject positions (e.g., street thugs, terrorists). These representational processes involve the mediation of a narrow range of images used to justify or rationalize the institutionalization and, at times, intensification of streetscape CCTV systems. They also specify how socially constructed problems become recognizable and actionable through the limits and modalities of media framing.

Prior to, and contemporaneous with, the production of rationalizing and legitimizing discourses in news media, however, images or typifications of social problems requiring CCTV surveillance solutions also result from definitional struggles among groups of people with different interests and goals. Although diverse groups of people may seek to influence or interpret public policy and/or public opinion on CCTV surveillance in some way, they are not all driven by material or instrumental objectives, and they do not all enjoy institutional positions of power and influence. Theoretical arguments pertaining to structural or cultural advantage as the independent variable in mediated definitional struggle are, consequently, insufficient to explain the dynamics of framing contests over social problems and CCTV policy solutions.

To formulate a sufficient framework to explain how Canadian streetscape monitoring programs are designed, it is important to attend to the varied alliances, rationalities, techniques, and antagonisms that characterize the promotion and implementation of monitoring systems in the context of the diffusion of governance structures and privacy protection frameworks (see Chapter 1). Developing certain streetscape monitoring systems involves the primary definitions of business partners, who identify specific segments of the population (e.g., panhandlers, prostitutes, loiterers) or specific spatial areas as problems requiring extraordinary attention and policing. But police, politicians, and ordinary citizens also attempt to establish monitoring systems using similar techniques of problematization that cannot be explained in terms of business and material interests. Moreover, attempts to establish monitoring programs are as much about enabling citizens to go about their lives free from real or imagined threats in public areas as they are about managing the population to serve certain materialist ends. This is not to suggest that attempts to enact monitoring programs are always benign; rather, there are many reasons involved in the promotion of monitoring systems, not all of which can be reduced to business interests and the pursuit of profitability.

One of the main challenges of investigating the ways that streetscape CCTV surveillance systems are promoted and implemented is to explain how knowledge about social problems is produced in different cities across the country. Knowledge about social problems not only includes ideas about criminality and other undesirable behaviour in public spaces but also entails a wide range of associations (people, geographies, activities, events, news production, bureaucratic structures) that figures into the promotion and contestation of streetscape CCTV systems – within and beyond the privacy policy sector. Knowledge, in this regard, is conceptualized broadly to entail systems of thought as well as systems of action.

Another challenge of the investigation is to explain how streetscape CCTV surveillance is negotiated as a viable response to knowledge about social problems. The problematics of establishing public-area streetscape CCTV surveillance monitoring systems involve "assorted attempts at the calculated administration of diverse aspects of conduct through countless, often competing, local tactics of education, persuasion, inducement, management, incitement, motivation and encouragement" (Rose and Miller 1992, 175). This analytical strategy requires an examination of the programs, documents, claims, myths, images, people, formal policies, informal governance structures, geographies, activities, moral justifications, and forms of evidence that embody and give effect to streetscape monitoring ambitions.

The chapters to follow describe configurations of persons, policies, structures, legislation, organizations, and events that comprise attempts to establish streetscape CCTV surveillance monitoring systems, and they examine the many ways that diverse groups of people attempt to make streetscape CCTV surveillance operable through systems of thought and action. By foregrounding the construction or negotiation of social problems and their perceived surveillance solutions, however, the argument is not that the production of cultural meaning is only about semiosis – that is, the intersubjective production of meaning (Jessop 2004). To be sure, semiosis plays a constitutive role in the production of social order, but processes of signification articulate with economic, political, legislative, and material forces that cannot be reduced to semiosis. It is a sociological truism that human meaning is socially constructed and discursively transmitted; it is also a sociological truism that processes of signification are embedded in material practices that are not reducible to discourse.

On the one hand, therefore, analyzing streetscape monitoring programs requires attending to the ways in which they are enacted as a viable response to perceived social problems. Especially salient in promotional activities are the ways that monitoring initiatives are indexed to the mediation of local, national, and global episodes that function primarily as warning signals for future crime risks. Signal crimes are typically unexpected and often violent events that become the focus of intensified attention because they serve as a proxy for engaging more nebulous popular fears and concerns (Innes 2004, 2001). Not only are signal crimes a main component of promotional efforts, but they are also often used to interpret the significance of, and sometimes to challenge, privacy protection principles, organizational safeguards, and existing governance structures.

On the other hand, it is necessary to focus on the politics of contention or resistance to CCTV promotional efforts. Especially salient in resistance activities are the ways that streetscape monitoring initiatives are indexed to the mediation of national and global episodes that function as signalling events and operate in a similar manner to signal crimes; they articulate some of the problems with streetscape monitoring systems, whether ethical, financial, or practical. The main national signal event in the history of public-area CCTV surveillance promotion was Commissioner Radwanski's Charter challenge in Kelowna (see Chapter 5). But global signalling events, such as the publication of the infamous Home Office report (see Chapter 8), also exercise an important influence on promotion and design processes, and they comprise part of the diffusion of surveillance policy and monitoring programs. Data are presented on pragmatic forms of resistance (e.g., use of privacy protection guidelines) as well as more direct forms of resistance (e.g., protest coalitions) to streetscape CCTV surveillance initiatives – not to examine how various people seek to liberate individuals who are targeted by CCTV surveillance programs from the oppressive power of camera networks but to better understand struggles against the government of individualization (Foucault 1982, 212). Put differently, the focus is on how various forms of resistance to streetscape CCTV initiatives represent struggles over knowledge about social problems and proposed surveillance solutions. They are not struggles, in other words, staged by one group of people against other groups who lay claim to problems and the merits of surveillance solutions.

Finally, the social construction and contestation of social problems and their perceived CCTV surveillance solutions take place in the cultural and structural context of antecedent governance structures – developed inside and outside the privacy policy sector – that accompanied the early ideational and administrative diffusion of streetscape monitoring programs across the country. That is, promotion and design processes in specific Canadian cities (particularly after 1996) were shaped by a set of heterogeneous influences that diffused unevenly and inconsistently to enable a variety of promotional and planning processes. As outlined in Chapter 1, the voluntary nature of compliance characterizing CCTV surveillance privacy protection guidelines adopted by the privacy policy sector has partially contributed to a variety of responses to social problems and their perceived CCTV surveillance solutions. But other influences, especially the promotional claims pertaining to the administrative design of Sudbury's monitoring program, have also strongly contributed to the development and dissemination of operational structures through networks of governance (see Chapter 10). Combined with a set of contingencies in the form of time- and space-specific national and regional signal crimes and events that contribute to the reinforcement, re-configuration, and interruption of the tripartite diffusion of streetscape monitoring programs across the country, processes of establishing Canadian monitoring systems are aptly characterized as an assemblage of factors that cannot be reduced to any single interest or intention.

Part 2
The Rise of Streetscape Monitoring Programs

3
Monitoring Programs in French Canada

The social construction and contestation of social problems on the streets of Canadian cities comprise a key dimension in the process of establishing streetscape CCTV surveillance monitoring programs. Emotive claims about the risk of violent crime, set against the backdrop of specific examples of past wrongdoing, are especially influential in promoting monitoring programs. The importance of emotion in the promotion of public-area monitoring programs is recognized in the CCTV surveillance literature (e.g., Hier et al. 2007; Hier, Walby, and Greenberg 2006; Hier 2004; Hay 1994). Less well understood, however, are the ways in which claims-making activities interact with the educational and regulatory efforts of privacy advocates and the emergence of privacy protection policy frameworks (but see Webster 2004).

The purpose of this chapter is twofold. The first purpose is to examine the emergence of streetscape monitoring programs in the province of Quebec. Between 1981 and 1993, the cities of Drummondville, Sherbrooke, and Hull introduced monitoring programs. The City of Baie-Comeau introduced a streetscape system in 2002, and the City of Montreal launched a monitoring program in 2004. Not only did the introduction of programs in three of these cities precede the proliferation of monitoring programs in the United Kingdom, but also they were largely if not exclusively overlooked in Anglo-Canadian promotional efforts in the 1990s. One consequence of the latter oversight was that the ideational and administrative diffusion of streetscape CCTV across Canada was forestalled by at least a decade.[1] A second consequence was that the Canada-wide privacy protection policy framework oriented toward fostering best practices in establishing CCTV surveillance did not develop to the extent that it could have.

The second purpose of the chapter, therefore, is to examine how a privacy protection policy framework for establishing and, to an extent, administering monitoring systems emerged in response to monitoring programs in Quebec. In the early 1990s, the Commission d'accès à l'information (the

Commission to Access of Information, or CAI), along with the Ligue des droits et libertés (the League of Rights and Liberties) and the Commission des droits de la personne (the Commission of Human Rights), ruled on the legality of recording images taken from public video surveillance cameras. The ruling was based on streetscape CCTV surveillance in Sherbrooke. The CAI's engagement with video surveillance in the early 1990s contributed to the formation of a policy protection framework that culminated in the adoption of *Minimum Rules Applying to the Use of Surveillance Cameras* in Quebec in 2002 (see Appendix 3.1).[2] These rules were designed as a guide to assist bodies governed by the Act Respecting Documents Held by Public Bodies and the Protection of Personal Information and the Act Respecting the Protection of Personal Information in the Private Sector to comply with privacy law, and the document represented a first step toward *regulating* public-area video surveillance practices. Yet in the aftermath of the privacy commissioner of Canada's unsuccessful constitutional challenge to public-area video surveillance (see Chapter 5), and the ensuing institutionalization of a pragmatic approach to CCTV systems across the country, the privacy protection policy response to streetscape monitoring programs assumed a conciliatory rather than regulatory orientation in Quebec and across the country.

Drummondville: Canada's First Streetscape Monitoring System[3]

The first public-area streetscape CCTV surveillance monitoring program in Canada was established in Drummondville. The city is located along the Rivière Saint-François in central Quebec. In 1920, the Hemmings Falls hydroelectric dam was constructed in Drummondville. Industrialization attracted immigrants, and population expansion facilitated further industrial development. Into the 1980s, the city's economy was primarily centred on textile production. Following a recession in the 1980s, Drummondville began to diversify economically, stimulating economic growth and population expansion. Today Drummondville is characterized by industrial growth and diversification, supporting a population of approximately 68,000 people.

The initial request to establish a public-area CCTV surveillance monitoring system was made in 1979. Members of the municipal council called for cameras to be installed in a frequently used pedestrian tunnel passage linking 10th Street to Mélançon Street. The underground tunnel (the tunnel of Sylvania), connecting a largely residential area with an area populated by several schools, enables pedestrians to pass under a train track. Following an assault that took place in the tunnel, representatives of the municipal council, in consultation with the Drummondville Police Service, called for the installation of cameras. Two cameras were installed in 1980, and they remained in the tunnel until 2008.

The cameras were visible to pedestrians passing through the tunnel, and images captured by the cameras were transmitted to a fire and police emergencies dispatcher who could monitor activity in the tunnel. Although images were available for viewing twenty-four hours a day, seven days a week, screens were monitored infrequently. Recordings of the images were not regularly maintained, but the system did have recording capabilities. The original purpose of the cameras was to respond to instances of physical threat and violence, but they soon became a passive instrument to survey minor youth transgressions and disturbances such as graffiti, loitering, and harassment. Public consultations were never considered prior to implementing the cameras. In fact, the tunnel cameras were installed prior to the creation of the CAI in 1982.

When the municipal council recommended installing tunnel cameras, they also called for the installation of two streetscape cameras in the downtown core to respond to troubles stemming from drinking establishments and problematic businesses. The streetscape cameras were mounted at the corners of Lindsey and St. Jean Streets and Marchand and Heriot Streets in 1981. Similar to images captured by the tunnel cameras, camera images from the downtown streetscape cameras were available for viewing twenty-four hours a day, seven days a week; they were neither constantly monitored nor regularly recorded, and no public consultation took place prior to installing the cameras. Images were transmitted to the public security office of the Drummondville Police Service, where a telephone dispatcher had access to monitors.

The downtown camera system was discontinued in 1988. One reason for discontinuing it was that the specific establishments that the cameras were intended to survey moved. Another factor was the changing character of the city. In the 1980s, downtown Drummondville (what is understood today as Old Drummondville) was the economic centre of the city. There were a number of banks and large businesses that attracted people into the core. Shifting demographics in the city led to a deterioration of the downtown area, and the arrival of large chain stores along the outer highway, such as Walmart, Zellers, and Costco, created problems for downtown businesses.

Economic and commercial flight from Drummondville's downtown core is significant. In a number of Canadian cities where streetscape CCTV camera monitoring programs have been established (Hamilton, London, Sudbury, Kelowna), it is business flight from downtown areas that contributes to perceptions of social disorder and necessary streetscape CCTV surveillance solutions. In Drummondville, however, it was business flight from the core that contributed to mitigating the perception of disorder in the core. Combined with a number of technical difficulties that created undesirable and unanticipated expenses for the city, and a feeling among city representatives that the cameras did not achieve the results envisioned, the program was terminated in 1988.

Currently, Drummondville does not run a streetscape camera monitoring system, and city representatives do not wish to revisit the issue. There have been recent developments with the tunnel cameras, however. From at least 2002 to 2007, these cameras were repeatedly vandalized. Until 2003, they remained under the jurisdiction of the Drummondville Police Service, which demonstrated continuing interest in passively monitoring the tunnel. In 2004, the Drummondville Police Service was replaced with the Sureté du Quebec (SQ) – Quebec's provincial police service. The SQ did not share an interest in monitoring the tunnel, and the cameras were neglected from 2004 to 2006. In the early portion of 2006, a group of young people allegedly vandalized the cameras to the point of inoperability. The tunnel remained unmonitored from 2006 to 2008, but the damaged cameras, and the vandalized signs notifying pedestrians that the tunnel was under video surveillance, remained in place.

In January 2007, representatives of the municipality became aware of the inoperability of the tunnel cameras, and the file was transferred from the SQ to the municipality. From January to August, the file pertaining to CCTV monitoring in the tunnel was passed around among city representatives until a news article appeared in *L'Express*, Drummondville's weekly newspaper. The article, "Insécurité et malpropreté: Des citoyens ont peur d'emprunter le tunnel sous la voie ferrée" (Insecurity and Uncleanliness: Citizens Afraid to Use the Tunnel under the Railway), centred on the experiences of a sixty-nine-year-old Drummondvillois who complained of young people loitering in the tunnel and strewing garbage along the walkway (*L'Express* 2007). The article also problematized the fact that signs indicated the tunnel was under police surveillance, but the cameras were not working.

Partially in response to the article, Steven Webkins, deputy directeur général in Drummondville, was charged with making recommendations to the municipal council concerning the future of the monitoring system. In November 2007, Webkins recommended that the city fund a new system to monitor the tunnel. He proposed installing two cameras on telephone posts outside each entrance to the tunnel that would be visible to pedestrians entering and leaving the tunnel. He also proposed installing a number of covert cameras inside the tunnel that pedestrians would not know about. The rationale for the hidden cameras was to police youth vandalism. Council approved the proposal and earmarked $20,000 to fund the project.

The new cameras were installed in February 2008. The monitoring system consists of two overt cameras outside each end of the tunnel and a number of covert micro- or pen cameras mounted inside the tunnel. Camera images are available for casual observation by staff members who work in the local fire hall. The monitoring screen is located in a high-traffic area, digital recordings are retained for thirty days, and tunnel activity is recorded twenty-four hours a day, seven days a week. Until November 2007, signs were posted around the tunnel indicating that video surveillance was being carried out.

With the introduction of the new monitoring system, however, the municipal council decided against posting signs to alert the public that CCTV surveillance was in effect. There were at least five reasons informing the decision not to post signs. First, the previous signs had been vandalized, and there was a considerable amount of graffiti on them. The feeling was that new signs would attract new graffiti. Second, council members agreed that signs would convey a false sense of security to pedestrians. Given that the cameras are not regularly or diligently monitored, the members of council did not want to convey the impression that the cameras are monitored. Third, councillors decided that members of the public do not need to be alerted to the cameras outside the tunnels because the cameras are clearly visible. Fourth, councillors decided that posting signs to notify people about monitoring inside the tunnel would defeat the purpose of the covert cameras. And fifth, privacy and public awareness were not considered serious issues by many councillors; the feeling was that one's right to privacy is surrendered in public.

Sherbrooke: Canada's Emerging CCTV Surveillance Privacy Protection Framework[4]

Sherbrooke is located in southeastern Quebec where the Rivière Magog and the Rivière Saint-François meet. Originally settled by anglophones in the nineteenth century, current-day Sherbrooke is composed mostly of a Catholic francophone population. A number of industrial sectors – micro-electronics and information technologies, environment, health – have experienced considerable growth in the city, facilitated in part by a large student population at four colleges and two universities. Until 2001, the city boasted a population of about 75,000 people. In 2002, a merger with Ascot, Bromptonville, Deauville, Fleurimont, Lennoxville, Rock Forest, and Saint-Élie-d'Orford increased the population to approximately 145,000 people.

Sherbrooke's experience with streetscape CCTV surveillance has unfolded over four general phases.[5] The first, conception phase ranged from 1989 to 1991. In 1989, the Sherbrooke Police Service installed four CCTV surveillance cameras on Wellington Street South, between King and Ball Streets. The Wellington Street South cameras were installed primarily to improve safety for women in the downtown core. They were also installed to police drug activity, vandalism, theft, and hit and runs in what was commonly understood as the bar district. The area under surveillance was populated with more than a dozen nightclubs and strip bars in the conception phase – a widely perceived source of nuisance, criminality, and social disorder. In April

1992, an additional camera was installed to monitor the parking area at the centre of city hall in an attempt to reduce or deter vandalism to parked cars.

The Wellington Street South cameras were mounted to pedestals on steel poles and hardwired to the police station with a rented cable from Vidéotron (Labréque 1992). The tube-shaped cameras rotated 270 degrees from left to right and 60 degrees up and down. The monitoring system enabled continuous surveillance of the designated areas through a small television screen located in front of the console of the communications officers in the communications room at the police station. The cameras operated on an automated monitoring system, whereby images from each camera would appear sequentially on the monitoring screen; an area would be recorded for thirty seconds before panning to and recording a new area. Overriding the automated system was possible, and the cameras had zoom capabilities. Images were recorded on videotape and retained for seven days. Until March 1992, the cameras were not accompanied by signage notifying members of the public that the areas were under video surveillance.

In 1992, the Ligue des droits et libertés initiated an investigation into the legality of the Wellington Street South cameras. The investigation marked the beginning of a second, justificatory phase of streetscape CCTV surveillance in Sherbrooke. Part of the investigation involved filing a complaint with the Commission des droits de la personne. It also involved a request for the CAI to rule on the legality of using CCTV surveillance cameras to record images of public places.

The Commission des droits de la personne's investigation, which commenced in February 1992, was informed by the principles set out in Quebec's 1982 public sector privacy legislation, the Act Respecting Access to Public Documents and the Protection of Personal Privacy (hereafter the Quebec Act). Following an in-depth investigation, which took into account the Canadian and Quebec charters of human rights and freedoms, the commission opined that video surveillance of a public road, independent of recording, could be understood as an extension of human visual surveillance. But continuous recording of public images, they ruled, represents a form of intrusion contemplated by the Canadian and Quebec charters of human rights and freedoms. To avoid abuse of camera monitoring, therefore, the commission maintained that recording should only be used in instances where an offence has been committed, is about to be committed, or is likely to be committed.

The investigation launched by the CAI concerned access to information as stipulated under sections 1, 54, 64, and 67 of the Quebec Act.

1   This Act applies whether the documents are recorded in writing or print, on sound tape or film, in computerized form, or otherwise. (1982, c. 30, s. 1)

54 In any document, information concerning a natural person which allows the person to be identified is nominative information. (1982, c. 30, s. 54)

64 No person may, on behalf of a public body, collect nominative information if it is not necessary for the carrying out of the attributions of the body or the implementation of a program under its management. (1982, c. 30, s. 64)

67 It shall be the duty of every municipal police force and each member thereof to maintain peace, order and public safety in the territory of the municipality for which it is established and in any other territory in which such municipality has jurisdiction, to prevent crime and infringements of its by-laws and to seek out the offenders. (1982, c. 30, s. 67)[6]

The matter under investigation was whether or not the Sherbrooke Police Service (a public body) was collecting personal (i.e., nominative) information on citizens and, if so, whether the collection of nominative information was necessary to carry out law enforcement duties. Members of the CAI concluded that, because the cameras enabled police to identify people walking or driving on the streets, they were collecting nominative information. They also concluded that video surveillance images were covered under section 1 of the Quebec Act.

Ruling on sections 1 and 54 of the Quebec Act was straightforward for the CAI. Greater difficulty was experienced in interpreting section 64 (and section 67) of the act: Do the police, as a public body, need to collect/record nominative information using video surveillance camera images to fulfill their duties of maintaining peace, order, and public safety? During the CAI's investigation, police representatives cited statistics suggesting that the crime rate had fallen from 125 instances of criminality in 1989 to 97 in 1992 (a 22 percent decline). The latter statistic purportedly represented criminality for the months of January to May. However, a follow-up, on-site investigation by the Ligue des droits et libertés inquired into the actual utility of the cameras. The police confirmed that, in two years of operation, the videotapes had been screened only once or twice and that declining crime rate statistics pertained to theft, impaired driving, hit and runs, and break and enters, not to violent crime (Labréque 1992).

In their final investigation report (Labréque 1992), the Ligue des droits et libertés concluded that the Sherbrooke Police Service was contravening section 64 of the Quebec Act. The ruling was consistent with the decision offered by the CAI. The league determined that declining crime rates were related to the presence of the cameras but not to the visual recording of surveillance camera data.

Interestingly, the final decision offered by the Ligue des droits et libertés cites video surveillance in Drummondville. The director of public security in Drummondville (as of 1992), Marcel Lefebvre, informed Alice Labréque that in an eleven-year period public-area camera images had been recorded only once or twice (recall that Drummondville cameras were not regularly recorded). Based on anecdotal evidence from Drummondville, therefore, combined with findings from the investigation in Sherbrooke, it was concluded that the Sherbrooke Police Service should record camera images only when a crime is being committed or is about to be committed. Following a meeting between Mayor of Sherbrooke Paul Gervais and city and commission lawyers, representatives of the City of Sherbrooke announced in October 1992 that they were in compliance and not recording general camera images.

Expanding and Intensifying the System
From 1992 to 1995, the old-model, tube-shaped cameras surveying Wellington Street South and the parking lot at city hall remained under the control of the Sherbrooke Police Service. In September 1995, the police replaced all of the old-model cameras on Wellington Street South with up-to-date models (four cameras). They also expanded the monitoring system by installing two cameras on Wellington Street North and a camera on the King Street Bridge.[7] Following the upgrade and expansion, camera images were routed to a newly established 9-1-1 emergency dispatch centre that also became the CCTV surveillance monitoring centre. Until 2004, 9-1-1 call operators whose primary responsibilities were to attend to police, fire, and paramedic emergencies passively monitored non-recorded camera images. After 2004, designated camera operators were hired to monitor recorded camera images.

The addition of three new cameras to the monitoring system ushered in a third, expansion phase of streetscape CCTV surveillance in Sherbrooke. The expansion of the system entailed adding several new cameras in the years spanning 1996-2002. Between 1995 and 1999, for example, six police-monitored cameras were installed in a variety of locations: a pedestrian passage between Wellington Street North and a parking lot (a camera was also added to monitor the parking lot at the intersection of King Street and Camirand Street), a back alley on Wellington Street North, inside and outside Société Transport de Sherbrooke (the Sherbrooke bus/train terminal), and at the intersection of King Street and Wellington Street. In 1999, a camera was also installed at the front of the courthouse, and the camera in front of city hall was replaced. Furthermore, in 2001, the Sherbrooke Police Service installed four cameras to monitor four city parks (primarily to discourage vandalism), and they installed a camera to monitor a major radio system antenna located on city property. By the end of 2001, the system supported nineteen public-area CCTV surveillance cameras, six of which were streetscape cameras (see Figures 1 and 2).

1   Public-area surveillance camera, City of Sherbrooke, Quebec

2   Streetscape surveillance camera, City of Sherbrooke, Quebec

The primary justification for expanding the CCTV surveillance system was the physical and sexual assault of three women on Wellington Street North in 1994. The assaults were compounded by non-specific concerns about drug dealing, loitering, assault, vandalism, and car theft in the downtown area (Mennie 1997). After the sexual assaults took place, the Sherbrooke Police Service began to focus on the downtown area. Among other things, they expressed concerns that municipal parking lots located behind Wellington Street were accessible only through alleyways. The police wanted to demonstrate to members of the public that steps were being taken to address fears about crime in the downtown area.

Throughout the expansion phase, the cameras remained under the coordination of the police. Camera images were passively monitored by 9-1-1 dispatch centre operators, and they were recorded only when an offence was committed or was likely to be committed. Because the camera images were not recorded, and because the police maintained transparent information handling and disposal protocols, the CAI's involvement was minimal during this phase of monitoring.

Toward the end of the expansion phase, however, the CAI took a renewed interest in video surveillance across the province. The CAI's renewed interest – which posed implications for monitoring practices in Sherbrooke – was sparked in 2001 when Quebec City hosted the Summit of the Americas. The summit took place between 20 and 22 April; it was the third summit (since 1994) designed to bring together democratically elected heads of state and government from the Americas to discuss the liberalization of free-trade barriers. Yet, despite the historical, political, and economic significance of the summit in Quebec City, the event is widely remembered for its intense security preparations and the protests that it attracted.

One reason why security measures were so intense in Quebec City was that the summit came on the heels of the infamous 1999 anti-globalization protests against the World Trade Organization in Seattle. Inspired by these protests, as well as similar protests in Prague and Montreal (staged the previous year), the so-called Second People's Summit of the Americas took place from 16 to 21 April in Quebec City. The collective action entailed upward of 150,000 people marching in the streets of Quebec City in protest of the summit, some of whom managed to tear down a security fence erected by security personnel (the so-called wall of shame). Security authorities responded to the removal of sections of the fence with tear gas and rubber bullets, allegedly targeting many peaceful protesters, media representatives, and medical personnel.

In the weeks leading up to the summit, representatives of the CAI anticipated that peaceful protesters and conference site workers would be subjected to an excessive amount of surveillance and privacy infringement. In an attempt to encourage responsible and fair information-gathering practices, they publicly expressed concerns about the privacy rights of peaceful and democratic protesters. They also expressed concerns that privacy advocates would be denied access to security documents and conference preparations (Commission d'accès à l'information 2001-2).

The CAI was especially concerned with security personnel's use of surveillance cameras to record protesters who were legally and peacefully demonstrating. To ward off the potentially negative consequences of indiscriminate video surveillance, the CAI published and promoted *Minimum Rules Applying to the Use of Surveillance Cameras* in April 2001 (formally adopted in 2002 – see Appendix 3.1). The *Minimum Rules* set out ten general privacy protection principles resembling Flaherty's (1998) recommendations in British Columbia (e.g., needs assessment, time-specific monitoring, non-continuous recording), and it stipulated in clear language that at any time the CAI – an organization that enjoys enforcement powers over public bodies within its jurisdiction as well as over the personal information practices of private businesses – may make public recommendations, issue an order, or initiate penal proceedings. The *Minimum Rules* protocol in essence provided the CAI with a coherent policy framework to apply to existing monitoring systems and to proposed ones.

The 9/11 attacks on Washington and New York motivated the CAI to take further action on the use of public-area CCTV cameras. Its specific concern was that the aftermath of the 9/11 attacks brought into focus the extent to which increasingly inexpensive surveillance technologies and capabilities were outpacing and, in some cases, eclipsing debates about the importance of privacy and the ethical dimensions of surveillance (Commission d'accès à l'information 2003). Searching for a reasonable balance between camera surveillance and the protection of personal privacy, in late 2002 the CAI announced plans to hold public meetings on the use of public-area surveillance cameras.

The meetings were the first and the last of their kind in Canada. Under the stewardship of then-CAI President Jennifer Stoddart, the hearings were designed to gather opinions of specialists and members of the public; to gauge the necessity for public bodies to resort to CCTV surveillance in public places; to establish better guidelines for the use of surveillance cameras in public places; to produce a report on the use of surveillance cameras by public bodies in Quebec; and to initiate dialogue and debate on a major public policy concern.

To prepare for the September 2003 hearings, Commissioner Stoddart appointed Commissioner Michel Laporte to co-ordinate the proceedings. A presentation document was sent to 150 organizations, along with an invitation to present their opinions and points of view.

The hearings were held in Montreal (22 September) and Quebec City (25 September); they started from the premise that the use of surveillance cameras invades the privacy of persons under surveillance (a premise that was subsequently rejected in Sherbrooke – see below), and much of the discussion centred on the necessity for video surveillance as a last resort to policing public places. Twenty-one organizations contributed to the dialogue, representing cities, health-care units, unions, interest groups, government departments, and the OPC.

The parameters for discussion were informed by Quebec's revised public-sector privacy legislation, the Act Respecting Access to Documents Held by Public Bodies and the Protection of Personal Information (hereafter the Access Act).[8] Similar to the inquiry held by the Ligue des droits et libertés in Sherbrooke in 1992, the CAI was concerned with the necessity of collecting confidential nominal information on citizens, as stipulated under sections 53, 59, and 64 of the Access Act. In line with the 1992 ruling, the CAI argued that video surveillance images that are not recorded fall outside the law on access. Yet testimonies gathered during the hearings indicated that public bodies regularly record and retain camera surveillance images. The testimonies gathered from the ministries and public bodies that participated in the hearings, a small number of which ran streetscape programs, revealed that at least 5,000 CCTV surveillance cameras were used in the province to record everything from traffic violations to activities taking place in washrooms used by kindergarten students (Laporte 2004).

Based on the findings of the proceedings, the CAI called on the government for legislation to enable it to act as an independent evaluation body. As an independent body, it would focus on generating alternative means of addressing real or perceived problems prior to installing cameras; on analyzing risks to personal privacy prior to monitoring; and on developing a set of unified rules that could be applied across cities and organizations. These principles or orientations, combined with the *Minimum Rules,* informed the adoption of *Rules for Use of Surveillance Cameras with Recording in Public Places by Public Bodies* in June 2004 (see Appendix E).

The release of the final report on the public hearings in 2004 coincided with the beginning of a fourth, intensification phase of CCTV surveillance monitoring in Sherbrooke. What is interesting about the intensification of monitoring in Sherbrooke is that, as the CAI adopted a stronger regulatory stance, with the ultimate intention of curbing the use of public-area CCTV surveillance across the province, the City of Sherbrooke intensified its streetscape monitoring and *recording* activities. Part of the intensification of recorded monitoring entailed appointing a municipal security committee to co-ordinate the monitoring program and to address the CAI's *Minimum Rules.* In contrast to the CAI's "privacy first" orientation, however, which is founded on its mandate to authorize video surveillance as a last resort, the committee adopted an explicit, even defiant, "security first" position.

The impetus for intensifying recorded monitoring activities in Sherbrooke was the murder of Julie Boisvenu. A twenty-seven-year-old resident of Sherbrooke, she was abducted, sexually assaulted, and murdered on 23 June 2002. It took police a week to locate her body near Bromptonville (north of Sherbrooke), and it took them several months to arrest Hugo Bernier (on 21 September). During the investigation, it was revealed not only that Bernier was on parole for a sexual assault conviction when he murdered Boisvenu but also that he had been stopped twice by police on the morning that Boisvenu was abducted. During both stops, which took place immediately prior to the time that Boisvenu left a downtown Sherbrooke bar, police officers noted that Bernier was acting unusual and that he was intoxicated (a violation of his parole conditions).

In the days following Boisvenu's murder, her father, Pierre-Hugues Boisvenu, inquired to city officials about why video surveillance camera images could not be used to assist in the investigation. He made the inquiry after representatives of the Sherbrooke Police Service publicly stated that recorded camera images could have saved Julie's life. City officials informed Boisvenu – a high-ranking official in the provincial government of Quebec – that the camera images were not continuously recorded (tracing back to the 1992 CAI ruling) and that, if the images had been continuously recorded, they could have helped to save Julie's life (or at least facilitated the quicker capture of her killer).

As the legal proceedings into the murder later revealed, Julie Boisvenu was abducted on Meadow Street, a main downtown artery near Wellington Street. At the time, this area was covered by city-owned streetscape CCTV surveillance cameras. Her vehicle collided with a fire hydrant on Wellington Street in the early morning hours of 23 June. Although the collision took place in an area within the range of CCTV surveillance cameras surveying Wellington Street, the police officers investigating her disappearance could not determine who was in the abandoned jeep found at the scene because the CCTV surveillance camera images were not recorded.

After Julie's murder, Pierre-Hugues Boisvenu and his wife made a donation to CALACS Estrie, which had an office in Sherbrooke.[9] Soon he formed a relationship with the head of prevention and awareness for CALACS, Josée Anctil, and he started to work on CALACS' annual fundraising campaigns. Boisvenu and Anctil also became involved with the Mont-Bellevue Neighbourhood Security Committee, which oversaw security matters in downtown Sherbrooke. The committee enacted training regimens for young people working in parks; they hired a theatre group to dramatize security concerns as a public-awareness strategy; they put in place two students from the police foundations program at the local college to patrol the downtown area and escort people to automobiles; and they began to examine critically the purpose and applications of the city's CCTV surveillance system.

As members of the Mont-Bellevue Security Committee focused their energies on a variety of public safety initiatives, debate about surveillance and security in the downtown core continued to escalate. In January 2003, for example, the Sherbrooke Police Service issued a press release explaining how the surveillance cameras were used to apprehend a drug dealer in the core. The service also assigned six new police officers to run interventions in the downtown core on a daily basis between 7 p.m. and 4 a.m. Simultaneously, debate among representatives of the municipality centred on the importance of recording camera images in light of Julie Boisvenu's murder. And in September 2003, *La Tribune* published survey results suggesting that 91.9 percent of Sherbrooke residents supported recorded camera images in the downtown area (Legault 2003). The latter claim was used repeatedly to bolster support for streetscape video surveillance in the years that followed.

It was in the context of growing support for recorded CCTV surveillance in the core, or at least the perception of growing support, that Pierre-Hugues Boisvenu and representatives from the City of Sherbrooke prepared to participate in the CAI hearings. Part of their participation involved depositing a memoir or dossier on the importance of recording camera images, and both submissions summarized discussions that were taking place in Sherbrooke in the months leading up to the hearings. Boisvenu's dossier encouraged the CAI to authorize the City of Sherbrooke to implement continuously recorded CCTV surveillance and to establish a surveillance vigilance committee to oversee the camera project. Boisvenu argued that recorded camera images would have discouraged Hugo Bernier from abducting and murdering Julie or at least facilitated his capture. Boisvenu also argued that the Human Rights Commission's position on recorded camera images, prioritizing the privacy of citizens over their safety, is extreme. Anticipating resistance from the CAI, he recommended that the CAI should at least authorize the city to run a two-year experimental pilot project to test the effectiveness of recorded camera images.

Similarly, the City of Sherbrooke's memoir encouraged a greater focus on monitoring and recording camera images. The city's dossier recommended that the CAI establish a clear position with respect to digital recording and storage of camera images. City representatives drew on the murder of Julie Boisvenu to bolster their case for recorded monitoring activities, and they explained how recorded monitoring was being seriously considered for some areas of the city. City representatives also used their dossier to bring attention to the civilian foot patrol that was established by the Mont-Bellevue Neighbourhood Security Committee; they argued that committing a greater number of resources to the monitoring system was a better solution than using student/civilian police forces to secure the downtown area.

The recommendations made by Boisvenu and city representatives for intensifying CCTV surveillance materialized the following year. In the summer of 2004, city representatives introduced the first phase of what they called a CCTV surveillance pilot project. The project was designed to measure the effectiveness of CCTV surveillance prior to seeking city council's approval (and authorization of funds) for a fully operational, long-term monitoring program. The primary goal of the pilot program was to generate data on the utility of camera surveillance in the downtown core. During the CAI hearings, it was revealed that the City of Sherbrooke and the Sherbrooke Police Service relied on anecdotal evidence to justify the use and placement of public-area CCTV surveillance cameras. City council agreed to fund two phases of the pilot project in the summer months of 2004 and 2005 to gather data, thereby addressing the CAI's stipulation that camera surveillance is necessary to achieve a specific, serious, and well-defined purpose.

The first phase of the pilot project entailed hiring a police foundations student to monitor sixteen cameras between May and August. During the first phase, continuous recording was added to the program. The city and the Mont-Bellevue Security Committee wanted to assess specifically how well a person could monitor sixteen cameras. They also wanted to understand the kinds of activities that camera operators attend to. Over a nine-week period, the cameras were usually monitored on Wednesdays, Fridays, Saturdays, and Sundays between 6 p.m. and 4 a.m. The student monitor recorded observations on standardized observation tables so that city representatives could understand the types of information, observations, and interventions being made. Before and during the first phase of the project, 9-1-1 operators continued to monitor the cameras, and the Mont-Bellevue Security Committee collected and summarized data on the effectiveness of camera monitoring.

At the end of the first phase of the pilot project, the committee concluded that the surveillance monitoring equipment and physical design worked well. However, they found that the activities observed by the student monitor were minor (bar fights, public drinking, drug use) and that it was not entirely clear (from observation tables) what the student was doing. Based on these findings, the committee expressed concern that the CAI would not approve a fully operational, long-term CCTV surveillance program that entailed continuous recording of camera images. As a result of the committee's reservations, city council decided to terminate the pilot project and withdraw authorization for the second phase of monitoring.

When city council announced the termination of the pilot project, Pierre-Hugues Boisvenu publicly challenged the decision. He argued that security concerns in downtown Sherbrooke are the responsibility of the municipality and not the CAI. Collaborating with representatives from CALACS and the downtown business community, he began to lobby the city to form a Public Safety Vigilance Committee that would have the sole mandate to oversee (and reinstate) the pilot project. Advocates of continuation of the project, including Police Chief Gaétan Labbé and the chair of the city's Public Safety Committee, Robert Pouliot, maintained that the system could be managed effectively to render transparent and positive results and that the CAI's general concerns about privacy could not jeopardize the actual safety of Sherbrooke's citizens.

In response to the perception of growing pressure, city council agreed to revisit the matter of video surveillance in the downtown core and hold a second vote in May 2005. At the meeting, city council took into consideration some recent favourable news coverage (including the 2003 public survey results), the lobbying efforts of Boisvenu and his colleagues, several requests for video surveillance from downtown business owners, and a small rally held in front of the courthouse leading up to the vote. In mid-May, city council reversed the decision to terminate the pilot program.

A newly appointed Public Safety Vigilance Committee co-ordinated the second phase of the pilot project. The committee developed out of the Mont-Bellevue Security Committee; it was composed of Pierre-Hugues Boisvenu, Josée Anctil, Police Chief Labbé, Gilles Marcoux, two city representatives (including the mayor of Sherbrooke), and a few commercial business representatives. The committee adopted the specific mandate to ensure safety in the downtown core, with a secondary concern for privacy rights and the CAI's mandate. In fact, in the aftermath of city council's decision to reinstate the pilot project, several members of the Vigilance Committee publicly proclaimed their willingness to act in defiance of the CAI's *Rules* (Legault 2005). Nevertheless, the point of the committee was to address the *Rules* and to generate evidence that recorded images are needed and useful.

The second phase of the pilot project stretched over fifteen weeks, from 16 June to 25 September 2005. In addition to 24/7 recording of seven cameras in the downtown core, passive monitoring by 9-1-1 call operators persisted, and a designated student camera operator was hired to monitor camera screens for thirty-three hours per week. The student operator performed twelve weeks of surveillance, and 9-1-1 agents covered designated monitoring for three weeks.

Live monitoring by the designated operator took place from 7 p.m. to 4 a.m. on Thursdays and Fridays, from 6:45 p.m. to 4 a.m. on Saturdays, and from 6:45 p.m. to 1 a.m. on Sundays (all recorded observations were transferred to 9-1-1 call-centre operators). The city also authorized the release of funds to purchase a digital recorder and multiplexer for the sixteen monitored cameras and to create a secure storage box in which to lock the surveillance equipment. To realize a higher degree of accountability and respond to the CAI's *Rules,* hiring and training protocols were developed, regulations for access to images were established, and a general set of directives for the system was adopted. Protocols were put in place, whereby the designated camera operator was required to fill in revised standardized observation tables during each shift, and call-centre (i.e., 9-1-1) agents were required to use a calling card each time an observation was transferred from the student monitor. The latter enabled better data gathering on instances of police interventions.

When the second phase of the pilot project concluded, the Sherbrooke Police Service produced a final report on the results (see Dubois and Mercier 2005). The document was sent to the Vigilance Committee and the CAI. In addition to preliminary descriptive commentary on the structure of the pilot project, the results are presented in three main sections: "Les observations et interventions" (Observations and Interventions), "Les demandes de visionnement des enregistrements" (Demands of Viewing and Recording), and "La qualité des equipments" (Equipment Quality). The results produced by the police are important for understanding the consolidation of the establishment process in Sherbrooke.

According to the report, 506 hours of designated monitoring took place over fifteen weeks. The designated camera operator recorded 172 observations during the monitoring intervals (by comparison, 9-1-1 operators made eleven observations during the monitoring intervals). Designated camera operators also made twenty-four observations that led to "police interventions with results" (observations made by 9-1-1 operators resulted in five police interventions). Police interventions entailed issuing tickets, making arrests, filing reports concerning public drinking/intoxication (nine of seventy-nine observations) and drug activity (six of forty-six observations), as well as investigating "suspicious persons" (seven of thirty-eight observations) and rendering public assistance (two of nine observations). Most police interventions took place at the intersection of Wellington Street South and Therrien Street, Grenouillere Station, and outside the bus terminal. Observations were distributed over the four days of monitoring, with the greatest number recorded between the hours of 12 a.m. and 4 a.m.

Members of the Sherbrooke Police Service interpreted the data on observations and interventions to indicate the usefulness of the pilot project, particularly where the designated camera operator was concerned. But what they deemed more valuable was the preventative success of the pilot project. In its second phase, they added the category "prevention" to their analyses. Prevention data represented instances where a suspect of a crime was identified, where police spoke to suspicious people, or where suspicious people were expelled from an area under surveillance. Of the 172 observations made by the designated monitoring operators, eighty-eight (51 percent) were recorded as instances of prevention. The majority of preventions were related to alcohol consumption and bar activity during the monitoring intervals between the hours of 12 a.m. and 4 a.m.

In addition to maintaining data on monitoring activities during the second phase of the pilot project, the city asked the police to analyze data on criminal activity in the downtown area between 2000 and 2004. In May 2005, the Statistics and Operation Data Section of the Sherbrooke Police Service used data from the General Index – Police Information Module compiled by the SQ to develop a portrait of criminal activity in the downtown core, on Wellington Street, and in Sherbrooke generally. The police found that, although crime rates in the downtown area remained consistent throughout the year, they peaked on Fridays, Saturdays, and Sundays between 8 p.m. and 4 a.m. (crimes against property peaked from 8 p.m. to 12 a.m., and crimes against persons peaked from 12 a.m. 4 a.m.). When they focused exclusively on Wellington Street, they found a disproportionally high number of assaults, property crimes, and drug-related offences on weekends between midnight and 4 a.m. in relation to its population density (Brien 2006).[10] The report attributed the increased activity in the core largely to a high concentration of bars and nightclubs.

The combined influence of the criminal activities analysis and the data compiled by the Vigilance Committee led city council to authorize the monitoring program. Since 2005, the system has continued to record images from cameras in the downtown area. Images are passively monitored around the clock by 9-1-1 operators on two monitoring screens (the number of operators changes throughout the day), and designated student operators have manned the cameras from approximately 6 p.m. to 4 a.m. in the summer months (June-September). The monitoring station is located in an isolated area of the police station, and recorded images are retained under lock and key for seven days. The Vigilance Committee convenes three times per year to review statistics, decide on placement of cameras, and ensure that CAI's *Rules* is adhered to. An annual report is produced by the Sherbrooke Police Service, which is sent to the committee and the CAI.

From 2005 to 2008, the Vigilance Committee continued to conceptualize the monitoring program as a pilot project. In April 2008, however, the committee decided to reconceptualize the monitoring program as the Surveillance Camera Vigilance Project. The main reason why the Vigilance Committee decided to stop calling it a pilot project was that they submitted documents to the CAI for years but received no feedback.[11] The committee also received data on monitoring from 20 June to 22 September 2008 that led them to formalize the program. Using specialized data analysis software, the police reported 19,752 observations (up from 10,007 in 2006) leading to 123 police interventions (compared with 129 in 2006). Despite the increased reporting of observations, however, the number of interventions with results remained constant, and alcohol- and drug-related interventions dropped significantly.[12] The Vigilance Committee accepted Mercier and Racine's (2008) recommendation to continue the program in the summer of 2008.

Sin City: Hull and the Promenade du Portage[13]

At the same time that the CAI released its ruling in 1992 on the legality of recording camera images, representatives of the City of Hull started to establish a streetscape CCTV surveillance monitoring program. Hull (a.k.a. Gatineau-Hull) is situated on the west bank of the Gatineau River and the north shore of the Ottawa River in southern Quebec (across from Ottawa). Before amalgamation with Gatineau, Aylmer, Buckingham, and Masson-Angers in 2002, the city's population was approximately 66,000 people. Today Hull constitutes the central business, government, and entertainment district of the Gatineau region.

A unique configuration of historical, legal/political, and geographical factors led to the installation of streetscape CCTV surveillance cameras in the downtown district of Hull in 1993. The primary reason was to police a set of undesirable behaviours associated with drinking establishments along the Promenade du Portage (tracing primarily to the mid-1980s). The multifaceted campaign to regulate drinking establishments that escalated in the 1990s, however, took root in the context of a long history of alcohol regulation in the city.

As Brosseau and Cellard (2003) explain, there were three discernible "peaks" in Hull's anti-bar regulatory activities in the twentieth century. Anti-bar regulatory activities involved "local elite" campaigns designed to close or control drinking establishments. During peaks in anti-bar campaigns, which traced primarily to differences in alcohol sale and consumption laws in Ontario and Quebec, drinking establishments would be closed or displaced for a short time, only to resurface when regulatory activities petered out.

The first peak came in 1918. From the early 1900s, laws regulating the sale of alcohol were more permissive in Quebec than in Ontario. The influence of fundamentalist Protestant churches in Ontario contributed to a more restrictive attitude toward alcohol consumption compared with attitudes that predominated in Catholic Quebec. Restrictive drinking legislation (e.g., hours of operation) in Ontario motivated Ontarians to frequent drinking establishments in nearby Hull, and when prohibition hit Ontario in 1916 the number of Ontarians drinking in Hull, and the number of alcohol-related arrests, escalated.

Prohibition touched the provinces of Ontario and Quebec differently. Whereas Quebec lived under prohibition from May 1918 to July 1919, Ontario endured thirty years of prohibition (1916-46).[14] Although prohibition overlapped in both provinces for a period of about fourteen months, the flow of Ontario-to-Quebec drinkers did not wane. Rather, a black market developed in Hull, whereby clandestine bars and bootlegging activities took root. Still, underground bars and the production of illegal moonshine were shortlived in Hull; public morality movements were strong enough to bring prohibition into effect by 1918, but they were not strong enough to make it stick.

One consequence of differential provincial approaches to alcohol regulation after Quebec repealed prohibition in 1919 was that large numbers of Ontarians headed to Hull to drink. This led to a sharp increase in the number of Ontarians arrested for alcohol-related offences. Through the 1920s and early 1930s, three-quarters of the people arrested in Hull were from out of province (Brosseau and Cellard 2003). The differential legislative environment also gave rise to increased surveillance of bridges: Ottawa police surveyed the bridges to ensure that Ontarians did not bring alcohol into the province.

Although the 1930s ushered in a more respectable night culture centring on jazz music, the decade also witnessed the resurgence of public morality campaigns. By 1936, citizens' organizations led by the Catholic diocese were demanding that policy makers end drinking on Sundays, that drinking establishments close at midnight, and that drinking at floorshows be banned. The second regulatory campaign culminated in 1940 with a petition signed by 17,000 people – the total number of voters in Hull – but its success was shortlived (Brosseau and Cellard 2003).

By the late 1940s, prohibition had been repealed in Ontario. The number of Ontarians arrested in Hull declined after 1946, but the city remained a destination for Ontario residents in part because the hours of operation for Quebec's bars were more liberal than for bars in Ontario (3 a.m. closing versus 1 a.m. closing). Developments in the 1960s, however, set Hull on the path that eventually led to the installation of streetscape CCTV surveillance cameras in 1993.

Zero Tolerance

Until 1965, the bars in Hull were clustered in the downtown area close to the Alexandra and Chaudière bridges connecting Hull and Ottawa. Concerns pertaining to the rise of Quebec nationalism motivated federal politicians to transform the industrial character of Hull and, concomitantly, to link better the city centres of Hull and Ottawa. One step toward achieving this goal was to open the McDonald-Cartier Bridge in 1965. The bridge contributed to the displacement of the central bar district in downtown Hull farther north to Saint Raymond and Saint Joseph Boulevards. But construction of the bridge was also part of a wider project to build several office complexes (Place du Portage) to facilitate federal government bureaucracy (more than 20,000 workers). It was believed that construction of the Place du Portage would revitalize the decaying downtown core and reduce nationalist tensions by increasing the number of federal employees in Hull.

When Place du Portage was completed in downtown Hull in 1979 – a four-phase office complex that today comprises the largest office complex in the National Capital Region – it left a large number of vacant buildings, many unemployed people, and a dearth of business activity. The complex also contributed to the displacement of a residential community of about 4,000 people. To stimulate economic activity in the core, Hull City Council began to encourage the establishment of several bars in the early 1980s. Within five years, a large number of discos and strip clubs opened along the Promenade du Portage (formerly Principale Street).

Throughout the early 1980s, city councillors and members of the Hull Police Service struggled with a number of issues associated with alcohol consumption and nightlife along the Promenade du Portage. The main issue was the difference in closing times for drinking establishments in Ontario and Quebec. It was widely accepted as fact that Ontarians would drink in Ottawa until 1 a.m. before heading to Hull to continue consuming alcohol. It was also widely accepted as fact that the thousands of people who frequented drinking establishments in the core between 1 a.m. and 4 a.m. on Fridays, Saturdays, and Sundays contributed to a sharp increase in criminality, rowdiness, and violence.[15]

Between 1984 and 1987, city councillors staged a series of debates centring on closing times in Hull. The debates entailed a ten-member committee set up to hear presentations on the possibility of reducing closing time to 1 a.m. The debates took place at the same time that bars in Hull paid for free shuttle service to transport patrons from Ottawa's Byward Market to Aubry Street in Hull on Thursday through Sunday, between 11 p.m. and 4 a.m. Demand for the shuttle service was so great that twenty-one buses crossed the river every fifteen minutes (Aubry 1987). Council debates also took place in the context of a number of promotions designed by Hull bar owners to attract customers to their establishments (e.g., free drinks to any woman who appeared in establishments without a bra, three-for-one drink specials, wet-T-shirt contests, mud-wrestling events).[16]

The campaign to reduce drinking hours in Hull lost intensity in 1988 following several attempts by city council to reduce bar closing times and several challenges staged by bar owners. The problems in Hull, however, did not end. A sequence of high-profile murders associated with bars had taken place in the core in 1984, 1987, and 1988; violence in the core after 1 a.m. was a major concern for police; and drug dealing became increasingly associated with the bar district. By the mid-1980s, local news media (the *Ottawa Citizen, Le Droit,* and the French-speaking television station CHOT) started to dispatch journalists to cover the activities of the bar crowd after 11 p.m.

News coverage of post-closing activities (fights, excessive noise, vandalism, public drunkenness) facilitated the perception of downtown Hull as Sin City: disorderly, dangerous, and drunk.

By the early 1990s, city representatives were voicing greater concerns about the city's image (the Museum of Civilization opened in 1989) and about the costs associated with policing nightlife in the core. City Council created working committees as early as 1985 that recognized the economic benefits of nightlife in the core but that also weighed profitability and job creation against the excessive costs of policing and cleaning up. Part of the campaign to clean up the core, which gained momentum in the early 1990s, involved liquor-licence suspensions, undercover police operations in bars, and efforts to develop police/bar-owner partnerships. It also involved an English-language media component to inform young Ontario drinkers that disorderly behaviour would not be tolerated.

The campaign to clean up the core culminated in the adoption of the zero-tolerance policy. It was implemented by the Comité du renouveau de la Promenade du Portage (the Downtown Renewal Committee) in 1991. It was composed of citizen, council, police, and city representatives. Zero-tolerance strategies to reduce problems on the Promenade du Portage included an increased police presence (new police officers were hired), parking and driving bans on certain city streets, a campaign to close several bars, reducing bar closing time to 2 a.m., closure of high-traffic streets at certain times of the night, and an aggressive ticketing policy. The last measure entailed issuing tickets for as much as $400 for public urination, excessive noise, and public intoxication.[17]

Part of the zero-tolerance policy entailed installing streetscape CCTV surveillance cameras along the Promenade du Portage. The Comité du renouveau de la Promenade du Portage started to discuss the possibility of installing surveillance cameras on the promenade in early June 1992. The committee president, Claude Bonhomme, visited Sherbrooke with then-Chief of Police Lorrain Audy. During their half-day visit, Bonhomme and Audy examined Sherbrooke's monitoring system and decided that CCTV surveillance would positively contribute to policing efforts in the core of Hull. Their decision was based on the argument that Sherbrooke's system had been introduced in 1989 to address similar problems facing Hull in 1992, that Sherbrooke's system had significantly reduced crime in the downtown area, and that it was a cost-saving measure for police.

In September 1992, Bonhomme and Audy reported to Hull City Council on the benefits of introducing a streetscape CCTV surveillance camera monitoring program in Hull. They argued that CCTV surveillance was cheaper than deploying police officers to the core and that it was a proven tool in crime reduction (based on experiences in Sherbrooke). Yet neither Bonhomme nor Audy championed CCTV surveillance as a crime control measure in the way that most other Canadian proponents of it have done. Unlike most advocates for CCTV surveillance, who tend to foreground its merits in crime reduction, they understood and explained CCTV as one of the many components in the fight to clean up the core. Bonhomme in particular identified the main problems as late closing times for bars in Hull and the excessive number of Ontario patrons. As a result, the monitoring program was poorly designed and implemented and lasted only six years.

City council accepted in principle the proposal to install surveillance cameras, earmarking $75,000 to purchase video surveillance equipment. The provisional approval was based on a tentative proposal for a three-camera system. It was understood that three cameras would be mounted to lamp-posts at the three busiest intersections along the Promenade du Portage and that the cameras would be controlled by the police. Bonhomme's committee was charged with developing a detailed plan for the surveillance system, part of which involved addressing the CAI ruling on recording camera images of public places.

In April 1993, the Comité du renouveau de la Promenade du Portage presented a report to city council that made a number of recommendations for curbing social disorder under the zero-tolerance policy. The report called for council to invest public money to install video surveillance cameras, to ban street parking, to increase policing on the strip, to improve lighting in parking lots, and to transform a vacant lot into a park. On 4 May 1993, council accepted some of the proposals made by the committee (banning street parking downtown between 12 a.m. and 5 a.m., increasing the number of police) but rejected several others. Among the rejected proposals was the CCTV surveillance system. Council concluded that the money needed to install a CCTV surveillance system would be better spent on lighting in parking lots and that the money needed to establish a video surveillance monitoring system should be invested in a match-funded revitalization project with Heritage Canada.

Following the rejection of some of the recommendations made under zero tolerance, Claude Bonhomme resigned as president of the Comité du renouveau de la Promenade du Portage. He argued that his work on the committee was valued neither by city council nor by the new mayor, Yves Ducharme, and that he could not continue without the support of his colleagues. Only days after his resignation, however, a woman's face was slashed with a broken bottle on the promenade in a random act of stranger violence. The publicity garnered by the attack, combined with the attention granted to Bonhomme's public declarations that city hall was not committed to cleaning up the core, led to a reversal of the decision not to install a CCTV surveillance system.[18]

In November 1993, four surveillance cameras were installed at four of the five streets that intersect with Promenade du Portage: at Leduc Street, Laval Street, Saint-Jacque Street, and Aubry Place. The camera locations covered a one-kilometre stretch of the street and the area surrounding at least twenty-four drinking establishments. Cameras were housed in semi-transparent domes, and signs notifying members of the public that the area was under video surveillance were posted. Camera images were transmitted to the police station, where 24/7 monitoring was available. Images were recorded by police officers only on an event-specific basis, and no police officers were ever assigned to surveillance camera duty. The police force, moreover, showed no interest in evaluating the system or producing reports for council; police conceived of the system as a dispatch tool that could help to prioritize 9-1-1 calls, reduce the demand for foot-patrol officers, and identify troublemakers on an ad hoc basis (Leman-Langlois 2003).

From 1993 to 1996, city council continued its attempts to reduce bar closing times and to have certain establishments' liquor licences revoked. These efforts met with mixed success: in the early 1990s, for example, two of the more high-profile bars shut down based on pressure by council and the police – including special hearings before Quebec's liquor licensing board. But the problems on the strip persisted. Brawls, vandalism, and drug dealing remained high priorities for police and council leading into 1996, and there was a general perception among police that the CCTV surveillance cameras did not work to deter undesirable behaviour. Bar patrons, moreover, would openly flout the cameras, and city representatives were particularly bothered by young women who repeatedly exposed their breasts in front of the cameras.

The difficulties associated with nightlife in the core came to a head on 3 October 1996 when an eighteen-year-old man was beaten by a group of six men. The beating was filmed by a news crew from CHOT and quickly came to signify the continuing problems on the promenade. Following the televised beating – which entailed the victim sprawled out on the street while the group of young men repeatedly hit him on the head with a skateboard – city representatives began to pressure the province to grant special powers to reduce closing time in Hull. In late 1996, the province announced that legislation would be changed to allow Hull City Council to close bars at 2 a.m. This was particularly significant because on 1 May 1996 Ontario changed the closing time of bars to 2 a.m.

Despite the decade-long efforts to clean up the core, therefore, the primary factor contributing to reduced disorder on the Promenade du Portage, and to the demise of the CCTV surveillance system, originated in Ottawa. Less than a year after Ontario increased closing time to 2 a.m., Hull City Council reduced closing time from 3 a.m. to 2 a.m. (in February 1997). Tellingly, the harmonization of closing hours quickly precipitated a decline in the number of predominantly English-speaking drinking establishments. Only eight months after harmonization, four bars near the strip closed. As a component of a broader strategy to ensure the closure of bars, city council began anonymously to purchase buildings and drinking establishments. These establishments were soon replaced with cafés and computer stores, and the decline of the bar district was met with a rapid revitalization project (sidewalk expansion, new lamps, building renovations). In 1999, the police removed the video surveillance system. Yet the red-and-white signs notifying the public that the area was under video surveillance remained for three more years (Leman-Langlois 2003).[19]

The Fires of Baie-Comeau[20]

The industrial city of Baie-Comeau is located along the St. Lawrence and Manicouagan Rivers in northeastern Quebec. Limited employment prospects for Baie-Comeau's population of approximately 22,000 people are mitigated in part by opportunities at the Manicouagan-Outardes Hydro-Electric Complex, one of several hydroelectric dams in the region. Restricted industry and educational opportunities motivate younger members of the city to migrate to larger urban centres (Montreal, Quebec City), and in recent years Baie-Comeau's population has started to decline.

Examining a single-camera streetscape CCTV surveillance monitoring program in Baie-Comeau is important not only to understand the empirical scope of monitoring programs in Quebec but also the ways in which the CAI responded to the city's monitoring system. The CAI's decision to hold public hearings in Montreal and Quebec City in September 2003 was partially motivated by an investigation conducted in Baie-Comeau in 2002. The City of Baie-Comeau installed a streetscape camera at the same time that *Minimum Rules* was formally adopted by the CAI. The city therefore became an important test site to apply *Minimum Rules,* and the investigation contributed to the formation of the CAI's policy position on the use of public-area monitoring systems in the province.

The establishment of a streetscape monitoring system in Baie-Comeau was set in motion in 2001 when the municipal police force received a growing number of complaints from shopkeepers in the Mingan neighbourhood (City Block 3)[21] about vandalism, graffiti, and loitering. This neighbourhood is located in the old Autry downtown region of west Baie-Comeau. The downtown core is a small hybrid commercial-residential area, offering a limited number of retail outlets and rented dwellings. Two parallel commercial streets, Rue Bosse and Rue De Puyjalon, constitute the boundary for the downtown area, where two-storey buildings (commercial on the main floor, residential on the second floor of some buildings) line the streetscape.

In March 2002, the directeur général of the City of Baie-Comeau, Jeannot Mainville, was presented with a proposal to install or consent to the installation of two CCTV surveillance cameras to monitor the area surrounding the alleyway running behind Rue Bosse and Rue De Puyjalon. Members of the Plateau Division of the Société de développement commercial (the Commercial Development Society) forwarded the proposal based on shopkeepers' claims that youth commonly loitered in the vicinity, that they harassed pedestrians/customers, and that, most of all, they used cardboard discarded by businesses to set fires in the alley.

The initiative to install surveillance cameras was also set in the broader context of claims about a growing crime rate in and around the Mingan neighbourhood. In 1999 and 2000, for example, police statistics indicated that City Block 3 accounted for 33 percent of total crime in Baie-Comeau; by 2001, police statistics indicated that the crime rate in the area had increased to 41 percent. Police attributed the growing crime rate there to gangs of youth who loitered in the parks on Rue Jalbert and Rue De Puyjalon and to a concomitant escalation in drug use and trafficking in and around the library and four local drinking establishments.

Representatives of city hall agreed in March 2002 to fund and oversee the installation of two streetscape CCTV surveillance cameras and related monitoring equipment.[22] On 3 May 2002, the first CCTV surveillance camera was installed at the intersection of Rue Jalbert and Rue De Puyjalon in the Mingan neighbourhood. At the same time, a post was erected in the alley that runs between Rue De Puyjalon and Rue Joliet with the intention of installing the second camera. Installation of the second camera was delayed when technicians encountered electrical problems.

Centrealarme, a private security firm that held the contract to manage 9-1-1 calls from the Manicouagan area,[23] administered the single-camera system used to monitor the area surrounding the corner of Rue Jalbert and Rue De Puyjalon. Camera images were routed to mini-computers that digitally recorded surveillance images 24/7. The password-protected mini-computers were stored in an office that was not accessible to employees of Centrealarme. Two agents were on duty at all times to answer 9-1-1 calls; the agents were able to view images on the surveillance monitors, but the CCTV surveillance contract with the city did not stipulate live-monitoring activities (Bilodeau 2002).[24]

On 3 July 2002, two months following installation of the first camera, members of the CAI learned through a Radio-Canada report that a CCTV surveillance camera was going to be installed in the alleyway running behind Rue Bosse and Rue De Puyjalon. Laurent Bilodeau of the CAI visited Baie-Comeau in late July to evaluate the monitoring system using the CAI's recently adopted *Minimum Rules*. The evaluation primarily entailed interviews with city, police, business, and social services representatives during the full-week, on-site investigation.

The *Final Inquiry Report into the Installation of a Surveillance Camera in the City of Baie-Comeau* (Bilodeau 2002) begins by considering Baie-Comeau's monitoring system in light of the CAI's 1992 findings in Sherbrooke. Recall the CAI's ruling that Sherbrooke was justified in its use of streetscape CCTV surveillance cameras to extend the normal visual capabilities of the human eye but that it was not justified in recording general public activity. The CAI permitted the Sherbrooke Police Service to record camera images when a crime was committed or about to be committed; it also ruled that the commission possessed regulatory powers to verify recordings without prior notice.

Bilodeau's investigation in Baie-Comeau concluded that CCTV surveillance monitoring generally conformed to the specific principles set out in *Minimum Rules*. However, beyond the minimal standards pertaining to public-area CCTV surveillance (and inspired by Commissioner Radwanski – see Chapter 5), Inspector Bilodeau sought to determine, in the context of the spirit of *Minimal Rules,* if the collection of surveillance camera images was indispensable to ensuring the safety of the citizens of Baie-Comeau.

Bilodeau's attempt to address empirically the spirit of *Minimum Rules* illustrates some of the limitations that privacy inspectors encounter when they rely on CCTV surveillance advocates' interpretations of, and concomitant claims pertaining to, protocols for minimal rules. In some ways, it also addresses some of the problems with the generality of such protocols published by information and privacy commissioners across the country. During the course of his investigation, Bilodeau learned that the city's main objective for using CCTV surveillance was to discourage or prevent youth criminality. Observing *Minimum Rules,* city, police, and business representatives informed Inspector Bilodeau that a variety of failed strategies (foot patrols, extra policing operations) to combat youth criminality had been deployed prior to installation of the streetscape CCTV camera. In accordance with *Minimum Rules,* CCTV advocates claimed that reasonable steps had been taken to address criminality in City Block 3 prior to using video surveillance and that multi-year police statistics indicated a clear need for establishing a monitoring system.

Bilodeau responded to the city's stated intentions for using CCTV surveillance by examining whether or not discouraging potential youth criminality was an appropriate justification for streetscape monitoring. Much of the investigation centred on the actual youth crime problem, its origins, and its solution. According to *Minimum Rules,* representatives of public bodies must conduct a study of the risks and dangers requiring the use of surveillance cameras, and they should examine alternative solutions to reducing risks and dangers prior to introducing CCTV surveillance systems. When the camera system was established in Baie-Comeau, advocates of the system noted a significant and growing crime rate in City Block 3 based on statistics tabulated by the municipal police force. However, Bilodeau's investigation revealed that City Block 3 borders on City Block 4; the latter is a sector of the city where a number of schools and housing centres for the Département de protection des jeunes (Youth Protection Services) are located. According to police statistics, City Block 4 had the second highest crime rate among the city blocks in 2001.

Problems with the interpretation of official police statistics are important. In addition to interviewing police, business, and city representatives who favoured video surveillance, Bilodeau interviewed social services workers who were not involved in establishing the monitoring system. He did so to try to understand better why an escalating crime rate was observed in City Block 3. The common understanding of the rising crime rate among social services workers pertained to a shift in drug consumption patterns in the city. Early in 2001, the SQ and the RCMP seized a large quantity of cannabis in the region. The seizure of cannabis (the drug of choice at the time among youth in the city) led to a spike in the street price. Faced with higher street costs, youth turned to phenylcyclohexylpiperidine (PCP) in the summer of 2001. PCP was cheaper and easier to find than cannabis, yet it also produced aggressive behaviour in users.

Importantly, in addition to facilitating a more complete understanding of the reasons why the crime rate was growing in City Block 3, interviews with social services representatives revealed contradictory evidence concerning the city's attempt to explore alternative strategies to fight crime. The representatives interviewed in the investigation were not able to confirm an escalation in police foot patrols prior to installation of the surveillance camera, and they were not able to support the argument that everything had been done to address the perceived problems in City Blocks 3 and 4. Members of the downtown community associated with social services argued that community consultations would have produced a number of alternative, community-based strategies that could have been put in place before turning to CCTV surveillance.[25]

Although city and community representatives failed to agree on the solutions to problems faced in the city, they did agree on the problematic nature of policing in the city. At the same time that PCP was circulating among youth in and around City Blocks 3 and 4, the municipal police force was being transformed. In 2002, the minister of public safety under the Parti Québécois, Serge Ménard, promised municipal police services in the province that they would benefit financially by renting police services from the SQ rather than maintaining their own police services. In June 2002, all of the towns in the province east of Quebec City "shifted from blue to green" and subscribed to the SQ. What this meant for Baie-Comeau was a sharp decline in the perceived presence and effectiveness of the police service.

Prior to incorporation of the SQ, Baie-Comeau's municipal police force was composed of five patrols and thirty-five members. After incorporation of the SQ, six patrols composed of thirty-seven members were responsible for the entire Manicouagan territory. In practical terms, this meant that the new police force was responsible for policing a much larger area, yet the size of and the funding for the new police force were similar to that of the old ones. Coupled with the fact that crime activity tends to concentrate in certain towns (e.g., Chute-aux Outardes), it is believed that the effectiveness of the policing services in Baie-Comeau was diminished with introduction of the SQ.

Beginning from the CAI's foundational orientation that surveillance cameras constitute an intrusion into the private lives of people under surveillance, the final investigation report concluded that the City of Baie-Comeau observed many of the stipulations set out in *Minimum Rules* but that it was not justified in using CCTV surveillance to monitor public space. This conclusion was based on the argument that the collection of video surveillance images must be proven to be indispensable for ensuring the security of citizens. Bilodeau maintained that neither the city nor social services representatives had explored alternative means to address the problems experienced in the city. Despite his critical comments on social services, however, the investigation of CCTV surveillance centred on the city's actions, not on the activities of social services agencies.

In September 2002, a copy of the preliminary report was sent to the mayor of Baie-Comeau and to city hall to solicit feedback. The comments returned by the city clerk and the director of public security, fire division, asserted that Inspector Bilodeau falsely claimed that alternative strategies had not been employed prior to installing the surveillance camera and that a displacement effect had occurred.[26] City respondents also pointed out that, after Bilodeau's visit, they had posted signs notifying the public that the area was under video surveillance (responding to one of several problems flagged by Bilodeau in his assessment).

Still, the reactionary commentary failed to address Bilodeau's argument that the city had failed to address the first stipulation of *Minimum Rules:* to conduct a study of the risks and dangers of a surveillance camera as well as an analysis of the criminal behaviour necessitating video surveillance. Bilodeau reasoned that, if the city had attended to this stipulation, it would at least have considered more appropriate alternatives to mitigate youth criminality. Accompanying this conclusion were Bilodeau's arguments that the city had failed to consult the community and to rationalize the need to record surveillance images, that a displacement effect had occurred, and, most important, that the city had failed to demonstrate the indispensable need to record and retain general public images.

In October 2002, Bilodeau filed two primary final recommendations with the CAI: to order the city to unplug the camera at the corner of Rue Jalbert and Rue De Puyjalon and to halt any further plans to install cameras until the city was able to demonstrate the indispensable need for video surveillance in the territory. On 12 December, CAI representatives commented on the recommendations in a communiqué to the city. The CAI accepted the general findings of Inspector Bilodeau's investigation and ordered the city to halt plans to install a new CCTV surveillance camera. The CAI did not, however, order the city to unplug the camera at the corner of Rue Jalbert and Rue De Puyjalon.[27] Alternatively, the CAI directed the city (within six months) to review the appropriateness of the continued use of the camera, to consider restricting its use to certain times of the day and certain parts of the year, and to consult with community representatives and stakeholders in the area under surveillance (Stewart 2002). In other words, the CAI adopted a conciliatory rather than a regulatory position in Baie-Comeau.

The city responded to the CAI's ruling by establishing a consulting committee to oversee the single-camera monitoring project. The committee was composed of social services workers, police, and city representatives, and its mandate was to evaluate the camera system on a continual basis. When the committee was initially established in 2003, its main task was to establish terms of reference to present to the CAI within six months of the latter's ruling. Among other things, the committee developed rules on recording, viewing, and retaining surveillance images, and specific times when images were to be recorded were established.

In 2004, the committee adopted a mandate to meet annually. Meetings were held in 2004 and 2005. Since 2006, however, representatives at city hall have sent letters to committee members prior to meetings to inquire if a meeting is desired. This was also the year that the camera stopped working. Faced with an expensive repair bill that the city could not afford in 2006, the committee met to discuss the temporary status of the camera. Even though only half of the members attended, it was decided to leave the inoperable camera in place to create/maintain the perception that the area was under surveillance. The camera was repaired in 2007.

The single camera in Baie-Comeau, therefore, is operated with the explicit purpose of deterring youth criminality. In other words, it is not used to attend to actual crime. In fact, over the past eight years, camera images have never led to an arrest because images of crimes in progress are always captured in the evening when it is dark. Images are also routinely difficult to use because trees, clutter in the alley, and containers get in the way.

Although the consulting committee has never considered introducing a second camera to the monitoring system, there are recent developments in public-area CCTV surveillance in the city. In 2007, the director of services at the local library approached the city to propose installing a surveillance camera to monitor the entrance to the library to monitor youth entering and leaving the premises. Library representatives were concerned with a growing problem of drug dealing in the washroom of the library as well as accompanying disturbances (graffiti, harassment, defecating on the floors).

In 2008, a camera was installed at the front entrance of the library. The camera is equipped with a monitor in view of the patrons entering the library, and the images are recorded. The camera system is governed by a small group of city and library representatives associated with the director of leisure, arts, and culture. The committee used the terms of reference developed for the streetscape camera to form its regulatory policy.

Conclusion

This chapter examined the empirical foundations of public-area streetscape CCTV surveillance monitoring programs in Quebec, including the privacy protection policy framework that emerged with the rise of French Canadian monitoring initiatives. Streetscape CCTV surveillance began and ended quietly in Drummondville, but it attracted the sustained attention of the privacy policy sector when the City of Sherbrooke introduced surveillance cameras to monitor sections of Wellington Street. The Wellington Street cameras led to the CAI's ruling that monitoring without recording is permissible, effectively setting an influential, pragmatic precedent for reacting to and regulating aspects of streetscape CCTV surveillance monitoring practices.

Tracing to the inception of streetscape monitoring programs in Drummondville, Sherbrooke, and Hull, a number of patterns that have been repeated across Anglo-Canada from 1996 to the present emerged in Quebec. The most salient patterns concern the uneven ideational, administrative, and privacy protection policy diffusion of streetscape monitoring programs. There is no definitive evidence to suggest an ideational or administrative diffusion from Drummondville to Sherbrooke. The inception and termination of Drummondville's program preceded Sherbrooke's system, however, and the CAI was aware of public-area video surveillance in Drummondville when it evaluated Sherbrooke's system in 1992. There is clear evidence of an ideational and, to an extent, administrative diffusion from Sherbrooke to Hull and Baie-Comeau. The administrative diffusion of streetscape surveillance not only entailed representatives of Hull and Baie-Comeau emulating parts of Sherbrooke's system but also took place in the broader context of the CAI's 1992 ruling on recording camera images (i.e., policy diffusion). The latter contributed to variation in designing, establishing, and deploying systems.

Beyond the context of diffusing privacy protection policies/rulings, the examination of streetscape systems in Quebec is important for three reasons.

First, streetscape CCTV surveillance in Drummondville, Sherbrooke, and Hull preceded the proliferation of public-area video surveillance in the United Kingdom. This is important for understanding the rise of streetscape monitoring practices in Canada and around the world. In fact, despite the early rise of monitoring initiatives in Drummondville and Sherbrooke, Canadian monitoring activities are not even mentioned in Norris, McCahill, and Wood's (2004) assessment of the international diffusion of public-area video surveillance. Second, despite the fifteen-year history of streetscape monitoring in Quebec, when streetscape CCTV surveillance appeared in the Anglo-Canadian cities of Sudbury and Kelowna in 1996 and 1998 respectively, no program in Quebec was acknowledged or mentioned in promotional and planning materials (see Chapters 4 and 5). And third, the failure of streetscape monitoring practices and experiences to diffuse from French to English Canadian cities posed implications for the sophistication of governance structures and monitoring practices in Anglo-Canada. At the least, the diffusion of the policy rulings on recording camera images could have influenced the ways in which Anglo-Canadian systems were designed in the late 1990s.

In addition to the significance of examining French Canadian monitoring programs noted above, in the period spanning 1981-93, many of the themes repeated across Anglo-Canada appeared in Quebec. The commonality of themes is especially interesting in light of the absence of ideational and administrative diffusion from French to English Canadian systems and in the context of the Canada-wide diffusion of a pragmatic policy orientation.

- *Shifting justifications:* Tracing to Drummondville's shifting rationale for maintaining a public-area monitoring system – from preventing violence to responding to instances of vandalism in a pedestrian tunnel – shifting priorities repeated themselves in Sherbrooke. Its monitoring system was initially introduced to survey activities associated with downtown drinking establishments. Within a decade, the primary justification had shifted from disorder stemming from drinking establishments to reduction in violent crime in the aftermath of a high-profile signal crime.
- *Signal crimes:* In all of the cities analyzed in this chapter, signal crimes were used to promote monitoring systems at various (sometimes multiple) stages of development. The most powerful example is the murder of Julie Boisvenu. Promotional activities oriented toward introducing recorded surveillance in Sherbrooke exemplify how signal crimes can be used by proponents of CCTV surveillance to defy or challenge privacy protection regulations.
- *Needs assessment:* Particularly in Sherbrooke and Baie-Comeau, CCTV advocates invoked police statistics to bolster support for monitoring

systems. In Sherbrooke, for example, a pattern that reappears across the country was observed: invoking police statistics, usually in the context of a pilot program, to demonstrate the success of monitoring practices. Especially relevant is the observed pattern (in Sherbrooke and Baie-Comeau) when police statistics fail to substantiate claims to the need for video surveillance.

- *Pilot programs:* Tied to the invocation of police statistics to bolster support for monitoring initiatives is the implementation of pilot projects. Implementation of a pilot project implies a serious commitment to assessing the utility of surveillance cameras and making an informed decision about the usefulness of continued monitoring. A pilot project was first introduced in Sherbrooke in 2004 to assess the effectiveness of streetscape monitoring in a wider effort to convince councillors to endorse the program and provide operational funding. The use of or reliance on pilot programs, not all of which clearly demonstrated comprehensive efforts to assess the utility of monitoring systems, was repeated in Sudbury (Chapter 4), Kelowna (Chapter 5), London (Chapter 6), Hamilton and Windsor (Chapter 7), and Thunder Bay (Chapter 9).
- *Monitoring activities:* The only city analyzed in this chapter that introduced a live-monitoring component was Sherbrooke (after 2004). In most cities, passive monitoring by 9-1-1 call operators has been the norm. Moreover, all of the programs, save for the system in Baie-Comeau, have been operated by police.
- *Drinking establishments:* Bars and nightclubs figure prominently in promotional efforts. For example, Sherbrooke's system was introduced to survey activities associated with drinking establishments, and Hull's system was based entirely on monitoring late-night drinking activities.
- *Other strategies:* CCTV surveillance has been among several strategies deployed to address problems and concerns in at least three of the cities analyzed in this chapter. Sherbrooke's Mont-Bellevue Security Committee introduced several safety initiatives alongside video surveillance, Baie-Comeau representatives laid claim to several strategies, and Hull adopted a wide range of tactics to reduce disorder along the Promenade du Portage. The extent to which all strategies were deployed is not clear, however, and at least in Baie-Comeau (based on Bilodeau's findings) claims to the deployment of strategies other than CCTV surveillance were used as a rhetorical promotional strategy.
- *Oversight committees:* In Hull, Sherbrooke, and Baie-Comeau, oversight committees were developed to evaluate monitoring systems and make recommendations for further monitoring activities. The committees were composed of volunteers primarily from the business community, police, and city administration.

- *Mixing public-area and streetscape systems:* In Sherbrooke and Drummond-ville, public-area systems were linked. A similar pattern is found in Sudbury, Kelowna, and Thunder Bay.

In addition to common trends in French Canadian monitoring initiatives that appear across Anglo-Canada, there were a number of rare occurrences that did not appear in Anglo-Canadian establishment efforts (including reactions from the privacy policy sector).

- *Aggressive pragmatism:* The most prominent policy response to streetscape monitoring in Quebec was the ruling against recording camera images in the absence of a crime in progress. The CAI's policy ruling was accompanied by an aggressive form of pragmatism that involved a critical, on-site investigation in Sherbrooke, the staging of public hearings in 2003, and the recommendation to shut down the camera in Baie-Comeau. Also rare in the external oversight of monitoring programs were on-site investigations, seen in Sherbrooke and Baie-Comeau.
- *Signal events:* In addition to the signal events of the 1991 ruling in Sherbrooke, the introduction of *Minimum Rules* in response to the Summit of the Americas, and the 2003 public hearings, perhaps the most interesting set of signal events that influenced the establishment process in Quebec was the post-9/11 security environment. The CAI was motivated by responses to the 9/11 attacks to search proactively for a balance between privacy and security.
- *Council support:* Council support across Anglo-Canada is far from homogeneous, but it is rare to find city councillors who are willing to terminate programs after they are introduced. In Sherbrooke, however, councillors temporarily withdrew support after the first pilot project, and councillors in Hull and Drummondville terminated programs.
- *Signage:* One of the more unusual features of monitoring programs in Quebec is the lack of willingness to post signs informing members of the public that areas are under video surveillance. No signs were posted in Sherbrooke until 1992, and Drummondville councillors decided against posting signs for their public-area system in 2008. No signs were posted in Baie-Comeau until the CAI's involvement, and, conversely, signs remained up in Hull for three years after the program was discontinued (see, too, Chapter 4 on the lack of signage in Sudbury). Posting signs is one of the easiest ways to bolster support for claims to transparency among proponents of monitoring programs (see Lippert 2009).

Streetscape monitoring programs in Quebec between 1981 and 2005 involved a range of individuals, claims, policies, signal crimes, and events in various configurations. The privacy policy sector exercised a significant influence on how monitoring systems were designed, but the pragmatic policy orientation also contributed to diversity in establishing systems. The early French Canadian examples could have provided some bases to design monitoring programs in English Canada. As the chapters to follow demonstrate, however, French Canadian programs failed either ideationally or administratively to diffuse to English Canada.

APPENDIX 3.1

Minimum Rules Applying to the Use of Surveillance Cameras

A study of the risks and dangers as well as a crime survey, in cooperation with insurers or the police if need be, should be carried out before using cameras as surveillance tools.

- Alternatives to the use of such cameras, less invasive of privacy, should be examined.
- If required, such devices should be used for a limited time on limited occasions (public festivities, particular events, period of the year, hours of the day, etc.).
- The public targeted by such surveillance should be informed by any appropriate notice: information and the name, address and telephone number of the owner or user of the equipment should be provided, on a sign for instance.
- The equipment selected should only keep the necessary information, for instance: if these devices operate under someone's immediate supervision, this person should only record pictures in case of an offence. On the other hand, in cases where continuous recording is required, the material should be kept only for a limited period.
- Surveillance cameras should never be aimed at points like: house windows, showers, bathrooms, dressing rooms, etc.
- Persons assigned to the operation of such devices should be well aware of the rules designed to protect privacy. Likewise, where outsiders are hired instead of regular employees.
- Precise rules for storing the recordings should govern the management of the information collected. Access, within the organization or the company, should be restricted.
- The rights of access and correction should be recognized to any person targeted by the recordings.
- An evaluation of the use and effects of this technology should be made regularly.

Respect of the Minimum Rules

The Commission expects and requires scrupulous respect of the minimum rules applying to surveillance cameras. Non-compliance with these rules could entail serious consequences.

In this regard, here is a reminder: under the terms of the *Act respecting documents held by public bodies and the protection of personal information* and the *Act respecting the protection of personal information in the private sector*, the Commission may, at any time, verify whether the law is respected, and inquire. If it is not satisfied, the CAI may make recommendations, issue any order, make non-compliance with such orders public, or even undertake penal proceedings.

Source: Authorization to reproduce granted by Les Publications du Québec.

4
Sudbury's Lions Eye in the Sky

This chapter examines the City of Sudbury's Lions Eye in the Sky video surveillance monitoring program.[1] Sudbury (Greater Sudbury as of 2001) is the largest city in northern Ontario (population is about 151,000), situated approximately 400 kilometres north of Toronto. During construction of the Canadian Pacific Railway in the 1880s, the discovery of high concentrations of nickel-copper ore led to the intensification of mining/smelting activity and increased settlement in the area. After the Second World War, the population of Sudbury grew significantly, in part based on US demand for so-called non-communist nickel. By the 1960s, sulfur dioxide emissions from the smelting process had damaged the environmental landscape to such an extent that NASA astronauts planned for lunar landings on shattered cones (i.e., fragmented rocks) in the region.

In an effort to alter the city's reputation as a toxic wasteland, municipal and industry representatives initiated a re-greening effort that eventually earned the city a United Nations environmental rehabilitation award in 1992. In 2004, the Greater Sudbury Development Corporation also initiated a revitalization campaign to preserve the city's historic buildings, create a vibrant residential community, and enhance the arts and culture. Revitalization was set in the context of economic diversification in finance, tourism, health care, and the amalgamation of the towns and cities that made up the former Regional Municipality of Sudbury.

Today the city is characterized by a distinction between Old and New Sudbury. New Sudbury is a commercial and residential area populated by a number of big-box stores and expansive suburbs located outside the city centre to the northeast. By contrast, a mix of specialty stores, banks, games rooms, professional offices, and vacant buildings distinguishes downtown Sudbury, located in Old Sudbury. Among the notable demographic groups residing in Old Sudbury are seniors, who inhabit at least seven housing complexes, and homeless people, whose support facilities are located in the downtown core.

In 1996, members of Sudbury's business community and police force became the first community representatives in Anglo-Canada to introduce a streetscape CCTV surveillance monitoring system. Although monitoring programs had been running in Quebec since the 1980s, neither proponents nor designers and a professional auditor of Sudbury's monitoring program demonstrated awareness that Canadian cities used surveillance cameras to monitor city streetscapes prior to Sudbury. In fact, as late as 2005, members of the Lions Eye in the Sky Advisory Committee claimed that the Sudbury Police Service comprised the "first police service in Canada to test Closed Circuit Television (CCTV) as a law enforcement tool" (Greater Sudbury Police Services Board 2005).

Admittedly, information about streetscape CCTV surveillance in Canada was extremely limited on, if not entirely absent from, the World Wide Web (Web) in the mid-1990s, and the Web had not yet become a taken-for-granted source of information. Nor was CCTV surveillance as widely discussed in popular media as it is today. Still, by 1995, the City of Sherbrooke's monitoring program had attracted the attention of the CAI (and information and privacy commissioners outside Quebec), the City of Hull's system had generated significant coverage in the English-language press, and an English-language Canadian Broadcasting Corporation investigative report of Sherbrooke's system was available (Canadian Broadcasting Corporation 1992).[2]

There were several implications of Sudbury's failure to build on representatives' experiences with, and privacy developments pertaining to, CCTV surveillance practices in Quebec. Unlike streetscape CCTV surveillance in the United Kingdom, for example, where the quick accession of monitoring programs left little time to develop reflexively and collaboratively a set of fair information principles (Maguire 1999; but see Webster 2004 and Chapter 10), monitoring systems in Canada developed slowly. The slower development of Canadian streetscape systems provided a potential set of opportunities for information and privacy commissioners to work proactively with community representatives to develop a cumulative and comprehensive privacy protection policy framework for establishing public-area CCTV surveillance monitoring programs from the outset. In other words, the development of streetscape monitoring programs in English Canada during the late 1990s could have built proactively on the fair information principles developed in the context of monitoring experiences in Quebec years earlier to elaborate and strengthen the design and administration of monitoring systems.

The introduction of Sudbury's monitoring program was a pivotal missed opportunity to standardize how streetscape CCTV surveillance is designed at the municipal, provincial, and national levels. Throughout the late 1990s, Canadian provincial information and privacy commissioners formed their pragmatic position on streetscape CCTV surveillance. Prior to 2001 – the year that the Ontario OIPC adopted *Guidelines for Using Video Surveillance Cameras in Public Places* – pragmatism in Ontario involved interpreting a set of fair information principles where institutions governed under the Freedom of Information and Protection of Privacy Act (FIPPA) and the Municipal Freedom of Information and Protection of Privacy Act (MFIPPA) are concerned.[3] FIPPA and MFIPPA offer definitions for personal information, collection of personal information, record keeping, and data access rights, with the aim being to balance institutional needs and desires against the protection of personal privacy. The privacy protection acts, which are the statutory privacy documents governing the Sudbury Police Service and the municipality, do not provide proactive guidance for community representatives seeking to establish public-area CCTV surveillance monitoring systems. Rather, they are designed to protect personal privacy, to inform decisions on the disclosure of personal information, and to enable access to information.

The Ontario OIPC's passive approach to the regulation of surveillance generally and public-area CCTV surveillance particularly had implications beyond Sudbury. After Sudbury's streetscape monitoring system was introduced, it became the main point of origin for the ideational and administrative diffusion of streetscape CCTV surveillance monitoring programs across English-speaking Canadian cities. The Lions Eye in the Sky became a primary reference point for representatives of cities considering streetscape monitoring not only because Sudbury was the first Anglo-Canadian city to introduce streetscape monitoring but also because an independent audit of the program (the KPMG report) was posted on the Sudbury Police Service website in 2000. The audit legitimized Sudbury's monitoring program in the eyes of the representatives of the Sudbury Police Service and members of a municipal oversight committee, and it created the sense outside Sudbury that the Lions Eye in the Sky was an exemplar to follow. At the least, the audit provided rhetorical support for advocates of streetscape CCTV systems in other cities to promote their own monitoring programs (see Chapters 5, 6, 7, 8, and 9).

The Elgin Street Underpass

Sudbury's experience with public-area CCTV surveillance began in the early 1990s when the Sudbury Police Service, collaborating with the City of Sudbury, installed a surveillance camera system in the Elgin Street underpass. The underpass is a busy thoroughfare used by visitors, labourers, shopkeepers/merchants, and students to access the downtown area. The underpass is also periodically used as shelter for homeless people during the extremely cold winter months in northern Ontario.

In the late 1980s and early 1990s, several robberies, disturbances, and other criminal incidents allegedly took place in and around the underpass. In response to several assaults on women in the area, the Sudbury Women's Centre approached the police to propose installing a video surveillance

3   Public-area surveillance camera signage, City of Sudbury, Ontario

monitoring system in the underpass. Police representatives, in turn, approached Sudbury City Council for procedural and financial support. Following consultation with police and community representatives, city council
agreed to purchase the equipment.

In 1992, four cameras were installed to monitor the Elgin Street underpass:
one at each entrance to the underpass and two in the underpass itself (see
Figure 3). The cameras, which remain in the underpass at the time of writing
(July 2009), are fixed models; they lack zoom, pan, and tilt capabilities. The
camera images were originally transmitted over coaxial cables through part
of the city's cable television network to a single monitor located in the old
police station on Larch Street. The camera images were available for monitoring twenty-four hours per day, seven days per week, in the communications centre of the police station. A second monitor located in the staff
sergeant's office was subsequently added to the system.

The surveillance equipment used to monitor the underpass was supplied
and installed by Sudbury-based Northern Voice and Video (later renamed
Northern Video Systems, hereafter referred to as Northern Video). When
Northern Video, one of the largest CCTV companies in Canada, installed
the Elgin Street underpass system, the company specialized in creating,
installing, and maintaining CCTV networks for mining and power companies throughout North America. Northern Video remains the sole supplier of
CCTV camera equipment in Sudbury, and the company has donated over

$30,000 worth of free software, training, and equipment to sustain public-area monitoring practices in the city.

The BMOB Streetscape Pilot Project

The initiative to install streetscape CCTV surveillance cameras to monitor sectors of downtown Sudbury originated with Alex McCauley. McCauley was Sudbury's chief of police from 1994 to 2002. In the early 1990s, he became aware of the Strathclyde, Scotland, Police Service's use of streetscape CCTV surveillance cameras after he read a review of the program published by the International Association of Chiefs of Police.

The historical region of Strathclyde is composed of a number of towns and cities in west central Scotland. The first locale in Strathclyde to introduce streetscape CCTV surveillance was Airdrie (in November 1992), a market town east of Glasgow with a population of approximately 36,000 people. In the early 1990s, a few other towns and city centres established streetscape monitoring programs, but the systems in Strathclyde remained small-scale, regional, and locally funded into the mid-1990s.

In 1995, Police Chief McCauley visited the Strathclyde Police Service headquarters in Glasgow while he vacationed with his family in Scotland. The CCTV surveillance systems in Strathclyde appealed to McCauley because they were used in jurisdictions similar in size to Sudbury. They also appealed to him because the systems were funded by local community partnerships.

Following his visit to the police headquarters in Glasgow, McCauley was convinced that streetscape cameras would positively complement existing policing practices in Sudbury – with negligible costs to police. In the early to mid-1990s, many downtown Sudbury business representatives shared the perception that the police lacked a visible presence in the core. Funding was not available to hire police officers to address complaints about theft, violence, public intoxication, prostitution, and aggressive panhandling in the downtown area, and claims that the economic and social conditions of the downtown core had declined were growing.[4]

McCauley understood streetscape CCTV surveillance as a viable way to address perceptions about crime and disorder among businesspeople in general and among seniors residing in the downtown area in particular.[5] He informally proposed the idea to his deputy chief and director of administration, Sharon Baiden, of installing a streetscape monitoring system in the core. McCauley also approached Mike Lawson, co-owner of Northern Video, for consultation on the technological logistics of installing surveillance cameras in Sudbury's downtown area. To solicit long-term funding for the program, and to develop a wider community support network for the proposed camera system, McCauley entered into discussions with members of the Sudbury Metro Centre. He presented informal arguments in favour of installing surveillance cameras in the downtown core to members of the Metro Centre's Downtown Safety and Security Committee (DSSC). McCauley's arguments were based on his perceptions of Glasgow's City Watch program.[6] To measure support for the proposed system, the DSSC conducted a small survey of downtown businesses. The survey revealed that many downtown business owners strongly supported the proposal to install surveillance cameras in the core.

On 6 November 1996, an ad hoc CCTV committee met to finalize plans for a CCTV surveillance pilot project. The committee was composed of Chief McCauley, Maureen Luoma (executive director, Metro Centre), Mike Lawson (Northern Video), and eight representatives from the Sudbury Police Service and the business community. Members of the committee decided to launch a pilot project during the Christmas shopping period to provide shoppers with an increased sense of security in the downtown core. To minimize the negative connotations associated with security cameras, the committee attempted proactively to manage potentially disapproving news coverage by linking the pilot project to existing CCTV surveillance practices across social spaces (e.g., banks, stores) and to the effectiveness of the Elgin Street underpass cameras; they framed the pilot project as a community safety rather than a policing issue (Sudbury Metro Centre 1996).

With support from the ad hoc committee, and specifically from Northern Video (Mike Lawson agreed to supply a camera free of charge during the test phase), McCauley proposed the introduction of a community-based CCTV surveillance monitoring pilot project to the Police Services Board. The research that informed the design, rationale, and structure of the proposal was based on McCauley's personal experiences in Scotland, the Sudbury Police Service's experiences with the Elgin Street underpass cameras,[7] the review report of the Strathclyde systems, data from the Metro Centre's survey of downtown business owners, and technical consultation with Lawson. No formal written proposal was produced, and the only public consultation conducted was with owners and managers of downtown businesses.[8]

In December 1996, a single CCTV surveillance camera on the Bank of Montreal Building (BMOB) became operational. The BMOB is located on Durham Street to the north of the downtown core (see Figure 4). The camera was mounted on the BMOB for three reasons: the property owner consented to have the camera mounted on the building, the location enabled easy access to the city's fibre optic infrastructure,[9] and the area under surveillance was perceived as a main location for anti-social behaviour (panhandling, loitering) – particularly close to banks.

The BMOB camera images were initially transmitted to police headquarters over fibre optic cables supplied by Northern Cable Holdings (a company associated with Northern Video). The camera was a globe-style model, equipped with pan, zoom, and tilt capabilities. Although the camera was

4   Streetscape surveillance camera, City of Sudbury, Ontario

mounted on the corner of the building, it had 360-degree viewing capability. During the pilot phase, restricted-duty police officers periodically monitored the camera images. Systematic data on viewing patterns and interventions were not collected, and no signs were posted to notify the public that the area was under video surveillance.

The pilot project spanned approximately four months (December-March), but the camera was operational for only one month (December) to test the technological components of the system.[10] Nevertheless, during the four-month pilot project, the camera remained on the BMOB; it was pulled back and out of sight in March 1997. The inoperable camera was left in public view from January to March to enable committee members to assess whether the presence of the camera contributed to a reduction in anti-social behaviour (e.g., aggressive panhandling) and to gain a better understanding of public perception of the camera. The committee reported a 10 percent reduction in anti-social behaviour during the pilot phase (Greater Sudbury Police Services Board 2005).

At the close of the pilot project, the ad hoc CCTV committee concluded that the technology worked well: images were successfully transmitted to the police station. The committee also concluded that the system contributed to community policing efforts (e.g., identifying missing persons) to the detection of several criminals and that it enjoyed high levels of support among downtown businesses and seniors (no systematic data were collected on the opinions of seniors).

The pilot project did not, however, meet with total approval. For example, Maureen Luoma and Police Chief McCauley received unsolicited copies of George Orwell's *Nineteen Eighty-Four,* and the *Sudbury Star* carried a series of editorials in 1996 and 1997 that criticized the pilot project. The criticisms centred on potential threats to privacy and civil liberties, the notion that cameras are a cheap substitute for an increased police presence, and doubts about the efficacy of the cameras (e.g., *Sudbury Star* 1996). Critical news coverage was an important reason why the committee concentrated heavily on public relations when the monitoring program was expanded (see below). Despite criticism, however, the committee concluded that voices of resistance were marginal and restricted to a small group of people and a few news items.

Establishing the Lions Eye in the Sky Streetscape Monitoring Program

In March 1997, the ad hoc CCTV committee decided to expand the monitoring system to cover a greater area of the downtown core. The first task for the committee was to establish terms of reference for developing a long-term monitoring system, and its first priority was to reconfigure the composition of the advisory committee to reflect adequately the community. The ad hoc CCTV committee created the Video Monitoring Advisory Committee (VMAC) to manage and steer the monitoring program and to report to the Sudbury Police Services Board on matters pertaining to applications, effectiveness, funding, and expansion of the system. The VMAC, which remains functional at the time of writing under the auspices of the Lions Video Monitoring Advisory Committee (LVMAC), was initially composed of representatives from the Sudbury Police Service, the Metro Centre, the wider business community, Northern Video, a local seniors' advocacy group, community groups, and four "non-aligned members" from the community.[11]

In 1997, the newly established VMAC started to plan expansion of the downtown video surveillance monitoring system. Using funds from the Metro Centre, it purchased the camera used in the pilot project. It also set a target to expand the system by one camera per year in an effort to establish maximum video surveillance coverage in the downtown area. The VMAC expected to generate enough money to buy two additional cameras through a promotional package distributed to businesses and insurance companies in the downtown area, but only eight insurance companies donated funds, totalling $7,500. The rental fee for fibre optic cables was estimated at $7,000 in 1997, and equipment maintenance (e.g., cleaning domes, camera sticking) was estimated at $2,100 (Lions Eye in the Sky 1997).

To generate funds to purchase equipment and maintain and upgrade the system, the VMAC approached the Lions Club of Sudbury. The club is affiliated with Lions Clubs International, which is composed of 45,000 non-profit clubs located in 202 countries. The mandate of Lions Clubs International is to establish business clubs devoted to the betterment of local communities. Regional segments of Lions Clubs International support youth charity work, aid for disabled people, seniors, and other community causes. Part of the reason why members of the VMAC approached the Lions Club of Sudbury was that its president, John Hollinger, was affiliated with the Metro Centre.

Following a presentation by Chief McCauley in June 1997, the Lions Club of Sudbury agreed to donate $48,000 to cover costs to purchase surveillance cameras and related equipment (cabinets, colour monitors, video recorder, fibre optic video receiver data transmitter, outdoor heating houses with defrost kits, auto zoom lens, variable speed pre-position pan tilt). Members of the Lions Club believed that the surveillance system would deter crime and make citizens, particularly seniors, feel safer in the core. They were specifically encouraged by the fact that the VMAC planned to use volunteers rather than police officers to monitor the cameras (see below) and that the system was a community-based initiative.

In addition to the original camera on the BMOB (reactivated by August 1997), two cameras were installed on the Carrefour francophone building at the corner of Elgin Street and St. Anne Road (this camera was moved to the corner of Elgin and Beech Streets in the summer of 1998) and in front of Sudbury News Service at the corner of Elm and Durham Streets in the summer of 1997 (see Figure 5). The three CCTV cameras were fully operational by October 1997.[12] All camera images were routed to the communications centre in the police headquarters, where images were continuously recorded on three VCRs. Images were transmitted along fibre optic cables

5   Streetscape surveillance camera, City of Sudbury, Ontario

supplied by Sudbury Hydro at half the market cost (Video Monitoring Advisory Committee 1997). Images appeared on two colour television monitors, and image recordings were retained for about two months. Limited-duty police officers continued to perform periodic live-monitoring duties while the committee explored ways to recruit volunteers. When camera images were not monitored by limited-duty police officers, the cameras panned along downtown streets using an automated function.[13]

Public Relations, Promotion, and Fundraising

Once the system became operational, the Lions Video Monitoring Advisory Committee (renamed to commemorate the Lions Club donation) started to develop a public relations strategy. Its goal was twofold: first, to promote a positive public image of the system as a cost-effective way to reduce crime and increase public safety; second, to generate money through donations and local fundraising to cover the costs of maintaining and upgrading the system (fibre optic rental fees, upgrades).

To achieve these goals, the LVMAC formed a public relations subcommittee on 7 November 1997. To promote the system, the subcommittee developed a media strategy to increase public understanding of the system and to showcase its effectiveness. For example, it held press conferences to foster a positive image of the program as a community safety initiative. The first press conference was held on 1 December 1997 to launch the system formally, and members of the LVMAC framed the program as a community safety project. The subcommittee also started to collect police crime statistics and anecdotal incident reports using a monthly auditing process. Public presentation of the data, communicated as monthly press releases, was intended to demonstrate the tangible benefits of the cameras (Video Monitoring Advisory Committee 1997). The subcommittee's promotional efforts even included "Lions Eye in the Sky" stickers distributed to downtown businesses (but not until 2001).

To generate money for maintaining and expanding the program, the public relations subcommittee developed a number of fundraising strategies. In addition to the promotional package used to solicit initial funds for maintenance and expansion costs, on 10 July 1998 the subcommittee held the first "hot dog day" fundraiser for the camera system (designated as Video Monitoring Day); a profit of $200 was made. The subcommittee also developed a more complete information package intended to solicit donations. This package included a five-minute promotional video; it was initially distributed to financial institutions, service clubs, and small businesses, and later it was sent to some police forces around the country.

Despite the various fundraising strategies adopted by the LVMAC, attracting sufficient operating capital remained challenging. In fact, fundraising proved to be so challenging that the subcommittee held a Christmas gift-wrapping fundraiser. From 1997 to 2000, the LVMAC continued to attract small donations from local businesses, but it also started to look beyond the city for funding. In 1998, for example, the LVMAC began to explore funding opportunities through the province's Partners Against Crime Community Crime Prevention program, and it began to explore the possibility of outsourcing the monitoring facilities. The latter entailed a proposal to carry out monitoring services for local businesses. In 2001, the committee even explored the possibility of outsourcing the monitoring facilities to surrounding institutions and communities; it considered approaching the nearby cities of Sturgeon Falls and North Bay as well as Laurentian University, Cambrian College, the local hospital, and Sudbury Hydro, with the intention of becoming a centre for CCTV monitoring in northern Ontario.

There is evidence that the public relations campaign was effective. For instance, the *Sudbury Star* reported regular updates of the varied uses of the cameras – the "Downtown Camera Highlights" – particularly when the cameras were put to unexpected uses (locating missing children, intervening in suicide attempts). The monitoring system attracted favourable news coverage beyond Sudbury as well *(Thunder Bay Chronicle, Toronto Star)*. The image fostered by the public relations subcommittee was positive enough that police representatives from several other Ontario cities (Espanola, Toronto, London, Barrie, Oshawa, Ottawa, Elliot Lake, Thunder Bay, Windsor, Hamilton, Sturgeon Falls, and North Bay) contacted representatives in Sudbury to gather information about streetscape monitoring. By 1999, the Lions Eye in the Sky was emerging as the primary reference point for streetscape monitoring programs in Anglo-Canada.[14]

Expansion and Legitimization

With the public relations promotional and fundraising strategies in place by 1998, the LVMAC engaged in a number of mutually reinforcing activities oriented toward expanding and legitimizing the monitoring system. Expansion of the system entailed foremost ongoing efforts to attract funds to add more cameras as well as to introduce a regular live-monitoring component. Legitimization of the system entailed foremost continuing public relations campaigns to foster an image of the monitoring system as both a viable community safety initiative in Sudbury and an exemplary Canadian community safety initiative beyond Sudbury.

In 1998, the monitoring program was expanded in two main ways. The first set of developments leading to expansion of the program gained momentum in June 1998, when the LVMAC entered into an agreement with the Ontario government's workfare program. Formalized through the Ontario Works Act on 1 May 1998, the workfare program, implemented by the Conservative government of Ontario, obliged able-bodied, working-aged recipients of social assistance to perform unpaid work duties in return for remuneration. The Sudbury Police Service entered into an agreement with Ontario Works Sudbury, whereby social assistance recipients were assigned to monitor the cameras. Using people on social assistance to monitor cameras not only contributed to expansion of the system but also helped to legitimize the monitoring program by enabling representatives of the LVMAC to claim that the camera images were regularly monitored.[15]

The second way that the LVMAC expanded the program in 1998 was by attracting sponsorship funds for a new camera. In June 1998, representatives from Canadian Pacific Rail (CP Rail) informed members of the LVMAC that they wished to make a donation either to install a camera on their property or to contribute to the cost of installing a camera that could monitor their property (Lions Video Monitoring Advisory Committee 1998a). CP Rail is located on Elgin Street to the south of the downtown area. The property overlooks the railway tracks and the surrounding public streets, including the Elgin Street underpass. CP Rail pledged $6,000 toward the purchase and installation of a camera as well as the cost of laying fibre optic cables to transmit images to the communications centre at police headquarters. The total cost of adding a new camera to the system was estimated at $10,000, and the outstanding funds were raised by the LVMAC.[16] When the camera was added to the system in January 1999, CP Rail became the first community sponsor to fund a private camera to be added to the five-camera system.

Three other developments significantly contributed to the legitimization, and subsequent expansion, of the Lions Eye in the Sky monitoring program. The first development transpired in 1998, when the Ontario OIPC received a complaint under MFIPPA about the downtown cameras. Inspector Brian Beamish of the Ontario OIPC reviewed the monitoring program and for-warded two recommendations to the LVMAC: to post signs in the areas where cameras are mounted, and to commission an independent audit of the system to justify its continued operation.

The response of the Ontario OIPC reflected the ways in which streetscape monitoring was approached in English Canada, and to a lesser extent in French Canada, in the 1990s. Exemplifying the response to streetscape monitoring among information and privacy commissioners in Anglo-Canada was the position taken by the information and privacy commissioner of British Columbia, David Flaherty, in Investigation Report P98-012 (published on 31 March 1998). Flaherty's investigation focused on video surveillance practices by public bodies throughout British Columbia. As a "privacy prag-matist" (Flaherty 1998, 2), he argued that video surveillance is neither good nor bad and that a balanced approach that weighs crime prevention measures against an individual's right to be left alone is apt. The main strategy that Flaherty employed to achieve this goal was to formulate guidelines for the establishment and application of video surveillance systems. In effect, the precedent set by Flaherty reinforced the role of privacy commissioners in English Canada as advocates and educators rather than regulators where public-area CCTV surveillance is concerned (Bennett 2003; see, too, Cavouk-ian 1998). It also reinforced the pace set in Quebec years earlier: namely, to work toward best practices in public-area monitoring rather than seek to regulate the activities of public bodies.

Responding to the recommendation to post signs was straightforward for members of the LVMAC: the Lions Club donated $420 to post six signs on major access routes to the downtown core (see Figure 6). But it was the recommendation to commission an independent audit that proved highly significant not only to the legitimization of the Lions Eye in the Sky but also to the legitimization of other initiatives around Canada. When Inspector Beamish completed his review of the Lions Eye in the Sky in August 1998,

6   Streetscape surveillance camera signage, City of Sudbury, Ontario

the monitoring program was attracting attention from other Canadian municipalities (e.g., Toronto, Hamilton, London). Members of the LVMAC repeatedly claimed that the CCTV surveillance cameras produced positive results pertaining to crime rates, fear of crime, and economic revitalization, and their claims were being reproduced outside Sudbury. Members of the LVMAC felt pressure to validate their claims that the program was effective at reducing crime and enhancing public safety.

In 1999, the Sudbury Police Services Board voted in favour of commissioning an independent review of the monitoring program. The board secured $30,000 from the Ontario Ministry of the Solicitor General and Correctional Services to finance the review. The accounting and consultancy firm KPMG was commissioned to audit the program. Oscar Poloni of KPMG conducted the audit, and the final report was presented to the LVMAC in June 2000 (Poloni 2000).

The KPMG report evaluated six aspects of the Lions Eye in the Sky: the anticipated benefits of the program, the impact of video surveillance in the downtown area, the impact of the monitoring system on areas outside downtown Sudbury (i.e., the displacement effect), the costs and benefits of camera monitoring, community acceptance of and response to the program, and the future direction of the program. Several data-gathering and analysis techniques were employed. To assess the benefits and the impacts of the program, for example, interviews with members of the LVMAC and the camera operators were conducted, statistical and empirical crime data from Sudbury and other Canadian communities were reviewed, and the impact of public CCTV programs in the United Kingdom was summarized to establish the "reasonableness" of evaluation results. Poloni also carried out interviews with business and community representatives to gather information on perceptions of the cameras, and a survey of fifty downtown merchants and fifty-eight residents in the downtown area was conducted.

The most influential findings contributing to the legitimization of the Lions Eye in the Sky – and to streetscape monitoring initiatives in other Canadian cities – pertain to the impact of monitoring on crime in the downtown core. Poloni concluded that, in the three-year period following introduction of the monitoring system, detectable criminal activity in the downtown area decreased dramatically. Between 1996 and 1999, he argued, assaults and robberies decreased by 38 percent, and property crimes decreased by 44 percent. Using a comparative framework, whereby crime rates in Sudbury were compared to those in other Canadian communities close to or similar in size to Sudbury (North Bay, Timmins, Sault Ste. Marie, Hamilton, and Ottawa, Ontario; Regina, Saskatchewan; Saint John, New Brunswick), Poloni concluded that Sudbury's crime levels had declined at greater rates without evidence of displacement.

Beyond claims about the impact of camera monitoring on the crime rate in Sudbury, the KPMG audit concluded that the monitoring system was beneficial to both the safety and the perception of safety of law enforcement officers and members of the public. For instance, 79 percent of downtown resident survey respondents and 98 percent of business respondents approved of the Lions Eye in the Sky monitoring system. Furthermore, 65 percent of residents reported that CCTV did not invade privacy, compared with 98 percent of business respondents. In terms of CCTV monitoring increasing business revenues, KPMG concluded that 9 percent of residents had increased their shopping habits since the cameras were installed; 6 percent of business respondents reported that CCTV had improved business.

Based on the findings of the KPMG investigation, Poloni's report presented several recommendations. First, drawing on interviews with members of the Sudbury Police Service, the report recommended installing cameras on Larch Street and St. Anne Road, purportedly where large numbers of seniors are targeted by criminals and aggressive panhandlers. Second, the report criticized the community-funding approach on the grounds that it was unable to generate the resources needed to expand the program. Third, the report recommended finding long-term camera operators.[17] And fourth, the report was critical of the lack of signage in and around the locations of the cameras themselves (the LVMAC responded with stickers).[18]

The KPMG report was presented to the Sudbury Police Services Board and the LVMAC in June 2000. The findings were well received by the board and committee members, and there was enthusiasm that the KPMG audit validated the monitoring program (Lions Video Monitoring Advisory Committee 2000). The findings of the report, particularly the statistics regarding the drop in crime rates, were circulated in the media, and the report was posted on the Sudbury Police Service website. The LVMAC was particularly keen to promote claims presented in the report that 300-500 criminal offences were deterred by the cameras, that no displacement effect had occurred, that violent and property-related crimes had declined after the cameras were installed, that downtown Sudbury had saved between $600,000 and $800,000, and that the system was used to assist in locating missing children (see Lions Club 2002).

After the KPMG Report

Following completion of the KPMG audit, the Lions Club of Sudbury pledged $10,000 to add a new camera to the system, and representatives from the City of Sudbury approached the LVMAC to install a camera to monitor the Teletech parking lot at 40 Elm Street (to provide security for employees of a local marketing firm). In 2001, a new camera, funded mostly by the Lions Club, was installed on a building at 65 Larch Street, and another, city-funded camera was installed to monitor the Teletech parking lot and surrounding area.[19]

Despite the addition of two cameras to the system, however, the LVMAC continued to experience difficulty generating sufficient capital to maintain the program. In 2001, the Greater Sudbury Police Service incorporated the ongoing costs of the system in its own budget (Lions Video Monitoring Advisory Committee 2002). Since the initial three-camera system was established in 1997, the Greater Sudbury Police Service invested labour and limited funds to keep the system operational, but it maintained more of a formal partnership than a leadership role. Bolstered by the KPMG report's claims about the importance of the system for crime reduction, and empowered by a favourable second review from the OIPC in 2002 (see below), the Greater Sudbury Police Service increased its yearly contribution to approximately $60,000 and started to assume greater control of the program. In 2002, under the new leadership of Police Chief Ian Davidson, the police service sought to formalize its financial contribution to the system by requesting $300,000 from the police budget to update the entire system to digital monitoring. The system was upgraded using police funds when the Police Services Board approved funds totalling $100,000.

Although the Greater Sudbury Police Service was assuming an increasingly active role in the monitoring program, the LVMAC continued to pursue funds to maintain and expand the system. Encouraged by the City of Sudbury's expressed willingness to pay for private monitoring services (and CP Rail's funding for a camera), the LVMAC elected a Strategic Planning Subcommittee to assess the future of the program and to explore strategies to attract paying customers before soliciting further funds through community donations in 2001. Part of the strategy to attract paying customers entailed creation of a business plan by the Greater Sudbury Police Service (2001). The business plan set out a five-year goal to offer public and private video surveillance monitoring services as an adjunct to existing security practices and as a stand-alone security measure. The business plan identified areas, including parking lots and recreational facilities, and it targeted utilities (fire stations, hydro, arenas) as potential subscribers; the Strategic Planning Subcommittee estimated that 168 cameras could be linked to the existing system (Lions Video Monitoring Advisory Committee 2001).

The main goal of promoting the system to public and private interests was to attract paying customers to generate a stable, long-term funding source by selling expertise and consulting services (Greater Sudbury Police Service 2001). Both proposals were rejected for two main reasons: first, they involved breaking the LVMAC's mission statement to provide monitoring in the downtown area; second, police representatives concluded that it was neither practical nor appropriate for the Lions Eye in the Sky to compete with private-sector security agencies.

As the subcommittee generated strategies to attract paying customers, a number of businesses in the downtown area approached the subcommittee to explore installing cameras to monitor their premises. Plans to expand the system, however, were forestalled by interrelated local and extra-local developments. First, on 21 June 2002, Privacy Commissioner George Radwanski launched a challenge under the Canadian Charter of Rights and Freedoms after the RCMP ignored a ruling under the Privacy Act to cease streetscape CCTV monitoring practices in Kelowna (see Chapter 5). The Charter challenge generated a significant amount of news coverage across Canada (Greenberg and Hier 2009), and the editorial board at the *Sudbury Star* revisited the implications of the CCTV program for privacy and civil liberties. In response to the heightened attention to public-area video surveillance in Canada, the LVMAC concluded that the challenge was a federal issue (monitoring in Kelowna was conducted by the RCMP) but that they should nevertheless wait for the final ruling on the Charter challenge before expanding the system.

Second, at the same time that Commissioner Radwanski launched his Charter challenge in Kelowna, the Ontario OIPC was putting in place *Guidelines for Using Video Surveillance Cameras in Public Places*. A component of *Guidelines* required institutions governed by MFIPPA and FIPPA that conduct continuous or periodic video surveillance of the public to review their programs.

On 1 May 2002, Judith Hoffman from the Ontario OIPC reviewed the Lions Eye in the Sky. Inspector Hoffman forwarded a number of pragmatic recommendations to the LVMAC to improve the system, including a request for more adequate signage and for the development of protocols for the expeditious disposal of surveillance records (some surveillance tapes were being kept for up to six months without justification prior to the digital upgrade). Hoffman also called on the LVMAC to conduct a more focused external audit in the context of the principles noted in *Guidelines* to demonstrate the ongoing need and efficacy of the Lions Eye in the Sky monitoring program.

In response to Inspector Hoffman's review, the chair of the LVMAC, Tom Walton, developed an audit template in cooperation with the Greater Sudbury Police Service. The final audit, sent to the Ontario OIPC in September 2002, was presented in the format of responses to thirty-eight queries organized into six general sections: administration, public consultation, camera access, operator review, storage/accessibility, destruction of records, and system maintenance. The audit offered a brief explanation of each question posed by Hoffman, repeating information already available in promotional material and the KPMG report. Based on the audit and a subsequent OIPC review of the program in 2003, the LVMAC installed six additional signs (paid for by the city), and a new limit of seventy-two hours was adopted for tape retention.

In 2003, the LVMAC started planning for installation of the seventh Lions Club streetscape camera. Accompanying installation of the new camera was the creation of a public survey (public consultations were promoted by the Ontario OIPC after the adoption of *Guidelines* – see Chapters 7 and 9). The committee decided to conduct a survey about the downtown camera system partially to gather data on public awareness and opinions to comply with the provisions set out in *Guidelines* and because they thought that resolution of the Kelowna challenge opened the door for expansion efforts. The survey was initially designed to target business owners and seniors in the downtown area. After committee discussion, however, in March 2004, 2,000 surveys were distributed to downtown businesses, seniors, secondary school students, and a variety of other downtown agencies. A total of 557 surveys were returned.

The survey posed the following five questions:

1 Are you aware of the camera system in downtown Sudbury?
2 What do you think the purpose of the cameras are?
3 Since the cameras have been installed, do you feel safer during daylight hours in the downtown area?
4 Since the cameras have been installed, do you feel safer after dark in the downtown area?
5 Would you support more cameras in the downtown area?

Table 1

Lions Video Monitoring Advisory Committee public survey responses, 2004

	Age											
	14-25			25-55			55+			Unknown		
Questions	Yes	No	UD	Yes	No	UD	Yes	No	UD	Yes	No	UD
1. Aware of cameras?	257	130	0	53	2	0	92	3	1	11	8	0
3. Safer in daylight?	125	253	11	35	18	2	83	10	3	9	9	1
4. Safer after dark?	111	268	10	30	22	3	63	21	12	9	8	2
5. Support more cameras?	202	174	14	44	9	2	83	11	2	14	4	1

Note: UD = undecided.
Source: Courtesy of the Sudbury Police Service.

In June 2004, the Greater Sudbury Police Service assigned a summer student to summarize the findings of the survey. Given that at least 387 of the 557 (69 percent) surveys were returned by secondary school students, the LVMAC decided to analyze the data by age group (i.e., 14-25, 25-55, 55+). They did so to account for the anticipated skewing of the data based on responses from the students.

The final report on the survey consists of quantitative and qualitative findings. Quantitative responses were tabulated for questions 1, 3, 4, and 5 (see Table 1). Qualitative responses were recorded in full for questions 2 and 5.

As the findings presented in Table 1 indicate, the majority of respondents reported awareness of the cameras. What is notable about responses to the first question, however, is that 34 percent of respondents in the 14-25 age range (130 people) reported no awareness of the cameras. Notably, respondents in this age range also reported the lowest feeling of safety provided by cameras, regardless of time of day. At least three explanations can account for this set of findings. First, there could be a relationship between outreach and consultation on the part of the LVMAC and awareness of, and subsequent comfort with, the cameras, whereby young people were not deemed worthy of consultation and awareness in promotional campaigns. Second, regardless of reported comfort or safety levels, it could simply be that older members of the community are more engaged with news media and other community information sources. Third, young people might simply be skeptical of any project resembling police control. It is significant that so many respondents in the 14-25 age range thought that the survey was worth filling out.

Regardless of the responses from community members aged 14-25, members of the LVMAC received the overall findings from the survey in a positive light. They noted that seniors were happy with the program, particularly the increased feeling of safety provided by the cameras, and that strong support was expressed for the cameras among respondents over the age of twenty-five. In response to the lower levels of awareness, safety, and support reported among respondents 14-25, the LVMAC's conclusion was twofold: first, that some students' responses are unreliable; second, that students need to be educated about the purpose of the monitoring program (see Chapter 7 for a similar response to unfavourable public consultation data).

After completion of the public survey, LVMAC activity declined. Part of the decline can be attributed to the fact that Tom Walton, the long-term enthusiastic chair of the committee, stepped down. With the decline of committee activity, the system came under the regulation of the Greater Sudbury Police Service. From 2003 to 2006, the police aimed to establish live monitoring twenty-four hours a day, with two operators on duty at any given time. Staff shifts were assigned in four-hour blocks, spanning from 8 a.m. to 12 p.m., 12 p.m. to 4 p.m., 4 p.m. to 8 p.m., and 8 p.m. to 12 a.m.; the "graveyard shift" spanned from 12 a.m. to 8 a.m. The problem that the police encountered was securing camera operators.

From 2003 to 2006, there were four groups of monitors: 9-1-1 call operators, Ontario Works employees, police foundations and law and security students, and volunteers from the community. Monitors affiliated with Ontario Works could not work in excess of seventy hours per week and not more than seventeen weeks. The limited hours created problems with retention and retraining (the police had to retrain monitors every four months).

As 2006 approached, members of the Greater Sudbury Police Service experienced difficulty recruiting enough workfare clients who could pass the screening process. This meant unmanned cameras several times during the week. By 2006, the police had ceased accepting Ontario Works clients. To maintain live monitoring, the police arranged to have students from local colleges awarded course credits for volunteering to monitor the cameras (the police benefited from a community member who volunteered his time). In the spring of 2009, the police implemented a new program to attract volunteers from other educational institutions and the public.

The most recent camera added to the system was erected on the side of the Northern Mines building on Cedar Street, in the north part of downtown. The camera is positioned to view the Sudbury Transit transportation hub, a popular liquor store, and the downtown Tim Hortons restaurant. At the end of 2008, there were twelve individual public-area cameras in operation, eight of which qualify as streetscape cameras. With the exception of the Elgin Street underpass, all of the cameras are the same model: the Speed Dome Ultra, manufactured by Florida-based Sensormatic Electronics. The cameras are inside a glass sphere mounted in a cylindrical white housing. Each camera has zoom, pan, and tilt capabilties and swivels 360 degrees.

Conclusion

When the Lions Eye in the Sky monitoring program was established in 1997, neither federal nor provincial information and privacy commissioners offered published guidelines on the use of CCTV surveillance cameras in public spaces. Representatives of the City of Sudbury not only forged ahead with establishment of their system in the absence of a provincial CCTV surveillance privacy protection policy framework but also based it largely on selective interpretations of monitoring programs in the United Kingdom. In doing so, the LVMAC enacted a promotional and administrative design structure independent of the privacy policy sector that subsequently influenced promotional and administrative designs in other cities. Put differently, at least until 2001, it was the Lions Eye in the Sky monitoring program rather than the Ontario OIPC (and other provincial OIPCs) that exercised the strongest influence on the development of operational protocols, funding schemes, monitoring structures, and, especially, claims to effectiveness in Anglo-Canadian cities where monitoring programs were promoted. After 2001, the Lions Eye in the Sky was at least as influential as the privacy policy sector in the establishment of Anglo-Canadian monitoring systems, largely because of the exemplary status that the Lions Eye in the Sky assumed with release of the KPMG report.

The perceived exemplary status (or at least the claim to exemplary status) of Sudbury's program by representatives in cities across Anglo-Canada is significant. As I illustrate in the chapters to follow, in Anglo-Canadian cities that implemented monitoring programs after 2001, the recommendations presented in *Guidelines* (e.g., public consultations, data handling, and storage) were interpreted in various ways. Flexibility in the design and implementation process not only enabled the enactment of different monitoring systems and protocols but also fostered opportunities for a range of people to resist monitoring initiatives. Despite variation in the process, however, responses to the OIPC's recommendation that use of video surveillance cameras should be justified based on verifiable evidence attesting to public safety concerns have overwhelmingly relied on the LVMAC's claims about the effectiveness of surveillance cameras in reducing crime and disorder. Reliance on these claims has not only bolstered promotional support for monitoring initiatives in other cities but also encouraged proponents of streetscape monitoring systems across the country to model parts of their systems on the Lions Eye in the Sky.

Sudbury's monitoring system has been so influential for three reasons. First, as outlined above, the independent KPMG report was posted on the Sudbury Police Services website, and it presented favourable and usable claims and arguments. Ironically, it was the Ontario OIPC that encouraged the independent evaluation in an effort to gain stronger influence over monitoring initiatives in the province. Second, the LVMAC engaged in unparalleled promotional activities that were influential prior to the KPMG report (in Hamilton, Kelowna, and London). Third, the program was promoted as a community-based initiative, including community funding arrangements, oversight committees, and an ownership structure, which appealed to other Anglo-Canadian communities.

Admittedly, the VMAC and the LVMAC made many gains in the administrative design of streetscape monitoring: they developed terms of reference early in the design process, they introduced an auditing and oversight component, and they promoted public awareness of the system through a variety of means. Moreover, the activities of the LVMAC are unique among Canadian streetscape monitoring initiatives: in no other Canadian city has so much effort been devoted to community fundraising and public relations, and their level of engagement partially fostered a multilateral decision-making and responsibility-sharing structure. Yet it is the uniqueness of the LVMAC's commitments to promoting and expanding the Lions Eye in the Sky that has contributed to the consolidation of negative trends in the diffusion process. Monitoring programs that have ideationally and administratively diffused in part from Sudbury draw on certain aspects of the Lions Eye in the Sky. But other Canadian cities have been able to emulate neither the community-funding model nor the LVMAC's public relations strategies. Combined with the privacy policy sector's pragmatic orientation to balancing the desires of CCTV advocates with privacy protection measures, the result has been inconsistency in the diffusion and establishment process.

5

Kelowna and the Constitutional Debate about Public-Area Video Surveillance

A privacy protection policy framework on public-area CCTV surveillance began to emerge in the early 1990s in Quebec (see Chapter 3). Despite the more aggressive approach to pragmatism adopted by the Commission d'accès à l'information (CAI), the conciliatory approach taken in Sherbrooke in 1991 presaged an emerging pragmatic orientation that was endorsed across the country in the late 1990s and early 2000s. Since 1992, privacy protection advocacy concerning public-area video surveillance has been primarily educational rather than regulatory, and information and privacy commissioners have, since the late 1990s, sought proactively to encourage compliance with the fair information principles that were eventually institutionalized in the minimal rules and guidelines protocols in 2001-2. One problem with the latter approach, however, is that information and privacy commissioners across Canada tend to operate on a complaint-resolution basis, a function that is less useful in promoting proactive compliance with privacy legislation and guidelines (see Bennett 2003). Set in the context of a growing number of issues facing the privacy policy sector, public-area CCTV surveillance has been passively and reactively addressed, and this is a feature of the policy environment that inadvertently contributes to a variety of responses to monitoring initiatives across Canadian cities.

An important exception to the pragmatic educational/voluntary compliance approach adopted by the Canadian privacy policy sector transpired in 2002 when the federal information and privacy commissioner of Canada, George Radwanski, rejected privacy pragmatism and adopted a strong regulatory stance. Drawing on the principles stipulated in the Canadian Charter of Rights and Freedoms, the Privacy Act, and the United Nations Declaration on Human Rights, Radwanski challenged the RCMP's use of a single CCTV surveillance camera in Kelowna. The significance of Radwanski's Charter challenge reached beyond public-area video surveillance and raised issues and concerns about the role of appointed parliamentary commissioners in Canada. In other words, the problem with the constitutional challenge (from the point of view of the Department of Justice and other government agencies) was not so much the ethical and legal arguments that Radwanski presented about public-area video surveillance but the position from which he presented them. Nevertheless, the outcome of his challenge to public-area video surveillance in Canada – a challenge that could have changed the ways in which information and privacy commissioners respond to such surveillance – consolidated the institutionalization of a pragmatic policy orientation.

The Camera in Kerry Park[1]

Kelowna (approximate population of 110,000) is located beside Okanagan Lake in the centre of the Okanagan Valley in the interior of British Columbia. The third largest metropolitan area in British Columbia and the largest city in the Okanagan Valley, Kelowna sits between Calgary and Vancouver. Toward the close of the nineteenth century, the commercial potential of the city was realized when settlement and transportation development enabled expansion of the fruit and wine industry in the region. Today the combination of commercial development, temperate climate, and surrounding lakes and natural amenities attracts tourists and retirees from around the world.

Kelowna's experience with public-area CCTV surveillance began in 1998 when then-Mayor Walter Gray learned about Sudbury's three-camera streetscape monitoring system at a meeting of the Okanagan municipalities. Gray was interested in such surveillance because of growing concerns among city representatives about drug use and prostitution in and around Kelowna's waterfront parks.[2] The superintendent of the RCMP detachment in Kelowna, Gary Forbes, was also encouraged by claims made by members of Sudbury's Lions Video Monitoring Advisory Committee (LVMAC) about the efficacy of surveillance cameras in reducing anti-social and criminal behaviour.

Beyond specific concerns about drug dealing and anti-social behaviour along Kelowna's waterfront, interest in public-area CCTV surveillance was reinforced by a set of community transformations that came to a head in 1986 – the year that residents of Kelowna experienced the first major riot in the city's history. During the annual Kelowna Regatta – a cultural festival that encompasses a wide range of community activities – groups of youth took to the downtown streets and inflicted approximately $250,000 worth of damage to local businesses. When similar riotous activities broke out the following year, the regatta was cancelled in 1988 – the first time since 1886.

The regatta riots had a twofold effect on the city's self-image: not only did they focus attention on growing problems with drug dealing and drug use in the downtown core (see below), but they also signalled the fast-changing character of the city more generally. From 1986 to 1991, for example, the population of Kelowna increased from 61,000 to 76,000 people.[3] During this time period, population growth was especially accelerated in areas close to downtown Kelowna, where a number of apartments and seniors' facilities were built (City of Kelowna 1999). Population growth throughout the 1990s[4] encouraged suburban residential and commercial development, and the centre of cultural life and commercial activity was increasingly displaced from the downtown core to the suburban periphery.[5]

Hence, the regatta riots tapped into a broader set of concerns among many residents of Kelowna about the changing character of the city. In response to the riots, and to the perceived social and community deterioration that preceded them, a civic organization, Kelowna Pride, was formed in 1989. Kelowna Pride promoted various cultural events in the parks around the city in an effort to discourage drinking, drug use, and public violence. In 1998, Kelowna Pride started to organize and promote Parks Alive! It is a non-profit community program designed to draw Kelowna's residents to the city's parks (especially downtown) to participate in community, artistic, and musical events.

Despite the multi-year effort to rid the parks of drug use and other undesirable behaviour, however, concerns about safety in the parks and the downtown area more generally persisted. It was in this context that Mayor Gray consulted with Superintendent Forbes, as well as Ron Born (city manager), about installing a surveillance camera in Kerry Park – a waterfront park situated across from the intersection of Mill Street and Bernard Avenue in downtown Kelowna. Corporal Doug Brecknell was placed in charge of planning installation of the camera. He contacted representatives of the City of Sudbury to talk about establishing a video surveillance monitoring system, and he contacted Trojan Security – a downtown security company – for technical expertise. On 15 July 1999, an experimental CCTV surveillance camera was installed on a wooden pole in Kerry Park.

The camera was equipped with manual and automated monitoring and recording functions. The system was capable of recording set periods of time, but it was not capable of 24/7 recording. It could not record around the clock because of limited storage capabilities (the system recorded on S-VHS tape). Even though the system was periodically used to record set blocks of time (e.g., eight hours on a Friday evening), the sole operator of the system, Doug Brecknell, lacked resources to review videotape surveillance records. In practice, the RCMP used the camera a few times to perform targeted surveillance operations in conjunction with police officers on the ground.[6]

After a few weeks of operation, the wooden pole supporting the camera was dowsed with gasoline and set on fire; the camera, a demo from the manufacturer, was damaged but not destroyed. Although the camera was used infrequently during the experimental phase, representatives of the city and the RCMP found it to be useful for targeting specific activities. Images of a drug deal captured on 15 July, for example, were apparently used to expedite legal proceedings. Nevertheless, city and RCMP representatives also found that public awareness of the camera simply displaced criminal activity to other areas of the park after a press release from the mayor's office drew attention to the camera (after two weeks of operation). Based on comparisons with Sudbury's camera program, there was agreement that the camera monitoring system lacked the necessary human and financial resources to accomplish the desired goal of eliminating drug-related activity from the park.

Part of the process of mounting a camera in Kerry Park involved consultation with the OPC. The OPC was consulted rather than the provincial OIPC because, although the RCMP contracts policing services to the municipality, they are a federal police force that falls under the jurisdiction of the OPC/ Privacy Act. In fact, the Kerry Park camera became the first case of public-area video surveillance to engage the OPC under Commissioner Bruce Phillips (information and privacy commissioner of Canada from 1990 to 2000). Prior to investigating the Kerry Park camera, Commissioner Phillips' office had investigated video surveillance in government offices. The information and privacy commissioner of British Columbia, David Flaherty, had also published in 1998 *Investigation Report P98-012*, a report on video surveillance practices at the main branch of the Vancouver Public Library in downtown Vancouver and at the headquarters of the Insurance Corporation of British Columbia in northern Vancouver. Public-area and streetscape surveillance posed a new set of developments for Commissioner Phillips' office.

Following discussions with representatives of the RCMP in Kelowna, Phillips opined that public-area video surveillance, as an experimental crime-control measure, is legitimate. He maintained that, if the city could demonstrate that video surveillance reduced drug use and trafficking in the park, then it was justified in using the technology. His decision reflected the position adopted by Commissioner Flaherty, as well as the position adopted by the British Columbia Civil Liberties Association (BCCLA), pertaining to the camera in Kerry Park.[7]

The Queensway Camera and the Spirit of the Law

Although RCMP and city personnel experimented with the test camera in Kerry Park only for a short period of time, they concluded that video surveillance was a useful tool for policing social problems. They also concluded that public-area video surveillance enjoyed community support based on anecdotal claims from members of the business community and city hall (no formal public opinion survey was conducted until 2001).

In the fall of 1999, the RCMP began to explore ways to implement a streetscape CCTV surveillance system in the downtown core. Their desire to move quickly to establish such a system was driven by three sets of concerns. The first set involved drug activity, criminality, and vandalism in and around Kasugai Garden and the Queensway bus depot. Kasugai Garden (named after and donated by Kelowna's sister city in Japan) is an enclosed tourist and community attraction; it is located behind city hall on Water Street, adjacent to the Queensway bus loop. In the late 1990s, the grounds-keeper of Kasugai Garden complained to city hall that the park was being used as a site for drug dealers and users. Discarded needles were regularly found in the park, and its hours of operation were consequently scaled back due to the growing presence of drug dealers and users.[8]

The escalation of drug dealing and use in Kasugai Garden was related to a growing number of complaints about vandalism, intimidation, and harassment at the Queensway bus loop. The bus loop is a transit mall located at the east end of Queensway Avenue at the Ellis Street intersection. Not only did the city experience problems with vandalism (e.g., broken windows in the bus kiosks) and graffiti at the bus loop, but a set of complaints was also lodged with city hall about people panhandling and sleeping in the bus loop area. City representatives voiced particular concerns about women and seniors feeling intimidated to use the Queensway transit area.

The second set of concerns in the downtown area involved loitering, vandalism, panhandling, intimidation, and violence around the corner of Leon and Abbott Streets – an area directly across from City Park and close to the Gospel Mission. The mission is a non-profit Christian organization that provides food, lodging, and essential services (e.g., dental care) to needy men. The guiding philosophy of the mission is to provide food and lodging for all men irrespective of life circumstances or situations. The "open door" orientation of the Gospel Mission posed a problem for city officials because it attracted a variety of clients, not all of whom were legitimately needy in the eyes of city officials (e.g., drug users and "transients").[9] City officials were equally concerned with similar service provisions of the Drop-In and Information Centre, an organization a few blocks east of the Gospel Mission that provides food and shelter to men and women.

The third set of concerns in the downtown area centred on the bar flush between Leon and Lawrence Avenues – especially during the summer months. The bar flush entails hundreds of bar patrons in the 200 block of Leon Avenue leaving numerous drinking establishments at the same time. Certain members of the large groups of mostly intoxicated patrons who fill the streets allegedly vandalize parked cars and businesses, compete for a limited number of taxis, and come into conflict with one another.

In essence, the combination of concerns about drug dealing, homelessness, vandalism, and the bar flush, reinforced by a dearth of beat cops in the core, produced the perception among city representatives that the downtown area was out of control. Responding to this perception, Gary Forbes began to co-ordinate discussions with representatives of the city and the Downtown Kelowna Association (DKA) about establishing a six-camera monitoring system to cover the downtown area. Based on concerns expressed by the BCCLA, and by provincial Information and Privacy Commissioner David

Loukidelis,[10] the RCMP started to develop an operations manual to stipulate how the monitoring system would be administered. Following the approach taken in Sudbury, they also started to explore partnership funding with the city and the DKA. On 11 February 2000, the DKA pledged $5,000 toward the purchase of a camera to monitor "hot spots" in the areas of Queensway and Leon Avenues.

On 9 March 2000, the proposal to install cameras in the downtown core came before Kelowna City Council. Although the primary, long-term goal was to cover the entire downtown area, city, DKA, and RCMP representatives initially focused on Kasugai Garden. No formal written proposal was presented to council, and no public consultations were conducted prior to considering video surveillance in the Queensway area. After hearing arguments brought forth by Ron Born in favour of establishing a video surveillance monitoring system, a majority of councillors agreed in principle to endorse the monitoring program. However, they decided to wait for finalization of the RCMP's video surveillance policy (finalized in April 2000). Council earmarked $17,000 for installation of the camera.

On 22 February 2001, a "community safety camera" overlooking Kasugai Garden was activated. The camera, mounted to a fifty-foot torch-proof metal pole above the Bennett Clock, rotates 360 degrees and is capable of surveying the entire Queensway bus loop. Eleven signs notifying the public that the area is under video surveillance were mounted. Surveillance images were transmitted to RCMP headquarters, where four civilian watch commanders (hired by the city to work in the RCMP detachment) had access to camera images. Images from the camera were recorded twenty-four hours a day, seven days a week, on two recorders and retained for six months. Surveillance images were periodically monitored by watch commanders, whose primary duties were other than video surveillance monitoring; for reasons of liability, the RCMP decided that live monitoring would foster an unjustified expectation among the public that they would be able to respond to all crimes in progress (Royal Canadian Mounted Police 2001).

As city, RCMP, and DKA representatives began to plan for expansion of the monitoring program using reserve funds earmarked by the city (approximately $100,000), Commissioner Loukidelis wrote a second letter to the city (on 26 June 2001) to raise concerns about video surveillance in public places. Loukidelis also sent a letter to the new information and privacy commissioner of Canada, George Radwanski, to request an investigation into the lawfulness of the Queensway camera under the Privacy Act (and the lawfulness of the proposed installation of five other cameras). His letter, which constituted an official complaint to the OPC, was inspired by claims made by the BCCLA (on 18 June 2001) that the Queensway camera was simply displacing crime to the corner of Bertram Avenue and Lawrence Street.[11]

In response to Loukidelis' request, the OPC launched its second investigation into CCTV surveillance in Kelowna. Commissioner Radwanski sent two inspectors to Kelowna to assess the monitoring system. Part of the investigation involved consultation with Giuliano Zaccardelli, then commissioner of the RCMP, about the lawfulness of the camera. In a letter dated 4 October 2001,[12] Commissioner Radwanski informed Commissioner Loukidelis that the OPC's investigation concluded that the RCMP are not justified in recording general public activity 24/7. Set against the backdrop of the CAI's ruling in Sherbrooke in 1992 (see Chapter 3), Radwanski explained to Loukidelis that continuous recording violates section 4 of the Privacy Act[13] and that Commissioner Zaccardelli had ordered the RCMP in Kelowna on 28 August 2001 to stop recording continuous images to comply with the Privacy Act. On 27 November 2001, however, Zaccardelli wrote to Radwanski to explain that the RCMP did not agree with the arguments of his report and that, although continuous recording would not continue, they would continue to use the camera (Royal Canadian Mounted Police 2003).

Based on his investigation (which was presented in the form of a response letter to Loukidelis), Radwanski therefore concluded that the RCMP were in compliance with the letter of the law concerning video surveillance in Kelowna. However, he also concluded that the RCMP were in violation of the spirit of the law. The Privacy Act, argued Radwanski, was written in the early 1980s when real-time public-area video surveillance could not have been anticipated. The spirit of the law, he maintained, concerned the very presence of the camera and the constitutional rights of innocent Canadians to walk the streets free of police surveillance; it did not concern minor technicalities such as the use of a VCR to record camera images. Hence, Radwanski explained in his letter to Loukidelis why he thought that any public-area video surveillance carried out by the RCMP in Kelowna or elsewhere is unacceptable. Radwanski reasoned that, especially in the wake of the 9/11 attacks in Washington and New York, public-area video surveillance posed a punctuated threat to the privacy rights of innocent individuals. In a manner of argumentation never before publicly presented by an information and privacy commissioner in Canada, Radwanski outlined the enormous psychological impact of having to live with constant surveillance carried out by Big Brother-type policing agencies.

Constitutional Debate about Public-Area CCTV Surveillance

When Commissioner Radwanski published his opinion about the camera in Kasugai Garden in an open letter addressed to Commissioner Loukidelis, video surveillance monitoring practices had already attracted the attention of his office. For instance, on 15 June 2001, Radwanski responded to a complaint filed by the information and privacy commissioner for the Northwest

Territories, Elaine Keenan Bengts, under the newly created Personal Information Protection and Electronic Documents Act (PIPEDA).

The complaint focused on Centurion Security Services, a security company that mounted four streetscape CCTV surveillance cameras on its office building to monitor a downtown intersection in Yellowknife. Centurion staff members monitored the camera images for a little less than a week before public criticism encouraged company representatives to dismantle the cameras.[14] Under PIPEDA, Radwanski ruled (on 15 June 2001) that the monitoring system was unlawful.[15]

Commissioner Radwanski's efforts to resist public-area CCTV surveillance intensified in the months following his ruling on Centurion Security Services. Under the Privacy Act, the privacy commissioner's powers are limited to making recommendations to the heads of federal institutions under investigation and, if fruitless, to report to Parliament through a special report or, more usually, an annual report. Radwanski exercised both options. In the OPC's 2000-1 annual report (Office of the Information and Privacy Commissioner of Canada 2001), he reiterated concerns about the rights of innocent individuals being subjected to intrusive forms of surveillance by the RCMP. Moreover, in his annual report, he called on members of Parliament and senators to assist in pressing the RCMP to remove the Queensway camera. A few months later (15 March 2002), Radwanski sent a letter to the solicitor general of Canada, Lawrence MacAulay, to request an immediate order to the RCMP to dismantle the Queensway camera.[16] In the letter, Radwanski argued that it was unusual for the RCMP to ignore the recommendations of the information and privacy commissioner of Canada and that the RCMP's defiance potentially struck a crippling and irrevocable blow to the quality of privacy in Canada. Solicitor General MacAulay dismissed Radwanski's claims and refused to acknowledge his own jurisdiction over the RCMP in Kelowna as a contracted police force to the municipality.[17]

Radwanski subsequently intensified his efforts to halt monitoring practices in Kelowna by commissioning Justice Gérard La Forest, a former justice of the Supreme Court of Canada, to offer an opinion on the legality of the use of video surveillance by the police on public streets (i.e., "general video surveillance"). Radwanski commissioned La Forest because he had written the decision in *R. v. Wong* (1990),[18] where Toronto police officers had used CCTV surveillance cameras to monitor illegal gambling activities in a hotel room in the absence of a police warrant. The case went to the Supreme Court of Canada as a constitutional challenge under section 8 of the Canadian Charter of Rights and Freedoms: "Everyone has the right to be secure against unreasonable search or seizure."[19] The Supreme Court ruled that, although the police had a reasonable misunderstanding of the law, they were not justified in violating the privacy rights of Wong – regardless of the technologies used to gather information. Wong's appeal was dismissed, but the privacy rights of individuals (who enjoy reasonable expectations to privacy under the Charter), even when engaged in illegal activities, were affirmed.

In his assessment of warrantless general video surveillance in Kelowna, La Forest (2002) opined that the practice violates section 8 of the Charter. He equated general video surveillance with a police officer closely following a person in a given geographical space, and he argued that the constitutionality of general video surveillance should not hinge on recording. The latter interpretation of the Charter was significant: it essentially rejected the argument that non-recorded video surveillance can be understood as an extension of human visual capabilities (see Chapter 3), and it called into question the ethics of general public video surveillance *sui generis*. La Forest also opined that Solicitor General MacAulay did have jurisdiction over the RCMP in Kelowna, a declaration that reinforced Commissioner Radwanski's interpretation of the Privacy Act.

Publication of La Forest's legal opinion vindicated Radwanski's efforts to challenge public-area video surveillance practices by federal law enforcement agencies, and it ignited a chain of events that ultimately set the federal privacy agenda on public-area video surveillance in Canada. The first link in the chain involved a set of public engagements to clarify and promote the ethical and legal bases for challenging video surveillance in public places. On 17 July 2001, for example, Commissioner Radwanski sent an open letter to Southam News in response to a story that the news agency had printed on the front page of the Ottawa Citizen (and other Southam publications). Commenting on PIPEDA, Southam claimed that the new legislation could permit a robber to walk into a bank and demand that surveillance cameras be turned off before committing a robbery. Radwanski responded by explaining the normative bases of the reasonable person test (i.e., an organization may collect, use, or disclose information only for purposes that a reasonable person would consider appropriate under given circumstances) and by explicating a rarely seen distinction among privacy advocates concerning different types of situations where video surveillance occurs. Radwanski argued that the difference between private surveillance on private premises and private commercial surveillance of the public carried out by public agencies, on the one hand, and public-area video surveillance, on the other, is crucial to the reasonable person test (see Radwanski 2001). This argument draws attention to the important normative differences between public and private spaces, and between public and private interests, thereby resisting the all-too-common conflation of video surveillance in public, private, and hybridized public-private spaces (see Chapter 2).

Early the following year, Commissioner Radwanski visited the West Coast of Canada. On 6 February 2002, he addressed approximately thirty-five members of the Kelowna Chamber of Commerce (he also delivered an address to approximately thirty people at Okanagan University College the following year). His purpose was clear: to frame video surveillance as an imminent threat to the rights and freedoms of Canadians. Radwanski argued that the single camera in Kelowna represented a national test case – the thin edge of the wedge – that will "irrevocably change our whole notion of our rights and freedoms" (2002a). He did so by conceptualizing privacy as an innate human need, and by citing evidence and examples pertaining to function creep, displacement, and camera effectiveness. Significantly, Radwanski avoided voicing a polemical position on CCTV surveillance (i.e., CCTV surveillance is unacceptable in any situation), alternatively presenting a number of logical and empirically based arguments about the problems posed by public-area camera surveillance.[20]

The campaign against public-area CCTV surveillance heated up on 21 June 2002 when Radwanski filed a statement of claim against the solicitor general, the attorney general, and the commissioner of the RCMP with the Supreme Court of British Columbia. He sought a declaration that video surveillance by the RCMP in a public place is contrary to the Canadian Charter of Rights and Freedoms and that it breaches the United Nations Universal Declaration of Human Rights and the International Covenant on Civil and Political Rights.[21]

Reacting to Radwanski's statement of claim, the RCMP and the Department of the Solicitor General initiated strategic action to defend against the challenge (a statement of defence was submitted on 13 September 2002 by the Department of Justice). Immediately following the statement of claim, representatives of the Department of the Solicitor General began meeting with representatives of the RCMP (from July to September 2002) to discuss the use of public-area video surveillance cameras by federal law enforcement agencies. Representatives of each agency agreed to work together to develop an overarching national public policy position on the use of "public safety cameras" based on the RCMP's existing operations manual on closed-circuit video equipment (Blondin 2002). They decided to base the national framework on the principles laid out in the provincial policy frameworks adopted in Alberta, Ontario, and British Columbia but with stronger language in order to "effectively communicate that the Department and the RCMP are committed to enhancing public safety and crime prevention through the Public Safety Camera initiative while at the same time giving full consideration and respect to the privacy rights of Canadians" (Blondin 2002, 2).

Beyond concerns pertaining to the use of video surveillance by federal law enforcement agencies, however, Radwanski's actions touched a nerve among government agencies concerning the perceived growing assertiveness by parliamentary commissioners. Internal correspondence in the Department of Justice is worth quoting at length:

Parliamentary Commissioners such as the Privacy Commissioner and the Information Commissioner have shown increased interest in expanding their role beyond their statutory mandates as ombudsmen who are ultimately responsible to Parliament. This is confirmed in the pleadings of the Privacy Commissioner in this case when he states that he has the powers beyond those provided for in the Privacy Act. The Privacy Commissioner openly claims to be the protector of privacy interests of Canadians and asserts that it is his responsibility to bring to the courts issues which threaten the privacy of Canadians.

The Privacy Commissioner's view of his role in bringing forward this court challenge is incompatible with the role assigned by Parliament. It threatens a shift from Parliamentary accountability to judicial accountability and could lead to future court challenges to government actions or programs and even legislation. For example the Privacy Commissioner could initiate a Charter challenge to the CCRA database or to the proposed lawful access scheme ...

In addition, if the Privacy Commissioner's authority to bring this case is not challenged it will set a precedent that will be difficult to overcome both legally and in the public environment. This case, if it proceeds, is likely to make it to the Supreme Court of Canada. If that happens, it will be very difficult to argue in subsequent cases that the Commissioner does not have the authority to initiate an action of this kind. What is more, this precedent will not be limited to the Privacy Commissioner but would extend to other Parliamentary Commissioners (e.g., the Information Commissioner, the Human Rights Commissioner, the Auditor General, etc.) and possibly to other statutory office holders (Department of Justice n.d.b).

Hence, Radwanski's challenge to public-area video surveillance tapped into an existing set of concerns among government agencies concerning the perceived shift in the role of parliamentary commissions from advocates for parliamentary accountability to regulators pursuing judicial accountability.

On 12 March 2003, Commissioner Radwanski's Charter challenge began with the federal government's motion to the Supreme Court of British Columbia (Kelowna) to dismiss the case. The Department of Justice motioned to have the case dismissed on the grounds that Radwanski did not possess powers as a parliamentary officer to launch a court case. The Office of the Information and Privacy Commissioner, federal lawyers argued, is a statutory body under the Privacy Act, and no law makes explicit reference to the privacy commissioner's privileges to initiate legal action under the Charter. The commissioner's powers, argued federal lawyers, are limited to investigating and making recommendations in the capacity of ombudsman on behalf of Parliament and to keep the contents of the report confidential. In response, Radwanski's lawyer argued that the Privacy Act stipulates the commissioner's role as neither ombudsman nor litigator, yet the Supreme Court of Canada has previously granted the commissioner leave to argue cases in court.

The legal debate about the information and privacy commissioner of Canada's role partially reflects the structural dilemmas inherent in the very Office of the Information and Privacy Commissioner of Canada. The commissioner enjoys a flexible and complex set of powers as ombudsman, advisor, educator, and quasi-judge, yet the statutory frameworks outlining the commissioner's role are unclear. Consequently, the ways in which the powers of the commissioner's office get used are largely dependent on the styles, skills, and personalities of office holders (Bennett 2003). Commissioner Radwanski possessed personal characteristics such that he eschewed the hitherto existing educational- and advocacy-based policy approach favouring privacy pragmatism and challenged the very practice of public-area CCTV surveillance. He was so committed to challenging video surveillance that he publicly proclaimed that he expected federal lawyers to seek delays in hearing the substantive Charter issues pertaining to public-area video surveillance and that a set of appeals was inevitable.

The appeals never materialized. The BC Supreme Court ruled that Commissioner Radwanski did not have the legal authority to challenge the RCMP's use of video surveillance under the Charter. The court's ruling did not necessarily signal the end of the OPC's efforts to quell public-area video surveillance in Canada, and Radwanski planned to continue his fight against public-area monitoring practices. Yet on 23 June 2003, he resigned after a committee of members of Parliament claimed that he had falsified financial documents and violated standards of office and human management. The commissioner, cleared of charges on 13 February 2009, maintained that he had been discredited for his strong opposition to post-9/11 government surveillance initiatives in general and to CCTV surveillance in particular.[22]

In July 2003, Interim Privacy Commissioner Robert Marleau announced that the OPC was withdrawing an appeal to the BC Supreme Court filed by Commissioner Radwanski. The stated reasons for withdrawing the appeal were the costs associated with continuing to fight video surveillance as well as the low likelihood of success and the narrowness of the issue.[23] Marleau alternatively initiated discussions with the RCMP that were oriented toward developing a national policy framework on public-area video surveillance and intended to produce a set of guidelines to denote best practices. When Information and Privacy Commissioner Jennifer Stoddart took office in 2003, she claimed that it was not possible to re-initiate the appeal and continued to pursue a national policy framework (see below).

The consequence of withdrawing the appeal, then, was threefold: first, the substantive constitutional issues of public-area video surveillance were never debated in a Canadian court; second, the Charter challenge became associated with a discredited privacy commissioner;[24] and third, the pragmatic, reactive, complaints-based approach to addressing public-area video surveillance was institutionalized in the period 2003-6. The last consequence reinforced rather than transformed the already-existing policy framework that had taken hold across the provinces, and it inadvertently contributed to a diversity of responses to monitoring programs in various communities.

Toward a National Policy Framework on Public-Area Video Surveillance

When Commissioner Stoddart took office in December 2003, she was presented with a draft copy of terms of reference developed by the OPC-RCMP task force on video surveillance (Office of the Information and Privacy Commissioner of Canada 2003b). The terms of reference were focused primarily on the issues arising from the abandoned challenge to the RCMP's camera in Kelowna; they sought to strike a balance between RCMP policing duties and the OPC's commitments to minimizing privacy intrusions. Stoddart adopted the minimal rules orientation that she had endorsed as privacy commissioner of Quebec (recall that the public hearings were held in September 2003 in Quebec) as well as the more detailed frameworks in place in British Columbia, Ontario, and Alberta, and she began to formulate a set of guidelines to encourage "best practices" in video surveillance monitoring of public areas.

On 1 September 2004, the officer in charge at the National Contract Policing Branch (NCPB) and a representative from the Operational Policy Sector met with representatives from the OPC to discuss terms of reference for a task force on police surveillance of public places.[25] Earlier that year (in April), the RCMP contacted the Canadian Association of Chiefs of Police (CACP); the latter confirmed that it did not have a policy to govern provincial and municipal agencies' use of community surveillance cameras. The following day, a bulletin was forwarded to all divisions of the CACP to request that installation of community cameras remain suspended until further notice from the NCPB (Royal Canadian Mounted Police 2005).

On the recommendation of Commissioner Zaccardelli (Office of the Information and Privacy Commissioner of Canada 2004a), the OPC took the lead in developing national guidelines for the use of public-area video surveillance cameras. Zaccardelli recommended that the OPC develop the guidelines because he did not want the RCMP to be perceived as representing the diverse policing agencies in Canada. The OPC adopted a two-pronged approach. The first aim was to consolidate existing knowledge in house, with a view to commissioning an empirically based, independent study of the scope of public video surveillance through its contributions program, and to study data-protection policies around the world. The second aim was to educate Canadians about public video surveillance.[26] From the outset, members of the OPC recognized that they were limited in what they could say about public video surveillance because they did not even know the extent of public-area monitoring systems in Canada (Office of the Information and Privacy Commissioner of Canada 2004b; see, too, Chapter 10).

In 2004, the OPC finalized a draft set of guidelines and terms of reference for the use of public-area video surveillance cameras. Part of the terms of reference acknowledged the progressive steps that the RCMP took in response to the Queensway camera in Kelowna to develop a policy framework and to study the effectiveness of a second camera installed at the corner of Leon and Abbott Streets (see below).[27] In response to the proposed guidelines, the RCMP informed the OPC that they could speak in isolation of neither the Canadian police community nor other federal enforcement agencies. They also warned the OPC that it would be unwise to proceed with guidelines before gaining the endorsement of Canadian policing agencies.

After a number of delays by the RCMP and the CACP, the OPC announced that it intended to release final guidelines in January 2005 regardless of consent from the Canadian policing community (a draft of the guidelines was previously sent to the RCMP and the CACP). Reacting to the announcement, RCMP internal correspondence expressed several conflicting concerns about the legal ramifications of the guidelines where evidentiary standards for implementing surveillance cameras by the RCMP and other enforcement agencies in Canada are concerned; about the OPC developing policy for the RCMP; about the need to collaborate with the CACP; and about the importance of maintaining working relations with the OPC.

Although the OPC issued draft guidelines on 25 June 2004, it was not until 10 January 2005 that they were sent to the Community, Contract and Aboriginal Policing Services (CCAPS) for comments.[28] The conclusion of the analysis was that, if adhered to, the guidelines proposed by the OPC would entail significant resource expenditure by the RCMP and the wider Canadian policing community. It was concluded that, if adopted, the guidelines would lead to significant delays in the implementation of video surveillance systems. Especially problematic were principles pertaining to privacy impact assessments, restricting the use of video surveillance to serious exceptional circumstances, and responding to information-access requests for segments of video recording excluding other individuals. The analysis also warned of the potential danger that the guidelines – designed to apply to "community cameras" – might be extended to other forms of video surveillance (e.g., cell blocks).

By late 2005, the OPC had not received RCMP endorsement of the guidelines and consequently proceeded to finalize the guidelines alone. In March 2006, the OPC's *Guidelines for the Use of Video Surveillance of Public Places by Police and Law Enforcement Authorities* was released (see Appendix D). The OPC explains in the preamble to the fifteen principles that the guidelines were developed in the context of a discussion group of stakeholders established jointly by the OPC and the RCMP, following the 2001 investigation in Kelowna. By the time the federal guidelines were published in 2006, Alberta, British Columbia, Ontario, Nova Scotia, Saskatchewan, New Brunswick, Newfoundland and Labrador, and Quebec had put measures in place. In effect, publication of the OPC guidelines marked the institutionalization of the pragmatic policy framework on public-area video surveillance.

Therefore, the regulatory approach that Commissioner Radwanski adopted to address public-area video surveillance threatened to shift the emerging policy framework in Canada from a passive, complaints-based educational approach to an active regulatory one. The latter was to be informed by public consideration of the constitutional and ethical bases of public-area video surveillance. With Radwanski's challenge terminated, however, a pragmatic policy initiative was institutionalized concerning public-area video surveillance that had at least two interrelated consequences: first, it consolidated a policy framework worked out in the provinces; second, it reinforced the policy framework that inadvertently enabled a diversity of responses to monitoring initiatives in communities across Canada. In other words, if nothing else, Radwanski's efforts could have focused more attention on the ethics and pragmatics of public-area video surveillance. Instead, they were reduced to something perceived to be the ranting of an egomaniac that violated the standards of his public office.

After the Queensway Camera

While national attention was focused on the mounting tensions between the OPC and the RCMP/Department of Justice in early 2002, representatives of the Kelowna RCMP, DKA, and City of Kelowna developed plans to expand their monitoring system. On 22 April 2002, Kelowna City Council met with the RCMP to discuss the implications of the opinion offered by Justice La Forest. Two decisions were reached: first, that the Queensway camera would be turned off; second, that a new, RCMP-run camera would be installed at the corner of Leon and Abbott Streets. The latter was planned as a one-year pilot study to measure the effects of video surveillance monitoring on crime rates in and around the Leon-Abbott area.

As early as June 2001, however, Mayor Gray openly resisted Commissioner Radwanski's efforts to terminate the camera program in Kelowna. On 29 June, for instance, Gray wrote to Commissioner Loukidelis to explain how the camera system in the Queensway area was in compliance with the requirements set out by Commissioner Phillips. In October of that year, Gray publicized the results of a citizens' survey revealing that 80 percent of Kelowna's residents agreed that cameras are an effective crime prevention tool.[29] This was combined with claims presented in Sudbury's KPMG report that

7   Streetscape surveillance camera, City of Kelowna, British Columbia

crime had fallen dramatically in Sudbury after cameras were installed. Finally, in February and March 2002, Mayor Gray wrote to Commissioner Zaccardelli and Minister MacAulay to reaffirm the city's support for the camera, and he received supportive responses from both (City of Kelowna n.d.).

The second camera was installed at the corner of Leon and Abbott Streets on 16 October 2002 – the same day that the Queensway camera was returned to the city and simultaneously turned off (see Figure 7). Part of the promotional effort to shift monitoring activities to the Leon-Abbott location involved references to an assault that watch commanders picked up on the Queensway camera. In early July 2002, a beating took place in the parking lot of Memorial Arena (located across the street from the police station) after a failed drug deal. Watch commanders notified the RCMP, who intervened in the assault and made an arrest. RCMP officials subsequently claimed that they were able to prevent a probable homicide and that the taped assault constituted evidence for legal proceedings (Jones 2002).

Despite a series of technical difficulties, the new camera became operational on 17 September 2003. The RCMP issued a press release, informing the public that they would run a one-year pilot study to test the effectiveness of the camera. They also informed the public that, in consultation with the OPC, they had put in place a policy on public safety cameras respecting the privacy rights of Canadian citizens (Royal Canadian Mounted Police 2003). When the new camera was activated, Commissioner Zaccardelli promised the OPC that the RCMP would not install any additional cameras until the close of the pilot project.

Following further technical delays, the pilot project was initiated from April 2004 to April 2005.[30] When the project came to a close, the RCMP detachment in Kelowna reported its findings to RCMP E Division Headquarters. The findings indicated that the camera had failed to reduce crime in the downtown area. Kelowna RCMP attributed the failure to an unexpected influx of transients into the core. Transients, they argued, are not able to gain admission to the Gospel Mission, so they circulate around the downtown area and mix with intoxicated bar-goers, especially on weekend evenings. RCMP officers requested an extension of four and a half months to study further the effectiveness of the camera, and they requested approval to perform continuous recording due to limited human resources to monitor the camera. RCMP E Division headquarters granted the extension but denied the request to institute continuous recording (Royal Canadian Mounted Police 2005). The camera was reactivated on 1 August 2005 and ran until February 2006.

Meanwhile, on 22 August 2005, Kelowna City Council voted to reinstall the Queensway camera. This decision was based on recommendations from the City of Kelowna's Transportation Division following a 2004 meeting between officials from the Transportation Division and officials from Translink, the Greater Vancouver Transportation Authority.[31] Council endorsed a proposal to have images from the Queensway camera monitored by evening security staff at the Chapman Parkade, a parking facility on Lawrence Street run by the City of Kelowna, where the installation of additional cameras was planned. To appease Commissioner Loukidelis, council also decided that the city would develop a CCTV monitoring policy in accordance with the terms of the provincial Freedom of Information and Protection of Privacy Act.

There are several reasons why Kelowna City Council voted to reactivate the Queensway camera and bring it under city (as opposed to RCMP) control. Tracing to July 2004, the city adopted several strategies to combat problems in the Queensway and Leon-Abbott areas. For example, six additional beat cops had been hired to work the downtown area, and RCMP policing power was reinforced by DKA security patrols used to target transients. The city also hired security staff to patrol the transient station between the hours of 3 p.m. and 10 p.m., and a number of crime prevention through environmental design (CPTED) principles had been introduced into the transit mall (e.g., cutting down hedges, increasing lighting, cleaning graffiti, biweekly power-washing, playing classical music from the Bennett Clock) (City of Kelowna 2005).

Still, problems in the transit loop persisted. The RCMP promised to hold off on introduction of the cameras until the pilot project came to a close and until the national guidelines were completed. It was therefore decided that the antenna and monitoring equipment for the Queensway camera would be removed from the RCMP detachment and relocated to the Chapman Parkade. The total cost of the project was $13,609 ($3,848.75 to move the antenna from the RCMP detachment to the parkade, funded by transit funding, and $9,760.44 from the city's parking reserve to install cameras in the parkade). The city decided to install cameras in the parkade because it was previously policed by security staff who performed regular foot patrols. Once the security staff were charged with monitoring the Queensway bus loop, foot patrol was no longer possible. Council accepted the recommendation of the Transportation Division to install cameras in the parkade so that the area could also be constantly monitored.

Four stationary cameras were purchased and distributed throughout the parkade. The monitoring station is manned for sixteen hours a day. The cameras in the parkade, and the Queensway camera, are recorded onto a hard-disk drive that overwrites every twenty days, save for instances when the video is retained for legal proceedings.

At the time of writing (July 2009), Kelowna City Council was considering extending the system in the parkade (it had the technological capability to run sixteen cameras on the existing circuit). The RCMP detachment had also applied to the city to install four additional streetscape cameras. The proposal called for the city to take over the Leon-Abbott camera as well as the proposed cameras. If the latter took hold, then the system will fall under provincial jurisdiction. Yet as of May 2010, city representatives were rethinking their endorsement of all video surveillance (the Chapman Parkade contract had been revised) – even after receiving funds from the province (see Appendix A).

Conclusion

When the idea to establish a public-area CCTV surveillance monitoring system partially diffused from Sudbury to Kelowna in 1998, representatives of the city and the RCMP set out to model their system on the Lions Eye in the Sky. Advocates of CCTV monitoring in Kelowna were especially interested in Sudbury's community funding model and in CCTV surveillance as an adjunct to policing powers. The process of introducing a system in Kelowna, however, did not follow from that of Sudbury: there was no community oversight/steering committee that came together, no sustained fundraising or public relations campaigns, and few resources available to introduce live monitoring of surveillance cameras. Rather than reproduce or even approximate the scope and character of the Lions Eye in the Sky, then, Kelowna's system unevenly diffused from that of Sudbury.

The Charter challenge introduced by Commissioner Radwanski threatened to reconfigure the ways that streetscape monitoring was conducted in Kelowna and across the country. In response to the challenge, not only the RCMP in Kelowna but also representatives in other Canadian cities suspended efforts to promote or expand streetscape monitoring systems. On termination of the challenge, the pragmatic approach to public-area CCTV surveillance was consolidated, and information and privacy commissioners across the country (especially in Quebec) became more passive. The OIPCs' emphases in responding to monitoring initiatives shifted closer to encouraging compliance with the stipulations in minimal rules protocols, and CCTV advocates in cities across the country – including Kelowna – perceived resolution of the Charter challenge as a green light to proceed with monitoring activities. In other words, prior to 2003, the influence of the Charter challenge, as a signal event in the history of streetscape monitoring in Canada, led many proponents of CCTV surveillance to reduce efforts to introduce or expand monitoring systems. Yet diffusion of the challenge had the opposite effect, albeit with heterogeneous outcomes, after 2003. Indeed, although the consolidation of privacy pragmatism contributed to a variety of responses to establishing monitoring systems, it also further enabled the staging of resistance.

6
London's Downtown Camera Project

This chapter examines the City of London, Ontario's, Downtown Camera Project. The project became the country's largest monitoring program (in terms of the number of cameras) when it was launched in the fall of 2001. Some of the communications and promotional dynamics that contributed to the formation of the project have been examined elsewhere (Hier et al. 2007; Hier, Walby, and Greenberg 2006; Hier 2004); in those studies, the initiative was conceptualized as a form of streetscape CCTV monitoring that developed from the ground up. As the data presented in this chapter illustrate, however, the Downtown Camera Project involved a more elaborate set of relations than previously suggested.

The primary aim of earlier analyses was to understand better the promotional and fundraising efforts that gained momentum when a citizens' group formed in the immediate aftermath of the murder of a young person in London's downtown bar district. It is improbable that the monitoring system would have been launched in the absence of the sympathy and emotion evoked by the multi-pronged community- and police-driven educational and safety campaign that followed the murder, but the Downtown Camera Project entailed a broad configuration of government and extra-government forces that culminated in the country's most detailed operational and governance protocol, replete with institutional safeguards and accountability structures (regardless of their initial and ongoing effectiveness).

The governance structure developed to administer the Downtown Camera Project is significant for understanding how monitoring systems were developed after London's system was established. The progressive operational design of the project was based on a sequence of funding debates, signal events, liability concerns, and consultations/interactions with the Ontario OIPC, yet the administrative apparatus diffused inconsistently to other cities. As I explain in Chapters 7 and 9, for example, the Hamilton Police Service ignored London's organizational design, but the City of Thunder Bay modelled its Eye on the Street program after London's. Organizational developments in Sudbury and Hamilton, moreover, combined with the inconsistent diffusion of London's program, reinforced progressive and negative trends in the diffusion of streetscape monitoring programs in Windsor (Chapter 7), Brockville and Peterborough (Chapter 8), and Vancouver (Chapter 7).

The Downtown Camera Project[1]

London (estimated population of 450,000) is located in southwestern Ontario, situated midway between the Canada-US border at Detroit and Toronto (approximately 200 kilometres each way). The city is known as a university town, with a population of approximately 40,000 full-time students primarily attending the University of Western Ontario and Fanshawe College. In a manner similar to that of other cities examined in Chapters 3, 4, and 5, London's downtown core experienced an accelerated degree of business flight to suburban malls prior to installation of the Downtown Camera Project. Especially visible to Londoners has been the migration of businesses from the Galleria – the major downtown mall – and the concomitant hollowing out of the shopping centre.

The Downtown Camera Project became operational on 15 November 2001. Bolstered by claims made by members of Sudbury's Lions Video Monitoring Advisory Committee (LVMAC) concerning the economic and crime-reduction benefits of streetscape CCTV surveillance in northern Ontario (see Chapter 4), London's monitoring program was implemented under the official guise of providing and maintaining a safe environment for citizens and businesses in the downtown core and of deterring and/or improving the ability of police to respond to crime and anti-social behaviour (Corporation of the City of London 2001). Establishment of the Downtown Camera Project, however, was based on a number of diverse forces – not least of which was the desire to rejuvenate the downtown business economy – that configured to articulate the need for streetscape CCTV surveillance in the core.

The initial idea to install streetscape CCTV surveillance cameras in London came from the newly appointed chief of police, Albert Gramolini. In early 1999, Police Chief Gramolini instructed Steve Goodine, then-sergeant of community services, to investigate CCTV surveillance in public places. Goodine's investigation entailed examining Sudbury's Lions Eye in the Sky video surveillance monitoring program as well as monitoring programs in Glasgow, Scotland, and Ipswich, England.[2] His initial investigation did not entail detailed consideration of privacy protection law or consultation with the Ontario OIPC.

As Goodine was investigating monitoring programs in Sudbury and the United Kingdom, twenty-year-old Michael Goldie-Ryder was stabbed to death outside Ichabods, a bar close to the intersection of Richmond and York Streets in the downtown entertainment district. Goldie-Ryder, a

London-area student attending Regina Mundi College, was celebrating a friend's birthday party on 16 January 1999. Shortly after 2 a.m., when several drinking establishments let out simultaneously, Goldie-Ryder was stabbed in the neck after a fight broke out over access to a taxicab. The same evening, Jeremy Beebe, a student at Fanshawe College, was stabbed in the chest close to the same intersection.[3]

In the days following the stabbings, Police Chief Gramolini met with downtown bar owners to discuss ways to reduce violence in the core.[4] At the same time, local businessman David Tennant and local radio personality Jim Chapman met with Mayor Dianne Haskett to organize a public meeting to talk about violence in the downtown area – especially in the context of drinking establishments. The public meeting, held at London's Convention Centre on 11 February, attracted an estimated 200 people.[5] The meeting featured Mayor Haskett, Police Chief Gramolini, and Amanda Alvaro, who represented the newly created citizens' group Friends Against Senseless Endings (FASE). FASE was organized by friends of Michael Goldie-Ryder to develop strategies to resist community violence through education and awareness as well as to pressure the federal government to enact legislative changes pertaining to criminal assaults involving knives.

The focus of the public meeting was on knife violence in the context of Goldie-Ryder's murder as well as the murder of Jamie Williamson.[6] A number of responses to the perceived escalation of violence in the core were discussed, including the importance of introducing surveillance mechanisms (e.g., metal detectors) in downtown bars. After the public meeting, Police Chief Gramolini asked David Tennant to chair an ad hoc community-police initiative to address violence, social problems, fear of crime, and economic re-vitalization in the core. He also introduced Tennant to Amanda Alvaro at the meeting, and Tennant subsequently invited Alvaro to co-chair the ad hoc committee.

For the remainder of 1999, Tennant and Alvaro co-chaired what came to be known as the Coordinating Committee for Community Safety (CCCS). The CCCS was a volunteer-based group composed of the mayor, police officers, members of FASE, and representatives of the London Downtown Business Association (LDBA). The committee first met in late February to discuss strategies to reduce violence in downtown London and to produce recommendations for the City of London's Community and Protective Services Committee (CPSC) and the London Police Service Board (LPSB).

To formulate a multi-faceted set of recommendations to fight violence in the core, the CCCS was divided into three overlapping subcommittees: Police and Public Interaction, Education, and Legislative. Each subcommittee was charged with the task of reporting to the LPSB by May 1999. To achieve the latter goal, several legal and education experts were recruited for the purpose of consultation. From the outset, the committee, with its three branches, was formed as a short-term, community-based advisory group with a clear and limited mandate.

The CCCS subcommittees began meeting in late February. The mandate of the Legislative Subcommittee was to develop recommendations to amend the Criminal Code of Canada regarding weapons offences, particularly involving knives. Its primary recommendation was to increase penalties for crimes involving knives with the intention to deter violent and knife-related crimes (Coordinating Committee for Community Safety 1999a).[7] Based on the recommendations made by the Legislative Subcommittee, the Education Subcommittee's mandate was to communicate the recommended deterrents to young people aged ten to twenty-four in and around the London area.[8] Working with FASE, the Education Subcommittee developed an elaborate public education campaign (see below) to challenge and change attitudes about violence and weapons (Coordinating Committee for Community Safety 1999c).

Whereas the mandates of the Legislative and Education Subcommittees were to generate legal and educational strategies to prevent violence involving knives, respectively, the Police-Public Interaction Subcommittee (chaired by Steve Goodine) had a mandate to review current police programs, discuss the needs of the community as they related to safety, and work toward ensuring a safer downtown. In the Police-Public Interaction Subcommittee's report to the LPSB on 29 April 1999 (Coordinating Committee for Community Safety 1999b), three necessary factors for crime to occur were emphasized: a motivated criminal, a vulnerable victim, and the absence of a capable guardian. To address victim vulnerability, the subcommittee recommended adding a taxi stand on the west side of Richmond Street, north of York Street, to assist in dispersing crowds from the bar flush. Informed by CPTED principles, they also recommended increased lighting in the downtown area (put in place prior to installation of the cameras).

To address the absence of a capable guardian, and thereby reduce the motivation for criminality, the Police-Public Interaction Subcommittee forwarded two recommendations. The first recommendation was to increase foot patrols through the Downtown Community Patrol Officer Program (which was put in place). The second recommendation was to install monitored video surveillance cameras in the core. The latter recommendation was based on the claim that "surveillance cameras have proven to be a successful crime prevention tool for many communities throughout the world," that "the argument regarding the reduction in crime is irrefutable," and that "there is also a strong argument to be made regarding the positive economic impact the cameras create" (Coordinating Committee for Community Safety 1999b, 2). To bolster support for these claims, the subcommittee's report cited claims made by Sudbury's LVMAC that crime rates in monitored areas of downtown Sudbury dropped 20.4 percent after the introduction of surveillance cameras, in turn enabling economic rejuvenation.

While the CCCS subcommittees were preparing reports for the LPSB, the London Police Service's Crime Analysis Unit (CAU) prepared recommendations for surveillance camera locations based on a request from Steve Goodine (London Police Service 1999). The CAU completed a review of criminal activity at twenty-one major intersections in downtown London between 1996 and 1998, based on nine crime categories that were assigned weighted values (e.g., murder/attempted murder was assigned five points, and a liquor offence was assigned half a point). The review concluded that the intersections of and around Richmond and York Streets and Richmond and Dundas Streets (i.e., Clarence-Dundas, Talbot-York, Richmond-Central) experienced significantly more crime in the survey period. The CAU recommended that, if cameras were installed, the five aforementioned intersections were the most suitable locations.

Hence, in the immediate aftermath of the death of Michael Goldie-Ryder (February to May 1999), a multi-faceted community and policing initiative to address violence generally and violence involving knives particularly was under way in London. The *London Free Press* consistently and favourably reported on the momentum generated by the crime prevention initiative; the news reporting was set in the context of the murder of Goldie-Ryder (and that of Williamson), the championing of video surveillance by the CCCS, and the symbolic and practical importance of the emergence of FASE (see Hier et al. 2007). The London Police Service (LPS) and members of the LDBA had a clear interest in video surveillance as a crime prevention and economic rejuvenation strategy. It is inaccurate, however, to characterize establishment of the Downtown Camera Project primarily as a police- or business-driven initiative.

Promoting the Downtown Camera Project
In the days following the attack on Michael Goldie-Ryder, public discussion and debate about violence in the core did not address the need for video surveillance. Sergeant John O'Flaherty of the London Police Service, for example, was quoted in the *London Free Press* as saying that "the downtown, other than that area [where Goldie-Ryder was murdered], is a safe place to be ... There's weapons and there's testosterone and there's booze" (Berton 1999). Orlando Zamprogna, then-chair of the city's Police Services Board, added that "London's downtown is as safe as anywhere else in the continent" (cited in Sim and Schuck 1999). Councillor Joe Swan, then-chair of the city hall Committee to Revitalize Downtown London, stated in response to the murder that "this is not about location but a violent act that took place

in our society" (cited in Brown and Yasvinski 1999). And London's then-mayor, Dianne Haskett, responded to the murder primarily by lobbying the federal government to tighten penalties in the Criminal Code of Canada for carrying concealed weapons rather than pushing for implementation of CCTV surveillance in the downtown core (Brown and Yasvinski 1999). Despite initial reactions from police and city representatives, the Downtown Camera Project was established within three years of Goldie-Ryder's murder (Hier et al. 2007; Hier, Walby, and Greenberg 2006).

When the Police-Public Interaction Subcommittee reported to the LPSB on 29 April 1999, it estimated start-up costs for the monitoring program at approximately $200,000. The estimate was a projection to fund from thirteen to sixteen cameras based on crime-location data presented by the CAU. Representing the CCCS, David Tennant appeared before the LPSB on 23 July 1999 to promote the subcommittee's specific recommendation to install cameras in the core. The LPSB approved the concept of installing surveillance cameras and ordered the LPS to complete a feasibility study. Approval of the concept of CCTV surveillance in the core formalized a second promotional and fundraising phase of the CCCS that was already informally under way.

The two-year joint public-promotional campaign to raise awareness of violence and to raise funds for the Downtown Camera Project succeeded partially on the basis of a repertoire of political and communications activities centred primarily on FASE. Among the activities that members of FASE were involved in were open-forum discussions and presentations to students at local high schools; a poster campaign at high schools and bars; meetings with national advisory groups, such as the Federation of Canadian Municipalities (which members of FASE lobbied to increase criminal penalties for crimes involving knives); and a sustained letter-writing campaign to local news outlets to draw attention to violent crime on London's streets as well as to the proposed and preferred solutions of CCCS/FASE. In conjunction with a London-area school board, members of FASE also organized a "walk against violence" on 16 May 2001 to honour the memory of Goldie-Ryder. In what it was hoped would become part of the annual Goldie Ribbon Campaign,[9] the walk against violence initially raised $10,000 to support the CCTV surveillance initiative in the core (Hier et al. 2007).

The momentum generated by the initial CCCS/FASE promotional and fundraising activities culminated in a unique debate staged by the *London Free Press* (on 12 July 1999) between local lawyer Andy Rady and Police Chief Gramolini. The debate format was unique in two respects: first, it presented opposing opinions in response to these questions: "Should surveillance cameras be located downtown?" and "Is this a reasonable crime prevention measure or an infringement of civil liberties?"; second, the online version of the debate invited readers to submit a "yes/no" response to indicate support for the installation of CCTV surveillance cameras in the core.

Rady argued against surveillance cameras, presenting an ethical argument informed by Jeremy Bentham's ruminations on the panopticon. He differentiated the symbolic meaning of public and private space, and he qualified the use of surveillance cameras in certain social contexts. Gramolini, by contrast, presented an argument that relativized rather than qualified the use of CCTV surveillance in different social spaces. He argued that surveillance cameras have proliferated throughout public and private spaces and that the City of Sudbury achieved marked declines in crime rates after it introduced such cameras. The result of the vote – used subsequently by the CCCS to bolster support for the monitoring initiative and by the Ontario OIPC as a partial indicator of public consultation in accordance with *Guidelines for Using Video Surveillance Cameras in Public Places* (see below) – was that 80 of the 104 respondents (77 percent) voted in favour of installing cameras in the core.

Institutional Safeguards and Accountability Structures
Following the debate in the *London Free Press*, fundraising efforts for the educational campaign and the monitoring initiative continued. On 4 August 1999, for example, FASE hosted a benefit concert featuring the LPS band Duty Calls. By 28 October, the CCCS had generated enough support that David Tennant informed the LPSB that he had secured funding from London-area businesses for nine cameras and that he had commitments to fund all sixteen cameras.[10] Tennant's report to the LPSB not only signalled funding commitments to launch the monitoring program but also marked the beginning of an elaborate sequence of interactions involving community organizations and various branches of the City of London to establish a set of institutional safeguards and accountability structures.

The process of establishing institutional safeguards began when the LPS released the *Monitored Surveillance Camera Program Feasibility Study* in November (Goodine 1999). The study, which formed the template for the Downtown Camera Project proposal, outlines a plan to establish a monitoring site in downtown London that would be governed by a community-based agency and maintained by London Hydro. It starts from the premise, borrowed from Sudbury's LVMAC, that any monitoring initiative must be community- rather than police-based to avoid the attribution of Big Brother surveillance. The study recommends that the LPS enter into a partnership with existing organizations such as Neighbourhood Watch or Block Parent, both of which have established organizational structures and budgets. A major component of the community-based approach pertained to fundraising for the acquisition of initial hardware as well as a public relations campaign to articulate the utility of surveillance cameras. The study does not

comment on the important legislative reasons for having regulatory responsibilities assigned to a community-based group rather than the city (see
below), and the only comment on privacy protection in the study reads
thus: "Although Canadian law implies there is no reasonable expectation
of privacy in public places, one must consider the atmosphere of the community" (Goodine 1999, 16).

After the *Feasibility Study* was completed, the LPSB added the estimated
costs of the first year of operations to the police budget projections for 2000
($200,000 to cover half of the projected first-year budget in the study; the
total amount was estimated at $397,219.52). The LPSB's projected operational
expense was earmarked for release to the Environmental Services Department
(which would take control of budget management) pending approval from
municipal council. The budget amendment subsequently went before the
Board of Control for the first of three sets of approvals. After considering
the proposal, the board deferred approval and instructed the LPS and the
CCCS to produce further information pertaining to financial commitments
facing the city.[11]

This information was presented to the Board of Control by January 2000,
and the proposal went to the CPSC for a second round of approval on 31
January. The CPSC approved the proposal to install sixteen surveillance
cameras but requested further information from the LPS concerning what
became the estimated $210,000 in required start-up capital and $350,000
in annual operations expenses. A main reason why the CPSC sought further
information was based on the activities of certain city councillors, especially
Sandy Levin.

In late January, for example, Councillor Levin wrote to Police Chief Gramolini to assess how committed the LPS was to streetscape CCTV surveillance. In an e-mail,[12] Levin asked Gramolini the following question: "If you
had $350,000 at your disposal in the Police Services budget, would you invest
in CCTV surveillance?" The chief responded negatively, arguing that the
monitoring program was a community-driven initiative. Levin also sent
Gramolini the findings of Ditton's (1999) investigation of monitoring practices in Glasgow, where he found that fear of crime did not decline after the
installation of cameras and that concerns about abuse were significant.

On 7 February, the proposal, including the requested information on operational costs, went before municipal council for final approval. Until this
point, the proposal outlined the perceived utility of streetscape surveillance,
technological and hardware requirements, desired camera locations, and
start-up and operational costs. It did not address liability facing the city,
privacy protection, or operational protocol. Municipal council approved the
proposal subject to development of a governance structure (specifically a clear
statement on roles and responsibilities of stakeholders), a data-management
policy, and an assessment of the implications of the program under the

Municipal Freedom of Information and Protection of Privacy Act (MFIPPA). The last point was based on concerns raised by Councillor Levin concerning effectiveness and abuse (City of London 2001a). Council therefore instructed the city's Civic Administration to work with the CCCS and the LPS to clarify the finer details of the proposed monitoring system.

On 28 February, the CCCS reported on the roles and responsibilities of stakeholders in the proposed monitoring program. The major stakeholder identified in the report was Neighbourhood Watch (NW). The NW board of directors agreed to govern the monitoring program, in consultation with the LPS, under the guise of the Downtown Surveillance Camera Advisory Committee (DSCAC). The DSCAC, composed of representatives from NW, the CCCS, and the LPS, assumed responsibility for budgeting, operational matters, data-handling and storage protocols, auditing, and training.[13]

Following the CCCS submission of roles and responsibilities for the monitoring program to the CPSC, the city's Civic Administration reported on liability and privacy protection. Based on the proposal and clarification of roles and responsibilities, the city's legal department concluded that, with proper safeguards in place (e.g., confidential data handling and storage), liability of the city would be minimal. The legal department cautioned, however, that the city could incur costs if an individual sued the city on the basis that the cameras failed to deter a crime.

The city's freedom of information (FOI) co-ordinator reported on the implications of the proposed system under MFIPPA. MFIPPA applies to local government organizations, including municipalities and police services, and requires that local government organizations protect the privacy of individuals through the regulation and management of existing government records. Based on the privacy principles stipulated in MFIPPA, the city's FOI co-ordinator concluded that, because the NW board of directors is not appointed by municipal council, it is not a body that is considered part of the municipal corporation of the City of London.[14] The FOI co-ordinator also concluded that videotapes generated from surveillance activities would not constitute records of a municipal institution under MFIPPA, as long as the information collected was not under control and custody of the LPS. The FOI co-ordinator warned that the LPS could take control and custody of records if videotapes were used for law enforcement purposes. Nevertheless, the FOI co-ordinator explained that, "from the available IPC jurisprudence (Orders, Investigations and Judicial Reviews), this appears to be 'unchartered territory' at present."[15]

By the time the city's Civic Administration reported on liability and privacy protection concerns pertaining to the proposed monitoring system, several months had passed since the CCCS first forwarded recommendations to increase safety in the core. Members of the CCCS were growing increasingly concerned about the diminishing momentum of the proposed monitoring system as well as their ability to attract community donations. On 16 March, Tennant and Alvaro wrote to then-Deputy Mayor DeCicco. The letter outlined how, after seven months, three CCCS reports, the submission of a feasibility study, and endorsement from the LPS, the CPSC, and municipal council, the project had yet to gain final approval from council. Tennant and Alvaro explained that launch of the project was contingent on the ability of the CCCS to generate start-up funds from community donors and that the momentum that fuelled the project and public donations for cameras in the wake of Goldie-Ryder's murder was fading: "What we cannot accept is further procrastination. It is an unfortunate fact that as the memory of a tragedy lessens so does the motivation to prevent a recurrence, therefore our ability to raise funds for the capital costs [is] becoming increasingly more difficult and with further delays, in our opinion, will become impossible."[16] Tennant and Alvaro consequently called on the mayor's office to pressure council to make a decision on funding. The following week (22 March), Deputy Mayor DeCicco wrote to the CPSC and requested that it provide Tennant and Alvaro with a clear decision-making timeline.

On 27 March 2000, the CPSC recommended the release of $200,000 to municipal council for the annual operating expense of the monitoring program (earmarked in the LPSB's operations budget). In response to the significantly lower annual operating budget than requested ($350,000), Police Chief Gramolini wrote to the chair of the CPSC. He argued that the reduced budget required a reduction in the number of cameras and monitoring staff. The reductions, he maintained, posed liability issues for the LPS based on the reduced effectiveness in monitoring high-crime areas. Gramolini reminded the committee of the community-based consultation process that led to the proposed system, and he outlined how neither NW nor London Hydro could maintain the system on a reduced budget.[17] Gramolini also declared publicly that the project would not be viable on a reduced operating budget and threatened to terminate the proposal process.

On 3 April, a special meeting of the CPSC was convened to propose a revision to the initial proposal. It was decided that, on the provision that the CCCS generate $200,000 in start-up funds, the city would release $200,000 to the LPSB on an annual basis.[18] To address Police Chief Gramolini's concerns about scaling back the monitoring system, the CPSC proposed that the monitoring site be located in city hall, where the streetscape system could be integrated into the existing security system run by the city's Environmental Services Department and staffed by the Core of Commissionaires. The commissionaires were already under contract with the city to provide security services in city hall. Council reasoned that an additional commissionaire could be hired to facilitate 24/7 monitoring and that the revised monitoring arrangements would be viable with the $200,000 annual operating budget (City of London 2000).

The amendments proposed by the CPSC, which were accepted by all parties, posed implications for the design of the monitoring program, the city's accountability to the OIPC, and the influence that London's system had on systems yet to be developed in the country. The decision to locate the monitoring control centre in city hall meant, first, that London Hydro would no longer have control over the system and, necessarily, the surveillance records. When the city (a municipal institution under MFIPPA) assumed ownership of the program, it also assumed responsibility to manage surveillance records, thereby becoming accountable to the OIPC. The shift in ownership of the program not only inadvertently led to the development of an elaborate operational and privacy protection framework but also signified a shift in the establishment process from promotion and funding to governance.

Planning the Downtown Camera Project

Fundraising efforts continued following municipal council's provisional endorsement of the proposal, facilitated in part by news reporting on the one-week trial of Goldie-Ryder's murderer (June 2000), Michael Post, and by publicity generated by a memorial service held on Richmond Street to mark the second anniversary of the murder. Prior to completion of fundraising efforts and final approval of the proposal, however, city officials began planning for launch of the program. A request for proposals to supply equipment for, and to install, the monitoring system was published in the *London Free Press* on 11 November 2000. Mirtech International Security, a security company with an office in London, won the contract the following month.[19] Mirtech's estimated cost for the hardware and installation was $212,501.90.[20]

By the time municipal council granted final endorsement to fund the operational costs of the monitoring program on a "test basis" for two years (on 19 March 2001), the CCCS had raised $165,000 toward capital costs of the cameras.[21] Council's decision to endorse the program and purchase the equipment ($235,877) was based on the provision that the outstanding funds would be generated by the CCCS to reimburse the city and on the provision that positive evaluation results would be produced after one year of operation (including a six-month interim report). Municipal council planned to launch the Downtown Camera Project in June 2001, but a series of delays pertaining to formation of a privacy and accountability structure postponed the launch until November.

Building in Privacy and Accountability

The delays began on 25 June 2001 when councillors inquired at the regular council meeting into the implications of public-area monitoring practices in light of Privacy Commissioner Radwanski's ruling under PIPEDA in Yellowknife (on 15 June). Concern about privacy among some councillors was also informed by the OIPC's *Practices #10: Video Surveillance: The Privacy*

Implications (Cavoukian 1998), where the OIPC outlines general privacy protection principles under FIPPA and MFIPPA.

The privacy protection issues raised at the 25 July 2001 meeting were again sent to the Civic Administration for adjudication. On 30 July, the deputy city manager reported to municipal council that the federal ruling did not apply to the proposed program in London but that, given the amendments to the design of the program in April 2001, and specifically the amendment for the city – a municipal institution under MFIPPA – to assume ownership of the program, they were bound by municipal privacy legislation. Civic Administration informed councillors that housing and retention of surveillance records by the city's Environmental Services Department constitute "records" retention by a municipal institution under MFIPPA and that the requirements of MFIPPA must be met (City of London 2001b).

Civic Administration's adjudication was partially informed by a meeting held between representatives of Civic Administration, the LPS, NW, and the Ontario OIPC on 27 July 2001. The purpose of the meeting was to review the recently created London Downtown CCTV Code of Practice and to address the requirements set out for municipal institutions under MFIPPA. At the meeting, it was determined that the City of London was legally responsible for disclosure of surveillance records and therefore had to assume overall governance of the entire monitoring program. What this meant in practice was that the city, as the municipal institution responsible for surveillance records, could not legally pass videotapes or digital files to institutions that are not recognized under MFIPPA. Brian Beamish, director of policy and compliance at the OIPC, advised the city on the contents of signage, data collection and retention, advertising (website), and the importance of developing a legal information-sharing agreement with the LPS and NW in accordance with the OIPC's model Data Sharing Agreement.[22] The agreement was recommended to ensure that surveillance records remained under the jurisdiction of MFIPPA, thereby reducing liability to the city.

Based on the determination of the city's legal responsibility, London's manager of corporate security, David O'Brien, was assigned the role of program manager under the jurisdiction of the Department of Environmental Services. The city also appointed a Management Steering Committee to assist the manager of corporate security with operations of the program. The Management Steering Committee was composed of the manager of corporate security (Department of Environmental Services), the manager of licensing and elections (Corporate Services Department), and representatives from NW and the LPS. The mandate of the Management Steering Committee was to oversee the monitoring program in terms of operations, codes of practice, and disclosure of records under MFIPPA as well as supervision, financing, effectiveness, auditing, and maintenance (City of London Steering Management Group 2001). NW retained the responsibility to perform quarterly

8 Streetscape surveillance camera, City of London, Ontario

audits as a community-based, independent agency, albeit one that was bound by a data-sharing agreement with the city and under MFIPPA.

Operational Turbulence

From July to October 2001, the Management Steering Committee responded to the recommendations made by the OIPC by revising the Code of Practice, developing terms of reference, establishing legal data-sharing agreements with NW and the LPS, and amending the city's retention bylaw to conform to data-sharing practices under MFIPPA. On 15 November 2001, the Downtown Camera Project became operational. Fourteen of the sixteen wireless cameras covered an eight-block grid between Queens Avenue, Ridout Street, York Street, and Wellington Road in the downtown core (see Figure 8). The two outlying cameras were mounted at the corners of Pall Mall Street and Richmond Street and Central Avenue and Richmond Street (see Figures 9 and 10).

The cameras rotated 360 degrees, and they were equipped with privacy-enhancing programming to block out private residences and transparent windows. Sixteen signs notifying members of the public that the areas were under video surveillance were posted at each camera location (see Figure 11). Wireless signals were transmitted to sixteen monitors located in the city

9   Streetscape surveillance camera, City of London, Ontario

10   Streetscape surveillance camera, City of London, Ontario

11   Streetscape surveillance camera signage, City of London, Ontario

hall security office, where two commissionaires were on duty twenty-four hours per day, seven days per week. An additional monitor was located in the police station for the 9-1-1 operator's access, but it did not have recording capabilities. Surveillance images were recorded and retained for seventy-two hours.

In the first six months of operation (leading up to the interim report required by the CPSC), the system experienced recurrent problems. For example, the playback and viewing of recorded information required the use of a special viewer; the system failed to record in real time, resulting in poor visibility of data images recorded on the hard drive; cameras malfunctioned on a daily basis with long repair periods; and camera lenses required constant cleaning (City of London 2002). Nevertheless, the LPS reported that in the first six months of operation the camera images assisted in eight police investigations and twenty-eight interventions.

Immediately following the launch of the Downtown Camera Project, at their regular meeting, members of the CPSC requested an update on the system, along with a statement on the role that NW was playing as a community partner in the program. During the meeting, it was revealed that all of the required conditions to minimize liability of the city and NW, as stipulated in the Code of Practice, had not been met. The CPSC members were especially concerned that the data-sharing agreement between the city and NW had not been finalized. Members of the Management Steering Committee, NW, and CPSC understood that all data-sharing agreements needed to be finalized prior to the launch of the program.[23]

The data-sharing agreement between the city and NW was finalized the following month, and the NW audit team conducted preliminary audits in January, February, and April 2002. During each of the three audits, the NW audit team experienced difficulties with the playback function. Members of the audit team were able neither to access surveillance data requested nor to verify that the Code of Conduct had not been breached because the viewer program did not show real-time footage.

On 25 July 2002, Arthur Horrell, president of Neighbourhood Watch London, wrote to the Board of Control to raise a variety of concerns about the operational structure of the Downtown Camera Project. Horrell highlighted three major concerns held by members of NW. The first pertained to the "operational denial of a community voice in the supervision of the CCTV program, as per the *Code of Practice.*" Horrell complained that NW and other community members had been denied voice in the program because regular monthly meetings were not held (as stipulated in the Code of Practice). The second concern focused on the six-month interim report to the CPSC. Horrell maintained that the report did not involve input from the Management Steering Committee, and he questioned why the CPSC would be willing to receive a report that was not developed based on input by all partners. The third issue was that the Board of Control was not getting accurate information about the monitoring program. The letter concluded by warning that, if the operational rules stipulated in the Code of Practice continued to be ignored, the community-based participation component of the program would become "unsubstantive 'window dressing'" for the project.[24]

As the CPSC considered the technical and operational problems with the Downtown Camera Project, Information and Privacy Commissioner of Ontario Ann Cavoukian wrote to the FOI co-ordinator in London. Cavoukian explained that the OIPC had published *Guidelines for Using Video Surveillance Cameras in Public Places* in October 2001, and she presented the city with a full draft report of the Downtown Camera Project in light of *Guidelines.*[25] Cavoukian requested feedback from the city by 27 March 2003 before completing the OIPC's final report on the Downtown Camera Project.

The OIPC's draft assessment starts from the premise that municipal institutions governed by MFIPPA should regularly review and update existing monitoring programs and that they should regularly review and evaluate programs to ensure that they are still justified in relation to *Guidelines*. Eight recommendations are offered in the review. Four of the recommendations concern amendments to the Code of Practice to address secure disposal of surveillance records, inadvertent disclosure of personal information, violations of the Code of Practice or MFIPPA, and how non-municipal institutions dealing with records need to enter into and adhere to MFIPPA. Three other recommendations concerning data handling by NW, refinement of surveillance training, and creation of an information brochure were also identified. The major recommendation required that all aspects of section 4 of *Guidelines* ("Preliminary Considerations") be addressed and submitted to the OIPC for review and comment and to consider the necessity of the scope of the program.

Meanwhile, the Management Steering Committee's annual evaluation of the Downtown Camera Project was submitted to CPSC in February 2003. The evaluation was composed of five primary criteria: crime reduction, displacement, public opinion, cost, and administration. Based on a downtown crime study conducted by the LPS, the Management Steering Committee reported that the police had reviewed 100 recordings between November 2001 and November 2002 and that 25 reviews had been beneficial to policing activities. According to the report, crime in the downtown area experienced a 25 percent increase in the first year of operations (particularly robbery and assault). Pre- and post-camera criminal instances were compared to three-year statistical evaluations published by Sudbury's LVMAC to bolster the argument that a longer evaluation period was necessary.

The other criteria in the report were treated in a more cursory manner. Whereas a set of tables and statistics was presented on criminal incidents in the downtown area during the evaluation period, for example, the evaluation of displacement was provided in a single paragraph, claiming that crime in the core was not significantly greater than that in other areas of the city. The report on administration of the program revealed that camera or equipment failure had been experienced 451 times, resulting in 201 service calls to Mirtech, and that ongoing revisions were under way concerning auditing, the Code of Practice, and a response to the OIPC. The cost of operations and ongoing maintenance was estimated at $240,000 without explanation.

The report on public opinion briefly indicated that information had been requested from the general public (six times), for school projects (four times), from other municipalities (ten times), and from the media (fifty times). It also indicated that signs had been posted at each of the camera sites and that the Code of Practice had been posted on the city's website. To gauge a broader range of public opinion, the report cited findings from the 2002 LPS Public Needs Survey that most residents felt safe in areas other than the downtown and that 27 percent of residents did not feel safe at night. It also cited findings from a NW telephone survey that asked members, "do you feel the Downtown Surveillance Camera Program has improved your feeling of safety when you are downtown?" Approximately half of respondents indicated that they did not feel any safer, primarily because they did not frequent the downtown area. Based on data from the five criteria, the annual report concluded that the Downtown Camera Project had enhanced community safety, crime prevention, and the desirability of the downtown area.[26]

In response to the evaluation, Councillor Sandy Levin wrote to the city clerk prior to the 10 February 2003 meeting of the CPSC. Levin argued that data collection informing the annual report's findings had been done inconsistently and that it failed to replicate more useful data on a variety of areas in the city that were presented in the 1999 *Feasibility Study*. He also inquired into why, despite assurances in the *Feasibility Study*, data on crime tape admissibility and number of convictions based on tapes had not been included; why no data were presented on the NW survey to enable proper evaluation; why the budget had increased by $40,000; why the CPSC had not been presented with the OIPC review; and why the report reached the tenuous conclusion that community safety and crime prevention were enhanced by the cameras.[27]

The concerns raised by Councillor Levin were added to the 10 February agenda and adjudicated over the following months. Part of the response entailed accepting all of the recommendations made by the OIPC. On 26 March 2003, the city informed Commissioner Cavoukian that a number of amendments had been made to the Code of Practice to address the OIPC's recommendations and that ongoing reviews and audits would address these recommendations under section 4 of *Guidelines*.

Shifting Priorities: From Prevention to Investigation

The city's response to concerns raised by the OIPC effectively ended the OIPC's involvement in London (the OIPC conducted periodic updates via telephone). But the Downtown Camera Project continued to experience problems with governance, funding, and image transmission and storage. In 2003, for example, 506 camera failures were experienced that resulted in 453 service calls to Mirtech. The system continued to experience difficulty recording in real time, resulting in poor visibility of surveillance images. As of 23 February 2004, the CCCS still owed the city $70,877, and budget projections for 2004 called for the elimination of continuous monitoring to reduce costs to fund commissionaires. The 2004 budget cuts transformed the monitoring schedule, whereby a commissionaire, already responsible for security at city hall, periodically monitored camera images Monday to Friday 9 p.m. to 3 a.m. and twenty-four hours on weekends (City of London 2004a).

Significant changes to the governance of the program were also made in 2004. On 1 December 2003, Neighbourhood Watch London resigned from the Management Steering Committee based on resource limitations. In response to the resignation of NW partners, the Management Steering Committee recommended that the city's Management Support and Auditing Services assume auditing responsibilities. Since 2004, Management Support and Auditing Services has conducted monthly audits and produced reports two times per year. A computer program randomly selects time periods in the preceding seventy-two hours that are burned onto a disk and sent to Management Support and Auditing Services for evaluation. Audit evaluation reports are based on randomly selected monthly recordings over a six-month period as well as evaluations of entries in logbooks.

Due to the continuing technological problems with the camera system, the Management Steering Committee partnered with the city's Technology Services Division, which ran a fibre optic cable in the downtown area in 2004; the Management Steering Committee arranged for half of the cameras to be converted to fibre optic transmission (with two more by the end of 2005).

The following year, the CPSC requested a technological performance evaluation to enable comparison of surveillance images transmitted on wireless and fibre optic cables (October 2004-December 2005) (City of London 2004b). They also called for an evaluation of the number of incidents monitored before and after changes to the monitoring schedule and for the mounting of sixty signs in the downtown area (see Figure 12). The new signs were purchased in order to notify pedestrians approaching a camera from every direction that the intersection was under video surveillance. The estimated cost of the new signs was $4,000.

In the annual evaluation report (released February 2005), the Management Steering Committee concluded that the shift to fibre optic cables had significantly reduced the technological problems experienced with image transmission. Based on this finding, the committee recommended exploring a full conversion to fibre optic cables. A comparison of the number of incidents reported by commissionaires in 2003 and 2004 revealed not only that camera monitoring staff reported a greater number of incidents but also that police forwarded a small number of requests. The latter was based on the fact that the LPS assumed the right to have communications staff at the police station take control of the camera without going through city hall (City of London 2005). Nevertheless, the police do not monitor camera images, and the camera monitor is activated only in response to notification from dispatch.

In the midst of structural changes to the governance and operations of the program, David Tennant resigned from the CCCS (on 8 December 2005). He resigned because of the shifting mandate of the Downtown Camera Project from crime prevention to investigation. In his letter of resignation,

12   Streetscape surveillance camera signage, City of
London, Ontario

he explained that the initial recommendation of the CCCS was to introduce
CCTV surveillance monitoring in the downtown area only if 24/7 monitoring was part of the program. When the system was scaled back based on
budget constraints, he continued, the ability to market the system as a crime
prevention tool was compromised. The modified structure of the program,
Tennant maintained, posed implications not only for fear of crime in the
core but also for marketing the system as a worthy cause.[28]

Tennant also complained about the Management Steering Committee's
lack of effectiveness, and he recommended that the system be transferred
to the LPS. He reasoned that, in the wake of the 9/11 attacks on Washington
and New York, Londoners were no longer concerned with the LPS appearing
as a Big Brother figure. On 24 January 2006, the CPSC instructed the city
engineer to report back on Tennant's recommendations. The program was
never transferred to the LPS, and minor promotional activity was put in
place. For instance, the Management Steering Committee met with the

business community to explain the program in March 2006, and each year the city releases information on the monitoring program to college and university students.

As of May 2009, fourteen of the sixteen cameras had been converted to fibre optic transmissions. And, with updated cameras and new recording equipment, the difficulties with transmission were eliminated. Two commissionaires in city hall (a site supervisor and a duty commissionaire) passively monitor camera images from 8 a.m. to 5 p.m., and a dedicated commissionaire actively monitors images from 9 p.m. to 5 a.m. In mid-2009, the Management Steering Committee was also in the process of planning installation of a seventeenth camera, along Richmond Street, to cover the area between the Central Avenue and Queens Avenue cameras.

Conclusion

The City of London's Downtown Camera Project exemplifies a form of configurational convenience, whereby a number of discrete forces came together to introduce the country's largest streetscape monitoring system (as of 2001). The monitoring initiative began with the LPS investigating monitoring practices but soon intersected with the momentum generated by the murder of Michael Goldie-Ryder. The combined influence of local activism, a multi-faceted community safety initiative, sustained fundraising efforts, a provocative signal crime, favourable news coverage, and the LV-MAC's promotional campaign articulated the importance of establishing a streetscape monitoring system. At the same time, however, an existing set of organizational divisions within the city and between the LPS, the LPSB, city council, and Civic Administration, within the context of a set of signal events (e.g., Ditton's study of fear of crime, Radwanski's investigation in Yellowknife, the release of *Guidelines*) and the OIPC's pragmatic policy position, led to the formation of a multi-faceted responsibility-sharing and governance structure.

Although the City of London produced a multilateral governance structure, the administrative diffusion of the Downtown Camera Project has not been as influential as Sudbury's Lions Eye in the Sky. The Downtown Camera Project has contributed to the ideational diffusion of streetscape monitoring in conjunction with other cities running streetscape programs, but the detailed design of the Downtown Camera Project has not been emulated across the country – a failure of administrative diffusion and privacy protection policy diffusion. London's administrative and promotional structure did not diffuse to the extent that Sudbury's did for three reasons: first, the complexity involved in establishing the Downtown Camera Project has never been fleshed out by researchers or members of the OIPC; second, the amount of detail and interaction involved in establishing the Downtown Camera Project does not appeal to advocates of CCTV surveillance who strive to implement systems in the most straightforward manner possible; and third, the Downtown Camera Project was not promoted to the extent that the Lions Eye in the Sky was.

Finally, London's program is important for understanding some of the broader theoretical and explanatory dimensions of the establishment process. The design and implementation process involved in the Downtown Camera Project illustrates some of the explanatory problems with theorizing "the city" or "the state" as a homogeneous body characterized by singular interests and intentions. Data from interviews and documents show how funding decisions, operational policies, and privacy protection protocols for the Downtown Camera Project were developed through interactions with a variety of administrative units that comprise the Corporation of the City of London. The data also illustrate how the diffusion of responsibility across the city's administrative units can lead to greater accountability and transparency in streetscape monitoring practices, irrespective of the operational turbulence experienced after the launch.

Part 3
The Spread of Streetscape Monitoring Programs

7

The Expansion of Streetscape Monitoring Programs

The previous four chapters explored the processes involved in establishing streetscape CCTV surveillance monitoring programs in seven Canadian cities, including the development of a privacy protection policy framework by the privacy policy sector. Dating back to privacy protection advocacy in Sherbrooke in 1991, the basis for a Canada-wide, pragmatic privacy protection policy framework for public-area video surveillance started to emerge. The pragmatic policy orientation diffused to Anglo-Canada by the mid- to late 1990s, but it developed alongside a streetscape CCTV surveillance governance structure that initially emerged independently from the privacy policy sector (and that was subsequently enabled by it). The privacy policy sector began to exercise greater influence on how systems were established in the late 1990s, contributing to some progressive developments in the design of streetscape systems. The withdrawn Charter challenge in Kelowna, however, had a certain pacifying effect on OIPCs, as privacy pragmatism became further institutionalized.

This chapter continues to examine the strengths and limitations of Canada's (specifically Ontario's) pragmatic privacy protection policy framework for public-area CCTV surveillance in the context of the ideational and administrative diffusion of monitoring programs by examining streetscape systems in Hamilton and Windsor. These cities are similar in some ways: they are both industrial cities located in southern Ontario, they are home to Canadian colleges and universities, and they have experienced problems with (desirable) business flight from the downtown core. Moreover, streetscape monitoring initiatives in each city ideationally and administratively diffused partially from Sudbury's Lions Eye in the Sky program, and the systems were launched within weeks of one another.

Despite the similarities, however, there are also many differences in their processes of establishment. For example, the City of Hamilton's monitoring system was foremost a police-driven initiative, it was supported by city council from the outset, and it entailed the most elaborate public consultation process seen in Canada to date. Windsor's Video Guard monitoring program, by contrast, was established without participation of the Windsor Police Service, city council was not involved from the outset, and no public consultation was ever held. Neither system was substantially designed to build on the gains made in organizational design and privacy protection in the City of London's Downtown Camera Project, and, although representatives in both cities had interactions with members of the OIPC and designed their governance structures to comply with the OIPC's *Guidelines for Using Video Surveillance Cameras in Public Places,* each system was established on an idiosyncratic interpretation of what the privacy protection principles meant and which ones should be foregrounded.

Hamilton's Streetscape Monitoring Program[1]
Hamilton is an industrial port that encircles the western tip of Lake Ontario. In the 1930s, the Hamilton Harbour area was used to move raw materials and products into and out of emerging industrial sites (Ali 2003). Hamilton Harbour soon became recognized as a strategic site for industry, and the city quickly established itself as the steel capital of Canada.

Hamilton is home not only to two major industrial manufacturing plants, Stelco and Dofasco, but also to McMaster University and Mohawk College. The city supports a population of approximately 500,000 people distributed across a range of residential areas. Westdale, Ancaster, and Dundas, for example, are composed mostly of students and middle-class professionals. The city's north end, by contrast, is composed primarily of working-class Hamiltonians.

The initiative to install streetscape CCTV surveillance cameras in downtown Hamilton was set in motion with the recommendations outlined in the Hamilton Police Service's (HPS) *Challenging Our Patrol Priorities into the Next Century – C.O.P.P. 2000* (2000). In October 1998, a *C.O.P.P. 2000* project team, chaired by Superintendent John Petz, was given the mandate to produce recommendations to re-engineer the patrol function of the HPS by examining technological advances in policing and patrol officers' administrative and operational workload and to strive toward proactive policing. The project team produced nine sets of solutions; among the recommendations concerning the development of more efficient information management systems was the installation of closed-circuit television for the downtown core to help monitor and reduce crime and disorder (Hamilton Police Service 2000, 5.10, vii).

This recommendation was inspired by the City of Surrey, England's, streetscape monitoring program. In 1998, Superintendent Petz travelled with a colleague to the Surrey police headquarters, where he observed the Guildford Borough Council's monitoring system (Guildford Borough Council

1996).[2] Based on his observations, streetscape CCTV surveillance was identified in *C.O.P.P. 2000* as a way to address concerns about police budgeting,
human resource management, labour costs, and crime and disorder:

> Critical to the success of geographic policing ... will be our ability to free
> officers from inefficient processes and help establish beat integrity as the
> norm ... Technology in the form of Closed Circuit Television (CCTV) can
> both prevent and help us manage crime and disorder. Television cameras
> strategically placed in city and town cores can give us the advantage of many
> eyes covering high-crime districts or areas where people frequent. (Hamilton
> Police Service 2000, 60)

In *C.O.P.P. 2000*, human resources are identified as accounting for 82 percent
of the entire HPS budget, and CCTV surveillance is identified as a way to
reduce costs and increase efficiency.

Prior to the release of *C.O.P.P. 2000*, however, members of the International
Village Business Improvement Association (IVBIA) – one of two BIAs covering downtown Hamilton – learned about the role that Sudbury's business
community played in establishing of the Lions Eye in the Sky video monitoring system. Representatives of Sudbury's LVMAC discussed the Lions Eye in
the Sky – especially its purported contribution to revitalization and economic
rejuvenation – in a presentation at the annual general meeting of the Ontario
BIA in 1998. Members of Hamilton's IVBIA were attracted to claims made
about the success of Sudbury's program because of rapid changes taking
place to the culture and character of downtown Hamilton. As late as the
1980s, for example, Jackson Square was a major shopping attraction in the
downtown core, and the nineteenth- and early-twentieth-century Victorian
buildings lining the downtown streetscape were populated by successful
businesses and cinemas. By the 1990s, residential development in the outlying farmlands of the Greater Hamilton-Wentworth region, combined with
the concomitant development of major roadways, box stores, and shopping
plazas outside the downtown area, led to a sharp decline in commercial activity in the core.

After hearing a presentation on the Lions Eye in the Sky program and its
benefits concerning revitalization in downtown Sudbury, the executive
director of the IVBIA, Mary Pocius, approached the HPS to suggest the possibility of streetscape surveillance for Hamilton's deteriorating downtown
core.[3] The *C.O.P.P. 2000* project team had already compiled information on
streetscape monitoring, and they shared their findings with members of the
IVBIA.[4] Following the release of *C.O.P.P. 2000*, members of the HPS met with
board members of the IVBIA and the Hamilton Downtown Business Improvement Association (HDBIA) to mobilize community support for the CCTV
surveillance initiative (in early 2000). Subsequent meetings between members

of the HPS, the Hamilton-Wentworth Police Services Board (HWPSB), the IVBIA, and the HDBIA led to successful lobbying efforts to have capital costs for a pilot project added to the 2001 HPS budget.

Hence, the momentum to install cameras in Hamilton's downtown core was generated by two parties sharing overlapping interests. The HPS and the IVBIA took an interest in streetscape CCTV surveillance monitoring because of costs associated with policing disproportionally high crime rates in Beat 672 (particularly auto theft) and as a strategy to revitalize the downtown business culture, respectively. Revitalization was also a major concern for members of Hamilton City Council, who subsequently provided infrastructure funding to establish the monitoring project in response to lobbying efforts by the IVBIA and the HDBIA. Had the HPS implemented a monitoring program independently of support from the business community, it is unlikely that the city would have covered operational costs (fibre optic cable rentals, installation, maintenance).

Implementing the Monitoring Project

When members of the HPS and the BIAs met to discuss plans for CCTV surveillance in the core, Superintendent Terry Sullivan, command officer for Division 1 (downtown), was responsible for implementing the monitoring project. Following city council's approval of the HPS budget in early 2001, Sullivan consulted with and was granted permission by Police Chief Ken Robertson and representatives of the HWPSB to begin implementing formally a streetscape CCTV surveillance system to monitor certain intersections along King Street (East and West) in Policing Division 1. With an aim to have the monitoring system operational by March 2002, Superintendent Sullivan examined monitoring programs in England as well as the Lions Eye in the Sky program in Sudbury. Toward the end of the year, he also initiated consultations with the HPS Legal Department concerning Commissioner Radwanski's ruling on streetscape monitoring in Kelowna (released on 4 October 2001).

The first formal meeting to discuss operational issues among what became the CCTV Implementation/Steering Committee took place on 31 October 2001. At the meeting, the committee – composed of members from the DHBIA, IVBIA, HPS, and City of Hamilton – used Sudbury's monitoring program as a guide to explore public reactions, possible camera locations, live-monitoring possibilities, a partnership structure, and program goals. Inspired by Sudbury's use of volunteers to monitor camera images, the committee decided to recruit volunteer camera monitors through the HPS Volunteer Coordinator's Office.

For the remainder of the year, efforts to recruit a volunteer co-ordinator and volunteer monitors were finalized. A main strategy to recruit monitoring staff involved meetings with Mohawk College representatives to use Police

Foundations students and students registered in Mohawk's Law and Security Program. Meetings were also held with Hamilton Hydro to examine fibre optic cable transmission options and among police and city representatives to investigate plans for monitoring facilities. While Superintendent Sullivan co-ordinated the first phase of implementation in November, the HPS purchased four CCTV surveillance cameras and eight monitors (a fifth camera was donated by Panasonic Canada through the local supplier, Hill's TV and Audio).

On 6 January 2002, Superintendent Michael Shea became command officer of Division 1 and assumed responsibility for implementing the monitoring project.[5] When Shea assumed responsibility for planning and implementing the system, a strategy to model Hamilton's system on Sudbury's Lions Eye in the Sky was already in place. The Lions Eye in the Sky was used as a model for Hamilton's program for three reasons: first, the KPMG report (easily accessible on the Sudbury Police Service website by 2001) presented independent results lauding the value of streetscape monitoring (see Chapter 4); second, downtown Hamilton and downtown Sudbury were perceived by members of the CCTV Implementation Committee as relatively small regions of expansive cities that showed disproportionally high crime rates and commanded a disproportionally high number of service calls; and third, the LVMAC had apparently achieved remarkable success in reducing crime rates and stimulating revitalization in the core (based on claims presented in the KPMG report). The CCTV Implementation Committee also used the Lions Eye in the Sky rather than London's Downtown Camera Project as a model because the latter was perceived as a community- rather than police-driven initiative (but see below).

The day after Superintendent Shea assumed responsibility for implementing the monitoring initiative, Alexandre Hamel, an eighteen-year-old skater from Quebec who was competing in the Canadian Figure Skating Championship at Copps Coliseum, was robbed of $100 at a downtown ATM. The robbery was reported across local media outlets, and it brought to public attention for the first time the HPS plans to install cameras in the core (including the attention of members of the OIPC). On 9 January, the *Hamilton Spectator* reported that six closed-circuit television cameras were expected to be operational by the end of March and that the HPS planned to follow the OIPC's *Guidelines* to ensure that the system adhered to the province's privacy standards (Burman and Walters 2002). The following day, an editorial appeared in the newspaper lamenting the silence that had characterized the monitoring initiative:

> There's no doubt that some people sometimes find parts of downtown scary. But a supportable program is based on public airing of facts and discussion of concerns, and that hasn't happened to date ... The police service appears

to have decided to proceed without any opportunity for significant public comment or questions. A project advisory committee, made up at least partly of downtown businesspeople, is not broad enough in scope to support what appears to be almost unilateral action ... The mugging this week of a visiting Canadian figure skater will no doubt be mentioned repeatedly by reporters and commentators covering the national championships at Copps Coliseum. Aside from giving Hamilton-bashers a further opportunity for snorting derision, the incident does nothing to help Hamiltonians feel comfortable in their downtown ... The camera project was approved by the Hamilton board of police commissioners in the fall of 1999. That's more than two years in which police could have sought public comment or questions.

Equipped with the knowledge that a reporter from the *Hamilton Spectator*, Joan Walters, was preparing an article on privacy concerns in the context of the national attention generated by Commissioner Radwanski's investigation in Kelowna, Superintendent Shea arranged a meeting with Judith Hoffman of the Ontario OIPC (on 25 January 2002). At the meeting, Hoffman reviewed the OIPC's *Guidelines* with Shea, and she stressed the importance of signage, data retention and use policy, and especially broad public consultation.

News reporting on Alexandre Hamel's robbery and the HPS plan to install CCTV surveillance cameras in the core not only attracted the attention of the provincial OIPC but also drew Commissioner Radwanski to the city. On 13 February, Radwanski (2002c) spoke at McMaster University. He argued that, although the privacy commissioner of Canada does not have jurisdiction over the HPS, as an officer of Parliament she or he does have the mandate to oversee and defend the privacy rights of Canadians. As in speeches he delivered in Kelowna and Vancouver (see Chapter 5), Radwanski framed the proposed HPS monitoring system as the thin edge of the wedge that would irrevocably change the whole notion of rights and freedoms in Canada. He cited statistics suggesting declining crime rates in the City of Hamilton, and he relayed the contents of an OPC interview with a criminologist, Jason Ditton, about the limited effectiveness of streetscape monitoring in the United Kingdom.

Radwanski's visit to Hamilton, combined with the recommendations of the OIPC, significantly influenced the course of implementation and delayed launch of the program by two years. The shift in focus began on 18 March 2002, when Police Chief Robertson reported to the chairman and members of the HWPSB on behalf of the HPS (Hamilton Police Services Board 2002a). In his report (submitted to the board as an "information item"), Robertson conceptualized the monitoring initiative as a community- rather than police-driven program. He provided background claims about the usefulness of video surveillance in Sudbury (based on claims presented in the KPMG report) and an overview of the purpose and goals of the CCTV monitoring project in Hamilton. Robertson also outlined the OIPC's *Guidelines* to facilitate compliance with MFIPPA, and he presented a point-counterpoint response to Commissioner Radwanski's speech on 13 February.[6] The primary purpose of the report, however, was to notify members of the HWPSB that the HPS was entering a new phase of the implementation process designed to enhance the community consultation process (beyond the business community) by hearing from the general population.

The Community Consultation Process

Part of the community consultation process entailed soliciting feedback from citizens of Hamilton through letters, faxes, e-mails (to the HPS website), and a telephone survey as well as through newspaper media monitoring (e.g., letters to the editor).[7] A CCTV Evaluation Committee (an offshoot of the Implementation Committee) was appointed by the HPS to evaluate data gleaned from the multi-faceted community consultation process and to make a recommendation to Police Chief Robertson about the future of monitoring in the city based on community support for the camera initiative.[8] In its final report to Robertson (on 12 March 2003), the Evaluation Committee reported on eighty-five e-mails sent to the HPS website (eighty-one expressed support for the monitoring initiative), nine positive letters/faxes, three favourable voice messages, and six (of eleven) favourable news items (including letters to the editor). Partial results from the telephone survey revealed that 183 of 223 respondents expressed support for the cameras.

In addition to soliciting feedback through a telephone survey, media monitoring, and various communications directed to the HPS, the community consultation process entailed twelve public forums held between April and June 2002. The public forum series was designed as a city-wide engagement with Hamiltonians based on the OIPC's recommendation to consult broadly with members of the community (the fourth recommendation in *Guidelines*). Hamilton is composed of diverse geographic, economic, and cultural regions, ranging from the restaurant, bar, and residential periphery of the downtown core to the predominantly residential areas of Dundas and Ancaster. The logic informing consultations across the city was to reach out to all sectors of the community.

At every forum, a representative from the HPS handed out an information package that included a comprehensive description of the program goals, developments, projected costs, and the point-counterpoint document assessing Commissioner Radwanski's speech at McMaster University. The meetings also featured a small panel of community representatives from the CCTV Evaluation Committee, each of whom spoke about the importance of surveillance in the core. Attendees at each meeting were provided with a brief overview of certain activities leading up to the community consultations, including statistics drawn from the KPMG report and Beat 672 in downtown Hamilton. Meetings concluded with a member of the HPS taking a "straw vote" via show of hands to assess support for the proposal. Estimates from these votes were included in the Evaluation Committee's recommendations to Police Chief Robertson and in subsequent reports to the HWPSB (the estimates were not presented in subsequent reports, however).

The public consultation forums – followed by a second set of forums in 2006 (see below) – represent the most elaborate community outreach strategy in Canada in terms of CCTV streetscape surveillance since the 2003 public hearings in Quebec (see Chapter 3). The staging of public forums was indisputably a progressive development in the establishment of streetscape CCTV surveillance monitoring programs in the country, and they seemingly complied with the OIPC's recommendations to hold broad public consultations. Such consultations not only demand hours of valuable police labour time for planning and execution but also are motivated by a desire to reach out to members of the community and to maintain positive police-public relations. Although the HPS forums addressed the OIPC's basic recommendation to hold broad public consultations prior to using a video surveillance system, they did not conform to the spirit of the recommendation to gather fully informed public opinion. The HPS admittedly neither had an example to base its strategy on nor a clear lead from the OIPC on what exactly a public/community forum should entail. Given that the HPS effectively developed the first example of broad public forums in Canada on CCTV streetscape surveillance, it is important to examine some of the limitations of the process.

At least five interrelated problems limited the effectiveness and integrity of the 2002 forums. The first problem was that they did not entail fully informed debate among members of the police and Implementation and Evaluation Committees, on the one hand, and members of the public, on the other. Rather than "public consultations," the forums are better conceptualized as information sessions, whereby members of the HPS and Implementation and Evaluation Committees informed a very small number of Hamiltonians about their intentions and goals. The forums entailed police officers and businesspeople dispensing a narrow range of information about crime and CCTV surveillance and then asking members of the audience for questions and feedback.

On the surface, inviting members of the community (broadly conceived) to attend open public forums to learn about the monitoring initiative and provide critical feedback was a positive development. The problem, however, concerned the information provided to members of the community before they formed their opinions and comments – the second problem with the forums. The monitoring initiative was framed by CCTV advocates as a policing strategy that would effectively address crime in the core (and one that was proven to work in Sudbury). There was no effort by co-ordinators of the forums to inform attendees fully about research findings from the United Kingdom (see Chapter 10), ethical and privacy debates, the nuances of Commissioner Radwanski's many arguments, or the complex factors contributing to downtown problems. If the primary goal of the forums was to equip attendees with resources to make fully informed decisions about streetscape video surveillance, rather than have a few members of the Evaluation Committee (who were mostly downtown businesspeople facing high insurance premiums in the core) voice a small range of opinions, it would have been responsible to assemble a more balanced panel of privacy experts or informed persons to comment on a range of issues.[9] Admittedly, inclusion of a broader range of panel discussants probably would not have changed the outcome, but it would have helped the HPS to realize its goal of reaching out to the community.

The third, and perhaps most damaging, problem observed with the public forum series was how Evaluation Committee members approached the notion of community consultation and how some members dealt with disagreement over and resistance to the monitoring initiative. For example, when the HPS held the first public forum on 4 April 2002 at the Central Library in downtown Hamilton, almost 100 people attended. During the forum, a group of what appeared to members of the Evaluation Committee to be an organized movement of political science students from McMaster University voiced opposition to the proposed monitoring system. Members of the perceived protest group lined up at the microphones and expressed concerns about privacy invasion and Big Brother surveillance. Forty-five minutes into the meeting, a member of the Evaluation Committee, David Blanchard, left in protest after he tired of listening to concerns about privacy invasion (Morse 2002). Resistance to the proposal was dismissed by at least some committee members as the concerns of young university students who had been inspired by Commissioner Radwanski's speech in February, who did not understand the purpose of the proposed program, and who closed down opportunities for other concerned citizens to express their serious and supportive voices at the meeting.[10]

The fourth problem with the forums followed from the third. By the time the consultations began, Evaluation Committee members had no sense of how to evaluate a consultation, save for a show of hands among meeting attendees. Members of the Evaluation Committee did not attend every meeting, data gathering was inconsistent, and the onus of responsibility for forming a well-rounded opinion about video surveillance was placed on the public. In fact, the Evaluation Committee had not even met by mid-April, and it had no terms of reference for approaching the forums in a responsible and fair manner. This says nothing of the impartiality of the committee, composed mostly of businesspeople from the downtown area. Indeed, at the start of the forum process, two of eight members of the committee publicly declared their intention to support the initiative (Bell 2002).

The fifth problem concerned the way in which community consultations were conceptualized by the OIPC as much as the HPS and how the consultation design related to the interpretation of results. When the OIPC recommended that the HPS conduct broad public consultations, it did not mean only public forums. When it came to designing public forums as an innovative way to facilitate dialogue among police and the public, however, the OIPC encouraged the HPS to reach out not only to Hamiltonians who live in and/or frequent the downtown region but also to those who only occasionally visit it. The logic of the latter recommendation is that streetscape CCTV surveillance can affect all members of the city at some time.

The recommendation to consult broadly is an admirable one, and in some cities broad public meetings/consultations might work well to gauge public opinion about video surveillance. But Hamilton is so diverse and fragmented that consultations in areas outside the core yielded results very different from findings in the core. Indeed, at the close of the forum series, the HPS reported that a total of 259 people attended the meetings. Of the 259 attendees, 216 (83 percent of all attendees) were present at the two forums held in the downtown area: an estimated 96 people attended the first forum held at the Central Library, and an estimated 120 people attended the second forum held at First Place. The latter is a seniors' residence located on King Street East at the corner of King Street and Wellington Street North (in the jurisdiction of the IVBIA). The forum was held on Monday, 29 April, at 2 p.m. to accommodate the residents' schedules, and it exemplified the only targeted forum held by the HPS. Whereas the result of the straw vote at the first meeting was represented as 50 percent of people in support, the result of the straw vote at the second meeting was represented as 95 percent of people in support.

In their final report to Police Chief Robertson, the Evaluation Committee argued that most meeting attendees supported the initiative to install cameras in the core (approximately 77 percent of people participating in the twelve straw votes). Yet they failed to take seriously the fact that only forty-three people attended ten consultations held outside the downtown core. By taking all forums collectively, they effectively equalized the findings (meetings ranged from 120 people to 1 person) even though proximity and attendance numbers are important. Moreover, they never targeted groups in the downtown core such as youth, students, bus users, or homeless persons – all groups that would come into daily contact with the cameras. In the end, the consultation process appeared to be an exercise to appease the OIPC and manufacture a public safety image, regardless of how much the HPS intended to stage rigorous public consultations.

Launching the Pilot Project

A few days after the Evaluation Committee finalized its report on the entire consultation process (on 12 March 2003), Police Chief Robertson recommended to the HWPSB that it seek the support of Hamilton City Council to run a two-year CCTV surveillance pilot project in downtown Hamilton prior to declaring its own support for the initiative (on 17 March 2003). His recommendation was based on the findings presented by the Evaluation Committee as well as recently released findings from a city-wide telephone survey. The latter entailed responses to a set of questions on the CCTV surveillance proposal added to a survey being conducted independently of the HPS but in relation to *C.O.P.P. 2000* (Hamilton Police Services Board 2002b). Robertson reported that 84.3 percent of telephone survey respondents believed that CCTV surveillance is an effective crime deterrent and detection device and that 82.1 percent supported the use of cameras by the HPS.

On 3 June 2004, the HPS launched the two-year pilot project. Five streetscape CCTV surveillance cameras were installed along King Street East and West at the intersections of James, John, Catherine, Walnut, and Ferguson Streets. Digital camera images were transmitted via fibre optic cables to eight monitors located in the call management area of HPS headquarters (see Figure 13). Camera images were recorded twenty-four hours a day, seven

13 Streetscape surveillance camera monitoring station, City of Hamilton

14 Streetscape surveillance camera signage, City of Hamilton, Ontario

days a week, and passively monitored in the CCTV workstation by members of the Call Management Branch (7 a.m. to 2 a.m.).[11] The cameras rotated 360 degrees with pan, zoom, and tilt functions, and the system was equipped with a pixel function to block out residential windows. In accordance with recommendations by the OIPC, images were saved for seventy-two hours, and signs were posted under cameras notifying the public that the area is under video surveillance (see Figure 14).[12]

To meet minimal recommendations set out by the OIPC, the Implementation Committee developed an interim CCTV policy. Among other things, the policy entailed a logbook and an application approval process for officers to gain access to surveillance recordings. Part of the pilot project also entailed forming a Citizens' Review Committee (an offshoot of the CCTV surveillance Evaluation Committee) chaired by Superintendent Petz. The Review Committee met quarterly to discuss statistics and to assess the strengths and weaknesses of the program and the equipment. The ultimate purpose of the committee's meetings was to prepare data to inform recommendations for the future of the program at the end of the pilot project.

Table 2

CCTV camera effectiveness, phase 1, City of Hamilton, Ontario	
Criminal arrests	19
Drug arrests	12
Found persons	4
Emotionally disturbed persons	5
Provincial offences	13
Transportation truck company notifications	5
Requests for CCTV recordings for investigation	39

Source: Hamilton Police Services Board (2005).

After the first year of operations, the newly appointed chief of police, Brian Mullan, reported to the HWPSB on the status of the program (Hamilton Police Services Board 2005). Mullan argued that the system had proven very successful in observing crimes in progress, in dispatching officers, and in providing visual oversight for officers on the ground. He presented descriptive statistics for the whole of Area 6703,[13] suggesting that the cameras contributed to a reduction in crimes and calls for service, ranging from robbery and auto theft to assault (see Table 2).

Chief Mullan's report to the HWPSB not only presented a set of statistics but also explained how, during the first year of the pilot project, several other policing initiatives were put in place. For example, in January 2004, the HPS implemented cross-squad goal-setting and problem-solving initiatives to co-ordinate better policing operations among the four squads of the HPS (based on recommendations set out in *C.O.P.P. 2000*). The HPS also implemented a sixteen-week "summer blitz" (i.e., Project Crack Down) in the summer of 2004, entailing eight plain-clothed officers devoted to drug enforcement activity in the core. The HPS increased officer visibility downtown by assigning nine auxiliary foot patrol officers and four bike officers during this period, and it assisted the RCMP in training recruits by having RCMP trainees run foot patrols in the core over a six-week period. Despite the multi-faceted policing initiative, however, Mullan attributed crime reduction and reduced service calls to Area 6703 to the success of the cameras.[14]

Toward the end of the pilot project, the CCTV Review Committee announced that it would hold eight public forums between 29 May and 22 June 2006. In the months leading up to the forums, volunteers were recruited to conduct 2,000 telephone surveys to supplement information gathered during the forums. Like the first set of community meetings, the 2006 forums were not well attended. Meetings began with a sixteen-minute overview of the program by Staff Sergeant Ken Weatherill to inform attendees of main

Table 3

CCTV camera effectiveness, phase 2, City of Hamilton, Ontario		
Criminal arrests	24	(19)[1]
Drug arrests	13	(12)
Emotionally disturbed persons	6	(5)
Missing persons	4	(4)
Provincial offences	15	(13)
Transportation truck company notifications[2]		N/A
Requests for CCTV recordings for investigation		N/A

Notes:
1 The numbers in parentheses represent data reported in the first-year review (Hamilton Police Services Board 2005). These data were not presented in the community forums.
2 The City of Hamilton passed a bylaw to restrict large trucks from exiting Highway 403 and driving through the downtown area along King Street. The cameras were used to monitor traffic violations of this kind.
Source: Weatherill (2006).

developments in the program since 2000. The information overview was accompanied by a list of descriptive statistics paralleling data used in the first-year update report (see Table 3).

As with the first set of forums, the HPS failed to comment on a number of issues that would have helped attendees understand these issues better. For instance, the year prior to the forums, the Home Office's *Assessing the Impact of CCTV* report (Gill and Spriggs 2005) was published and readily accessible on the Web. The report evaluates thirteen CCTV programs and fourteen public-area systems. It outlines several dimensions of public-area monitoring, ranging from organizational structure to crime reduction, and it challenges many of the common claims about the usefulness of public-area monitoring. By 2006, the Home Office report was available alongside a growing body of literature assessing – and calling into question – the effectiveness of streetscape monitoring systems, and closer to home, London had produced reports on crime reduction. The HPS also failed to mention that it had increased core patrol by 20 percent (thirteen to seventeen) from 2004 to 2005.

On 29 June 2006, the Review Committee completed its mandate when it presented recommendations to Police Chief Mullan. Based on its assessment of the public consultation data, it recommended not only the continued use of CCTV surveillance cameras but also their expansion to other areas of the city. Part of its recommendation was to abandon the possibility of using volunteers to monitor cameras and to keep the system under HPS control.

On 23 October 2006, Mullan submitted a report on the pilot program to the HWPSB (Hamilton Police Services Board 2006). Half of the report consists of background to the program, and the other half assesses the usefulness of cameras in the core. Mullan argues that, over the two-year period, the HPS witnessed a downward trend in crime rates in the areas where the cameras were deployed. He also provides data from the community consultation surveys, suggesting that 92 percent of respondents believe that cameras show a positive effect on the deterrence, detection, and suppression of crime and that 89 percent of respondents support the use of CCTV by the HPS. He concludes by informing the board that the CCTV Implementation and Steering Committees supported the use and expansion of CCTV cameras in Hamilton.

Post-Pilot Monitoring

At the time of writing (July 2009), the HPS continues to operate five streetscape CCTV cameras in the original locations. The camera images are monitored four hours a day by limited-duty officers. The screens are also subject to casual monitoring from passing police officers, who take control of the cameras when they see fit. A logbook is used to record officer-camera image interactions, but due to the sporadic nature of the monitoring and to the large number of potential monitors the logging system is not fully adhered to.

Tracing to the launch of the pilot project, the HPS envisioned expanding the program to include wireless movable cameras with regular monitoring intervals. Wireless cameras were desired because of costs associated not only with fibre optic rentals but also with laying fibre optic cables outside the downtown area. Regardless of the specific structure of the system, however, there was an understanding among committee members, business representatives, and the HPS that expansion of the program would necessitate ongoing city funding.

In September 2008, the initiative to expand the program came to public attention. The HPS announced that it had secured approval from the HWPSB to install ten to twelve new cameras that would transmit camera images over a wireless network to the police station. The HPS also aimed to have cameras accessible on laptops via wireless signals in patrol cars. Capital costs for the expansion were estimated at $100,000, and four new areas of the city were targeted for cameras: James Street North, Hess Village (Hess Street), Concession Street, and Ottawa Street.

On 19 June 2009, the HPS announced the installation of four new cameras in Policing Districts 2 and 3. The cameras were installed on Concession Street at the intersections of Summit and Hamilton Streets and on Ottawa Street at the intersections of Cannon Street and Britannia Avenue. Images from the cameras are transmitted over radio waves to police headquarters. The rationale for the expansion is the security and peace of mind for the businesses and visitors in the areas.

Kiddie Bars, Downtown Revitalization, and Windsor's Video Guard Monitoring Program[15]

As the HPS staged public forums across Hamilton, momentum started to build around establishing a monitoring program in Windsor. The latter city (approximate population of 216,000) is located in southern Ontario, about 200 kilometres southwest of London (about 300 kilometres from Hamilton). Windsor sits along the Detroit River, adjacent to the city of Detroit. As home to one of Canada's major automotive companies (Chrysler Canada), Windsor is commonly understood as the automotive capital of Canada. In the mid-1990s, however, city officials and members of Windsor's City Centre Business Association (CCBA) sought to transform the city's image from an industrial automotive centre into a post-industrial entertainment and tourist destination.

Revitalization of Windsor's centre was set in motion with the interim opening of Casino Windsor in 1994 (the casino was moved to its permanent location in 1998).[16] As Ontario's first casino, Casino Windsor created jobs, attracted millions of tourists and visitors from Canada and the United States, and marked the beginning of efforts by representatives of the city and members of the CCBA to rebrand Windsor by diversifying the economy and re-invigorating commercial activity in the downtown core.

A primary component of revitalization entailed the relaxation of land-use regulations and the introduction of economic incentives to create new businesses in the downtown area. Leading into the mid-1990s, business-licensing practices were relatively restrictive. The downtown area was populated with coffee shops, restaurants, retail outlets, and several late-night drinking establishments. Set in the broader context of the provincial Conservative government's discouragement of increasing licensing restrictions on business activity (see Knight 1998 for a general overview of the Conservative government of Ontario), however, and following completion of the City of Windsor's (1994) city centre revitalization report, few limitations were placed on the creation of new businesses. Among other things, what the deregulation of land use in downtown Windsor led to was the proliferation of youth-oriented, retail alcohol establishments (so-called mega bars).

From 1996 to 2004, the number of bars in the downtown core increased from fewer than twenty-seven to fifty-four (City of Windsor 2004). The sizes and patron capacities of bars also increased, to the extent that the downtown core offered 23,000 drinking seats by 2002 (Lippert 2008). Many of the newly created establishments came to be referred to euphemistically as "kiddie bars": large venues offering cheap drinks and a variety of promotional events (e.g., wet T-shirt contests) that catered to young people within and around Windsor as well as nearby Michigan, Ohio, and Indiana. Young Americans from across the Detroit River were particularly attracted to Windsor's bars and nightclubs to take advantage of the lower drinking age in Ontario (nineteen; Michigan's is twenty-one).[17]

The increasing number of young drinkers in the core was accompanied by an increasing number of problems for police, business owners, and downtown residents. In the early 2000s, for example, police received a growing number of complaints about noise, vandalism, traffic congestion, public urination, and street violence. Policing, especially after 11 p.m. on weekend evenings and mornings, increased significantly, taxing the ability of police to maintain a preventative presence on downtown streets. Several business owners and members of the CCBA, too, complained about increasing costs of insurance due to vandalism (e.g., broken windows) in the area and the concomitant decline of the retail sector. Downtown residents lamented the transformation of the downtown streets from retail outlets and local shops to crowded restaurants and entertainment venues.

By 2002, cleavages between certain bar owners (who were members of the CCBA) and other members of the business community and city council were growing. In addition to driving up insurance premiums for some downtown business owners and driving away other downtown retail businesses, the proliferation of kiddie bars along the so-called kiddie block started to work against the city's revitalization efforts. One of the main aims of revitalizing the core was to cast it as a safe place to attract a diversity of businesses, retail outlets, and visitors. Rather than working toward reducing late-night problems associated with the intoxicated bar crowd, however, in late 2001 some bar owners started running radio advertisements in Detroit suburbs that depicted Windsor as "bartown," replete with hot body contests and one-dollar drink promotions (Lippert 2008).

To address the perceived impediments to revitalization in the core, Windsor City Council hired a Maryland-based consultant, Peter Bellmio, to assess the social and physical conditions in Windsor's city centre. Bellmio was hired based on a recommendation from the mayor's joint city-police Scanning, Analysis, Research, and Action (SARA) committee, designed to assess security problems in the downtown area. Bellmio visited Windsor between 6 and 9 November 2002 with a mandate to assess quality-of-life problems and economic development issues in the city centre (Bellmio 2003). His assessment entailed interviews with city, community, police, business, and media representatives, a physical site inspection, and a working session to generate discussion about the problems facing Windsor's city centre (see below).

Surveying the Kiddie Crowd

As the SARA committee waited for Bellmio's final report (submitted on 13 January 2003), a local man, William Jentzel (twenty-one years of age), was attacked near the corner of Ouellette Avenue and Wyandotte Street in the downtown core. On 29 December 2002, Jentzel intervened to stop four men from beating another man in the early morning hours. Jentzel (who was later identified in news reporting and CCTV surveillance promotional materials as a Good Samaritan) subsequently spent eight days in a coma; he endured four brain surgeries and was left with brain damage, no sense of taste or smell, and reduced strength and control in his right hand.[18]

Following the attack on William Jentzel, his father, Tristan Jentzel, contacted Michael Hurst, mayor of Windsor, and Police Chief Glenn Stannard to inquire about what could be done to address violence in the downtown core. He held two meetings with Mayor Hurst – one alone and one in consultation with members of the Windsor Police Service (WPS) and Windsor City Council. As a result of the meetings, Jentzel joined the newly created City Centre Security Enhancement Resource Team (CCSERT).[19]

The CCSERT was assembled as a security subcommittee of the Mayor's City Centre Revitalization Task Force (CCRTF). One of the main goals of the CCRTF was to find ways to restrict the development of increasingly problematic drinking establishments and to reduce violence and disorder associated with the late-night drinking crowd. The CCRTF appointed two security committees – SARA and subsequently CCSERT – to generate possible solutions to the problems experienced in the downtown area and to formulate tangible recommendations to realize them, respectively.

The primary data source used by both committees was the Bellmio report. The fourteen-page report outlines a set of problems and needs facing the city centre. The primary problem highlighted in the report was downtown bars and associated undesirable activities. Especially salient in the report is the alleged busloads of young American drinkers (not all of whom are nineteen) from Indiana, Ohio, and Michigan who come to Windsor to take advantage of the lower drinking age and to "meet members of the opposite sex and to have a good time" (Bellmio 2003, 3). Increasing numbers of American drinkers, argues Bellmio, are not only associated with increasing incidents of violence, vandalism, noise, public urination, traffic congestion, and litter in the downtown area. The growing presence of young Americans also attracts greater numbers of Canadian patrons to downtown bars, which in turn fuels the drive to develop larger drinking venues. To remedy the problems associated with mega bars in the city centre, then, Bellmio offers a set of short- and long-term solutions. Among the long-term solutions is to consider installing cameras to allow for public-area streetscape surveillance similar to that in London and Sudbury (14).[20]

Members of SARA assembled on 23 January to discuss the recommendations in the Bellmio report, and they completed their assessment (destined for city council's approval) on 30 January (City of Windsor 2003). Leading up to a special meeting of city council the following month, members of

SARA publicly announced that they agreed with all of Bellmio's recommendations and that they were recommending that city council approve revised zoning bylaws, the creation of a task force to address problems with the bar scene (i.e., CCSERT), and the establishment of an on-site surveillance camera system (Hall 2003). In reaction to news reporting on the forthcoming SARA recommendations, however, Police Chief Stannard publicly stated that he did not want police to be associated with a video surveillance system. The Windsor Police Service Board chairman, Councillor Bill Marra, claimed that it was an extreme measure. The deputy chairman of the Windsor Police Service Board proclaimed that he was totally against the proposal. And Mayor Mike Hurst stated that surveillance cameras would be an extraordinary response to problems in the downtown area (Schmidt 2003).

The SARA committee's assessment of the Bellmio report was presented to city council in February. To examine strategies to implement the short- and long-term recommendations of the Bellmio report, city council formally created the CCSERT as an extension of SARA and instructed members to generate specific short- and long-term recommendations for the CCRTF. The CCSERT produced fourteen recommendations and submitted them to the CCRTF by June. In addition to recommending safety initiatives such as a one-year freeze on kiddie bars, improved lighting, after-hours washroom access, and a series of bylaws (e.g., anti-fighting, anti-littering), the committee encouraged installation of the streetscape CCTV surveillance monitoring program.

After the CCSERT formally recommended establishment of such a monitoring program, members of the CCBA moved to implement a pilot project. At a CCBA board meeting, Larry Horwitz (also a city councillor) suggested that cameras could be mounted on his building on Pelissier Street (the old YMCA building) and that Elite Protection Security Specialists (hereafter Elite Security) could supply the equipment. Horwitz subsequently approached Glen and Sherry McCourt of Elite Security and began to finalize plans to launch a pilot project.

In February 2004, Fran Funaro, managing director of the CCBA, publicly announced that the CCBA intended to have surveillance cameras mounted on the YMCA building by March. The following month, Elite Security presented a contract to Larry Horwitz (representing the CCBA) to install three CCTV surveillance cameras at 511 Pelissier Street. The CCBA was responsible for covering the basic start-up costs (signs, network connectors, service fees), and camera-monitoring equipment was supplied by Elite Security. The six-month pilot program was designed to include live monitoring by Elite Security's staff on Friday and Saturday nights between 11 p.m. and 4:30 a.m.[21]

Prior to the formal launch of the pilot project, the CCBA sought city council's approval/endorsement through the CCSERT. During council's deliberations in early June, Councillor Joyce Zuk voiced concerns about privacy protection and civil liberties. She posed questions to the delegates who were supporting the proposal (including Councillor Horwitz, Tristan Jentzel, and Glen McCourt from Elite Security) about the storage and disposal of surveillance images, and she requested evidence showing that streetscape cameras reduce crime. She also asked the city solicitor about liability facing the municipality and whether it was even appropriate or necessary for the CCBA to seek council's approval to establish a monitoring system. When suitable answers failed to materialize in response to Councillor Zuk's and other councillors' questions, council moved to defer ruling on the pilot project until further information was available. Following the meeting, the legal advisor to the City of Windsor, Patrick Brode, was assigned the responsibility to review existing legislation and draft a report to assess the city's liability concerning the proposed monitoring system.

On 18 June 2004, the six-month "Video Guard" CCTV surveillance pilot project was launched without city council's endorsement. The purpose of the program was to monitor late-night activity in the core. Four streetscape CCTV surveillance cameras (two stationary cameras and two panoramic ones) scanned the length of Pelissier Street from Wyandotte Street to Park Street (see Figure 15). Three signs notifying the public that the area is under video surveillance were posted (see Figure 16), surveillance images were recorded in real time from the premises of Elite Security on three monitoring screens, and surveillance images were retained for seventy-two hours. The cameras were monitored live from 11 p.m. to 4 a.m. during a Friday-Saturday shift and from 12 a.m. to 5 a.m. during a Sunday shift. To carry out live-monitoring duties, Elite Security hired Tristan Jentzel. The CCBA-funded pilot project was not governed by terms of reference or a formal operational manual, and no data-gathering/analysis system was put in place to assess the effectiveness of the system. Nevertheless, the goal of the pilot project was to demonstrate to members of city council that CCTV surveillance cameras would contribute to the reduction of problems in the core.

Immediately following the launch of the pilot program, a complaint was laid with the Ontario OIPC. Following up on the complaint, Judith Hoffman from the OIPC contacted the City of Windsor, primarily because two members of city council sat on the CCBA board. The connection between the city and the CCBA, claimed the OIPC, qualified the latter as a municipal institution under MFIPPA. After initial consultation with Patrick Brode, Hoffman encouraged the City of Windsor to remain involved with the monitoring initiative and to develop an operations policy in co-operating with the CCBA. Brode and members of the Chief Administrative Office began researching camera operations in Sudbury and London, and they started to draft privacy regulations and an operations policy. To assist city representatives, Hoffman forwarded a copy of *Guidelines*.

15   Streetscape surveillance camera, City of Windsor, Ontario

16   Streetscape surveillance camera signage, City of Windsor, Ontario

As the end of the pilot project approached, members of the CCBA started calling for a four-month extension of the program. They also called for an expansion of the program to include two additional cameras at the corner of Ouellette Avenue and Wyandotte Street. Part of the effort to expand the system included publicized arguments that the CCBA was not connected to the City of Windsor and that it was not accountable to the OIPC under MFIPPA. The main concern of the CCBA was that the pilot project would be halted because of bureaucratic red tape concerning interactions among city representatives and the OIPC. The CCBA board therefore unilaterally approved a four-month extension of the pilot program. At city council's 20 December meeting, Brode's final report (Brode 2004) was formally received, and council instructed the City of Windsor's administration to assist the CCBA in adhering to operational standards outlined in *Guidelines*. Council did not, however, debate extension of the pilot project.

On 12 January 2005, members of the CCBA met with representatives of the City of Windsor, Elite Security, and Deborah Grant of the OIPC. At the meeting, Grant authorized continuation of the pilot project under MFIPPA based on the understanding that the city's Legal Department was working to develop a privacy policy based on those of other cities in Ontario running streetscape monitoring programs. At the meeting, Grant informed the CCBA and city representatives that the CCBA could not run the monitoring program independently. On behalf of the OIPC, Grant encouraged the CCSERT to take ownership of the program using city funds.

Expanding Video Guard

The following month, the CCSERT created a surveillance camera subcommittee to report on the success of the pilot project and to oversee the possible expansion of Video Guard. The subcommittee's report to the CCSERT in March 2005 could not offer statistical support for the effectiveness of the cameras because no reporting protocol had been set up during the pilot period. Nevertheless, committee members argued that meetings between the WPS and city administrators gave support to continue the program (City Centre Security Enhancement Resource Team 2005a). Also noting claims about the perceived effectiveness of London's and Sudbury's monitoring programs, the subcommittee recommended the addition of two cameras to the system.

On 9 June 2005, the CCSERT recommended to city council that the existing pilot project on Pelissier Street be adopted, continued, and maintained by the City of Windsor. They also recommended expanding the system to include cameras at the corner of Wyandotte Street and Ouellette Avenue and Wyandotte Street and Park Street; that the system be supported by joint funds from the CCBA and the City of Windsor; and that policies, procedures, instructions, and responsibilities be developed to support the program, including an audit/evaluation function to regulate and assess its effectiveness (City Centre Security Enhancement Resource Team 2005b).

When the City of Windsor assumed ownership of Video Guard in June 2005, councillors' first priority was to finalize an operations protocol. Members of the Chief Administrative Office collected information from Sudbury's KPMG report and information from the City of London. They were specifically interested in gathering information on the rationale for using video surveillance, the structure of monitoring programs, and protocols about confidentiality and privacy.

The Chief Administrative Office submitted a final report on public-area video surveillance (including an operations policy) to Windsor City Council on 16 January 2006 (City of Windsor 2006). It had already been sent twice to the OIPC for review. Council approved a motion that the City of Windsor enter into an agreement with Elite Security and the CCBA to expand the scope of the program subject to final approval by the OIPC of the video surveillance policy.

Accompanying the proposal for the new cameras was a two-minute tape that Tristan Jentzel and Glen McCourt presented to council. The tape illustrated what an average weekend night entailed in the downtown core. The tape depicted a man outside a bar shooting a gun in the air five times, and it showed two young women being approached by a group of menacing men. The images included close-ups of people's faces in order to illustrate the quality and zoom capacity of the cameras. During the presentation, Mayor Eddie Francis became agitated and asked the representatives from Elite Security to turn the video off. He claimed that it was not proper to be showing people's faces to city councillors or to have the images broadcast on local television (council proceedings were broadcast live on a local cable television station). Still, the footage contributed to the consolidation of the 9-1 vote in favour of expanding the program.

The downtown video surveillance privacy policy – a hybrid of the City of Sudbury's promotional materials and the City of London's operational policy – was finalized and sent to the OIPC for approval in April. The City of Windsor Downtown Video Surveillance Policy identifies the city clerk as the head of the program under MFIPPA; the City of Windsor is identified as the service provider. The policy calls for live monitoring and recording of surveillance images on Fridays-Saturdays from 11 p.m. to 4 a.m. and Sundays from 12 a.m. to 5 a.m. and for recording of images at other times. The policy also calls for establishment of a Surveillance Audit Committee composed of representatives from Public Works, Corporate Facility Planning, Health and Safety, the WPS, and City Planning. Audits of the program are performed annually to assess the system's impact on crime, crime displacement, cost, and public opinion. The public input process entails a statement about the appropriate contact person to handle complaints from members of the public.

In mid-June, city council granted final approval to install four additional cameras to monitor Pelissier Street and Maiden Lane, Ouellette Avenue, Wyandotte Street, and Park Street, and the video surveillance policy received final council approval in September 2006. In late 2006, the four original cameras were replaced, and four new cameras were installed at the corners of Ouellette Avenue and Park Street and Ouellette Avenue and Wyandotte Street.[22] Tristan Jentzel continued to operate cameras, but an additional operator was also hired. At the close of the pilot project, the CCSERT was disbanded because members thought that they had met all of their objectives in reviewing Bellmio's report and implementing strategies to address crime in the core. The governance structure put in place by the City of Windsor calls for the program to be reviewed in 2009 when the contracts expire. The planned review process will include all cameras that are owned by the city, including those mounted on or within city-owned buildings and those monitoring traffic on freeways.

Conclusion

This chapter examined the ways that representatives in Hamilton and Windsor established streetscape systems in the context of the tripartite ideational, administrative, and policy diffusion of streetscape monitoring programs across Anglo-Canada. Despite certain similarities, the process of establishing a system in each city was substantially different. Part of the variation in the establishment process pertains to the different interests in CCTV systems in each city (e.g., beat integrity versus kiddie bars), to ownership structures (e.g., police versus city ownership), to the influence of signal crimes and events, and to the ways in which proponents of streetscape systems in each city interpreted and acted on the stipulations presented in *Guidelines*.

Hamilton is particularly important in the rise and diffusion of streetscape CCTV surveillance programs for several reasons. First, from 1998 to 2001, the monitoring system was designed based on the administrative diffusion of LVMAC promotional materials. Until the end of 2001, the design and implementation process did not involve public consultations, and there was little innovation in the operational structure beyond the Lions Eye in the Sky. Following a signal crime early in 2002, however, critical media attention attracted the interest of both the OIPC and Commissioner Radwanski. The signal crime was used in promotional rhetoric (Hier 2004), but it also focused attention on matters pertaining to operational protocol and privacy protection. The increased attention led to the staging of public consultations to appease the OIPC, and the consultations were significant for at least two reasons: they were designed entirely by the HPS, involving little actual interactive consultation with the public, and they developed a precedent that was invoked in Thunder Bay the following year (see Chapter 9). In other words, in a manner similar to the Lions Eye in the Sky governance structure, the HPS developed a template for consultations without guidance or direction of the OIPC. The limited integrity of the consultation process, consequently, is attributable not only to the failure of the HPS to stage rigorous consultations but also to the OIPC to provide clear guidance (a failure of policy diffusion) – another pivotal missed opportunity.

In contrast to Hamilton's emphasis on the public forum process, no public consultations were staged in Windsor. Although the streetscape systems in Hamilton and Windsor were launched within weeks of each other, the operational structure of each was very different. Unlike the establishment of Hamilton's system, the WPS had little involvement in the monitoring system in Windsor, and the city assumed ownership of the program. The ownership structure exercised significant influences on the administrative structure, but similar to how the OIPC encouraged the consultation process in Hamilton, its involvement in Windsor was primarily educational. The pragmatic orientation adopted in Hamilton and Windsor contributed not only to diversity in the design and establishment processes but also, as I illustrate in the following chapter, to flexibility in efforts to resist monitoring initiatives.

APPENDIX 7.1

Hamilton Police Service
Leading the Way Together

CCTV Community Forum Surveys
The Hamilton Police Service is committed to providing quality service.
We care what you think!

1 Would you feel safer in Hamilton knowing that the Police Service was monitoring the area on CCTV in addition to police patrols?

Yes ___   No ___   Undecided ___

2 Would you be more inclined to visit an area that had CCTV cameras installed?

Much more inclined ___   Somewhat more inclined ___
Not more inclined ___   Less inclined ___   Undecided ___

3   Do you support the use of closed circuit televisions?

   Yes ___   No ___   Undecided ___

4   Do you believe that closed circuit televisions are an effective tool for deterring and detecting crime?

   Yes___   No ___   Don't Know ___

5   Do you oppose the use of closed circuit televisions for any reason?

   Yes, state reason: _____   No ___

6   Note responders gender

   Male ___   Female ___   Transgender ___

7   What is your age range?

   18-30 ___   31-44 ___   45-64 ___   65-over ___

8   What city, town or township do you reside in?

   _____

9   Comments:

   _____

_____

Source: Reproduced with permission of Hamilton Police Service, Corporate Services Division.

8
Thwarted Efforts to Establish Streetscape Monitoring Programs

The previous five chapters analyzed the complex relations that contributed to establishing streetscape CCTV surveillance monitoring programs in nine French- and English-speaking Canadian cities. Save for Drummondville and Hull in Quebec, where monitoring programs were discontinued after several years of operation (see Chapter 3), all of the cities analyzed continue to operate monitoring systems.

This chapter examines three Canadian cities where efforts to establish streetscape CCTV surveillance monitoring systems have been thwarted: Vancouver, British Columbia, and Brockville and Peterborough, Ontario. Hier et al. (2007) reported on some of the communications dynamics that led to the defeat of monitoring proposals in Brockville and Peterborough, so the chapter focuses mostly on Vancouver. Admittedly, there are dozens of cities in Canada where streetscape CCTV surveillance proposals of varying complexity have been considered and rejected. The primary reason why such proposals are rejected is the obligation to long-term funding. The thwarted establishment efforts examined in this chapter, however, entail a mix of critical newspaper coverage, community activism, signal events, the absence of signal crimes, and resistance by civil libertarian and information and privacy commissioners.

The chapter begins by examining efforts of the Vancouver Police Department (VPD) to establish a streetscape CCTV surveillance monitoring program in the Downtown Eastside (DTES) and in the entertainment district. The first of three phases in Vancouver began in 1998, when the VPD attempted to establish a monitoring program to survey the area surrounding the corner of Main and Hastings Streets. The proposal was abandoned in 2005 after a multi-year effort to resist streetscape monitoring by the Carnegie Community Action Group, the British Columbia Civil Liberties Association (BCCLA), and the information and privacy commissioner of British Columbia intersected with the release of the Home Office report (Gill and Spriggs 2005). Following the thwarted attempt to establish a monitoring system in the

DTES, the VPD initiated efforts to introduce streetscape cameras in the entertainment district. This initiative was also resisted by the BCCLA and Information and Privacy Commissioner David Loukidelis, but plans to introduce streetscape CCTV surveillance during the 2010 Olympic Games gave rise to a third phase that is currently under way.

The second city examined in the chapter is Brockville. The 1999 proposal for CCTV surveillance in Brockville is significant because it is the only monitoring initiative that has been defeated based on a critical editorial campaign staged by journalists working for the local press combined with, or in addition to, a volatile manifestation of civic resistance. The thwarted effort in Brockville illustrates how alternative definitions of video surveillance can be expressed in the context of a poorly articulated rationale for introducing public camera surveillance and in the absence of a signal crime or other event that could be used to galvanize public support for a monitoring program. However, in 2008 the Brockville Police Service initiated a renewed effort to establish a monitoring program based in part on the newly established monitoring program in nearby Trenton/Frankfort (see Appendix A). Combined with Vancouver's current initiative, the recently renewed effort in Brockville suggests that arguments about failed attempts to establish monitoring programs should be received with caution.

In the third city examined in this chapter, Peterborough, a community-based resistance campaign ended efforts by the city's business community to install streetscape cameras in the downtown core. Following a proposal put forth by the Peterborough business community to address problems related to the bar flush, a community group formed to articulate a set of counter-definitions to primary claims made by advocates of the proposal. The campaign was enabled by the absence of a signal crime and a relative degree of apathy among businesspeople in downtown Peterborough. Unlike promotional efforts in Vancouver and Brockville, there has been no attempt to revive Peterborough's thwarted proposal.

Shifting Priorities for Streetscape Monitoring in Vancouver[1]
Located in the Lower Mainland of southwestern British Columbia, Vancouver is the largest city in the province. With a population of approximately 600,000, Vancouver is composed of several diverse ethnic and cultural neighbourhoods.[2] It is regularly ranked as one of the most livable cities in the world, in part because of its proximity to the Pacific Ocean, its temperate climate, and its surrounding forests and mountains. Significant for the analyses to follow, Vancouver is not only home to what is commonly understood as Canada's poorest postal code; it is also, at the time of writing, preparing for the 2010 winter Olympic games.

In April 1999, the VPD released *CCTV: A Community Policing Option for the Downtown Eastside* (Fredericks 1999).[3] The ninety-page discussion paper called for the installation of sixteen streetscape CCTV surveillance cameras to survey fifty-nine blocks in the DTES.[4] The DTES is composed of seven official over-lapping communities – Chinatown, Gastown, Oppenheimer, Victory Square, Strathcona, Thornton Park, and the Industrial Area – and it is home to ap-proximately 16,000 residents (City of Vancouver 2001a). The DTES lies ad-jacent to Vancouver's business and retail district, and it is Canada's poorest urban area (Haggerty, Huey, and Ericson 2008). The DTES is widely perceived as a skid-row community given the high numbers of drug addicts, criminal activities, and mentally ill persons. But the community is also home to working-class people and residents of diverse ethnic backgrounds.

The initiative to establish a streetscape CCTV surveillance monitoring program was caught up in Vancouver's efforts to revitalize the DTES. In July 1998, Vancouver City Council endorsed the principles set out in *A Program of Strategic Actions for the Downtown Eastside* (City of Vancouver 1998b). The report was part of a six-report submission that addressed drug treatment, housing, land use, the creation of legitimate businesses, and strategic actions for policing and community development in the DTES.[5] Among other things, a recommendation was presented in the report on strategic actions that the city manager, the general manager of community services, and the chief constable of the VPD seek council's approval to apply for funding through the federal government's National Crime Prevention Program[6] Safer City Initiative funded through the Crime Prevention Investment Fund to address concerns in the DTES (City of Vancouver 1998a).

The ensuing application, "Building a Future Together: The Downtown Eastside Community Revitalization Program," built directly on the strategic policing and community development actions set out in the reports. In March 1999, council approved a five-year revitalization program; the first phase included a community crime prevention initiative jointly funded by the Department of Justice and the Crime Prevention Centre. Responding to council's endorsement, former VPD chief Bruce Chambers identified a community-based streetscape CCTV surveillance project as consistent with council's strategic actions initiative, and the CCTV surveillance discussion paper was circulated to city officials.[7]

The monitoring project was conceptualized as a $400,000 community crime reduction initiative to address the open-air drug market at the inter-section of Main Street and Hastings Street in the heart of the DTES.[8] Tracing to the early 1990s, pervasive drug dealing and use among the evening crowds outside the Carnegie Centre[9] at the corner of Main and Hastings were a primary concern for city officials. A set of programs, ranging from safe injec-tion sites to affordable housing, was proposed in the early to mid-1990s, and streetscape monitoring was tied to these initiatives.

On 28 May 1999, Sergeant Fredericks and Inspector Gary Greer spoke at a public meeting at the Carnegie Centre, hosted by the Downtown Eastside

Residents Association (DERA). The VPD representatives explained that they wanted to install more than twenty-five streetscape CCTV cameras in the DTES to reduce the violent crime rate around Main and Hastings Streets (the discussion paper called for sixteen cameras). The VPD representatives described how the program would entail live monitoring by civilian monitoring staff, and the program would include a civilian oversight committee. The spokesmen relativized continual police video surveillance monitoring by linking the proposed system to other forms of public and private video surveillance on the SkyTrain system and in the Cassiar Connector and Deas Island Tunnel (now the George Massey Tunnel). They also presented arguments based on interpretations of data from the United Kingdom, Australia, and the United States that CCTV surveillance could reduce crime and public disorder.

Following the meeting at the Carnegie Centre, the VPD installed a preliminary test camera on the roof of the former Royal Bank Building that sits directly across from the Carnegie Centre. The camera was installed without public notification to assess the technological aspects of the system. Critical reaction to the camera, and to the proposed system, came from a variety of sources. Provincial Information and Privacy Commissioner David Flaherty, for example, argued that streetscape cameras in Vancouver would be a major step toward the creation of a surveillance society, and he raised concerns about function creep and the possibility of linking CCTV surveillance data to existing databases such as PharmaNet.[10] Local activists posted and circulated pamphlets warning of displacement, and in interviews they speculated about attaching helium balloons to a bed sheet to float in front of the camera (Haggerty, Huey, and Ericson 2008). And local news coverage was balanced but sympathetic to the complex issues facing the DTES. Local news media articulated concerns about privacy, displacement, and the appropriate allocation of public funds to address the concerns facing residents of the DTES.

Following initial critical reaction to the monitoring initiative, the BCCLA (in June) and the Carnegie Community Action Project (in July) released position papers to provide broader context for the VPD's discussion document. The BCCLA's response starts by pointing out that, between April and June 1999, the number of proposed cameras grew from sixteen to twenty-five and that the main demographic target group for surveillance in the DTES – males aged sixteen to thirty – was declining. The response proceeds to outline and analyze eleven key principles informing the use of public-area CCTV surveillance cameras by institutions governed by British Columbia's Freedom of Information and Protection of Privacy Act (FIPPA). Among the issues critically analyzed include effectiveness, displacement, need, and privacy infringement (British Columbia Civil Liberties Association 1999).

The Carnegie Community Action Project adopts a position similar to the one developed by members of the BCCLA. The Community Action Project's shorter position paper identifies five key issues: effectiveness, displacement, rapid expansion, actual uses/target practices, and rejection of CCTV proposals in US and UK cities. Yet the report more directly addresses how CCTV surveillance in the DTES fails to address the actual concerns facing the community:

> The use of CCTV in this situation potentially brings the worst of all possible worlds to the Downtown Eastside. It provides no new housing or employment opportunities to the people who live in the neighbourhood. It offers no means of improving living conditions inside SRO [single room occupancy] hotels. Indeed, some people have suggested that it might push illegal activities off the street and into people's living spaces. (Carnegie Community Action Project 1999)

The report also praises the VPD's community-based innovations in areas such as housing and drinking-establishment regulation but concludes that "CCTV offers police a long-term means of monitoring behavior with minimal presence. Unfortunately, this is not what the Downtown Eastside or Vancouver presently need[s]" (Carnegie Community Action Project 1999).

The multiple reactions to the monitoring initiative were effective in bringing a broader set of issues about CCTV surveillance to the attention of the public and especially city councillors. Expanding the scope of public discussion about streetscape monitoring was significant in 1999 because the city was heading into a municipal election, and councillors did not want to link themselves with a project associated with ignoring the needs of people in the DTES (e.g., drug treatment, affordable housing).

Still, despite the multiple critical reactions to the monitoring initiative from community-based organizations, Haggerty, Huey, and Ericson's (2008, 43) argument that the concentration of social problems in the DTES enabled established community activists to secure media attention and effectively oppose policing practices should be received with caution. It is true that organizations, including the Carnegie Community Action Project and the BCCLA, took a clear stand against the streetscape monitoring initiative, but service providers and community activists in the DTES were not singularly opposed to the proposal to install cameras along Hastings Street. Conversely, several representatives of community groups – many of whom operate video surveillance systems in and around their organizations and offices – welcomed the cameras, believing that they would capture police harassment and violence against innocent addicts, homeless people, children, and the poor.

Following release of the BCCLA and Carnegie Community Action Project position papers, the CCTV proposal went before the Vancouver Police Board (VPB) for adjudication. The VPB returned the proposal to the VPD and requested further study – especially concerning public opinion and privacy concerns. A meeting was held between the newly appointed information and privacy commissioner, David Loukidelis, Mayor Philip Owen, and members of the VPD's Senior Management Team. At the meeting, Loukidelis stressed the importance of developing clear operational policy and of holding meaningful public consultations. The VPD subsequently announced plans to hold a number of public meetings to explain its goals to community stakeholders, and it organized a research trip to the United Kingdom to gather data on operations and governance (Vancouver Police Board 2000).

In July 2000, Sergeant Fredericks completed his second and final discussion document: *Neighbourhood Safety Watch: Closed Circuit TV – A Safer Community Option for the Downtown Eastside, Strathcona, Chinatown, and Gastown Area* (Fredericks 2001). The 129-page discussion document (dated September 2001) proposes twenty-three fixed overt colour cameras in targeted high-crime areas in the DTES as well as two mobile cameras. The number of fixed cameras increased from sixteen to twenty-three because businesses outside the original fifty-nine-block area complained about possible displacement to their immediate surroundings.

The proposed Neighbourhood Safety Watch Program (NSWP) was presented under the ownership of the VPD. The VPD's Forensic Video Unit was charged with administering the program, and the Citizens' Advisory Committee for Urban Safety Enhancement (CAUSE) was designated to oversee the program. CAUSE – composed of private citizens, professionals, representatives from targeted communities, and a VPD liaison – was responsible not only for governing the management and use of surveillance data but also for making recommendations on expansion and positioning of surveillance cameras. The proposal called for continuous recording of camera images in a CCTV monitoring room located in the Emergency Communications Centre for South Western British Columbia on East Pender Street, where twenty-four-hour live monitoring by civilian CCTV emergency communications operators (i.e., 9-1-1 operators) would take place. A master control room located in the Forensic Video Unit office on Main Street would enable access not only to camera images but also to the Emergency Communications Centre, where CCTV emergency communications operators worked.

The NSWP Code of Practice included in the discussion document stipulated that all written, recorded, or videotaped information constitutes a record under FIPPA. Surveillance images were to be retained for thirty-one days, and changes to the Code of Practice were to be made in consultation with CAUSE. The VPD was required to produce an annual report on the monitoring system that would be submitted to CAUSE, city council, and the VPB. The NSWP proposal called for signs to be posted in areas where surveillance cameras were mounted, and it outlined procedural policy pertaining to installation, accountability, public information, assessment, staffing, complaints, breaches of the code, and access to surveillance information and equipment.

Prior to the public release of the NSWP discussion document on 26 October 2001, the existence of the revised proposal was leaked to local media (by Sergeant Fredericks). On 31 July, the *Vancouver Sun* reported that a revised version of the 1999 proposal had been presented to the VPB and the mayor's office in 2000 and that a series of public consultations was planned for the fall of 2001 (Sorensen 2001). In response to the news coverage, journalists working for the *Vancouver Courier* and members of the BCCLA requested copies of the new proposal to facilitate open public dialogue about installing cameras in the DTES. The VPD denied the requests, claiming that the proposal was under development (O'Connor 2001).

Leading up to the public release of the NSWP document in late October, two sets of developments influenced the VPD's efforts to establish a monitoring program in the DTES. The first set of developments entailed local activist groups and media focusing increasingly critical attention on the VPD's plan to establish a monitoring system. In August 2001, for example, representatives of the BCCLA not only requested a copy of the report but also complained to Mayor Owen and Deputy Police Chief Greer that the secrecy of the proposal infringed on the public's right to debate openly the merits of the proposal. Failure to release the proposal in a timely manner, they claimed, placed limitations on the length and scope of the public consultation process.

Members of the Carnegie association, too, took a public stand against the proposal. On 18 September 2001, the association wrote to the VPB to voice concerns about the status of the proposal's author, Grant Fredericks. Reiterating arguments made in response to the first public meeting at the Carnegie Centre, they argued that Fredericks was closely associated with the CCTV security industry and that the VPD had erred when it assigned him the task of designing the monitoring proposal.[11] The Carnegie association's letter also raised concerns after a fibre optic cable was installed between the Main Street Police Station and the Emergency Communications Centre on Pender Street a few months earlier (O'Connor 2001).

Despite growing resistance to the revised proposal to establish a monitoring program, a second set of developments partially worked against this resistance. On 8 August 2001, using the city's portable CCTV camera system, the VPD captured images of a multiple stabbing.[12] During the Celebration of Light fireworks display at English Bay in the city's west end, surveillance images were used to identify two men who had stabbed four other men at the corner of Davie and Denman Streets. The images, after they were released to the public, led to apprehension of the two men and were used to support the efficacy of streetscape CCTV surveillance; they were also linked to the importance of video surveillance during the infamous "riot at the Hyatt."[13]

In the aftermath of the 9/11 terrorist attacks in Washington and New York, the debate about privacy versus security was decidedly tipped in favour of the latter.

When the NSWP document was released on 26 October, the VPD initiated what it conceptualized as a two-pronged public consultation phase. The first part of the phase entailed soliciting written responses from members of the community by 31 December 2001. The VPD mailed copies of the NSWP document to community groups in targeted areas, and it posted the report on its website. The second phase of consultation entailed planned public meetings before a neutral facilitator to be held early in 2002. On release of the NSWP discussion document, the VPD also declared that, if there was support for the proposal, a final report would be produced by the new point man on the monitoring initiative, Inspector Axel Hovbrender, and submitted to the VPB and then to city council to approve $500,000 in start-up funds.

Members of the BCCLA immediately reacted to what they called the flawed consultation process. They argued that the VPD granted only two months to respond to the 129-page document in the context of global debate about civil liberties in the aftermath of the 9/11 attacks. The BCCLA also criticized the VPD for handling the consultation process rather than hiring a neutral agency. The association subsequently complained to the VPB about the forced consultation process, which in turn extended the deadline for written submissions to 28 February 2002.

In early January 2002, Information and Privacy Commissioner Loukidelis wrote to Vancouver Police Chief Terry Blythe to urge caution in proceeding with the proposal to install cameras in the DTES. Loukidelis argued that the NSWP report lacked evidence to support the need for a CCTV system and how it would alleviate the many problems found in the DTES. The following month, Commissioner Radwanski spoke in Vancouver at an event co-sponsored by the Canadian Bar Association and the BCCLA, where he rehearsed his argument that streetscape CCTV surveillance represents the thin edge of the wedge.

In late February, Hovbrender submitted a proposal to the VPB for the first stage of approval. Part of the proposal entailed holding community forums in the fall of 2002. The VPB decided not to proceed with the initiative, including public meetings, until Commissioner Radwanski's Charter challenge was completed (Vancouver Police Board 2002). When the Charter challenge ended in July 2003, the VPD renewed its efforts to establish a monitoring program. At this time, Commissioner Loukidelis became more forceful. In addition to arguments about cost effectiveness, evidence of crime reduction, and compliance with FIPPA, Loukidelis drew attention to an in-progress investigation into the effectiveness of streetscape monitoring in the United Kingdom. At the 15 October VPB meeting, it was decided that the second phase of the public consultation would again be deferred until the results of the Home Office evaluation by the University of Leicester were available.

The Home Office report was published in February 2005 (Gill and Spriggs 2005). The study involved analyses of fourteen CCTV systems that were designed to survey a variety of social spaces. The study examined time-series police crime statistics and public attitude survey results, complementary policing initiatives introduced alongside CCTV surveillance, reasons for installing CCTV systems, technical specifications, control-room operations, and economic impacts. The main findings were that CCTV surveillance had no overall effect on crime rates. The researchers found that CCTV systems were more effective at reducing vehicle-related crimes than violent crimes, and they were not able to find a significant reduction in fear of crime.

The combined influence of Commissioner Loukidelis' efforts to promote compliance with the BC OIPC's *Public Surveillance System Privacy Guidelines* (and FIPPA) and the Home Office report was significant. On 18 May 2005, Inspector Hovbrender submitted a recommendation to the VPB that the NSWP proposal be abandoned (Vancouver Police Board 2005). He argued that the Home Office report provided evidence to suggest that the original NSWP proposal was overly ambitious and that in the period spanning 1999-2005 policing and community service conditions in the DTES had changed. Hovbrender accepted the conclusion of Gill and Spriggs (2005) that CCTV surveillance does not achieve the results commonly attributed to it, but he also qualified their findings by arguing that, although the Home Office report draws a positive correlation between the scope of monitoring systems and the reduction of crime, it also suggests that displacement is not an issue. Gill and Spriggs argued that displacement was not common but that it did occur across the fourteen systems analyzed. Nevertheless, Hovbrender used his interpretation of the report to recommend that the VPD target a smaller area of the city to run a pilot project. He reasoned that the initial proposal was broad enough to control for displacement, but in light of the Home Office report displacement was no longer a concern.

The VPD's Streetscape Monitoring Aspirations, Take Two

Almost exactly a year to the day that the VPD abandoned the NSWP proposal, newly appointed Police Chief Jamie Graham announced that he wanted the city to reconsider plans for streetscape monitoring in light of the fast-approaching 2010 winter Olympic games in Vancouver and Whistler. On CKNW's talk-radio program *The Bill Good Show*, for example, Graham explained that the VPD wished to get back into the business of video surveillance cameras (early May). Based on preliminary discussions with Mayor Sam Sullivan, he explained that the VPD was revisiting the proposal to establish a monitoring program. Graham argued that his colleagues in Chicago and the United Kingdom attested to the usefulness of video surveillance, and he claimed that carefully and strategically placed cameras in different areas of the city would be a huge step in emergency preparedness and counter-terrorism during the 2010 Olympic games.

Reaction to the re-emergence of the streetscape CCTV surveillance monitoring initiative was swift. On 12 May 2006, Information and Privacy Commissioner Loukidelis wrote to Police Chief Graham to reiterate his position on public-area video surveillance.[14] Loukidelis explained that, based on the principles laid out in FIPPA, the VPD should seek solutions to crime and disorder that have the least possible impact on privacy. Invoking stipulations presented in *Public Surveillance System Privacy Guidelines* (see Appendix C), he maintained that public-area video surveillance should be a last resort; that the VPD should complete a privacy impact assessment; and that rules for use and disclosure of surveillance data should be formulated. Loukidelis drew attention to the main findings of the Home Office report, and he pointed to a study by researchers at the University of Alberta that assessed behavioural changes under CCTV cameras (see Carson et al. 2004).

In the context of a growing set of critical news stories in the local media, Police Chief Graham contacted Micheal Vonn, policy director at the BCCLA, after she was cited across news reports. Graham explained that he was not entirely sold on CCTV surveillance and that he envisioned a broad public consultation process. The following day, however, he announced at the VPB meeting that he would present the board with a business plan to move forward with the initiative.

On 25 May, the chair of the BCCLA's Privacy and Access Committee, Richard Rosenberg, wrote to Police Chief Graham, Commissioner Loukidelis, and members of the VPB.[15] Rosenberg raised concerns about the VPB's approval of Graham's submission to produce a business plan for public-area CCTV surveillance. He argued that public consultation is very important but that members of the BCCLA were disappointed that the business plan would precede consultation with community members. Rosenberg therefore requested that the consultation be based on a concrete proposal that outlines where cameras will be placed, for what purpose, their cost, and data supporting their implementation. He also requested that Loukidelis' request for a privacy impact assessment be met and that organizations such as the BCCLA be permitted to present the VPB with a written response to a concrete proposal (the BCCLA never received a proposal).

On 7 November 2006, the VPD announced at a press conference that it planned to install streetscape CCTV surveillance cameras in the Granville Mall entertainment district of the city, between Robson and Davie Streets. The Granville Mall is a transit and pedestrian mall populated by fifty-seven bars, pubs, nightclubs, and cabarets. In the early 1990s, Vancouver City Council sought to reduce the growing number of sex shops along Granville by rezoning the area and encouraging nighttime entertainment. Council's largely successful attempts were complemented in 2003 when drinking hours were extended in the city from 2 a.m. to 4 a.m. By 2006, the area had become known for late-night disorder, including rowdiness, public drunkenness, vandalism, and physical altercations.

On 13 December, Sergeant Sheila Sullivan delivered a presentation on the proposed monitoring project before the VPB. She examined the potential benefits, costs, advantages, and disadvantages of CCTV surveillance as a crime reduction tool. Her presentation outlined how the first phase of the initiative would examine the legal framework, identify key social concerns, consult key stakeholders, review existing technology and best practices, and make recommendations based on a detailed business case analysis for cameras in the entertainment district. Sullivan noted that a report would be submitted to the VPB in May 2007, and if approved a budget request could go to council by October, and implementation could begin in 2008 (Vancouver Police Board 2006).

The VPD subsequently announced that it would present a proposal at the 20 June meeting of the VPB to install cameras in the entertainment district, but the proposal never came. The VPD never consulted with the BCCLA, and it remained silent on its desire to establish a monitoring system in the Granville Mall. There were two potential reasons why the VPD abandoned the renewed initiative. The first reason concerns security preparations leading up to the 2010 winter Olympic and Paralympic games in Vancouver and Whistler. As early as 22 February 2005, members of the Office of the Information and Privacy Commissioner of Canada started meeting with RCMP representatives to discuss surveillance at the Olympics. The RCMP were working with the Vancouver Organizing Committee to develop a security system, and a primary component of the security system was establishment of a satellite-controlled CCTV surveillance system. The International Olympic Committee favoured an approach whereby host countries leave a legacy of Olympic infrastructures and facilities behind for community use, and the RCMP expected to leave the CCTV surveillance system to municipal and provincial agencies.[16]

The second potential reason that the VPD abandoned its efforts to establish a monitoring system in Granville concerns the 27 October 2008 announcement by BC Solicitor General John van Dongen and Attorney General Wally Oppal that the province would provide $1 million in initial funding to the Cities of Vancouver, Surrey, and Kelowna to examine the use of CCTV surveillance in high-crime areas. On 3 April 2009, the provincial government announced not only that Vancouver would receive $440,000 to fund a redeployable CCTV surveillance unit for special events and emergencies but also that the City of Williams Lake would receive $50,000 for a streetscape program (see Appendix A). One month prior to the funding allocation announcement, Vancouver requested $2.6 million in CCTV funds from the province and the RCMP Vancouver 2010 Integrated Security Unit (V2010-ISU) handling security for the Olympics. The V2010-ISU recommended that cameras be deployed along the Granville Mall entertainment district, at the cruise ship terminal area, and at two live sites hosting large crowds during the games. The VPD planned to test the system during the 2009 Celebration of Light fireworks events in July.

Civic Resistance to Streetscape Monitoring in Brockville[17]

The City of Brockville (approximate population of 21,000) is located along the St. Lawrence River, about 100 kilometres south of Ottawa, and an hour's drive from the Canada-US border at New York State. Commonly known as the City of 1,000 Islands, Brockville promotes tourism based on its strategic location for boating and water activities. Ongoing downtown revitalization has encouraged population growth and expansion of the manufacturing sector as well as retail businesses and accessibility of waterfront parks and trails.

The initiative to establish a public-area streetscape CCTV surveillance monitoring program in Brockville came from Police Chief Barry King. After becoming aware of public-area video surveillance in Sudbury, as well as in Hull, Quebec, and Ipswich, United Kingdom, King applied on behalf of the city for a Proceeds of Crime/Frontline Policing provincial government grant to implement a public-area CCTV monitoring program. Under the auspices of the Safe Community Coalition (SCC), King requested $158,000 to install eight to ten cameras to monitor fifteen city blocks in the downtown core. The initial proposal called for monitoring to be carried out by law and security students at the local college, and the aims of the camera system were to lower vandalism, reduce the prevalence of break and enters, respond to altercations in the bar district, and identify suspects and stolen vehicles.

In December 1998, the Ontario solicitor general approved a grant of $70,000 under the Futuristic Crime Prevention Initiative. The grant enabled the SCC to develop a proposal that would see three to five cameras implemented under the auspices of the Safe Streets Program. On 19 January 1999, Police Chief King presented the Safe Streets Program proposal to the City's Economic Development and Community Services Committee (CEDCSC), composed of three city representatives. King's presentation, and the accompanying *Safe Streets Program: CCTV Surveillance of the Downtown Core* report (1999), boasted of operational efficiency in an era of fiscal restraint and laid claim to the potential utility of the cameras in addressing social issues such as violence, vandalism, and aggressive panhandling. The proposal called for cameras to be passively monitored from the police station by 9-1-1 dispatchers, and it stipulated that recordings would be stored for sixty days. Based on the presentation and report, the CEDCSC voted two to one in favour of establishing a monitoring program in Brockville.

By the time the Safe Streets Program proposal was endorsed by the CEDCSC, several critical news articles addressing CCTV surveillance in Brockville had appeared in the local newspaper, the *Recorder and Times*. Under such headlines as "Are City Residents Ready for Big Brother?" (Phillips 1998), "Invading Our Spaces" (Coward 1998), "There's a Better Way to Keep Our Downtown Safe" (Maclean 1998), "Cop Better than Camera" (Mather 1998), "We Don't Need Video Surveillance" (Taylor 1999), and "Cameras Should Be Last Resort" (*Recorder and Times* 1999a), the Safe Streets Program was scrutinized in two interrelated ways. The first way identified a perceived need to have a greater police presence in the downtown core. Members of the editorial board of the *Recorder and Times* decided that video surveillance represented a poor substitute for community policing. This decision was based on the fact that city council had struggled with the Police Service Board for several years prior to 1999 over maintaining a police presence on downtown streets; also, the city had funded a $10 million revitalization project spanning the years 1998-2004 that focused on, among other things, street lighting and visibility. In a series of daily editorials and articles, from 10 to 26 January 1999, the editorial board and staff writers made it clear that the Brockville Police Service had received a second grant through the Ontario Community Policing Partnership Program that would see the hiring of two new downtown beat patrol officers. The position of the editorial board was thus "how much more money is council going to keep committing to the so-called crime problem at a time the crime rate is falling across Canada, including Brockville?" (*Recorder and Times* 1999b).

The second way that members of the editorial board at the *Recorder and Times* redefined the Safe Streets Program was through a hybrid discourse, pitting small-town community privacy against big-city intrusive state surveillance. They used a discourse of Big Brother policing as a proxy for the erosion of small-town community living. Although the newspaper published two letters to the editor that supported the initiative, the editorial board adopted a critical stance in relation to the program. For example, after questioning both the privacy-related ethics and cost-effectiveness of the proposal, the editorial board challenged the police chief's claims to problem behaviour in the downtown core: "King Street is hardly the Paris Commune. Where's the apprehended insurrection that requires full-time video surveillance?" (*Recorder and Times* 1999a). A local criminal lawyer also took advantage of the availability of column space: "Such cameras get one thinking of *Big Brother* and *1984*. The thought of law-abiding people being spied upon in an outdoor public place is rather ominous" (*Recorder and Times* 1998). Letters to the editor expressed the view that increasing the use of a technological quick fix to address perceived social problems was "an abdication of duty and an admission of not being able to cope with the problems" and "a colossal waste of money" (*Recorder and Times* 1999c). But the most emphatic opposition came directly from the editorial board: "A living, breathing human, exercising the good judgment of a well-trained police constable is light years ahead of a student sitting five kilometers away watching through the blinkered lens of a video camera" (*Recorder and Times* 1999a).

Following the CEDCSC's endorsement of the Safe Streets Program proposal, it was not necessary for the Brockville Police Service to secure the consent of city council before moving ahead with the program. Members of the Police Services Board, however, believed that council approval would legitimate the program and that council members could provide community input. Brockville's mayor, Ben TeKamp, who was supportive of the proposal, also called for council approval following the critical articles and editorials published in the *Recorder and Times* (Brockville Police Service 1999).

City council was scheduled to meet on 26 January 1999, when they would vote on the Safe Streets Program proposal. In the week leading up to the vote, councillors remained evenly divided on the CCTV proposal. Days before the meeting, however, councillors and the mayor were inundated with an estimated 500 phone calls from citizens who expressed concerns about the implications of camera monitoring in the downtown core. The night before the meeting, for instance, Councillor Jason Baker fielded phone calls for two straight hours, and Mayor Ben TeKamp took thirty-two calls at his home. The callers objected to state surveillance in their small community. The efforts of the callers were enough to secure a unanimous "no" vote against implementing the initiative (the vote was taken on 26 January).

Possibly because the proposal was adjudicated less than a month following its inception, an official, organized Brockville citizens' movement failed to materialize (or at least failed to appear openly in public). It is not clear if the phone calls and letters to the editor were based on the actions of an organized grassroots movement or if they merely represented spontaneous acts of individual dissent. What is clear is that these indicators of citizen resistance to the CCTV proposal did not surface publicly until the *Recorder and Times* articulated concerns about the proposal. It is also apparent that support on city council for the project was evenly divided in the week leading up to the vote. Indeed, the drive to establish CCTV surveillance in Brockville demonstrates how, in the absence of a clearly articulated policy position, local authorities may be vulnerable to sustained critical media attention.

The Return of a Streetscape Monitoring Initiative

Four years after the initiative to establish a streetscape CCTV monitoring program in downtown Brockville was defeated, the possibility of mounting cameras in the core returned. Throughout 2002 and 2003, the Downtown Business Improvement Association complained about vandalism in the downtown area. At the 24 November 2003 annual general meeting of the

DBIA, the chairperson of the meeting, Kimberly Horton, put the question of video surveillance cameras on the floor and called for a show of hands in support of reviving Police Chief King's 1998-99 initiative. No response was received (Zajac 2003).

The suggestion to revisit the possibility of installing cameras in the core was spurred on not only by persistent acts of vandalism but also by the end of a disruptive sixteen-week downtown reconstruction project accompanied by a sharp decline in tourism in the aftermath of Toronto's severe acute respiratory syndrome (SARS) outbreak. Despite the brief increased attention to streetscape monitoring, however, the proposal did not materialize until August 2008, when Councillor Louise Severson called for cameras in response to a number of assaults and break-ins in the downtown area (Jiggins 2008). In October 2008, the Brockville Police Service assembled a report on video surveillance. Part of the report was a study conducted by Sergeant Peter Buell: *Video Surveillance in Downtown Brockville* (Buell 2008).

The report, written as a component of a leadership course that Buell took at the Ontario Police College, begins from the premise that "video surveillance of Brockville's downtown core is generally accepted by citizens and will provide a financially manageable solution to improve security and safety of our citizens" (Buell 2008, 3). The latter claim was based on a survey of 106 business owners in the core, a survey of 61 pedestrians, and the commonly cited statistics from the KPMG report that robberies and assaults decreased in Sudbury by 38 percent after video surveillance was introduced and that property crime declined by 44 percent. Interestingly, the history provided on Brockville's 1999 experience with proposing video surveillance is abstracted from Kevin Walby's (2006) overview of public-area CCTV surveillance in Canada.[18]

The report concludes with an overview of the nine-camera monitoring system in Trenton/Frankfort, Ontario, as well as the OIPC's *Guidelines*. The proposed Brockville system calls for an initial four wireless cameras to be mounted at locations along King Street and for a monitoring facility in a city-owned building. The report notes that the impetus for the proposed system, unlike the 1999 initiative, came from the business community and that public support would be strong if the proposal did not come from the Brockville Police Service. At the time of writing (July 2009), cameras had not been installed to survey the downtown streetscape.

Organized Resistance to Streetscape Monitoring in Peterborough[19]
Peterborough (approximate population of 78,000) is located in the Kawartha cottage region of north-central Ontario, equidistant by approximately two hours from Toronto (to the west) and Ottawa (to the east). Peterborough is home to Trent University and Sir Sandford Fleming College. The initiative

to establish a streetscape monitoring program in Peterborough was not motivated by revitalization efforts, but it was influenced by problems stemming from the late-night downtown bar crowd.

Peterborough has operated a public-area CCTV surveillance system since 2001. The city operates twelve cameras that monitor areas around the local marina, museum, library, and Millennium Park. The cameras were installed after windows were broken at the Boat House – a restaurant and meeting area in Millennium Park – and after a new fountain in the park attracted unwanted clientele.

In 2002, the Ontario OIPC reviewed the system to ensure that it was in compliance with the newly released *Guidelines*.[20] A number of recommendations were made pertaining to operational policy and the importance of signage, and the city responded favourably to the recommendations (Information and Privacy Commissioner of Ontario 2004).

In June 2004, however, the OIPC received twenty registered complaints that the city had failed to adhere to *Guidelines*. Responding to the large number of complaints, the OIPC sent inspectors to Peterborough to examine the system and interview city staff. The result of the investigation was an additional set of recommendations concerning signage, data handling and storage, and operational policy.

During review of the existing surveillance system, members of the OIPC also learned about an initiative to expand the system to include streetscape cameras in the downtown core. On 9 December 2003, the Peterborough Restaurant and Bar Association, in accordance with its zero-tolerance policy for anti-social behaviour in the downtown core, recommended the expansion of video surveillance by establishing a downtown security camera system. A motion to bring a formal proposal before Peterborough City Council had been passed by the Peterborough Downtown Business Improvement Association's (PDBIA) Board of Management and Vandalism Committee – a committee composed of BIA members, police officers, municipal politicians, and some residents. The executive director of the PDBIA, Walter Johnstone, introduced to committee members the possibility of establishing a monitoring system as a cost-effective way to deal with ongoing problems of vandalism and violence stemming from the bar flush.[21]

On 16 February 2004, Johnstone presented a proposal to city council that called for the expansion of closed-circuit security camera surveillance into the downtown core. The proposal cited the success of video surveillance in London and Sudbury, and it called for the PDBIA to pay $85,000 to purchase equipment and install cameras at five intersections along George Street in downtown Peterborough. The proposal not only sought to expand the number of cameras monitoring public space in the city but also called for twenty-four-hour coverage of the city's business and entertainment district (monitored by existing city operators). Among other things, the proposal identified vandalism, petty crime, public urination, graffiti, litter, and aggressive panhandling as problems requiring surveillance (Sherk 2004, 2). Although the PDBIA was expected to pay the initial costs of purchasing the equipment, the report to council stipulated that taxpayers would cover all operational and maintenance costs.

Following Johnstone's presentation to council, the proposal was approved in principle. Concerned with costs, effectiveness, and privacy issues, however, councillors appointed the city's central area facilitator, Lance Sherk, to work with the PDBIA and the city's Planning and Development Services Department to produce a comprehensive assessment of expanding security cameras and to provide specific recommendations to council for expanding CCTV surveillance in Peterborough.

Sherk began researching monitoring programs in the United States and the United Kingdom, and he consulted with representatives in London, Hamilton, and Sudbury. He also decided to conduct public consultations to solicit community feedback about the proposal.

The first public consultation involved community forums. Four community forums were held in May and June 2004. The four meetings attracted between fifteen and thirty people each. The meetings were designed as sessions to inform the public why the PDBIA wished to expand video surveillance in the city and to review the OIPC's *Guidelines* and gather feedback about the initiative.

The second public consultation involved a survey of the downtown business area. The survey was distributed on 11 March 2004. Of the 483 surveys sent to downtown business and property owners, only 59 were returned (12 percent). Of the respondents, forty-nine (83 percent) supported the expansion of video surveillance (Sherk 2004, 10). The survey was also distributed by representatives of the Peterborough Chamber of Commerce (composed of 820 members). Approximately 6 percent of the constituents responded, with an approval rate of about 80 percent.

Throughout the public consultation and data-gathering process (February-May 2004), concerns pertaining to privacy, effectiveness, cost, and motive were frequently articulated in the local press, the *Peterborough Examiner*. Similar concerns were raised by councillors when the proposal was approved in principle, and these concerns motivated councillors to commission the report. In sharp contrast to London and Sherbrooke, however, where the murder of a young person precipitated formation of a sustained grassroots advocacy campaign, no event of equal public significance had occurred in Peterborough. And in contrast to Brockville, where an accelerated decision-making process provided little time for the crystallization of citizen opposition but raised opportunities for sustained critical media attention, the consultation process in Peterborough afforded local interest groups time to mount public resistance to the expansion of video surveillance.

Resistance to the business-led camera initiative came principally from Stop the Cameras Coalition (STCC), an alliance of the Council of Canadians, the Social Justice Coalition, the Peterborough New Democratic Party, the Peterborough Coalition Against Poverty, and other concerned citizens. The STCC staged an effective communications campaign that entailed actions designed to undermine the rationale for the camera initiative and ultimately defeat its final approval at city council. The STCC used three strategies to resist the expansion of CCTV surveillance in Peterborough, the first of which was to maintain a visible presence at the four community forums. In fact, of the fifteen to thirty attendees reported to have attended meetings, a significant proportion were affiliated with the STCC. At the meetings, members of the coalition held Sherk to account for claims made in the Planning and Development Services Department report. For example, at the final forum meeting held on 17 June 2004, Sherk was publicly pressed to answer questions about the relationship between CCTV surveillance and crime reduction; about the composition of the Vandalism Committee that originally brought forward the idea to expand CCTV surveillance; and about the long-term costs of maintaining the system (Peesker 2004a).

The STCC's second strategy was to gather data on, and attempt to sway, public opinion. For example, on 29 April 2004, representatives of the STCC held a public information and debate session. Jane Burns of the STCC invited members of the PDBIA to debate openly the merits of public video surveillance. The request was refused (Peesker 2004b). Members of the STCC also collected a petition with over 1,000 signatures opposing the cameras, and they conducted a survey of local businesses. Volunteers also visited 110 businesses in the downtown core to ask three questions: Do you support the cameras? Do you oppose the cameras? Undecided? (Stop the Cameras Coalition 2004, 7). Their data indicate that 20 percent of respondents supported cameras, 54 percent opposed cameras, and 26 percent were undecided. Furthermore, the STCC developed a website that greeted viewers with blinking eyes and a caption reading thus: "Do you like feeling as if you're being watched all the time? We don't."[22] The site provided the phone number for the PDBIA and encouraged readers to voice their concerns, and it provided contact information for city representatives.

While the first two communication strategies were significant in resistance efforts, the most influential strategy involved submitting a counter-report to council on 12 October 2004 (Sherk 2004). The report offers research findings on costs of the cameras, on their lack of effectiveness, and on abuse and privacy violations. More damaging, the STCC report addresses directly the claims made in Sherk's report. The former report criticizes the latter report for failing to substantiate the need for CCTV surveillance; for remaining indeterminate on long-term costs to maintain the system; for offering invalid data on the support of downtown businesses; and for conducting a flawed community forum process. The STCC report concludes that surveillance cameras are not the answer to Peterborough's alleged problems and that the results of Sherk's report lack credibility.

Faced with growing dissent, as well as council's unwillingness to endorse the expansion without further consultation, the PDBIA considered unilateral action by instituting a private surveillance scheme that would be paid for entirely by and responsible only to local merchants. This scheme raised the ire of the information and privacy commissioner of Ontario, who subsequently registered opposition to any non-statutory policing initiative (*Peterborough Examiner* 2005). Sherk's final recommendation was for a designated committee of stakeholders from the city, DBIA, and STCC to be assembled. This new committee would be responsible for investigating alternatives to cameras, defining further the need for monitoring the downtown area, and, if cameras were ever agreed to be necessary, the form that the system should take. At the time of writing (July 2009), the committee had met once and failed to reach agreement. Expansion of the public-area camera surveillance program is not currently being considered in Peterborough.

Conclusion

This chapter examined thwarted and abandoned efforts to establish streetscape CCTV surveillance monitoring programs in three Canadian cities. The data presented here are important for several reasons. Among the obvious reasons is that the data illustrate how streetscape CCTV surveillance monitoring initiatives are not inevitable in the context of available technologies, business/police interests, and existing monitoring initiatives. The data also illustrate how various factors configure to influence the course and outcome of efforts to introduce monitoring systems.

Thwarted efforts in the three cities show how resistance comes in a variety of forms, ranging from spontaneous public outcry to forceful advocacy by the privacy policy sector. In Vancouver, resistance took the form of established community groups and organizations mounting resistance to the VPD's plans to install cameras in the DTES and the entertainment district. Peterborough witnessed a more spontaneous small group of people who came together to articulate the problems with the monitoring initiative. And in Brockville, a short-lived burst of citizen outcry temporarily forestalled plans to install cameras to monitor the downtown streetscape.

Although thwarted efforts to establish streetscape CCTV surveillance monitoring programs are significant, we should be careful not to fetishize resistance efforts. Resistance is a recurrent feature of the establishment process – exemplified primarily by OIPC efforts to encourage compliance with privacy protection principles and by efforts among councillors to push for greater accountability in design structures – but organized community protest is a rare feature of the establishment process. This rarity limits the extent to which we can attribute explanatory power to protest groups, yet the recurrence of resistance in a variety of forms also indicates that streetscape monitoring initiatives are not inevitable – even if thwarted efforts return.

9
Thunder Bay's Eye on the Street

This chapter examines Thunder Bay's Eye on the Street public-area street-scape CCTV surveillance monitoring program.[1] Thunder Bay's sixteen-camera monitoring system became operational in November 2005, following eight years of promotion and preparation. The Eye on the Street is important in understanding streetscape initiatives in Canada because the design and implementation process was influenced by ideational and administrative diffusion from three different programs. When Thunder Bay's system was initially proposed in 1999, it was inspired by and promoted and designed based on Sudbury's Lions Eye in the Sky. Following Information and Privacy Commissioner of Canada George Radwanski's efforts to undermine public-area video surveillance, however, and the introduction of the Ontario OIPC's *Guidelines,* promotion of the program was modelled on Hamilton's public forum series, while organization of the program was modelled on London's Code of Practice.

This chapter represents the beginning as much as it does the end of the analysis of streetscape CCTV surveillance monitoring programs in Canada. The data presented here illustrate, first, the continuing importance of how the ideational diffusion of streetscape monitoring programs is linked to the administrative diffusion of operational policies and organizational designs. Second, the data illustrate how the diffusion of policy debates and protocols can disrupt the establishment process and introduce new dimensions into the administrative design of a monitoring program – especially in the context of the diffusion of multilateral decision-making and responsibility-sharing models. Third, the data illustrate the persistent selectivity of promotional and design tactics in the context of adhering to *Guidelines,* and they affirm the importance of committed individuals in promoting monitoring systems in the absence of sustained forms of resistance.

Planning the Eye in the Sky[2]

Thunder Bay (approximate population of 109,000) is located on the north-western shore of Lake Superior, about fifty kilometres north of the Canada-US border at Minnesota. In the past, Thunder Bay's economy has been based on forestry and manufacturing, but declining industrial activity, accompanied by a decline in downtown business prosperity, encouraged city representatives to promote the city as a tourist destination and an education centre.[3]

Historically, Thunder Bay is an amalgamation of two townships and two communities with two distinct downtown city centres. In 1970, Port Arthur (in the north end) and Fort William (in the south end) merged to form Thunder Bay, and a new inter-city centre was established.[4] Following amalgamation, the south-end city centre experienced a dramatic decline in commercial prosperity and a concomitant increase in incidents of vandalism, homelessness, and substance abuse. The decline of commercial prosperity in the north end was alleviated somewhat by construction of a large casino, but commerce in both city centres has been lost to expanding strip malls on the periphery.

The initial idea of starting a streetscape monitoring program in Thunder Bay diffused from two sources. First, Dick Waddington, a long-serving member of Thunder Bay City Council and a member of the Thunder Bay Police Services Board, attended a policing conference in the United States in 1997 that showcased CCTV as an innovative and effective mechanism to reduce crime and fear of crime. The following year, Sudbury Police Chief Alex Mc-Cauley invited Thunder Bay business and law enforcement representatives to inspect Sudbury's monitoring program. The Thunder Bay police chief, Leo Toneguzzi, and the chair of the Victoria Avenue BIA, Phil Jarvis, accepted the invitation to visit Sudbury. Waddington, Jarvis, and Toneguzzi subsequently reported on the merits of streetscape monitoring to members and representatives of Thunder Bay's business community. Their report was strongly influenced by statistical evidence produced by Sudbury's LVMAC attesting to the efficacy of streetscape CCTV surveillance in reducing and controlling crime in Sudbury and to the economic revitalization benefits of streetscape monitoring (Management Team 2001).

Representatives of Thunder Bay's business community responded favourably to the proposal to install CCTV surveillance cameras in the downtown areas, and members of the Victoria Street BIA started to broker a formal coalition among Thunder Bay's BIAs. The purpose of the coalition was to conduct further research on CCTV surveillance and to lobby city council to provide infrastructural and financial support for the program.

The Victoria Avenue BIA is one of three BIAs in Thunder Bay. Located in the south end of the city, it covers the Victoriaville Mall and a bus and transit terminal. The Simpson Street BIA is located in the old Fort William southern downtown core. Simpson Street is situated on the site of the original Fort William cart path; it is a commercial district of the southern core with a property occupancy rate of less than 50 percent, and it is known for its large concentration of bars, panhandling, prostitution, gang activity, and drug dealing. The Heart of the Harbour BIA is located in the north end of the city; it covers an area containing commercial businesses, banks, some of the city's tourist areas, and a second bus and transit station.

In 2000, representatives of the BIA coalition proposed to city council the idea of installing streetscape surveillance cameras. The proposal was framed as a community-based initiative that required council's support and funding. Councillors were reluctant to invest tax dollars to fund what they understood as a police responsibility (which should be funded through the existing police budget), but they agreed to form an ad hoc Implementation Committee (a.k.a. the Steering Committee) to explore the practicality of installing a CCTV system in the city.[5] Council's decision was based on initial findings from the BIAs' data-gathering activities, especially data provided by Sudbury's LVMAC. Under the auspices of the Crime Prevention Reserve Fund, $135,000 was allocated to streetscape monitoring start-up in the 2000 Police Service's capital budget, subject to further reporting on the viability of a streetscape monitoring initiative.[6]

The City of Thunder Bay's Internal Audit and Management Studies Team (hereafter the Management Team) was tasked with establishing and chairing the Implementation Committee. The committee consisted of representatives from the three BIAs, the Thunder Bay Police Service, the city's Transit Division, and TBayTel.[7] A representative from Thunder Bay's Transit Division was included in the committee's composition because the division had experience with conducting CCTV surveillance in the transit terminals; the intention was that the Transit Division would piggyback on the new technology and incorporate its existing system into the proposed, upgraded one. A TBayTel representative was recruited to advise and assist in planning cabling infrastructure for the cameras and to consult on appropriate camera locations. Finally, although a member of the Thunder Bay Police Service joined the committee, the Police Services Board was initially wary about the CCTV proposal tracing back to the initial BIA coalition; members of the Police Services Board were concerned that surveillance cameras would replace city funding for increased patrols in problem areas.

The first Implementation Committee meeting was held in December 2000, when committee members began to produce the first of several reports to promote the program to city councillors (Management Team 2001). The initial report to council provides a brief overview of Glasgow's City Watch monitoring program (inspired by Sudbury's references to and reliance on City Watch) as well as the Lions Eye in the Sky program (the latter is identified as Canada's only CCTV surveillance program). The report also identifies four main objectives of the program: to increase perceptions of safety, to increase pedestrian traffic in the downtown cores, to reduce the potential for violence and crime, and to reduce insurance claims and repair costs in commercial areas. Based on the stated objectives, the Implementation Committee established criteria for selecting suitable locations for the cameras. After considering the volume of pedestrian traffic, levels of crime (based on police-reported crime statistics), number of insurance claims, incidents of vandalism (based on a BIA members' survey), and perceptions of public safety (based on a review of a neighbourhood policing survey and the annual Thunder Bay Citizens' Survey), the committee designated eleven camera locations for sixteen cameras.[8]

The Implementation Committee's report to council also provides an overview of the anticipated program design. The organizational design calls for live monitoring of at least eleven cameras twenty-four hours per day, seven days per week. The committee reasons that three staff members would be required to conduct monitoring activities and that an additional two members would be required if the Transit Division's cameras were incorporated into the system. Based on the administrative design of Sudbury's Lions Eye in the Sky, Ontario Works recipients are identified as potential monitors, combined with the assistance of community volunteers. The report outlines how the police chief offered to provide police-based monitoring if the monitoring station were located in police headquarters.

On 23 April 2001, the Implementation Committee's report was presented to a newly elected city council. BIA representatives Bo Huk (Simpson Street BIA) and David Glover (Heart of the Harbour BIA), along with Kathleen McFadden (a management studies analyst with the City of Thunder Bay), explained the desire to install streetscape surveillance cameras and some of the findings disseminated from Sudbury's LVMAC. Councillors expressed support for the program and directed members of the Implementation Committee to identify additional sources of funding. Councillors also passed a resolution that the city's administration (i.e., the Management Team) would proceed with design and installation of the fibre optic network required to support the monitoring system, and they resolved to retain the Crime Prevention Reserve Fund ($135,000) to be used as start-up money for the program (City of Thunder Bay 2001). The system was expected to be operational within a year.

Forestalling and Reconfiguring the Eye in the Sky

As the Implementation Committee prepared to finalize the design and implementation strategies for the Eye in the Sky, a sequence of signal events forestalled launch of the program by five years and contributed to administrative refinement of the program. Until April 2001, the administrative structure of Thunder Bay's Eye in the Sky proposal was based on the information presented in the VMAC's and LVMAC's promotional and operational materials from Sudbury. The Implementation Committee had neither seriously considered privacy protection measures nor developed clear operational protocols or a code of practice. Thunder Bay's MFIPPA co-ordinator, Kathy O'Brien, was aware of Information and Privacy Commissioner of Ontario, Ann Cavoukian's, (1998) position paper on video surveillance from the outset, and subsequently of the OIPC's *Guidelines,* and she consulted with members of council and the Implementation Committee from 1999 on about privacy protection measures. It was not until Commissioner Radwanski started to garner public attention, however, that privacy protection provisions and data-handling and -storage concerns became a priority for committee members and councillors.

Delays in implementing the Eye in the Sky began after national media coverage of Commissioner Radwanski's 15 July 2001 ruling on streetscape CCTV monitoring in Yellowknife and his 4 October 2001 ruling on monitoring in Kelowna (see Chapter 5). Following his decision that the RCMP were violating the spirit of the Privacy Act by conducting public-area video surveillance, members of the Implementation Committee started to consult more closely with city councillors and Kathy O'Brien. When Radwanski filed a statement of claim with the Supreme Court of British Columbia on 21 June 2002, councillors and committee members decided to halt implementation activities until the Charter challenge was resolved.

For nearly two years, no formal promotion and planning took place, but members of council and the Implementation Committee continued to track developments in London, Hamilton, and Kelowna. While resolution of the Charter challenge in Kelowna in 2003 did not end efforts to establish a monitoring program in Thunder Bay, it did influence the organizational design of the program. The national attention garnered by Commissioner Radwanski's arguments about privacy violations posed by public-area video surveillance motivated city council to instruct the Implementation Committee to assess implications of the Charter challenge and to address stipulations in *Guidelines for Using Video Surveillance Cameras in Public Places* (released by the Ontario OIPC in October 2001). The committee's assessment of the latter led to a refined operational design.

The Implementation Committee reported to council on 25 August 2003. Responding to "positive developments with the Supreme Court's rejection of the Federal Commissioner's Charter Challenge" (Management Team 2003a, 14), the committee's report opens with the argument that Commissioner Radwanski's claim is no longer an issue, and it foregrounds the arguments that the City of London launched a streetscape monitoring program despite the Charter challenge, that the City of Sudbury's system continued throughout the challenge, and that the City of Hamilton planned its system while the challenge unfolded. The remainder of the report, which constituted the working proposal for the eventual launch of the program, presents a set of brief responses to the OIPC's five recommended considerations prior to using a video surveillance system set out in *Guidelines* (Information and Privacy Commissioner of Ontario 2001, 4).[9]

The first three OIPC considerations addressed in the report are dealt with in a cursory manner, affirming the selective uses and flexible interpretations that characterize responses to the OIPC's pragmatic *Guidelines*. Consideration 1, that methods of deterrence or detection other than video surveillance should be considered and rejected as unworkable before adopting a video surveillance system, is addressed in two sentences: "There are insufficient financial and police resources to maintain a high profile in these areas to act as a deterrent and create a climate of community safety. Currently, core violence projects are conducted, but are short in duration and temporary in nature due to cost constraints" (Management Team 2003a, 3). No data are presented to support the claim about insufficient resources, and no details are provided on other measures introduced to reduce criminal activities.

The second OIPC consideration, that CCTV must be justified by reference to verifiable, specific reports of incidents, crimes, or safety concerns in areas under question, is addressed with a graph depicting police data pertaining to service calls in the ten areas targeted for cameras. The data on the graph represent the time periods spanning January-December 2000, 2001, and 2002. The number of service calls remains relatively constant in each area during the sampling periods, with the number in two areas significantly higher than in the rest. The report to council offers no data, commentary, or analysis beyond the bar graph.

The OIPC's third consideration pertaining to conducting a privacy impact assessment is indirectly addressed by stipulations borrowed from the City of London's Code of Practice. Committee members report that Thunder Bay's Code of Practice would entail an annual review and quarterly audit of monitoring practices and data storage – a measure inspired by London's Downtown Camera Project. The report neither refers to nor uses the OIPC's privacy impact assessment tool.

In contrast to the first three OIPC-recommended considerations, the fourth consideration, to hold broad public consultations, was emphasized by the Ontario OIPC after the introduction of *Guidelines*, and members of the Implementation Committee responded to this recommendation by designing their public outreach strategy based on the Hamilton Police Service's public forums (see Chapter 7). Similar to forums held in Hamilton, those in Thunder Bay constituted the most elaborate promotional strategy designed to frame the monitoring program as a community-based public safety initiative. Councillors and members of the Implementation Committee deemed positive public consultation results essential both to satisfy the OIPC and to justify the program to the community. Therefore, they set out to stage a broad public consultation process.

In 2003, the Implementation Committee organized, promoted, and conducted public presentations at thirteen locations around the city. The three-month consultation process began on 31 March and concluded with a town hall meeting on 17 June. The meetings were held at each of the BIA headquarters, the Police Services Board facilities, the Chief of Police Advisory Board facilities, several seniors' residences, two local Rotary Clubs, a downtown condominium complex, Crime Stoppers headquarters, and a health centre. Each meeting was publicized through news releases, the city's website, and information pamphlets distributed around the city (see Appendices 9.1 and 9.2). A reported 80-90 percent of residents of the seniors' homes and the downtown condominium complex attended the meetings, and estimated attendance for the town hall meeting ranged from 175 to 360 people.

The consultations entailed a joint presentation delivered by Bo Huk and David Glover. They spoke about the reasons why the Eye in the Sky monitoring program was desired by the BIAs and about some of the events leading up to the public forums. Opportunities for public participation and feedback in the consultation process, which comprised the Implementation Committee's index for measuring public opinion, assumed two forms. First, a question period followed each presentation, and recurring themes in the question period were summarized and presented to council (see Appendix 9.3). Second, a guest book was circulated at all public forums to allow attendees to register positive and negative comments about the monitoring initiative (see Appendix 9.4). The committee reported on two negative comments and approximately 300 positive ones (Management Team 2003a).

Finally, the Implementation Committee's response to the OIPC's fifth consideration, to develop privacy-enhancing operational protocols, is addressed by stating that the committee planned to develop a Code of Practice and a regular auditing system and that signs would be posted to allow residents to avoid monitored areas. As explained below, such protocols were developed by introducing a multidimensional data-handling and evaluation structure based on London's operational policies.

Equipped with data suggesting community support for the system, and bolstered by the resolution of the OPC's Charter challenge and the attention granted to *Guidelines*, the Implementation Committee returned to city council with a revised proposal to begin implementing the program. Part of the proposal entailed responses to the withdrawn Charter challenge and to the OIPC's recommended considerations. The rest of the proposal outlined operational costs (see below) and staffing requirements to maintain live monitoring around the clock. The revised proposal outlined how Ontario

Works recipients were in short supply and how volunteers could not be used in the context of the privacy protection measures introduced into the revised administrative structure. Moreover, the proposal called for constant supervision of the monitoring station but outlined how the police could not supply continuous supervision.

When the Implementation Committee submitted the revised proposal, council had again turned over. By this time, the monitoring initiative had persisted over five years, thirteen public consultations, two city councils, a federal Charter challenge, and at least a dozen committee meetings. When the proposal was returned to council, frustration was growing among Implementation Committee members. Bo Huk and David Glover presented the final proposal to council in an all-or-nothing manner and warned councillors that they would protest any negative decision publicly. Councillors passed three motions pertaining to ratification of the program, finalization of the Code of Practice, and budgetary allocation (Transportation and Works 2005a), and they instructed the Implementation Committee to continue working with the city solicitor and members of the Management Team to ensure that the program adhered to provincial legislation.

Launching the Eye on the Street

Following city council's approval of the Eye in the Sky program proposal, the Implementation Committee immediately began installing surveillance cameras and monitoring equipment in preparation for launch of the program. Thirty-two signs designed by the city's Corporate Communications Department were posted in the camera areas (see Figure 17), and a brochure outlining the system was posted online and distributed around the city centres; a city newsletter officially announcing launch of the monitoring program was also produced, and promotional stickers resembling the ones adopted by the LVMAC were distributed among downtown businesses.

In preparation for launch of the program, the Implementation Committee finalized the operational structure of the system. Its first step was to transform itself into the Eye on the Street Steering Committee (ETSSC). The ETSSC consisted of the program manager (see below), a representative from each BIA, a representative from the Thunder Bay Police Service (who was not permitted to vote), and two members designated by the program manager (a TBayTel network engineer planner and the manager of Thunder Bay Transit). Between August 2003 and November 2005, the Implementation Committee continued to report to council on development of the Code of Practice, which constituted the governing document of the program; on interactions with the city's legal council and the Police Services Board, especially concerning formation of a memorandum of understanding with the police that stipulated the ways that the police must adhere to the Code of Practice; on the city's retention bylaws and the development of contracts with the owners

17 Streetscape surveillance camera signage, City of Thunder Bay, Ontario

of buildings where cameras were mounted; and on a request for proposals from potential service providers to manage the city-owned system.

On 22 November 2005, the Eye on the Street became operational. The program consisted of sixteen cameras mounted at twelve locations in the downtown areas (see Figures 18 and 19):

- corner of Victoria Avenue and May Street;
- corner of Victoria Avenue and Archibald Street;
- on Brodie Street near the parking lot of the Brodie Street Bus Terminal;
- corner of Donald Street and Syndicate Avenue;
- Brodie Street north of Donald Street;
- corner of Red River Road and Cumberland Street;
- corner of Red River Road and Court Street;
- corner of 215 Red River Road;
- corner of Simpson Street and Victoria Avenue;
- corner of Simpson Street and Rowand Street;
- at the Brodie Street Bus Terminal (three cameras); and
- at the Water Street Bus Terminal (three cameras).[10]

18   Streetscape surveillance camera, City of Thunder Bay, Ontario

19   Public-area surveillance camera, City of Thunder Bay, Ontario

The official explanation provided for the name change was that the Eye on the Street was "more consistent with the idea of the camera having the same view as a passer-by would" (Transportation and Works 2005b, 3) rather than the connotations associated with the Eye in the Sky as an authoritarian policing measure. The monitoring program was officially launched as a one-year pilot project, pending the results of a statistical review of the efficacy of the cameras (explained below).

Funding, Equipment, and Service Provision

The operational structure of the Eye on the Street was based on London's Code of Practice, and it entailed four main tasks leading up to the launch in 2005: to finalize funding responsibilities, equipment acquisition, and service provision; to finalize the Code of Practice as the governing document for the program; to finalize operational protocols pertaining to monitoring staff and data use and retention policy; and to design a system to evaluate effectiveness of the program.

Funding for the Eye on the Street fell into two categories: capital costs and operating expenditures. The initial capital costs included purchasing and installing sixteen cameras, monitoring equipment and software, fibre optic cable infrastructure, and street signs. The sixteen dome-style cameras were purchased from General Electric with city funds for $160,000 in 2004. The three BIAs and TBayTel absorbed street signage costs (approximately $1,000). Installing dedicated fibre optic cables to enable surveillance activities would have cost millions of dollars, but the program benefited from use of an existing fibre optic infrastructure belonging to TBayTel. TBayTel agreed to donate use of its fibre optic infrastructure to the program as well as to install additional cables to the main network at a reduced rate. Eventually, TBayTel also covered $50,000 of the $70,000 in cable costs as an in-kind donation to the project. Aside from TBayTel's donations, the city and the three BIAs provided capital funding. The total capital costs of the project amounted to $215,509 (Transportation and Works 2008), which was met by the original Crime Prevention Reserve Fund and an initial BIA donation of $12,000, with the shortfall absorbed by the city.[11]

Ongoing operating expenditures include staffing costs, maintenance, and yearly compensation to building owners who provide camera locations.[12] Operating expenses are roughly $165,000 per annum (Transportation and Works 2008). All operating costs are factored into the annual council budget aside from yearly donations of $2,500 from the BIAs. The Implementation Committee originally approached the city's information and resource co-ordinator to explore federal and provincial funding, but to qualify for government funding programs the committee required incorporation.

The service provider contract was awarded to APEX Investigation and Security in 2005 after a competitive tendering process. The Implementation Committee provided a description of intended monitoring practices to three security companies in contention. One of the companies wanted to negotiate part-time monitoring rather than 24/7 monitoring; the other company requested more money. Only APEX agreed to meet the conditions of the proposal within budget, and the Implementation Committee was adamant that the proposal should not be compromised. APEX's position as official service provider was ratified in September 2005.

The Code of Practice

Part of council's endorsement of the Eye on the Street was contingent on appointing a program manager (similar to the one in London), whose first task was to finalize the Code of Practice. Barbara Stacey – manager of central support for the Department of Transportation and Works – became program manager of the Eye on the Street in February 2005.[13] At that time, there was already a draft Code of Practice. Stacey's task was to develop the Code of Practice into a legally defensible code of conduct in compliance with the OPC's *Guidelines* and MFIPPA.

Stacey worked on the Code of Practice with the city's solicitor and its MFIPPA co-ordinator. The city solicitor was responsible for writing the final report and ensuring its legality. Because the city clerk is legally responsible for disclosure and protection of information from the monitoring program, the MFIPPA co-ordinator took an active role in recommending provisions for the Code of Practice pertaining to information management. The code also stipulated that the program manager and ETSSC must regularly consult with MFIPPA as part of normal operations.

In the final preparation phase, Stacey contacted representatives in London to develop the draft Code of Practice for Thunder Bay. Her draft materials were subsequently reviewed by members of the Thunder Bay Police, the city clerk, the MFIPPA co-ordinator, and other city officials before the city solicitor completed the document. A draft Code of Practice was presented to council in April 2005; council then referred it to the Police Services Board. The board reviewed and approved the Code of Practice following amendments pertaining to a memorandum of understanding between the Thunder Bay Police Services Board and the City of Thunder Bay in July 2005 (Transportation and Works 2005a). The memorandum of understanding comprises an agreement by Thunder Bay Police Service to observe the Code of Practice with respect to procedures for requesting stored information and accessing the security office.[14] The code was ratified in its final form in July 2005.

Operations

The Eye on the Street is housed in a government-owned building in an undisclosed location. The confidentiality of the monitoring facility (i.e., the security office) location reflects a general concern for control over access to the program. The Code of Practice limits access to the security office to certain personnel, approved at the program manager's discretion on burden of establishing necessity. In practice, approximately fifteen people are permitted to enter the security office: camera operators, the supervisor, cleaning staff, maintenance staff, and auditors. Members of the Thunder Bay Police

Service, councillors, and BIA representatives are not allowed access. All people who enter the facility must take an oath of secrecy.

Camera operators are employees of APEX Investigation and Security. All operators are graduates of the Department of Law and Security at Confederation College. Prior to deciding on the monitoring structure, the Implementation Committee explored three different staffing options. The first option considered was to use temporary rehabilitation placement personnel who were part of a modified work program (Management Team 2003a). Although the Canadian Union of Public Employees expressed interest in the idea, the Implementation Committee rejected this option on the grounds that the high turnover of new work placement staff would compromise privacy, incur additional training costs, lead to gaps in monitoring coverage, and prevent individuals from becoming well acquainted with the system. The second option involved permanent modified work placement personnel, but the city expressed concerns both about the remuneration that would be required to compete with the benefit that disabled workers would receive in any case and about the feasibility of securing enough workers to occupy the security office twenty-four hours a day. The final option – contracting the work to an external organization – was endorsed. Estimated staffing costs of $121,000 per annum were judged to be within the proposed operating budget.

The security office was originally intended to be manned for twenty-four hours a day, seven days a week, although at the time of writing live monitoring is conducted for the majority of the time but no longer 24/7.[15] The camera images are recorded all the time, and data are retained for seven days before being systematically erased in compliance with *Guidelines*. Inside the security office, images from the sixteen cameras are available for viewing on two dedicated monitors that can display video from any of the cameras or a projection unit capable of displaying all, one, or a configurable number of the cameras at any one time on a large white wall. Each camera is a pan, tilt, and zoom model housed in a dark-coloured globe. The on-duty camera operator is able to control any of the cameras via a control desk complete with joysticks and other functions, and the system includes a masking program that automatically obscures the video of areas predetermined to be invasions of privacy.

Information sharing between the security office and law enforcement agencies follows separate protocols for live and after-the-event situations. For live incidents, the security office has a dedicated communication line to the Thunder Bay Police Service's communications centre, and information may be shared in two ways. First, camera operators may contact the communications centre and advise the police regarding in-progress incidents. Camera operators can broadcast a live feed to a dedicated monitor in the police communications centre, although the police do not have the authority to request a live feed. Second, police may contact the camera operators and request that they use a camera to view a situation within the scope of the CCTV scheme.

For after-the-event CCTV footage, the Code of Practice outlines an information request procedure that the police must follow. A request form detailing the specific window of monitoring is filled out by the police officer who is requesting footage. This request is reviewed, signed, and faxed to the service provider by the staff sergeant. The service provider also reviews the request to ensure that it falls within the purview of the MFIPPA stipulations outlined in the Code of Practice before sending it to the camera operators. A copy is then burned to CD, bagged as evidence, and made available to the police to pick up. Ordinarily, this process takes a day, but there is a special request form that expedites the process to one hour.

Evaluation

The Eye on the Street has been, and continues to be, subject to multiple forms of evaluation, including monthly audits, public surveys, annual reviews, police feedback, and anecdotal evidence sourced from operations staff, supervisors, and the ETSSC. The Code of Practice includes an official "Program Evaluation Model" detailing the range of evaluation procedures from an administrative perspective. The Program Evaluation Model pairs each goal of the CCTV program with an appropriate mode of assessment. For example, success of the objective to deter violence, unlawful activity, and other anti-social behaviour is measured by reviewing police statistics, gathered before and after the cameras were installed, that pertain to clearance rates, number and type of crimes occurring, and number of referrals from the cameras leading to police action. The Program Evaluation Model also includes the expected results of the evaluation process as a means to assess the level of success of the program in the future.

The ETSSC reviews monthly statistical reports sourced from the observations of camera operators and requests made by the Thunder Bay Police Service. The statistics are compiled into annual reports. At the time of writing (July 2009), statistical reports for Eye on the Street are available for 2006 and 2007. The reports comprise the before/after statistical review of the program – an integral part of evaluation of the efficacy of the system – as well as offer details on the use made of CCTV footage by the police in the first two years of the program. Together, the reports are intended to provide evidence for the ongoing operation of the system.

On 10 December 2007, the Department of Transportation and Works reported to city council on how the goals and objectives of the monitoring program were being met (Transportation and Works 2008). The report consists of a detailed breakdown of reported crimes by area[16] in the downtown cores in 2005 and 2006. It also summarizes differences in the total number of crimes reported between 2005 and 2006 as well as indicates the number of times that CCTV cameras were used, per area, in 2006. In general, reported crimes increased in three of the four CCTV-monitored areas between 2005 and 2006. Total reported crime increased by 14 percent, with only ESZ112 (the area including the cameras at Red River and Cumberland) experiencing a decrease (of 10 percent) in reported crime. Cameras were used a total of 518 times across the four zones, although most of the use (482) was confined to a single area (ESZ404 – the south core area around the transit station and Victoria Avenue mall). The cameras were used an average of 1.5 times in the Simpson and Rowland area. The report also includes details of how cameras were used between November 2005 and April 2006, categorized as "medical intervention" (10 instances), "police defused" (67), "arrests" (37), "gone on arrival" (35), and "misc – no response, cancelled" (23).

In addition to estimates of crime prevalence by area, the report includes an analysis of the cameras' efficacy based on the statistics collected throughout 2006-7 compared with crime statistics for 2005. The analysis focuses on the requests from police for evidence, stating that, of ninety-three requests made in 2006, forty-three provided supporting evidence; in 2007, seventy-two requests for footage provided thirty-three instances of usable evidence. The analysis includes a statement by the City of Thunder Bay endorsing the success of the monitoring program. The increase in reported crimes (particularly in the south core) is attributed to the CCTV system's enhanced detection capabilities. The statistical analysis concludes that, because there are many factors within the community that impact these statistics and outcomes, it is difficult to draw conclusions about the program.

In addition to statistical evidence used to illustrate the system's efficacy, anecdotal and qualitative assessments of the effects of the cameras are provided in the report. It notes that the most recent camera installed, at 215 Red River Road, had an immediate impact in deterring loitering and soliciting, which had been common in the area. The Thunder Bay Police also provided feedback on the program to the Steering Committee, maintaining that Eye on the Street had developed into an integral part of policing in Thunder Bay. The report notes that the program aids police in quick response to potentially violent incidents, pinpointing specific problems as they arise and gathering evidence of crimes after the fact by reviewing footage.

In accordance with the Code of Practice, continuing solicitation of public opinion and support is integral to the program. Public opinion surveys were completed in 2005 and 2006 with the intention of comparing public opinion about crime, safety, and CCTV surveillance across time frames.[17] In December 2005, and again in November and December 2006, public opinion "benchmark" surveys were distributed to patrons of the north and south downtown cores to evaluate perceptions of the effectiveness of Eye on the Street. Surveys were distributed on the streets in five areas: the Heart of the Harbour BIA area (2005: 78 people; 2006: 72 people), the Victoria Avenue BIA area (2005: 61 people; 2006: 46 people), the Simpson Street BIA area (2005: 13 people; 2006: 22 people), the Water Street Bus Terminal (2005: 45 people; 2006: 52 people), and the Brodie Street Bus Terminal (2005: 38 people; 2006: 42 people). A total of 235 surveys were completed and returned in 2005, while 234 were completed and returned in 2006. Surveys were also administered to business owners in each of the BIAs, but so few were returned in 2006 (9) compared with 2005 (76) that the report omits these results.

The results of the surveys are broken down into responses by area and summarized collectively. Two types of questions related to the cameras are discussed in the report: first, questions specifically asking respondents to evaluate expectations of and responses to the cameras; second, questions related to assessments of crime and safety for comparative purposes between 2005 and 2006 (with the methodological assumption that any differences in opinion may be attributed at least partially to the CCTV program).

In terms of questions evaluating the CCTV cameras themselves, respondents were asked whether they felt safer with cameras in place. In 2005, 46 percent of respondents reported feeling safer, whereas only 38 percent in 2006 felt safer. In 2005, 57 percent of respondents thought that the cameras would result in a decreased crime rate; by 2006, 53 percent believed that the cameras had actually decreased crime rates, and 67 percent expressed belief that the cameras had increased actual convictions after a year of operation.[18] In terms of questions designed to assess the effects of the cameras on perceptions of safety and crime, visits to the downtown core (a factor that the CCTV scheme was intended to affect) remained identical, as seventy-eight respondents reported visiting the downtown two or three times a week in 2005 and 2006. Feelings of safety while walking after dark with others increased from 37 percent in 2005 to 50 percent in 2006.

The conclusion of the report to council casts Eye on the Street in a favourable light, although the report duly notes that 13 percent of respondents believed that the CCTV cameras had no effect whatsoever. Although an overall evaluation is not explicitly offered, the report emphasizes changes in reported feelings of safety as well as public opinion about effectiveness of the cameras. The public survey results were interpreted as legitimization of the program.

Finally, to ensure continuing compliance with the Code of Practice, Management Team staff complete quarterly audits. The audit reports on monitoring practices to ensure that they have not been used in a manner that constitutes a violation of the human rights code or that contravenes the stipulations of MFIPPA. Specifically, the audit team determines four time periods from four camera locations within a seven-day review period and requests recordings of monitoring activities for those time periods from the camera operators (based on London's Code of Practice). The video is then reviewed in accordance with the Code of Practice. The logbooks are also scrutinized to ensure that access to the security office, release of CCTV-gathered information, and compliance with correct logging procedures are observed in accordance with the Code of Practice. All audit reports suggest that the program is operating in compliance with the Code of Practice.

Conclusion

Although Thunder Bay's Eye on the Street ideationally and administratively diffused from the City of Sudbury's Lions Eye in the Sky, interactions among councillors and businesspeople concerning funding, and especially the influence of Commissioner Radwanski's Charter challenge in Kelowna, forestalled launch of the monitoring program by several years. Not only did the challenge delay launch, but it also set off a sequence of refinements that led to a public consultation process modelled on the City of Hamilton's public forums and an administrative structure modelled on the City of London's Code of Practice. In the end, the system was developed in a number of progressive ways, but there were also certain negative trends perpetuated in the context of the OIPC's pragmatic policy orientation (e.g., methods of gathering and evaluating public opinion, methods of gathering and interpreting statistical evidence).

Moreover, the cumulative or progressive administrative diffusion from Sudbury, Hamilton, and London to Thunder Bay is important for understanding the emergence of a discernible, albeit flexible, streetscape CCTV surveillance institutional anti-policy matrix (explained fully in Chapter 10). Canada's policy matrix in this regard entails a set of standard processes, including claims-making activities, community partnership and funding alliances, public consultation processes, codes of practice, ownership structures, auditing systems, and oversight committees, as well as policy protection advocacy, signal events, and municipal and federal privacy protection legislation. Application of the institutional anti-policy matrix as an increasingly standardized set of processes used to establish monitoring systems is neither comprehensive nor absolute, but it comprises a growing number of standardized patterns in the establishment process. Some of the standardized patterns diffused progressively from the privacy policy sector and from existing monitoring systems, and some of them diffused negatively from both sources. Important for the argument presented in the final chapter, the uneven tripartite diffusion of streetscape monitoring systems takes place in, and is facilitated in part by, the pragmatic policy framework on public-area CCTV surveillance monitoring programs.

APPENDIX 9.1

Eye in the Sky: Making Our Community Safer
Courtesy of the Thunder Bay Eye in the Sky Committee

Get Involved in Fighting Crime

Thunder Bay Eye in the Sky Project
Questions or Comments Contact:
Bo Huk: 626-4592
David Glover: 343-9032

Proposed Sites
- Victoria Avenue and May Street
- Victoria Avenue and Archibald Street
- North Brodie Street
- Donald Street and Syndicate Avenue
- Red River Road at Cumberland Street
- Red River Road at Court Street
- Court Street at Park Avenue
- Simpson Street at Victoria Avenue
- Charry's Corner
- Transit Terminals

Criteria for Site Selection
- Volume of pedestrian traffic
- Reported Crime
- # of Insurance Claims/$ value of repairs
- Incidents of Vandalism
- Perceived public safety

Source: Reproduced with permission of City of Thunder Bay, Transit Division.

APPENDIX 9.2

CCTV Systems
Downtown closed circuit television (CCTV) monitoring systems are widely used internationally and a growing trend in Ontario. Both Sudbury and London operate CCTV systems and Hamilton is in its final stage of consultation.

The Eye in the Sky initiative is *not* Police driven but an initiative of the local business community concerned with the safety and security of our downtown areas. The program will not be implemented without community support.

We want you to make an informed decision
The use of cameras would not mean a reduction in police patrols but serve as an additional tool to help provide better quality service to residents, businesses and visitors in downtown areas.

Voice your opinion
- Safer Streets
- Increased Pedestrian Traffic
- Reduced Property and Violent Crime
- Enhanced Economic Activity

Sudbury 1996
- First 3 years of operation deterred 300-500 robberies, assaults, thefts and other criminal offenses, saving as much as $800,000 in direct monetary loss
- Improved ability to deal with crime and anti-social behaviour
- Arrests due to prostitution and drug offenses increased by 18%
- Improved officer safety and public safety
- 79% of individuals and 98% of businesses agreed with the decision to implement CCTV monitoring downtown

London 2001
- Cameras have been used in police investigations
- Has led to enhanced community safety, crime prevention and attractiveness of the downtown

Hamilton 2003 (in progress)

Eye in the Sky Committee Thunder Bay
We need your Input

1999   Victoria Avenue BIA (Business Improvement Area) began to explore the installation of surveillance cameras to enhance public safety and encourage development in downtown areas.

2000   The Heart of the Harbour and Simpson Street BIAs were invited to participate and form the Eye in the Sky Committee

2001   Presentations made to City Council with $135,000 reconfirmed in the budget to contribute to capital requirements

2002   Federal Privacy Commissioner lobbying for protection of citizen privacy.

2003   In keeping with Ontario Privacy Commissioner guidelines, the Committee is asking for community input and plans to feed back information to City Council.

Source: Reproduced with permission of City of Thunder Bay, Transit Division.

APPENDIX 9.3

Presentation Schedule

Group Consultations	*Date*
Northwestern Health Centre	Monday, March 31st, 2003
Heart of the Harbour BIA	Tuesday, April 1st, 2003
Victoriaville BIA	Wednesday, April 2nd, 2003
Police Services Board	Thursday, April 24th, 2003
Lakehead Rotary Club	Thursday, May 1st, 2003
Simpson Street BIA	Thursday, May 1st, 2003
Paterson Building	Monday, May 5th, 2003
55 Plus Centre	Wednesday, May 14th, 2003
Brodie Street Condominiums	Tuesday, May 20th, 2003
Chief of Police Advisory Board	Wednesday, May 21st, 2003
Crime Stoppers	Friday, June 4th, 2003
Fort William Rotary	Wednesday, July 9th, 2003
Town Hall Meeting	Tuesday, June 17th, 2003

Common Themes

The following outlines the main recurring themes mentioned during community.

Community Concern & Committee Response

CC: Will Crime be displaced?

CR: The KPMG study in Sudbury indicated that there was no displacement.

CC: In general is Thunder Bay a high crime area?

CR: Although criminal activity as a whole may be decreasing in the City, the 10 areas we have focussed on indicate an overall increase in criminal activity in these areas. We also continue to have one of the highest incidents of crime in the province.

CC: Will there be any savings in the reduction of the police force?

CR: No. This program is meant to provide an additional tool to enhance public safety and desirability of the downtown cores.

CC: Will cameras be monitored all the time?

CR: We would like to ensure that there is one person in the monitoring room at all times for the program to be most effective.

CC: Will the cameras be taping all the time?

CR: Yes. The recording will be digital and records will be kept for a period of 7 days unless accessed or otherwise needed and approved for access.

CC: I would like to see other areas included.

CR: If we wanted it to, this could evolve into a very expensive project. The 10 core downtown camera locations proposed are based on the number of calls/dispatches, availability of fibre and BIA surveys. We would like to start small and make the project expandable.

CC: What about vandalism?

CR: The cameras will be installed roughly 20 ft above ground. They will have a bullet-proof enclosure.

Source: Reproduced with permission of City of Thunder Bay, Transit Division.

APPENDIX 9.4

Comments

The following are comments which were taken from a guest book circulated at consultation meetings. There were only two negative comments recorded.

Positive

We certainly need it! Excellent idea
Great plan
Highly support this initiative
Great concept
Interesting project
Very good presentation
This will be a positive addition to the community
Good project
We have the technology: use it
Worthwhile project, good luck
Wonderful idea
Hope the community responds positively to this good idea
I hope it's a go
Very impressed with the presentation. Will be of benefit
Ensure ongoing program evaluation
We support the program
Excellent idea. It will work here too
Hope to see it operating soon

Sounds like a good plan
Great idea. Keep rolling with this
Worthwhile project

Negative
I don't like the whole idea
Not convinced it's a good thing

Source: Reproduced with permission of City of Thunder Bay, Transit Division.

10
Panoptic Dreams: Arguments, Implications, and Recommendations

The preceding nine chapters documented the processes involved in establishing streetscape CCTV surveillance monitoring programs in thirteen Canadian cities. The purposes of the analyses were to assess how monitoring programs were initiated and implemented between 1981 and 2005 and to use specific case studies or regional developments to develop a set of general theoretical and conceptual insights into the rise of streetscape monitoring programs across the country.

This final chapter revisits the empirical, theoretical, conceptual, and political findings presented in the book and expands the analyses to address a broader set of implications and concerns. The chapter does not simply rehash the findings of the study, although a brief overview of the main arguments is provided. Rather, the primary aim is to move beyond the findings to glean insights into how future research on streetscape monitoring might be conceptualized and into how monitoring programs might be established, administered, regulated, and understood.

The chapter is organized into four sections. The first section not only recaps the arguments and central themes but also fleshes out some of the implications of the findings for existing and new monitoring programs. The second section addresses some of the conceptual and methodological implications of doing academic research on streetscape CCTV surveillance in the context of the explanatory framework presented in Chapter 2. Moving beyond the theoretical method developed to guide data analyses, the section argues that it is useful to conceptualize streetscape monitoring programs in terms of an institutional anti-policy matrix, and it further examines the problematics of establishing streetscape CCTV surveillance and the politics of diffusion. The third section formulates a set of ideal and pragmatic regulatory recommendations oriented toward maximizing progressive trends in the diffusion process. The recommendations do not challenge but build on the pragmatic policy orientation institutionalized by Canada's privacy policy sector. And the fourth section concludes the chapter by presenting responses to five critical public interest questions based on recurrent issues and dilemmas that emerged in interviews over the course of the investigation. The purpose of the final section is not to formulate a definitive set of arguments to apply to all monitoring initiatives but to encourage advocates and opponents of video surveillance systems to think differently, or at least more broadly, about the many dimensions of streetscape CCTV surveillance monitoring practices and programs.

Panoptic Dreams Revisited

In their assessment of public-area video surveillance and privacy protection law in Canada, Bennett and Bayley (2005) conclude that the future of video surveillance as a mechanism for crime prevention and detection is unclear and that the fate of the Canada-wide standardization of pragmatic policy protection guidelines is uncertain. Their conclusions are based partially on the arguments that public-area video surveillance is not as pervasive in Canada as it is in Europe and that the meaning of video surveillance is constantly changing with rapid developments and adaptations in imaging technologies. Although the fate of public-area video surveillance and the policy protection measures designed to counteract its most undesirable effects is not yet fully known, this book provides an empirical set of findings to understand better the direction of streetscape monitoring practices and the policies designed to ensure their accountability, transparency, legality, and utility.

The first step toward understanding the future of public-area video surveillance and its potential regulation is to understand how streetscape monitoring programs have been established to date. Deriving from empirical analyses of the dynamics involved in establishing monitoring programs in Canada, a set of interlocking arguments was presented to explain how these programs have been established, regulated, governed, and resisted/rejected. The primary argument is that there has been an uneven tripartite ideational, administrative, and policy diffusion of streetscape monitoring programs across the country. The idea to establish such programs has diffused from locations inside and outside Canada, but the ideational diffusion of Canadian programs has been the most influential. The primary source of diffusion has been the City of Sudbury's Lions Eye in the Sky program. Even before the KPMG report was posted on the Sudbury Police Services website in 2000, the VMAC's and LVMAC's promotional campaign (public presentations, a promotional video, statistical claims distributed through flyers) was a powerful force in the ideational diffusion of streetscape monitoring programs (in Kelowna, London, Hamilton, and Thunder Bay).

Accompanying ideational diffusion has been administrative diffusion. Not surprisingly, in the late 1990s (prior to the release and promotion of standardized privacy protection guidelines), there was a close relationship between ideational and rudimentary administrative diffusion of monitoring programs. As the number of monitoring programs grew in the context of increasing privacy protection advocacy, however, the relationship between ideational and administrative diffusion fragmented. Anglo-Canadian monitoring programs continued to draw inspirational, promotional, and administrative support from the LVMAC, but the administrative structures designed between 2000 and 2005 were increasingly influenced by the diffusion of privacy protection principles. They not only reconfigured the administrative designs of specific monitoring systems but also influenced the diffusion of a new set of administrative standards.

The diffusion of privacy protection policy on public-area monitoring has also been uneven. Tracing to Quebec in the early 1990s, the uneven ideational and administrative diffusion of streetscape monitoring programs was significantly influenced by the CAI's ruling on the Sherbrooke Police Service's collection of nominative information. The ruling constituted a rare example of assertive pragmatism in the history of establishing monitoring programs in the country (including critical on-site inspections in Sherbrooke and later Baie-Comeau), and it diffused across policy domains in Quebec and, to an extent, Anglo-Canada (the spirit of the ruling was especially discernible in Information and Privacy Commissioner of Canada George Radwanski's efforts to challenge video surveillance practices). Although information and privacy commissioners across Canada learned from one another and began to adopt a standardized privacy protection framework by 2002, applications of pragmatism in Anglo-Canada assumed a more conciliatory character than they did in Quebec.

Although the standardized pragmatic approach to public-area video surveillance is designed to encourage compliance with a set of fair information principles institutionalized in federal, provincial, and municipal legislation, it has partially contributed to and reinforced progressive and negative trends in the process of establishing streetscape programs. In some cities, governance structures in the form of operational policies, codes of practice, and data-sharing agreements have been strengthened through the progressive diffusion of administrative design protocols. In other cities, however, the administrative design process has resembled a cherry-picking exercise whereby CCTV advocates choose which privacy protection principles to endorse or emphasize (and how to do so) and which ones to ignore or downplay. The tendency to emphasize certain privacy protection principles is evident not only among proponents of public-area monitoring systems in Canadian cities but also among members of the privacy policy sector (e.g., emphasizing public consultations). And in still other cities, the pragmatic policy orientation has partially enabled various forms of resistance, ranging from political pressure from councillors to campaigns by protest groups. Combined with a set of influential contingencies in the form of signal crimes and signal events (whose influence is also partially enabled by pragmatism), the ways in which monitoring programs are established remain inconsistent.

These inconsistencies matter. Variability in the process of designing and implementing monitoring programs arguably poses implications for how systems are administered and deployed on a daily basis. It also poses implications for the extent to which monitoring systems will realize their stated objectives; for how long-term funding will be generated and secured; and for the legitimacy, transparency, and viability of monitoring initiatives.

Finally, it is important to reiterate an argument presented in the Introduction. Some readers will find the decidedly liberal interpretation of the findings unsettling; for them, the primary goal of critical sociological/criminological analysis is to expose the underlying interests and power relations that give rise to monitoring programs. I have emphasized the importance of material relations and power interests throughout the book, but I have also been clear that the process of establishing systems is far too complex to be reduced to a narrow set of interests and interactions. Indeed, my goal is neither to encourage nor to discourage monitoring systems but to produce useful recommendations and to identify theoretical, conceptual, empirical, and political places to begin analyzing streetscape CCTV surveillance in Canada.

Policy Proclivities and the Politics of Diffusion

Before I explore some of the ways that the privacy policy sector and the Canadian public might respond to streetscape monitoring initiatives, it is important to develop further conceptual insights into streetscape CCTV surveillance policy in its local, regional, provincial, and federal forms. I am using the term "policy" in a broad manner to refer to formal policy documents produced inside and outside governments, city administrations, and the privacy policy sector as well as to the regional co-ordinated deployment of resources among networks of community representatives in the context of myriad situational contingencies. *Panoptic Dreams* is neither a study of privacy protection policy nor public/municipal policy on crime prevention and social disorder, yet privacy protection policy and crime and disorder prevention policy have figured strongly into the analyses. Because crime and disorder policies at the regional and municipal levels have informed the bases for ideational and administrative diffusion of streetscape monitoring programs, and because the diffusion of federal and provincial privacy protection policy has exercised discernible influences on the ideational and administrative structures of monitoring systems, it is important to develop conceptual insights into how research might proceed in the context of policy proclivities.

Streetscape CCTV surveillance initiatives are usefully conceptualized as a form of "anti-policy." As Walters (2009) explains, anti-policy is a contemporary feature of international politics that entails an assemblage of discourses, schemes, policies, and practices whose purpose is to combat or prevent undesirable things. Anti-policy has no ultimate empirical or political referent: it ranges from global anti-poverty campaigns to anti-terrorism measures enacted by liberals and conservatives alike. What bonds specific anti-policy agendas together, however, is a common policy interest in counteracting the perceived negative dimensions of a set of heterogeneous phenomena under the guiding logic and practical orientation of "anti-" programs and strategies.

Anti-policy orientations are not part of a new political rationality or logic (e.g., neoliberalism) that is sweeping across Western societies. Nor are anti-policy orientations a form of anti-politics. On the contrary, anti-policy is a form of politics that seeks to act on the conduct, plight, and potential of certain population groups across a range of empirical settings. As a form or program of government that simultaneously enables and constrains actions, anti-policy denotes a class of phenomena that cannot be understood by simply analyzing the phenomena to which specific counter-agendas are opposed (e.g., crime). Rather, anti-policy needs to be analyzed in its own right, replete with its own institutions, agendas, orientations, and effects (Walters 2009). Indeed, the data presented in the previous chapters indicate that streetscape monitoring initiatives as anti-policy orientations have more to do with the strategies, tactics, alliances, and representations that give rise to monitoring aspirations (and to the forces of diffusion) than they do with actual instances of crime, disorder, and nuisance at which monitoring initiatives are directed. As I explained in Chapter 2, this is not to suggest that efforts to introduce systems are only about the enactment of crime and disorder; rather, the politics of enactment represents a domain of analysis – and necessarily of struggle – in its own right.

As an analytically distinct domain of the government of self and others, streetscape CCTV surveillance anti-policy analysis involves examining claims, myths, formal policies, informal governance structures, signal events/crimes, and regional contingencies that make CCTV policy solutions imaginable and actionable. But as I alluded to in the first portion of the book, it is unwarranted to explain the promotion and implementation of streetscape monitoring initiatives only in terms of the instrumental interests and agendas of community partnerships. The politics of enactment that gives rise to monitoring initiatives is no more reducible to the efforts of community partners to maximize profits and regulate certain population groups than it is to the objects and activities that monitoring systems are developed to address. What matters in the analysis of streetscape monitoring systems, at least as an initial step toward conceptualizing streetscape CCTV surveillance as an analytical domain of investigation, is to understand how knowledge about social problems is produced and how such surveillance is negotiated as a viable response to the construction of social problems.

Hence, it is useful to conceptualize the promotion, implementation, and administration of streetscape monitoring systems as an institutional anti-policy matrix. As such, these systems involve a set of standard (but not fixed) processes that can be explicated through detailed empirical examination. Among these processes are claims-making activities, community partnership and funding alliances, public consultation processes, codes of practice, ownership structures, auditing systems, and oversight committees, as well as policy protection advocacy, signal events, and municipal and federal privacy protection legislation. This is not to suggest that Canadian streetscape CCTV anti-policies do not technologically, ideationally, or administratively diffuse from other countries but simply that Canadian policy responses to perceived social problems and their preferred CCTV surveillance solutions cannot be reduced to the explanatory frameworks used to account for policy formation in different material, cultural, and political settings (see below).

Anti-Policy and the Politics of Diffusion

One of the main components in the rise of Canada's institutional streetscape CCTV surveillance anti-policy matrix is the politics of diffusion, which has been analyzed across a range of policy domains (see Rogers 2003). The primary focus of research on public policy diffusion has been the ways that governments learn from one another in a relatively consistent and vigilant manner. Policy makers, so the argument goes, exercise caution and restraint when developing or adopting new public policies. With the exception of a small number of innovations early in policy formation, most policy makers prefer to weigh the pros and cons of innovative policy initiatives before endorsing a new policy position (Nicholson-Crotty 2009; Walker 1969).

According to Rogers (2003, 14), diffusion occurs when "some innovation is communicated through certain channels over time among members of a social system" (see, too, Strang and Meyer 1993). Central to the typical policy formation process among governments is the communication of positive findings and benefits. Following a slow rate of adoption by a small number of governments, policy innovations are communicated, evaluated, and eventually adopted after a protracted learning process. There are also, however, various government policies that diffuse rapidly in the first few years of innovation and plateau as the number of adopters declines. Nicholson-Crotty (2009) explains that we know relatively little about policies that diffuse rapidly or about what causes variation in temporal diffusion patterns among governments, but he identifies issue salience and complexity, combined with electoral ambitions and regional reception, as the primary factors that motivate rapidly diffusing government policies. That is, government policy makers are more likely to discount or forgo the importance of the protracted learning process when policy adoption of highly salient, low-complexity issues holds out the promise of electoral success, especially when neighbouring regions also take up similar policy positions.

Although the tripartite diffusion of streetscape monitoring programs among Canadian cities has taken place outside the government policy arena, certain general insights can be gleaned from the literature on how policy diffuses among government agencies. Two insights are especially significant. First, in addition to arguments about the factors motivating the pace of diffusion, scholars of policy have documented how a process of reinvention takes place as policies diffuse, whereby adopters of policy introduce new dimensions into and broaden the scope of public policies as they evolve (Rogers 1995). The reinvention process does not necessarily equate to the increasing comprehensiveness of policy adaptation, however, and Hays (1996) introduces the suggestive argument that the reinvention or elaboration of policy on controversial issues tends to lack comprehensiveness to avoid or mitigate potential opposition to implementation efforts.

Second, government policy formation increasingly takes place through networks of actors and institutions within and beyond formal government. Policy networks are composed of and shaped by not only a range of government, non-government, and quasi-government actors and agencies but also by norms, values, beliefs, events, technologies, laws, and so on. Policy networks play an important role in shaping the diffusion of innovations and reinventions in the policy adoption process, and Rhodes (1996) argues that networks of governance informing the governmental service delivery process are based more on mutual adjustment, negotiation, and trust than they are on antagonism and conflict.

The rapid diffusion of public-area CCTV surveillance policy and its effects on establishing and administrating streetscape monitoring systems are not well understood – inside and outside formal government. As I explained in Chapter 2, most research on CCTV surveillance has theorized the disciplinary applications and effects of monitoring systems, usually seeking to link video surveillance systems to more general trends in the so-called surveillance society. Webster's (2004) account of CCTV surveillance policy diffusion through networks of governance in the United Kingdom is a notable exception to the strong emphasis on disciplinary power that pervades the CCTV surveillance literature (see, too, Webster 1996, 2009); it provides a comparative example to understand better the Canadian streetscape institutional anti-policy matrix.

According to Webster (2004), although monitoring programs in the United Kingdom were initially developed in the absence of formal government regulations and controls, standard approaches to self-regulation of operations and governance developed through policy networks of service providers, police, politicians, and policy makers. Ranging from the stated intentions of monitoring systems to the formation of codes of conduct/practice, an agreed-on set of standards emerged and evolved over the 1990s to shape the administrative structures of monitoring systems. Not only did an informal administrative structure emerge organically from networks of service providers based on the institutionalization of voluntary self-regulation protocols, but also co-regulatory measures involving service providers and policy makers subsequently emerged from the non-governmental CCTV policy environment. The paradox of regulating monitoring systems in the United Kingdom, then, is that the regulatory structures governing the operations and uses of CCTV surveillance systems developed from networks of service providers with little government intervention, yet government remains the dominant actor in the policy process.

To illustrate the process of CCTV surveillance policy reinvention and diffusion, Webster (2004) identifies three eras in the rapid diffusion of public-area CCTV surveillance in Britain. The first era, that of innovation, spanning the early to mid-1990s, was characterized by no formal regulation governing monitoring systems. Little was known about how to establish and administer such systems, and few technical standards or operational guidelines existed. By the mid-1990s, however, the second era, that of uptake, witnessed not only widespread ideational diffusion of monitoring programs but also accompanying administrative diffusion. The latter entailed the transmission of information about the use and impact of CCTV surveillance technologies, and it gave rise to voluntary forms of self-regulation (i.e., agreed-on standards among CCTV operators and administrators). When non-specific privacy protection legislation was introduced by the central government in the late 1990s,[1] the third era, that of sophistication, saw voluntary self-regulation give way to new forms of co-regulation that emerged from negotiations between operators and government representatives. Co-regulation brought forth a new set of relationships among stakeholders (government, service providers, industry representatives) focused on developing and implementing rules for the use of public-area surveillance cameras, and it rendered formal or specific CCTV policy unnecessary.

The rise of Canadian streetscape monitoring programs and their attendant regulatory/policy structures share certain similarities and a number of core differences with the rise of streetscape monitoring programs and attendant regulatory/policy structures in the United Kingdom. As in the United Kingdom, monitoring programs in Canada, especially in Anglo-Canada, were developed in a short period of time, primarily between 1997 and 2005. There was something of a rush to establish these systems in the late 1990s in cities such as Sudbury, Kelowna, Hamilton, London, and Thunder Bay. Although certain cities experienced greater success in launching systems by the early 2000s, a partial learning process took place among networks of representatives in the various cities that informed establishment efforts in the mid- to late 1990s. This is not to suggest that the learning process was thorough or uniform; rather, certain forms of ideational and administrative diffusion took hold in the late 1990s to comprise the bases for how monitoring programs are established and administered in Canada. By the time Commissioner Radwanski became a force to contend with in 2001, an existing policy framework had emerged largely outside the privacy policy sector, which had diffused unevenly alongside increasing privacy protection advocacy.

Despite these similarities, there are also core differences between the rise and diffusion of streetscape monitoring programs in Canada and the United Kingdom (beyond the sheer number of monitoring systems). The most salient difference is that British systems were encouraged by the central government's CCTV promotional policies and funding programs from the outset. Government sponsorship and funding not only provided an important sense of legitimacy to monitoring initiatives in the context of the highly resonant signal crime of Jamie Bulger's murder[2] but also contributed to standardization of the establishment process, especially after 1998, by encouraging the formation of community safety partnerships and, concomitantly, marginalizing dissenting voices.

In the absence of formal government promotional policy, governance structures pertaining to the promotion, design, and administration of monitoring systems in Canada have formed among small networks of local business, police, city, and community representatives. The rapid, uneven diffusion of streetscape programs across Canada – albeit only a limited number of which materialized (see Walby 2006) – entailed a process of policy reinvention that lacked a comprehensive or consistently cumulative character, even after the privacy policy sector started to encourage adherence to fair information principles and, eventually, privacy protection guidelines. Policy formation among local networks in the CCTV anti-policy matrix has diffused inconsistently based on a small number of available written documents and the promotional efforts of certain key proponents of streetscape monitoring. The privacy policy sector has contributed to progressive trends in the administrative diffusion of monitoring systems by promoting privacy protection guidelines but has also enabled variation in the reasons why monitoring programs are developed (including the actors and agencies that take up promotional efforts), in the selective endorsement of privacy protection principles (i.e., cherry-picking), and in the staging of various kinds of resistance.

Canada's experience in developing streetscape CCTV surveillance monitoring programs, therefore, is significantly different from Britain's experience, and this poses certain implications for how to promote greater consistency in the regulation of streetscape monitoring practices. Unlike the increasingly consensual character of establishing monitoring programs in the United

Kingdom, the establishment process in Canada is more antagonistic (conflict comes in a variety of forms, and it has resulted in a number of policy outcomes, including abandoning and forestalling monitoring initiatives). From 1997 to 2005, the emphasis on voluntary compliance and self-regulation was a growing feature of monitoring programs. But self-regulation in the establishment and administrative design structures has not been uniform, and it has not led to the standardization of co-regulatory structures. Admittedly, progressive trends toward co-regulation involving city officials, community partners, and police officers developed in London, Ontario, and diffused to Windsor and Thunder Bay. Yet how the enactment of co-regulatory measures among city representatives and agencies translates into daily applications of monitoring programs is a matter for empirical investigation.[3] What I am primarily concerned with below is how progressive trends in the regulation of streetscape monitoring programs can be strengthened through privacy protection policy and engagement.

Strengthening Policy Pragmatics

What might the future of public-area streetscape CCTV surveillance policy formation in Canada entail? One possibility is for the federal and/or provincial governments to develop a policy initiative on such surveillance. Given the nature of government policy formation discussed above (i.e., innovation, reinvention, learning, diffusion), federal and provincial Canadian policy makers would be wise to learn from the experiences in the United Kingdom. If Canadian governments were to follow Britain's lead, then the immediate, non-reflexive policy approach would be to build on the limited investments made by the federal government of Canada and the provincial governments of Ontario and British Columbia (see Chapter 1) and adopt a CCTV surveillance policy initiative to encourage the growth of monitoring systems. For some readers, this is no doubt an exciting prospect. But government representatives would be astute to consult the various studies that illustrate the limited effectiveness of CCTV surveillance cameras (see below). Given Webster's (2009) argument that the weak evidence for such cameras in reducing crime and disorder is posing problems for their continued use in the United Kingdom (especially ongoing funding), a Canadian governmental CCTV policy initiative is unwise.

In the absence of federal and/or provincial policy on public-area monitoring in Canadian cities, a more appropriate policy strategy is to strengthen the privacy policy sector's role in establishing and administering monitoring systems. The evidence suggests that streetscape CCTV policy will continue to be forged, reproduced, and disseminated among local networks in a piecemeal fashion, albeit with some influence from members of the privacy policy sector in the form of privacy protection guidelines. The privacy policy sector is in a position to build on progressive trends by revising the privacy protection guidelines and thereby contributing to reducing variation in the establishment process.

Privacy protection guidelines are self-regulatory instruments that operate to influence and shape public-area CCTV surveillance organizational design. Although adherence to the principles set out in the guidelines is based on voluntary compliance, they are neither optional nor foundationless. Several of the privacy protection guidelines are based on federal, provincial, and municipal privacy protection legislation that can be enforced by the privacy policy sector. But legal-authoritarian enforcement is not the only way to achieve compliance among proponents of streetscape monitoring programs: adherence to the more general principles provides monitoring program representatives with greater legitimacy in the eyes of the public and with a basis to develop operational protocols and avoid tensions stemming from data-gathering and -handling violations.

At least two amendments to the privacy policy sector's current approach to public-area CCTV surveillance would significantly contribute to the development of a stronger co-regulatory structure involving the OIPCs/OPC, service providers, stakeholders, and city administrations. The infrastructure for the first potential amendment is already available: commissioning original, empirical research to understand the scope and nature of monitoring programs across Canada to meet the needs of the privacy policy sector (and the needs of the OPC require clarification through empirical research). Members of the OPC realized the value of commissioning independent research on public-area CCTV surveillance at least as early as 2004, when they began formulating policy guidelines on such surveillance. In the policy formation process, the OPC considered a two-pronged research approach whereby it would consolidate existing knowledge on public-area monitoring practices and contract a researcher to investigate the nature and extent of video surveillance in Canada. The purpose of the data-gathering and -consolidation exercises was to educate Canadians better about the extent and effects of video surveillance, based on the realization that "we are limited in what we can say, in that we don't know the extent of video surveillance in Canada, and we have found to date very little solid empirical evidence, from Canada or anywhere else, as to the effect of video surveillance on human behavior" (Stewart 2004, 3).

Public education was conceptualized as the third product in a three-part strategy to gather and consolidate evidence on public-area monitoring. The other products entailed generating information capable of guiding OPC privacy impact investigations concerning the perceived necessity for video surveillance; of understanding the significance of claims to effectiveness, proportionality, and the absence of less discriminatory measures; and of generating guidelines for organizations on how video surveillance should comply with privacy protection legislation. The purpose was to provide auditors and organizations with a clear statement of what the OPC expects. From the outset, the OPC understood that the first two products were most important for advancing the regulation and standardization of monitoring programs and that the public education product was unlikely to reveal anything new (Stewart 2004).

Two projects were funded through the OPC's contributions program between 2004 and 2009. The first project, *L'utilisation des caméras de surveillance dans les lieux à accès public au Canada* (Boudreau and Tremblay 2005), is an investigation into public-area monitoring generally. Based on interviews, focus groups, and document review data, Boudreau and Tremblay provide an assessment of the scope, applications, efficacy, and regulations pertaining to public-area video surveillance. Their emphasis on regulation is especially important: not only does the study present an assessment of privacy protection regulations in seven provinces, but it also incorporates experiences with and perceptions of privacy protection regulations into the interview and focus-group process. Boudreau and Tremblay find widespread agreement among stakeholders and citizens that methods of governance are limited but necessary, especially with streetscape systems, ranging from meaningful public consultations to clarity of intention and purpose. What respondents and focus-group participants failed to agree on, however, was the role of the privacy policy sector in regulating governance structures (stakeholders expressed particular concerns about over-bureaucratization).

The investigation of Boudreau and Tremblay represents a significant and practical contribution to public-area CCTV surveillance monitoring programs in Canada that should have inspired and informed the direction of future empirical research into the applications and regulation of such programs (including OPC-funded research). The study engages many of the issues pertinent to public-area video surveillance, and it carves out a clear conceptual, methodological, and policy domain for subsequent investigations. Tellingly, however, like the many dimensions of streetscape monitoring programs analyzed in the preceding chapters, the insights into the establishment, administration, and regulation of public-area monitoring practices failed to diffuse to other studies (e.g., Lippert 2007; Walby 2006) – one of which was funded by the OPC (see below).

The second project funded through the OPC's contributions program (in 2008) was spearheaded by David Lyon under the auspices of the Surveillance Camera Awareness Network (SCAN) and the Surveillance Project at Queen's University. The aim of SCAN's first phase of reporting is to bring together research on camera surveillance within and beyond Canada to provide an accessible resource to promote awareness of surveillance camera issues (Surveillance Camera Awareness Network 2009). The first report is presented in four substantive subsections: "Camera Surveillance in Canada"; "Factors behind the Implementation of Camera Surveillance"; "Camera Surveillance, Privacy Regulation, and 'Informed Consent'"; and "Public Perceptions of Cameras." Each section is written by selected members of SCAN, and the information is presented to provide a report that is "not only evidence-based and accurate, but also attuned to the range of views held about surveillance cameras, and to finding appropriate ways of using such cameras, in whatever locations they are found" (Surveillance Camera Awareness Network 2009, 3).

For all the positive contributions that SCAN members are making to bringing about surveillance camera awareness, they do not provide the cumulative empirical data and analysis that the privacy policy sector requires to advance its knowledge and advocacy base about public-area monitoring programs in Canada. SCAN's literature reviews, combined with insightful commentary on signage and public opinion, can educate the Canadian public and facilitate dialogue among proponents and opponents of public-area video surveillance. Missing from the study, however, is an empirically informed, comprehensive critique of the scope, regulation, implementation, and perception of public-area monitoring systems. To be fair, SCAN is fulfilling the mandate that it carved out for itself prior to receiving OPC funding; the limitations of its study have more to do with the failure of the OPC to commission empirically based, cumulative research, which is itself based on the limited research foundation in Canada. In short, the OPC's decision to fund SCAN – followed by a second grant to build on the first phase of reporting, organize a workshop, and commission papers on privacy and camera surveillance to develop an edited volume – was a valuable but missed opportunity to build on research into establishing, administering, and regulating public-area CCTV surveillance in Canada.

Pragmatic Privacy Protection Scenarios

In addition to the continuing need for progressive, empirically based, cumulative, and original research, the second amendment that would strengthen the regulatory structure of public-area monitoring systems entails revising CCTV surveillance privacy protection policies and frameworks (i.e., protocols). Part of the process of revising and strengthening protocols should involve commissioning independent research to meet the product goals set out by, but not reducible to the needs of, the OPC in 2004. Another part of the process should involve consultations with representatives in communities running public-area monitoring programs. One possible strategy to facilitate consultation with program managers, members of auditing and oversight committees, police, community organizations, and the privacy policy sector is to design a public consultation process similar to the one held in Quebec in 2003. Considering that monitoring programs are currently running in eight Ontario cities, Ottawa or Toronto would be a suitable location to stage a first round of public meetings to gather information about public-area monitoring activities.

In terms of actually amending and strengthening the protocols to reduce variation in establishment and administration processes, it is important to continue balancing the desires of law enforcement agencies and public/municipal institutions with the interests of the privacy policy sector. In other words, it is important for that sector to undertake efforts at revision in the capacity of a partner and educator rather than an authoritative regulator and to maintain a system of voluntary compliance. Yet it is important to understand that reliance on voluntary codes has hitherto produced inconsistent results in establishment and administration processes, and the privacy policy sector's pragmatic approach has contributed to considerable variation in the design and application of monitoring systems.

The inconsistencies stemming from reliance on voluntary privacy protection codes are not unique to streetscape CCTV surveillance. Similar, albeit more far-reaching, problems appeared in generic Canadian private-sector privacy protection policy in the early 1990s, but a number of international, technological, and legislative developments convinced federal policy makers that policy refinement was necessary. As Bennett (1997) explains, the first comprehensive privacy standard was negotiated in Canada in 1992 (see also Bennett and Raab 2006, Chapter 6). Faced with the realization that OECD privacy protection guidelines were not successful in harmonizing compliance with privacy protection practices in Canada, representatives of major trade organizations entered into negotiations with industry representatives and government officials to build on existing private-sector privacy protection protocols and to standardize privacy protection processes.

The three-year negotiation process resulted in the Model Code for the Protection of Personal Information, and the Standards Council of Canada approved the code in 1995. The Canadian privacy standard is organized around ten principles, and organizations are advised that all principles must be adopted in their entirety to avoid cherry-picking. The standard can be adopted by any public or private organization that collects personal information, and the substance of the principles is expected to be incorporated into organizational codes of practice. Although the privacy standard is a voluntary instrument, a number of incentives, including the ability of organizations to strengthen policy and practice based on an existing template and to gain a seal of approval from a recognized external body, encourage compliance. To facilitate compliance, the standard comes with interpretive commentary and a workbook providing practical advice about the development and implementation of privacy policy.

In a manner similar to the formation of privacy protection policy on public-area CCTV surveillance, the primary challenge of implementing the

Canadian standard is to avoid excessive bureaucratization, on the one hand, and the possibility of organizations making purely symbolic claims that their policy measures are in accordance with the standard, on the other. To address this tension, the Quality Management Institute (QMI – part of the Canadian Standards Association [CSA]) developed a three-tiered recognition program for Canadian standards certification. As Bennett and Raab (2006) observe, there are interesting parallels between the goals of total quality management and the implementation of fair information principles. The first tier, declaration, includes obtaining a copy of the clearly specified standard expectations, the QMI application kit, and the privacy code work book, as well as reviewing organizational policies and practices. The documentation is then reviewed by the QMI. The second tier, verification, involves an auditing process whereby organizations are tested on the basis of their ability to conform to the privacy protection standards. The third tier, registration, entails recognizing organizations, including the signing of a privacy protection statement. The system is based on the simple adage "say what you do, do what you say, and be verified by an independent agency" (Bennett 1997, 354).

Although the CSA model was designed in a different context and for a different set of purposes than video surveillance privacy protection policies, it provides some important potential direction for the refinement of the privacy policy sector's approach to public-area video surveillance. The sector's present approach to encouraging compliance with the protocols is based on the assumption that public bodies or law enforcement agencies interested in establishing monitoring programs know about the privacy protection guidelines, will voluntarily address the principles in their entirety, and are able and willing to decipher and put into practice the overly simplistic explanatory notes accompanying each principle. Compliance with the guidelines often takes place after a complaint is laid with an information and privacy commissioner, and it usually entails strategically selecting and creatively interpreting what certain principles imply.

To develop a proactive, standardized set of privacy protection measures, an ideal three-tiered system of public-area CCTV surveillance privacy protection assurance could take the form of declaration, verification, and endorsement. Prior to launching such an endorsement system, whereby information and privacy commissioners would grant their seals of approval to monitoring systems after a set of privacy protection requirements is met (endorsement could be stated on street signage), the privacy policy sector could produce clear terms of reference, replete with clear examples and empirical references, to explain unambiguously what each stipulation in the guideline documents implies. One possible strategy to achieve clarity of purpose and intention is to use the OPC's contributions program, as well as a broad public consultation series (not mutually exclusive), to generate possible revisions/additions/templates based on empirical data and comprehensive understanding of monitoring practices and systems. A complementary strategy could be to appoint an action committee, composed of academics/researchers, community stakeholders/representatives, and members of the privacy policy sector, to facilitate the process. For monitoring bodies to receive the endorsement of the OIPCs and the OPC, they would need to conform to all principles in the revised privacy protection protocol.

The declaration phase could begin with the OIPCs and the OPC developing a set of unambiguous and fully conceptualized guidelines, replete with examples from cities where progressive trends in establishment and administration processes have been fostered, as well as making the purpose of the endorsement system widely known to police forces and municipal governments. The terms of reference would clearly explain the importance of public consultation and what it should entail (including evaluation of results); multilateral responsibility-sharing structures involving city administration, independent auditing committees, and oversight committees; needs assessment; and codes of practice. Importantly, the terms of reference would also offer a clear overview of international findings on the scope, use, and effectiveness of public-area CCTV surveillance systems. The latter should be presented not to discourage proponents of monitoring systems but to educate them as broadly as possible about the many dimensions of public-area monitoring practices. In the declaration phase, public bodies and law enforcement agencies would study the privacy policy sector's terms of reference and establish an initial relationship with the appropriate privacy protection agency.

The second tier, verification, could itself entail a multi-tiered process of establishing a monitoring system whereby an initial statement of intention is presented to all relevant parties (city administration, the privacy policy sector, community organizations, and members of the public). The statement of intention could be based on an OIPC/OPC template made available on the Web and in a comprehensive information package, and it would be followed by public consultations, needs assessment, privacy impact assessment, practical and verifiable short- and long-term funding strategies, as well as demonstration of the scope and effectiveness of public-area monitoring. The verification phase would also involve completion of a full proposal approved by all relevant parties before submission to the OIPC/OPC.

The final tier, endorsement, would include a comprehensive review of the proposal, including the proposed structural design, by the OIPC/OPC. Ideally, members of the privacy policy sector would be involved in the declaration and verification stages, so the endorsement phase would be an ongoing exercise oriented toward ensuring adherence to fair information principles. Similar to verification, endorsement would be multi-tiered. Initial endorsement of programs, which should take place in a relatively short time (one month), would entail a tentative or provisional endorsement to run a pilot program, and it would be followed by a period of assessment, modification, and revision. At the end of the assessment process, a final seal of approval would be granted.

The value of the multi-tiered system is at least fivefold. First, it could create a system of verification and endorsement that exists beyond specific regions/cities, where pressures from colleagues, councils, advocacy groups, and signal crimes and events do not exercise disproportionally strong influences on the establishment process. Second, it could remove responsibility from local representatives to decipher from guidelines what good practice entails, and it would provide clear terms of reference for establishing monitoring programs. Some readers might be tempted to argue that local representatives will be reluctant to surrender organizational responsibility, but the data presented in the book indicate that launching programs is more important to CCTV advocates than the specific organizational design process if excessive bureaucratization and "jumping through hoops" can be avoided from the outset. Third, the multi-tiered system promises to strengthen the integrity of the establishment process, thereby discouraging negative trends. For those parties truly interested in establishing monitoring systems that conform to the expectations of the privacy policy sector, they will endure the multi-year endorsement process (and the information presented in the book indicates that the process is often drawn out over many years anyway). The long endorsement process also promises to discourage parties that are not serious about adhering to fair information principles and astute organizational designs. Fourth, organizations and agencies that successfully negotiate the process can lay claim to and publicly promote the integrity of their monitoring systems (this could be disseminated among media outlets). At the same time, organizations and agencies that decide not to adhere to the process, or that drop out of the process, would be susceptible to negative publicity. The data in the book suggest that failure to conform to an endorsement system would provide ammunition for resistance groups and media outlets. And fifth, the endorsement process could diffuse across the country to reinforce best practices in public-area CCTV surveillance.

Admittedly, the multi-tiered endorsement system outlined above is an ideal form of CCTV surveillance governance; it would take a long time to develop, and it would require financial and human resources (and long-term commitments from many parties). The purpose of exploring the hypothetical structure is not to present a ready-made model to revise the guidelines and the privacy policy sector's existing governance protocols but to suggest a possible, empirically informed yet admittedly underdeveloped and overly idealistic alternative to strengthen the existing privacy protection framework. The hypothetical public-area CCTV surveillance endorsement system is offered not only to increase the integrity of privacy protection and actual monitoring practices but also to aid proponents of monitoring programs in designing the best possible systems. Short of introducing a model that conforms to something like the one presented above, the privacy policy sector should at least revisit the decidedly ambiguous and less than fully effective guidelines as they currently exist and work toward producing an instructive, comprehensive, and empirically informed guide for establishing public-area monitoring systems.

The Politics of Practice

To this point in the chapter, I have addressed some of the conceptual issues facing researchers who might be interested in investigating public-area monitoring systems. I have also addressed certain ideal aspects of the policy potential that lie before the privacy policy sector. I would be remiss to conclude the book without candidly addressing some of the issues that interest the public (including CCTV advocates and the privacy policy sector).

To this end, the focus of the book has increasingly shifted from analyzing what *has happened* in the establishment of streetscape CCTV monitoring programs to assessing aspects of what *should happen* in the establishment process. Responses to five critical public interest questions are presented; they are informed by the interviews conducted during the data-gathering phase of the investigation. The purpose of this final section is to encourage proponents and opponents of streetscape CCTV surveillance to think more broadly about the many dimensions of such monitoring by briefly discussing a wide set of issues, including findings in the international literature on public-area CCTV surveillance. I am fully aware that the sociological/criminological research base is still in its infancy, and the brief commentary that follows is presented not as an end to the analyses of streetscape monitoring programs in Canada but as a place to begin further exploration and development.

Question 1: Should streetscape CCTV surveillance monitoring programs be established to address crime, fear of crime, and social disorder?

When these programs are proposed in various Canadian cities, whether formally through monitoring proposals submitted to city councils and police boards or informally through statements of intention formulated by businesspeople or police, the debate quickly assumes an either/or form. That is, streetscape monitoring systems either should be established to address crime, fear of crime, and/or social disorder, or they should not. For reasons that I elaborate in responses to the interrelated critical public interest questions below, it is important to resist the temptation to think about and debate streetscape monitoring programs in either/or terms.

Debating the merits of public-area video surveillance in either/or terms only simplifies the difficult issues that we face as Canadians and community members. It is more helpful to think about preventative CCTV surveillance crime and disorder measures as both/and issues: they can have both positive and limited effects on the crime and disorder rate, and there are so many more issues to consider before we blindly accept greater public surveillance in our everyday lives. Some of the broader issues not commonly anticipated or considered include potential over-surveillance of some population groups, long-term funding concerns, and effectiveness (see below). They also include the ability of police to use surveillance cameras to increase officer safety on the ground and to respond to property and violent crimes after the fact. All of these issues are not ends but places to begin exploring the appropriateness of a streetscape surveillance system in a given community.

Hence, as elaborated in the response to the following question, two things should happen in the debate about establishing monitoring programs, regardless of the outcome. First, individuals who are opposed to monitoring programs and choose to speak out should try to appreciate that proponents of monitoring programs are usually motivated by genuine (even if unsubstantiated) concerns about safety and security on city streets. Conversely, second, individuals who promote monitoring systems should try to avoid becoming frustrated with various forms of resistance to the projects that they believe in and spend so much time working to develop. Individuals who oppose monitoring initiatives are motivated by genuine (even if unsubstantiated) concerns pertaining to privacy, ethics, social justice, and the appropriate allocation of human and financial resources.

Question 2: How should community members decide whether or not to support streetscape CCTV surveillance monitoring programs?

In community debates about establishing these programs, it is important to avoid polemical arguments that simplify valid concerns voiced by some community members in a wider effort to promote oppositional ones. Polemical argumentation is commonly used to simplify debates about establishing monitoring programs, and it can be found among the most extreme proponents and opponents of such programs.

On the one hand, opponents of streetscape monitoring systems exhibit tendencies to paint proponents of such systems with a single brush, maintaining that they wish only to increase business revenues or reduce policing costs by targeting homeless people, visible minorities, and youth. Aspects of this argument might be true in some cases, but proponents of monitoring systems are not diametrically opposed to upholding civil liberties and privacy protection measures (whose meanings are also open to interpretation and debate), and they usually promote monitoring programs with the good intentions of reducing crime/disorder and increasing citizen safety. Whether proponents' arguments about the crime and disorder rate are accurate, and whether streetscape CCTV surveillance is the best strategy to achieve their goals, are different matters.

On the other hand, there is a concomitant counterproductive tendency for proponents of streetscape monitoring programs to paint opponents of such programs with a single brush, rationalizing, minimizing, and sometimes trivializing civil libertarians' valid concerns as community members and Canadian citizens (sometimes by rationalizing public opinion data that contradict claims to public support). Opponents of monitoring programs are not always against any form of streetscape monitoring, but they tend to pose a set of un- or underaddressed questions pertaining to effectiveness, regulation, cost, and privacy. Whether opponents' arguments about privacy violations and the likelihood of camera abuse are accurate, and whether outright resistance to streetscape monitoring initiatives is the best course of action for ensuring community safety, are different matters.

Therefore, the establishment process should be characterized by transparent, respectful, interactive debates among opponents and proponents of monitoring systems. The establishment process should entail evidence-based dialogue and critique prior to purchasing equipment, locking in plans, and involving an OIPC (in some cases, the OIPC might facilitate early cordial discussion). Arguments such as "surveillance cameras are everywhere already, so a few more will not hurt" do not effectively address concerns among opponents of monitoring programs. There never was a community or national debate about the proliferation of CCTV cameras in a variety of social spaces, and such argumentation is no more productive than opponents' claims that surveillance cameras are used only to harass the poor, the racialized, and the young (but see below).

Question 3: If you have nothing to hide, do you have anything to fear?

One of the most common arguments presented by proponents of streetscape monitoring programs in Canada and elsewhere is that, if you have nothing to hide, then you have nothing to fear. When proponents make this claim, there is no absolute reason to believe that they are being disingenuous. However, international research suggests (but does not definitively demonstrate) that some members of the "nothing to hide" public have more to worry about than others.

Norris and Armstrong (1999) produced the most widely cited finding on public-area video surveillance targeting practices (i.e., the practices of focusing on members of some groups more than others). Based on their study of three British monitoring sites in the mid-1990s (including the data-gathering technique of shadowing camera operators), they argued that monitoring staff members – who watch over thousands of people on a daily basis – use categories of suspicion informed by racial, age, and gender cues to focus on some people and not others. In a more recent study, Goold (2004) confirmed that racial, gender, and age signifiers correlate with targeting practices. He concluded that young men were far more likely to be singled out for surveillance and that black and Asian males experienced disproportionately high levels of monitoring. However, Goold also introduced important qualifications into his interpretation; he concluded, for example, that there are important differences in targeting practices between police- and community-run systems and that the reasons why women are targeted tend to pertain to safety rather than suspicion.

Although the general findings on CCTV surveillance targeting have been widely cited in the surveillance literature, as Goold's study indicates, they should be received in the twenty-first-century Canadian context with caution. It might be true that camera operators focus on certain population groups and not others, but this has yet to be demonstrated in Canada. Although we do not have evidence of focused targeting in Canadian streetscape programs, there are nevertheless anecdotal evidence and findings from camera monitoring practices in retail stores that are worth considering.

In terms of anecdotal arguments, the discussion in Parnaby and Reed (2009) on natural surveillance and the politics of vision is interesting. They begin their discussion of the disproportional effects of surveillance generally by arguing that crime prevention consultants in Canada and elsewhere increasingly encourage natural forms of surveillance. Natural surveillance is informed by crime prevention through environmental design (CPTED) principles, and it entails measures such as enhancing public sight lines by cutting down hedges or removing fences. Parnaby and Reed reason that vision is a differentiated field, and when all members of a group of people become "visible" (e.g., people on a crowded downtown street) some members of the group get singled out for scrutiny and attention. Among the groups potentially targeted for surveillance, they argue, are black men and homeless people.

In terms of a more substantive evidential base, Walby (2005c) conducted ethnographic work with control-room operators in a shopping mall in Victoria, British Columbia. His focus is on how everyday forms of routine surveillance reproduce racialized assumptions about trustworthiness in the retail environment. Affirming Parnaby and Reed's presumptions and Norris and Armstrong's conclusions, Walby finds that two indicators attract the gaze of operators: perceived Native status and "bad shoes" (i.e., racial- and class-based biases). It is important to keep in mind that a retail store on Vancouver Island cannot be used as a proxy to infer monitoring practices on the streets of Canadian cities. Still, Walby's findings, taken in the broader context of anecdotal and international findings, should give the public in Canada pause to consider the potential inequitable applications of the surveillance cameras' gaze.

Question 4: Does it work?

The simple answer to this pertinent question is this: yes it does, and no it does not. As I have explained throughout the book, there is considerable variation in streetscape monitoring systems across Canadian cities. These systems vary in terms of monitoring practices (continuous versus discontinuous), numbers of cameras and monitoring staff, operational protocols, and oversight and auditing committees. Consequently, the "it" in the question signifies wide ranges of system features and design protocols that contribute to and make possible the "work" part of the question. That part, too, is open to broad interpretation, ranging from making people feel safer (inferred from responses to simplistic questions presented on public opinion surveys – see Question 5) to reduced crime rates assessed through police statistics and anecdotal claims from businesspeople.

Beyond these qualifications, the question of whether or not streetscape CCTV surveillance systems work is designed to assess the extent to which these systems reduce levels of crime, fear of crime, and social disorder. International evidence shows that public-area camera systems can contribute to property crime reduction in closed spaces (e.g., parking garages), especially when clear signage is posted, but there is no definitive evidence that cameras contribute to the reduction of violent crime. In the British context, Martin Gill and his colleagues have produced a sizable literature suggesting that the effects of surveillance cameras on crime rates generally are modest and that there is some evidence of the displacement of crime from one area to another (see Gill and Spriggs 2005; Gill 2003; and Ditton 2002). In the American context, Brandon Welsh and his colleagues have found that street lighting is more effective at reducing vandalism and theft than cameras and that there is mixed evidence that cameras displace non-violent crime to other areas (Welsh and Farrington 2005, 2004a, 2004b, 2003). Finally, Groombridge (2008), also writing in the British context, concludes that public-area video surveillance is not worth the investment, and Webster (2009) has recently warned that the weak evidential base is now posing implications for the continuation of monitoring in the United Kingdom.

Question 5: Do members of the public want streetscape cameras?

Whereas the empirical base for the effectiveness of CCTV surveillance in reducing crime and disorder is indecisive, the evidential base for levels of public support – at least judging from public opinion surveys – is not. Ranging from small-scale surveys distributed by police and business owners in Canadian communities to questions posed by the Canadian Strategic Council, the surveys are clear: when Canadians are asked if they support cameras, public opinion is unambiguously supportive.

Although findings on public opinion about the benefits of public-area CCTV surveillance are generally and consistently high, there are several important qualifications worth noting. In the International Survey on Privacy and Surveillance, for example, members of the Surveillance Project (2008) found moderate to high levels of international support for the effectiveness of "community CCTV cameras," but they also found that levels of support shifted across national contexts (49.8 percent of Canadian respondents moderately agreed that community cameras are effective, while 16.1 percent of Canadian respondents strongly agreed). Gazso and Haggerty's (2009) findings from public opinion polls of Albertans found similar levels of support but also illustrated that the ways in which questions were framed produced variation in responses. Especially suggestive is their finding that respondents tended to be more supportive of specific (e.g., CCTV) surveillance initiatives compared with general trends in the adoption of new surveillance technologies. Finally, the aforementioned findings are generally supported by focus group data collected by Transport Canada (2005) in the aftermath of the 7/7 attacks. The Transport Canada investigation found variation among residents of Canadian cities, with participants in Toronto showing higher levels of support for transit cameras (but more for crime reduction than anti-terrorism purposes).

Comprehensive, independent focus group data on public opinion about streetscape CCTV surveillance are not available in the Canadian context, but Lett's (2007) investigation of public opinion in Kelowna is suggestive. Lett found that residents of seniors' homes and clients at shelters generally support streetscape cameras *prior to being fully informed about variation in administration, cost, and effectiveness*. After being presented with even modest arguments that CCTV surveillance does not always achieve the results that proponents claim on its behalf, however, focus group participants changed their opinions. Especially unsettling and surprising to residents of seniors' homes was the fact that people other than police officers might monitor cameras and that cameras might not be monitored around the clock.

Based on the limited public opinion data available on attitudes about and perceptions of the effectiveness of public-area surveillance cameras, two preliminary conclusions can be drawn: first, Canadians show an initially moderate to strong tendency to support CCTV initiatives to reduce crime; second, public opinion data are complex, inconsistent, and incomplete. These two findings are significant: they point to some of the limitations of public opinion surveys in the form of a few basic questions, and they point to the need for more comprehensive public opinion-gathering techniques. To be blunt, presenting Canadians with the survey question "do you support community safety cameras to reduce terrorism?" is different from asking "do you support video surveillance cameras funded through tax dollars to monitor youth, homeless, and other populations deemed troublesome by the policing and business communities?" At the least, the findings point to the need to explore matters pertaining to CCTV surveillance in greater depth and to provide respondents with more information and broader context.

Conclusion

The introduction of public-area streetscape CCTV surveillance systems in Canadian cities has been limited but continual since the early 1990s. With some of Canada's major cities currently in the process of introducing monitoring systems (increasingly with government funding), the honeymoon with streetscape CCTV surveillance in Canada might be over. The sociological and criminological responses to monitoring programs in Canada have been surprisingly minimal. The time is long overdue for serious empirical investigation into the cultural nuances and practical complexities of streetscape surveillance systems in Canada. This study provides a place to begin developing further analytical and political insights into the processes of designing, establishing, and regulating the spread of streetscape CCTV surveillance in Canada.

Appendices

Public-Area and Streetscape CCTV Surveillance Monitoring Programs in Canada[1]

Ontario[2]

Thessalon

Thessalon is a small town (approximate population of 1,300) located between Sudbury and Sault Ste. Marie, on the north shore of the North Channel of Lake Huron. Thessalon operates a passive public-area CCTV surveillance monitoring program that consists of three cameras located in a parking lot at the community hall. The purpose of the camera system is to monitor vandalism in the parking lot. The cameras feed to a recorder and a single monitor locked in the basement of the hall, where surveillance images can be accessed by police officers. A local councillor proposed the system in 2000 to combat vandalism on and around the municipal office premises. Council provided funding from the general town levy, and three cameras were initially deployed at the municipal office, situated at the intersection of Main Street and Huron Street, in the spring of 2001.

Commenting on Thessalon's monitoring system is important because it attracted attention from the Ontario OIPC in 2002, prompting the town to draw up a code of practice in line with *Guidelines for Using Video Surveillance Cameras in Public Places*. Based on OIPC statements in published materials (e.g., see Information and Privacy Commissioner of Ontario 2004), it has been unclear whether Thessalon runs a streetscape system. When the municipal office changed location in 2006, the system lay dormant for a year before being redeployed in 2007 at the community hall. Representatives of the Town of Thessalon report that the cameras are rarely used; incidents of vandalism ceased when the cameras were installed, and police credit the cameras with having a deterrent effect.

Toronto

Toronto is located in southern Ontario. With over 5 million metropolitan residents, Toronto is the most populous city in Canada. The idea for a streetscape CCTV system originated in 2000 in discussions between members of Toronto City Council and Toronto Police Service. The original idea was shelved after councillors and police representatives decided that there was an inadequate policy framework in place and too few Canadian precedents to follow.

A contributing factor to renewed efforts to establish a streetscape CCTV monitoring program was the 26 December 2005 shooting of Jane Creba. Creba was caught in crossfire and killed in downtown Toronto when a gunfight broke out in the middle of the shopping day.

In 2006, the Toronto Anti-Violence Intervention Strategy (TAVIS)[3] secured a $7 million grant from the Ontario Ministry of Community Safety and Correctional Services to combat crime, violence, and gang-related activity. Convinced that the 2001 Ontario OIPC's Guidelines provided the necessary policy framework for streetscape CCTV practices, members of the Toronto Police Service obtained a $2 million grant from the ministry to explore video surveillance as a possible tool for crime detection and deterrence. An internal police committee comprised of staff familiar with policy, video technologies, public relations, corporate communication, and planning and design was assembled to plan a CCTV pilot project. Eight public consultations were held in early 2007.

In April 2007, the Toronto Police Service installed a fifteen-camera system to run a six-month pilot project. Eight cameras were installed in the entertainment district (in and around Yonge-Dundas Square in central Toronto), three were installed in the Jane and Finch area (a neighbourhood located in the former City of North York in northwestern Toronto), and four were installed in Scarborough (an area forming the eastern side of Toronto). To design the system, the committee referred to public-area CCTV monitoring programs in Britain, New Zealand, the United States, and Australia. Based on a lack of evidence that active or live monitoring deters or reduces crime, the police implemented a passive (recorded but non-monitored) program. The pilot project ran for two years (until May 2009), when Police Chief William Blair announced that the successful pilot would likely be redeployed on a permanent basis. Before final approval by the police board, the police service will produce a three-year implementation plan, design an annual audit system, and analyze further data from the pilot project. The cameras in the entertainment district and Yonge-Dundas Square continue to record public images.

Trenton/Frankford (Quinte West)

Trenton lies on the northern shore of Lake Ontario, 160 kilometres east of Toronto. Formerly an independent city, Trenton was incorporated into the Municipality of Quinte West (approximate population of 42,697) in 1998. In 2008, a nine-camera streetscape surveillance program was installed in downtown Trenton – with one additional camera located in the outlying village of Frankford.[4] The program was initiated by the Police Services Board to counteract crime in the downtown areas of Trenton and Frankford and to support a 2007–8 downtown rejuvenation project. The $80,000 installation fund (including all maintenance costs to date) was financed by unused policing funds paid by the City of Quinte West to the Ontario Provincial Police (OPP).

Footage from the cameras is transmitted over wireless Internet feeds to the dispatch office of the OPP building in Quinte West, where images are recorded. Live monitoring is possible by on-duty dispatch clerks and a downtown Trenton community policing office staffed by volunteers. Each camera has pan, tilt, and zoom capabilities and is set to a default patrol cycle that can be manually overridden. Trenton's cameras are equipped with motion detection technology set to interrupt usual patrol cycles and focus on nearby activity until all movement ceases for at least thirty-five seconds. The OPP building has both recording and manual override capabilities, whereas the community policing office has no recording facilities, and the cameras may be overridden only manually from that location if an OPP officer is present.

According to police representatives, Trenton's system has been favourably received by the public and local businesses. Footage from the surveillance cameras has apparently been used to secure convictions of a jewellery theft gang and a local armed robbery. Based on the perceived successes, an additional camera was installed in the spring of 2009, and the Police Services Board has recently switched service providers with the intentions of upgrading the system and adding four more cameras in Trenton and one camera in Frankford – the latter will likely be installed to monitor a soon-to-be-built children's play area. Monitoring practices are governed by a code of conduct based on London, Ontario's, Code of Practice. An auditing system involving three auditors is currently being implemented to monitor the success of the program.

Sturgeon Falls

Sturgeon Falls is the administrative and commercial centre of the small town of West Nipissing in northeastern Ontario. Approximately 7,000 people live in Sturgeon Falls, which is situated north of Sudbury. The streetscape monitoring program in Sturgeon Falls was established at a cost of $100,000 as part of the downtown BIA's beautification and rejuvenation project of

1998. The money was raised by representatives of the business community (partially through a public fundraising drive). There was no organized public consultation. The cameras were installed as a way to protect town renovations from vandalism, and members of the BIA also hoped that they would deter and control crime.

The West Nipissing Police Service administers the program, comprised of nine digital cameras located in a busy commercial area around King, Main, William, Queen, and Front Streets. One camera is located on the municipal building rooftop, providing a bird's-eye view of the core. The system entails both fixed and swivel, pan, and tilt cameras. The cameras feed to the police station, where they are recorded and sporadically monitored via a bank of monitors by on-duty police dispatch staff. The chief of police evaluates the program using annual crime statistics, but there is no official auditing process or published reporting system in place.

Owen Sound

Owen Sound is located on the shores of Georgian Bay, in Southwestern Ontario. In 2006, the Owen Sound Downtown Improvement Area (the business association) mounted two video surveillance cameras to monitor downtown city streets. The system was expanded in subsequent years to six cameras. Cameras were fixed models, and images were passively recorded to HD in the office of the DIA. In 2010, the DIA board faced costs associated with upgrading the system, and the Ontario Privacy Commissioner had requested a policy on public-area monitoring. At this time, only one of the cameras was functional and free of problems. The DIA voted to abandon the system in 2010.

Quebec

Montreal

In May 2004, the Service de police de la Ville de Montréal (SPVM) installed four surveillance cameras on Rue St-Denis between Rue Sherbrooke and Boulevard René-Lévesque – the city's Latin Quarter – in response to complaints by local businesses about drug-related activities in the area. The SPVM's three stated objectives for the system are to prevent violent crimes, drug trafficking, and gang violence. Although the SPVM consulted with the CAI before installing cameras, the CAI was later critical of the program. The CAI argued that the SPVM had failed to establish the need for CCTV, to consider the privacy implications of the system, or to investigate alternatives to CCTV. The SPVM ceased monitoring in 2005 in order to reconfigure the program and address the CAI's concerns.

Representatives of the SPVM consulted video surveillance systems in Lyon and Valoy, France, to design a twenty-four-camera system. Bolstered by the

Montreal Public Safety Commission's approval of the system for an additional year (in May 2005), the SPVM also resumed monitoring the original cameras. To address some of the CAI's concerns, an ethics committee was formed to oversee expansion of the program, and independent experts were consulted to assess the impact of CCTV surveillance on privacy.

New equipment was purchased and installed throughout 2006–7. In March 2006, six new cameras replaced the original four on Rue St-Denis. At that time, six additional cameras were installed on Rue St-Laurent south of Rue Sherbrooke between René Lévesque Avenue and Maisoneuve Avenue; twelve more cameras were installed on Rue St-Laurent north of Rue Sherbrooke.

The surveillance footage is transmitted to monitoring facilities via wireless microwave technology. Ten "technical surveillance agents" monitor the cameras seasonally. In response to the CAI's criticism pertaining to privacy infringement, the police implemented "masking" technology that blurs areas within the views of the cameras that would constitute an unnecessary invasion of privacy. Inspector Sylvain Lemay, supervisor of the program, reports that the initial 2004-5 monitoring reduced crime by 31 percent, property damage by 35 percent, and crimes against people (violence) by 9 percent.

Manitoba

Winnipeg

Winnipeg (approximate population of 700,000) is located in southern Manitoba, sixty kilometres north of the Canada-US border. In 2002, Winnipeg City Council rejected a proposal to establish a streetscape CCTV monitoring program put forward by the chief of police based on projected costs of $1.2 million. However, in April 2008, city council tasked the Winnipeg Police Service with researching and implementing a one-year pilot CCTV program.[5] The idea for streetscape CCTV surveillance was enthusiastically promoted by a councillor who had been impressed by the successful identification of arson suspects through the CCTV footage of a downtown gas station. Following both feasibility and privacy impact assessment reports – the latter conducted in liaison with the Manitoba ombudsman, who is responsible for access to information and privacy issues in the province – the police proposed and implemented an eleven-camera system. The cameras are located in the downtown area close to identified "hot spots" of crime activity.[6] The city provided startup and operating costs of $440,000 for the wireless system for one year, after which an audit will be conducted to judge the cameras' effectiveness.

British Columbia

In 2008, the Province of British Columbia introduced a $1 million funding program to provide CCTV technology to cities in the province. Four cities

– Vancouver, Surrey, Kelowna, and Williams Lake – submitted successful proposals. The funding is part of a pilot program to engage local governments and law-enforcement agencies in identifying possible applications of CCTV in high-crime areas. The program is a response to the 2006 "Reducing Crime and Improving Criminal Justice in British Columbia" report, completed by the BC Progress board, that specifically recommends the deployment of public CCTV in the province.[7]

Williams Lake

Williams Lake is a city of 10,000 people located in the central interior of British Columbia, approximately 400 kilometres north of Vancouver. The city reports the highest crime per capita rate in British Columbia since 2008. In response to an increase in property crime and vandalism, the Williams Lake downtown BIA proposed a public CCTV program in 2006, but the city refused to provide funding. In the fall of 2008, the mayor of Williams Lake contacted provincial authorities to inquire why Williams Lake had not been earmarked for provincial CCTV funding.[8] City representatives continued lobbying until the province agreed to reduce funding of the other BC cities in order to free up $50,000 for Williams Lake.

In line with conditions specified by the BC solicitor general, Williams Lake is currently tasking third parties with conducting a privacy impact assessment and preparing technical specifications of the proposed system. The intention is that the BIA itself will be responsible for administering the scheme – a proposal sanctioned by the solicitor general. In 2009, the BIA will relocate to an abandoned gas station that also houses the city's community police premises. The facilities will house the monitoring and recording equipment for what is intended to be a passive scheme.

Surrey

Surrey (approximate population of 390,000) is located in the Metro Vancouver area of British Columbia. Surrey is currently piloting a CCTV program using a provincial grant of $330,000. In 2006, Mayor Diane Watts noted the effectiveness of an informal video surveillance network mounted by local businesses. Watts signalled the city's intention to install CCTV cameras in crime hot spots around the city. A delegation was sent to England in 2006 to research public-area CCTV surveillance, and British police representatives promoted CCTV surveillance among Surrey and Vancouver authorities the same year. The city did not have the funds to install an extensive system, but a single camera was mounted on the city hall building to survey city-owned property, including the parking lot. In 2008, the city successfully applied for provincial funding for a one-year pilot project. The city is currently designing a system based in and around the Scott Road Sky Train station. One condition of the funding package is that researchers from Simon

Fraser University will monitor the progress and effectiveness of the program over the course of the year. Surrey is planning to continue funding and operating the program after funding expires, pending positive evaluation results from the pilot program.

Creston

Creston is located in the Creston Valley in the interior of British Columbia, between the Selkirk and Purcell Mountains. As early as 1999, city councillors installed four streetscape surveillance cameras on Main Street in downtown Creston. Between 1999 and 2009, the system expanded to parks and other public-area locations to address concerns about vandalism and property damage. The system was implemented in consultation with the local RCMP detachment, but it is a city-run system. Camera images from at least twenty-one CCTV surveillance cameras are not monitored live; digital images are recorded. There has been some resistance to the presence of cameras, whereby local residents have cut cameras off poles with long pruners.

Kitimat

The City of Kitimat is located in northwest British Columbia, adjacent to the City of Terrace. Motivated by concerns about vandalism, Kitimat's community safety committee examined streetscape video surveillance in 2008. The initiative was endorsed by council and driven by the Chamber of Commerce. Council earmarked $86,000 for cameras and equipment. At the time of interviewing (February 2010), certain city representatives were interested in exploring the possibility of buying cameras used in the 2010 Olympics.

Trail

The City of Trail is located in the west Kootenay region of the interior of British Columbia. In 2006, city council allocated $50,000 for video surveillance cameras to address concerns about vandalism and after-hours bar crowds. The system is composed of thirty-five cameras (one is portable), nine of which are streetscape cameras. Camera images are recorded by the city and periodically transferred to the RCMP detachment.

Nova Scotia

Antigonish

Antigonish is a small town of approximately 4,500 people located in northeastern Nova Scotia. Home to St. Francis Xavier University, Antigonish doubles in population during the academic term. The idea for a CCTV program in Antigonish first arose during a 2003 council meeting concerning increasing vandalism in the downtown area, particularly the destruction of parking meters. Despite some objections from town councillors, a vote to fund the system up to $10,000 passed in 2003. A single camera was installed in October 2004 on Main Street. The camera feeds to a monitor in the town hall, where it is recorded and passively monitored. An agreement exists with the RCMP detachment – responsible for policing Antigonish – requiring formal requests to access surveillance tapes.

Halifax

Halifax Regional Municipality is the capital of Nova Scotia (approximate population of 280,000 people). The Halifax Regional Municipal Police currently administer a six-camera streetscape monitoring program in downtown Halifax. The cameras are fixed models feeding via wire to the commissionaires' office in the downtown area. The feed is recorded permanently and live-monitored during the evening by a single commissionaire who performs other duties. Two cameras view the boardwalk/waterfront area, one camera is located at "pizza corner" (a busy eating district servicing patrons leaving many nearby bars and clubs), two cameras view the bar district itself along Argyle Street, and one camera is situated in the retail district on Spring Garden Road.

The idea to establish a streetscape monitoring program originated in discussions between Halifax City Council and the chief of police in 2006. City representatives were concerned about altercations in the downtown nightlife areas, specifically the robbery and assault of people leaving bars. The drive to install CCTV cameras came as part of a new overall deployment strategy involving increased numbers of officers in the downtown core. The overseer of the program since its inception, Superintendent Bill Moore, reports that the cameras, as part of the overall redeployment strategy, have reduced crime and increased detection in the downtown area. However, no auditing process exists to provide data on the specific role of CCTV in these results. The Halifax Police Service is currently considering expanding the system.

Alberta

Calgary

Calgary is the largest city in Alberta. Situated 200 kilometres north of the Canada-US border, Calgary has a metropolitan population of approximately 1.2 million residents. As early as 2006, representatives of the City of Calgary expressed interest in public-area and streetscape monitoring. In 2008, the Community and Protective Services Committee voted to implement a pilot project. The project involved a plan to install up to twenty-four streetscape cameras to monitor the downtown core. The following year city council approved a sixteen-camera pilot project to address drug use, graffiti, and assaults in the East Village and along Stephen Avenue Walk. The cameras are randomly monitored by the city's corporate security staff. Recordings from the CCTV cameras are retained for fourteen days, and the pilot project is administered by Animal and Bylaw Services.

Edmonton

Edmonton straddles the North Saskatchewan River in central Alberta, 500 kilometres north of the Canada-US border. Just over 1 million residents inhabit the metropolitan area, which incorporates downtown Edmonton on the north shore of the river and Old Strathcona. Old Strathcona is the nightlife district of Edmonton, and it was the site of the infamous 2001 Canada Day riots, which involved street fighting, vandalism, and traffic blockage after bars let out simultaneously, and it prompted police to deploy dogs, smoke bombs, and pepper spray to disperse the crowd. Partly in response to the riot, the City of Edmonton and the Edmonton Police Service drew up plans for a streetscape CCTV system as part of a new street management strategy for the area.

A pilot project deploying four cameras was put in place in Old Strathcona in 2003 (administered by police). It was hoped that the cameras would help to deter and detect crime and vandalism in the area, particularly in relation to the busy nightlife zone. The first year of monitoring coincided with a drop in crime as measured in the annual crime statistics review. Reluctant to draw a correlation based on these results, the police inspector in charge of the program repeated it for another year. Statistics for 2004 showed no reduction in crime in the areas covered by the cameras, and the inspector recommended withdrawal of the project. In 2005, the cameras were recalled and have not been used since.

APPENDIX B

Information and Privacy Commissioner of Ontario

Guidelines for the Use of Video Surveillance Cameras in Public Places

Ann Cavoukian, Ph.D.
Commissioner
September 2001

2 Bloor Street East
Suite 1400
Toronto, Ontario
Canada
M4W 1A8

416-326-3333
1-800-387-0073
Fax: 416-325-9195
TTY (Teletypewriter): 416-325-7539
Website: www.ipc.on.ca

Acknowledgements

This publication is an updated version of a paper released in 2001 by Dr. Ann Cavoukian, Information and Privacy Commissioner of Ontario.

Dr. Cavoukian gratefully acknowledges the work of Judith Hoffman in preparing the first report, and Catherine Thompson for her work on this updated report.

Table of Contents

1. Introduction

Government organizations are considering the implementation of video surveillance technology with increasing frequency for the purposes of general law enforcement and public safety programs. In limited and defined circumstances, video surveillance cameras may be appropriate to protect public safety, detect or deter, and assist in the investigation of criminal activity.

Organizations governed by the Freedom of Information and Protection of Privacy Act (the provincial Act) and the Municipal Freedom of Information and Protection of Privacy Act (the municipal Act) that are considering implementing a video surveillance program are encouraged not to view video surveillance as a "silver bullet." Although technological solutions to security challenges reflect an "urge for perfect fairness and perfect security, extended equally and automatically to all,"[1] no such world of perfection exists. Institutions must balance the public benefits of video surveillance against an individual's right to be free of unwarranted intrusion into his or her life. Pervasive, routine and random surveillance of ordinary, lawful public activities interferes with an individual's privacy.

These Guidelines are intended to assist organizations in deciding whether the collection of personal information by means of a video surveillance system is lawful and justifiable as a policy choice, and if so, how privacy protective measures can be built into the system.

These Guidelines do not apply to covert surveillance, or surveillance when used as a case-specific investigation tool for law enforcement purposes where there is statutory authority and/or the authority of a search warrant to conduct the surveillance.

These Guidelines are also not intended to apply to workplace surveillance systems installed by an organization to conduct workplace surveillance of employees.

2. Definitions
In these Guidelines:

Personal information is defined in section 2 of the Acts as recorded information about an identifiable individual, which includes, but is not limited to, information relating to an individual's race, colour, national or ethnic origin, sex and age. If a video surveillance system displays these characteristics of an identifiable individual or the activities in which he or she is engaged, its contents will be considered "personal information" under the Acts.

Record, also defined in section 2 of the Acts, means any record of information, however recorded, whether in printed form, on film, by electronic means or otherwise, and includes: a photograph, a film, a microfilm, a videotape, a machine-readable record, and any record that is capable of being produced from a machine-readable record.

Video Surveillance System refers to a video, physical or other mechanical, electronic, digital or wireless[2] surveillance system or device that enables continuous or periodic video recording, observing or monitoring of personal information about individuals in open, public spaces (including streets, highways, parks). In these Guidelines, the term video surveillance system includes an audio device, thermal imaging technology or any other component associated with capturing the image of an individual.

Reception Equipment refers to the equipment or device used to receive or record the personal information collected through a video surveillance system, including a camera or video monitor or any other video, audio, physical or other mechanical, electronic or digital device.

Storage Device refers to a videotape, computer disk or drive, CD ROM, computer chip or other device used to store the recorded data or visual, audio or other images captured by a video surveillance system.

3. Collection of Personal Information Using a Video Surveillance System

Any recorded data or visual, audio or other images of an identifiable individual qualifies as "personal information" under the Acts.[3]

Since video surveillance systems can be operated to collect personal information about identifiable individuals, organizations must determine if they have the authority to collect this personal information in accordance with the Acts.

Pursuant to section 38(2) of the provincial Act and section 28(2) of the municipal Act, no person shall collect personal information on behalf of an organization unless the collection is expressly authorized by statute, used for the purposes of law enforcement or necessary to the proper administration of a lawfully authorized activity. For example, the collection of personal information that is merely helpful and not necessary to the proper administration of a lawfully authorized activity would not meet the requirements of sections 28(2) and 38(2).[4]

Organizations must be able to demonstrate that any proposed or existing collection of personal information by a video surveillance system is authorized under this provision of the Acts.

4. Considerations Prior to Using a Video Surveillance System

Before deciding to use video surveillance, it is recommended that organizations consider the following:

- A video surveillance system should only be considered after other measures to protect public safety, detect or deter, or assist in the investigation of criminal activity have been considered and rejected as unworkable.

  Video surveillance should only be used where conventional means (e.g., foot patrols) for achieving the same law enforcement or public safety objectives are substantially less effective than surveillance or are not feasible, and the benefits of surveillance substantially outweigh the reduction of privacy inherent in collecting personal information using a video surveillance system.

- The use of *each* video surveillance camera should be justified on the basis of verifiable, specific reports of incidents of crime or significant safety concerns.
- An assessment of privacy implications should be conducted of the effects that the proposed video surveillance system may have on personal privacy, and the ways in which any adverse effects can be mitigated by examining the collection, use, disclosure and retention of personal information. Organizations may wish to refer to the Ontario Government's Privacy Impact Assessment tool.[5]
- Consultations should be conducted with relevant stakeholders as to the necessity of the proposed video surveillance program and its acceptability to the public. Extensive public consultation should take place.
- Organizations should ensure that the proposed design and operation of the video surveillance system minimizes privacy intrusion to that which is absolutely necessary to achieve its required, lawful goals.

5. Developing the Policy for a Video Surveillance System

Once a decision has been made to use a video surveillance system, an organization should develop and implement a comprehensive written policy for the operation of the system. This policy should include:

- The rationale and objectives for implementing the video surveillance system.
- The use of the system's equipment, including: the location of the reception equipment, which personnel are authorized to operate the system and access the storage device, and the times when video surveillance will be in effect.
- The organization's obligations with respect to the notice, access, use, disclosure, retention, security and disposal of records in accordance with the Acts. (See Section 7.)
- The designation of a senior staff member to be responsible for the organization's privacy obligations under the Acts and its policy.
- A requirement that the organization will maintain control of and responsibility for the video surveillance system at all times.
- A requirement that any agreements between the organization and service providers state that the records dealt with or created while delivering a video surveillance program are under the organization's control and subject to the Acts.
- A requirement that employees and service providers review and comply with the policy and the Acts in performing their duties and functions relating to the operation of the video surveillance system.

Employees should be subject to discipline if they breach the policy or the provisions of the Acts or other relevant statutes. Where a service provider fails to comply with the policy or the provisions of the Act, it should be considered a breach of contract leading to penalties up to and including contract termination.

Employees of organizations and employees of service providers should sign written agreements regarding their duties under the policy and the Acts, including an undertaking of confidentiality.

- A requirement that there is a process in place to appropriately respond to any privacy breaches.[6]
- The incorporation of the policy into all training and orientation programs of an organization and service provider. Training programs addressing staff obligations under the Act should be conducted on a regular basis.
- The policy should be reviewed and updated every two years or sooner if there is a change or upgrade to the video surveillance system.

6. Designing and Installing Video Surveillance Equipment

In designing a video surveillance system and installing the necessary equipment, the organization should consider the following:

- Reception equipment such as video cameras, or audio or other devices should only be installed in identified public areas where video surveillance is necessary to protect public safety, detect or deter, and assist in the investigation of criminal activity.
- The equipment should be installed in such a way that it only monitors those spaces that have been identified as requiring video surveillance. Cameras should not be directed to look through the windows of adjacent buildings.
- If cameras are adjustable by operators, this should be restricted, if possible, so that operators cannot adjust, zoom or manipulate the camera to overlook spaces that are not intended to be covered by the video surveillance program.
- Equipment should not monitor the inside of areas where individuals generally have a higher expectation of privacy (e.g., change rooms and public washrooms).
- The organization should consider restricting video surveillance to time periods when there is a demonstrably higher likelihood of crime being committed and detected in the area under surveillance.
- The public should be notified, using clearly written signs, prominently displayed at the perimeter of the video surveillance areas, of video surveillance equipment locations, so the public has reasonable and adequate warning that surveillance is or may be in operation before entering any area under video surveillance. Signs at the perimeter of the surveillance areas should identify someone who can answer questions about the video

surveillance system, and can include an address, telephone number, or website for contact purposes.

- In addition, notification requirements under section 39(2) of the provincial Act and section 29(2) of the municipal Act include informing individuals of the legal authority for the collection of personal information; the principal purpose(s) for which the personal information is intended to be used and the title, business address and telephone number of someone who can answer questions about the collection. This information can be provided at the location on signage and/or by other means of public notification such as pamphlets or the organization's website. See Appendix A for a good example of a city's sign.

- Organizations should be as open as possible about the video surveillance program in operation and upon request, should make available to the public information on the rationale for the video surveillance program, its objectives and the policies and procedures that have been put in place. This may be done in pamphlet or leaflet form. A description of the program on an organization's website would also be an effective way of disseminating this information.

- Reception equipment should be in a strictly controlled access area. Only controlling personnel, or those properly authorized in writing by those personnel according to the organization's policy, should have access to the controlled access area and the reception equipment. Video monitors should never be in a position that enables public viewing.

7. Access, Use, Disclosure, Retention, Security and Disposal of Video Surveillance Records

Any information obtained by way of video surveillance systems may only be used for the purposes of the stated rationale and objectives set out to protect public safety, detect or deter, and assist in investigating criminal activity. Information should not be retained or used for any other purposes.

Where records of personal information created using video surveillance are to be retained, the following policies and procedures should be implemented by the organization and should be included in the organization's policy discussed under Section 5:

- All tapes or other storage devices that are not in use should be stored securely in a locked receptacle located in a controlled-access area. Each storage device that has been used should be dated and labeled with a unique, sequential number or other verifiable symbol.

- Access to the storage devices should only be made by authorized personnel. Logs should be kept of all instances of access to, and use of, recorded material, to enable a proper audit trail. Electronic logs should be kept where records are maintained electronically.

- The organization should develop written policies on the use and retention of recorded information that:

  - Clearly state who can view the information and under what circumstances (e.g. where an incident has been reported, or to investigate a potential crime).
  - Set out the retention period for information that has not been viewed for law enforcement or public safety purposes. Recorded information that has not been used in this fashion should be routinely erased according to a standard schedule (normally between 48 and 72 hours). For example, images are not monitored from a video surveillance system in Toronto's entertainment district introduced in 2007. Images are overridden automatically every 72 hours and are not accessed unless an incident prompts an investigation.
  - Establish a separate retention period when recorded information has been viewed for law enforcement or public safety purposes. If personal information is used for this purpose, section 5(1) of Ontario Regulation 460 under the provincial Act requires that the recorded information be retained for one year. Although section 5 of Ontario Regulation 823 under the municipal Act contains this provision, a resolution or by-law may reduce retention periods.
  - Municipal organizations should consider passing a by-law or resolution, as contemplated by section 5 of Ontario Regulation 823, that makes their retention schedules explicit.

- The organization should store and retain storage devices required for evidentiary purposes in accordance with their own policies until law enforcement authorities request them. A storage device release form should be completed before any storage device is disclosed to appropriate authorities. The form should indicate who took the device, and under what authority, when this occurred, and if it will be returned or destroyed after use. This activity should be regularly monitored and strictly enforced.
- Old storage devices must be securely disposed of in such a way that the personal information cannot be reconstructed or retrieved. Disposal methods could include overwriting electronic records, shredding, burning or magnetically erasing the personal information. See Secure Destruction of Personal Information (Fact Sheet) available on the Office of the Information and Privacy Commissioner of Ontario's website (www. ipc.on.ca).
- An individual whose personal information has been collected by a video surveillance system has a right of access to his or her personal information under section 47 of the provincial Act and section 36 of the municipal

Act. All policies and procedures must recognize this right. Access may be granted to one's own personal information in whole or in part, unless an exemption applies under section 49 of the provincial Act or section 38 of the municipal Act, such as where disclosure would constitute an unjustified invasion of another individual's privacy. Access to an individual's own personal information in these circumstances may also depend upon whether any exempt information can be reasonably severed from the record. One way in which this may be achieved is through digitally "blacking out" the images of other individuals whose images appear on the videotapes. Video surveillance systems using wireless technology must securely encrypt the wireless transmission of all personal information. See Wireless Communication Technologies: Safeguarding Privacy & Security (Fact Sheet) available on the Office of the Information and Privacy Commissioner of Ontario's website (www.ipc.on.ca).

8. Auditing and Evaluating the Use of a Video Surveillance System

Organizations should ensure that the use and security of video surveillance equipment is subject to regular audits. The audit should also address the organization's compliance with the operational policies and procedures. An external body may be retained in order to perform the audit. Any deficiencies or concerns identified by the audit must be addressed immediately.

Employees and service providers should be aware that their activities are subject to audit and that they may be called upon to justify their surveillance interest in any given individual.

The organization should regularly review and evaluate its video surveillance program to ascertain whether it is still justified in accordance with the requirements in Section 4. This evaluation should occur at least once a year.

9. Other Resources

The personal information recorded by an organization's video surveillance system, and the organization's policies and practices respecting the personal information, are subject to the privacy protection provisions of the Acts.

Prior to implementing a video surveillance system or, for that matter, any new program with privacy implications, organizations should seek legal advice and consult with their Freedom of Information and Protection of Privacy Co-ordinator. The Ministry of Government Service's Access and Privacy Office is a useful resource for Co-ordinators.

The Information and Privacy Commissioner of Ontario monitors compliance with the privacy protection provisions of the Acts. If an organization intends to introduce, significantly modify or expand a video surveillance system, they should consult with the Office of the Information and Privacy Commissioner of Ontario.

Organizations should also consult the publications available on the Office of the Information and Privacy Commissioner of Ontario's website (www.ipc.on.ca), such as:

- Wireless Communication Technologies: Safeguarding Privacy & Security (Fact Sheet)
- Wireless Communication Technologies: Video Surveillance Systems (Fact Sheet)
- Secure Destruction of Personal Information (Fact Sheet)
- Breach Notification Assessment Tool
- What to do if a Privacy Breach Occurs: Guidelines for Government Organizations

Appendix A – *Example of a city's sign*

Attention

This Area May Be Monitored by Video Surveillance Cameras (CCTV) The personal information collected by the use of the CCTV at this site is collected under the authority of (an Act) and (by-law). This information is used for the purpose of promoting public safety and reduction of crime at this site. Any questions about this collection can be directed to the Manager of (Department) at (phone number), (City Hall address) (e-mail).

2 Bloor Street East	416-326-3333
Suite 1400	1-800-387-0073
Toronto, Ontario	Fax: 416-325-9195
Canada	TTY (Teletypewriter): 416-325-7539
M4W 1A8	Website: www.ipc.on.ca

Information and Privacy Commissioner of Ontario

Source: Guidelines for the Use of Video Surveillance Cameras in Public Places, Information and Privacy Commissioner of Ontario (2007). Reproduced with permission.

APPENDIX C

Office of the Information and Privacy Commissioner for British Columbia

Public Surveillance System Privacy Guidelines

OIPC Reference Document 00-01

January 26, 2001
(Replaces: June 21, 2000)
*Text changes from the immediately preceding version
of this document are italicized.*

1.0 Purpose of This Document

There is a very real risk that within a few short years British Columbians could find themselves subjected to pervasive, routine and random surveillance of their ordinary, lawful public activities. Surveillance systems have, in recent years, proliferated; they are operated by a wide variety of public and private bodies. The result is widespread surveillance of our ordinary lives. There is a very real prospect that this will evolve into a blanket system of automated surveillance. In and of itself, each system might be lawful and reasonable, but the synergy of all systems operating together is something the public is likely to regret.

It is not sufficient to say that citizens need not fear surveillance if they have nothing to hide. This misses the point. Privacy is a fundamental human and civil right that has constitutional dimensions, under ss. 7 and 8 of the *Canadian Charter of Rights and Freedoms*. It is also recognized, and protected, by the *Freedom of Information and Protection of Privacy Act* ("Act"). The right to privacy must not be eroded simply because there is supposedly nothing to fear if you have nothing to hide. Citizens have the right to feel, and to be, secure in their daily lives, but they also have the right to be free of unwarranted intrusion into their lives.

These guidelines are designed to assist public bodies in deciding whether collection of personal information by means of a video, audio or other mechanical or electronic surveillance system is both lawful *and* justifiable as a policy choice and, if so, how privacy protection measures should be built into the system. The Office of the Information and Privacy Commissioner ("OIPC") strongly encourages all public bodies that use, or are considering the use of, surveillance systems to comply with these guidelines.

These guidelines are intended to apply to surveillance systems in open public spaces (including streets, highways, parks) and public buildings (including government buildings, libraries, hospitals and educational institutions). They do not deal with workplace surveillance issues arising where a public body employer wishes to engage in surveillance of employees. Workplace surveillance issues will be addressed in a future OIPC publication.

These guidelines also apply, in a more limited manner, to covert surveillance. Covert surveillance is surveillance that is conducted through the use of hidden recording devices. It can be a highly intrusive and privacy invasive form of surveillance due to its secretive nature. A detailed and comprehensive assessment must be conducted prior to the decision to implement covert surveillance, to ensure that it is the only available option and that benefits derived from the material obtained far outweigh the violation to the privacy rights of the subjects being observed. If a public body regularly engages in covert surveillance as a case-based investigative tool for law enforcement purposes (including detection of insurance or other fraud) it should have a protocol in place that establishes the decision-making process to be followed before it is used in a given case. The guidelines in this paper, except those related to notification, placement of equipment and the preparation of a Privacy Impact Assessment, will still apply to covert surveillance. If a public body is undertaking a new form of covert surveillance, consultation with the OIPC should take place and a Privacy Impact Assessment should be developed respecting the new form of covert surveillance.

> Note: These guidelines do not constitute a decision or finding by the OIPC respecting any matter within the jurisdiction of the Information and Privacy Commissioner under the Act. These guidelines do not affect the powers, duties or functions of the Information and Privacy Commissioner respecting any complaint, investigation or other matter under or connected with the Act and the matters addressed in this document. ·

2.0 Our Role

All public bodies covered by the Act are required to comply with the privacy protection provisions of Part 3 of the Act. Those provisions govern the collection, use, storage and disclosure of personal information by public bodies. The Act defines personal information as recorded information about an identifiable individual. Personal information includes race, ethnic origin, colour, age, and sex. Any record of the image of an identifiable individual, including the characteristics of race, ethnic origin, colour, age, or sex, is a record of personal information.

Where a surveillance system records visual or audio information that is personal information, the record, and the public body's practices respecting that personal information, are subject to the privacy protection provisions in Part 3 of the Act. The OIPC has a regulatory role in monitoring and enforcing compliance with those provisions. The OIPC may conduct audits of public bodies' surveillance systems under the authority of s. 42(1)(a) of the

Act. These audits will review public bodies' compliance with the Act's requirements.

3.0 General Comments and Concerns

It is lawful for public bodies to collect personal information only in circumstances permitted by s. 26 of the Act. Before a public body can lawfully implement a surveillance system, any resulting collection of personal information must be expressly authorized by statute (s. 26(a)), must be for the purposes of "law enforcement" as defined in the Act (s. 26(b)), or must relate directly to and be necessary for an operating program or activity of the public body (s. 26(c)). The Act defines "law enforcement" as: policing, including criminal intelligence systems; investigations that lead or could lead to a penalty or sanction being imposed; or proceedings that lead, or could lead, to a penalty or sanction being imposed. A public body must be prepared to demonstrate to the OIPC, with specific evidence, that its proposed or existing collection of personal information by surveillance system is authorized under the Act in one of the ways just described.

More important from a public policy perspective, the OIPC considers the effectiveness of public surveillance systems for law enforcement purposes to be open to question in almost all cases. As is noted below in section 4.1(a), a surveillance system should be used only where conventional means for achieving the same law enforcement objectives are *substantially* less effective than surveillance *and* the benefits of surveillance *substantially* outweigh any diminution of privacy inherent in the system's existence and use. Cost-savings alone are not, in the OIPC's view, sufficient justification to proceed with a surveillance system. Surveillance systems are not a cure-all. Their privacy implications require extreme caution and avoidance of their use is desirable wherever possible, even where they are lawful. Further, where surveillance is used, the system should be designed so that it creates the least possible privacy impacts.

4.0 Guidelines

4.1 Factors in Considering Use of Surveillance

In considering whether to use surveillance, public bodies should take the following steps:

(a) A public body should only use surveillance as a last resort. Other measures of deterrence or detection must be considered before surveillance is entertained as a solution. A surveillance system should be used only where conventional means for achieving the same law enforcement objectives are *substantially* less effective than surveillance and the benefits of surveillance *substantially* outweigh any diminution of privacy inherent in the system's existence and use. A public body should be prepared to demonstrate that these factors have been satisfied.

(b) Public bodies must be prepared to justify the use of a surveillance system on the basis of verifiable, specific reports of incidents of crime, public safety concerns or other compelling circumstances.

(c) Before implementing a surveillance system, a public body should complete a Privacy Impact Assessment ("PIA"), to assess the actual or potential effects the proposed surveillance may have on privacy and on the ways in which any adverse effects are to be mitigated. The OIPC has developed a model privacy impact assessment and a blank assessment form for use by public bodies. These documents are available at http://www.oipc.bc.ca/sector_public/resources/pia.htm.

(d) A copy of the completed PIA, together with the public body's case for implementing a surveillance system as opposed to other measures, as outlined in this section, should be sent to the OIPC, to the attention of the Executive Director, for review and comment. These documents should be received by the OIPC well before any final decision is made to proceed with surveillance.

(e) It is recommended that the public body consider conducting consultations with relevant stakeholders, who may be able to assist the public body in making an informed decision as to the necessity for, and acceptability to the public, of the proposed surveillance.

(f) The implemented surveillance system should be designed and operated so that the privacy intrusion it creates is no greater than is absolutely necessary to achieve the system's goals.

4.2 Creating Surveillance System Policies

Once a decision is made to use a surveillance system, the public body should do the following in creating and implementing a policy for operation of the system:

(a) The public body should develop a comprehensive written policy to govern the use of the system's equipment. The policy should address the location of recording equipment, which personnel are authorized to operate the system, the times when surveillance will be in effect, and the location of reception equipment (i.e., the place where audio, visual or other signals received through the system are monitored). Where the system creates a record, the policy should also deal with the matters discussed in section 4.4, below.

(b) The policy should designate one (preferably senior) person to be in charge of the system, including as regards the public body's privacy obligations under the Act and the policy. Any power for that person to delegate his or her role should be limited, and should include only other senior staff.

(c) The public body should require employees and contractors to review and apply the policy in performing their duties and functions related to operation of the surveillance system. Employees should be subject to discipline if they breach the policy or the relevant Act provisions. Where contractors are used, failure to comply with the policy, or the Act's provisions, should be a breach of contract leading to penalties up to and including contract termination. Employees and contractors (and contractor employees) should sign written agreements as to their duties under the policy.

(d) The policy should be incorporated into personnel training and orientation programs and contractors should be required to do the same with their employees. Public body and contractor personnel should periodically (preferably annually) have their awareness of the policy and Act refreshed. The policy itself should be reviewed regularly and updated as needed, ideally at least once every two years.

4.3 Layout of Surveillance Equipment

In designing a surveillance system and installing equipment, a public body should follow these guidelines:

(a) Installation of recording equipment such as video cameras or audio recording devices should be restricted to identified public areas. Areas chosen for surveillance should be those where surveillance is a necessary and viable deterrent, as contemplated by section 4.1(a). Recording equipment should not be positioned, internally or externally, to monitor areas outside a building, or to monitor other buildings, unless necessary to protect external assets or ensure personal safety. Cameras should not be directed to look through the windows of adjacent buildings. Equipment should not monitor areas where the public and employees have a reasonable expectation of privacy (such as change rooms and adult *or children's* washrooms). (This requirement may not always apply where covert surveillance is used. See Part 1.0, above.)

(b) A public body should restrict use of surveillance to periods when there is demonstrably a higher likelihood of crime being committed and detected in the area under surveillance.

(c) A public body should notify the public, using clearly written signs prominently displayed at the perimeter of surveillance areas, of surveillance equipment locations, so the public has ample warning that surveillance is or may be in operation before entering any area under surveillance. (Public bodies should remember that signs almost certainly serve as a general deterrent.) This requirement does not apply to covert surveillance. A public body's signs should identify someone who can answer questions about the surveillance system. An address or telephone number should be given for the contact person.

(d) Only authorized persons should have access to the system's controls and to its reception equipment.

(e) Receiving equipment (such as video monitors or audio playback speakers) should be in a controlled access area. Only the controlling personnel, or those properly authorized in writing by those personnel according to the public body's policy, should have access to the receiving equipment. Video monitors should not be located in a position that enables public viewing.

4.4 Guidelines Regarding Surveillance Records

If the surveillance system creates a record, the following policies and procedures for access, use, disclosure, retention and destruction should be implemented (and should form part of the policy discussed in section 4.2):

(a) All tapes or other storage devices (such as computer disks or chips) that are not in use should be stored securely in a locked receptacle located in a controlled access area. All storage devices that have been used should be numbered and dated.

(b) Access to the storage devices should be possible only by authorized personnel. Logs should be kept of all instances of access to, and use of, recorded material.

(c) A public body should develop written policies on the use and retention of recorded information that address all of the following:

(i) Under what circumstances information is viewed and by whom. (For example, are all recordings viewed routinely or only when an incident is reported? Who is authorized to view the recordings?) The public body's personnel should only view information where there is a need to do so, either because an incident has been reported or is suspected to have occurred.

(ii) If viewing the information reveals no incident, or no incident is reported, how long is the recorded information retained? Recorded information should be routinely erased where no incident has been reported, or where viewing the recorded information reveals no incident, according to a standard schedule (e.g., every 24 hours, 48 hours or week). The OIPC considers retention periods of not more than 30 days to be preferable, although circumstances may necessitate different retention periods.

(iii) When the recorded information reveals an incident, how long is it retained? (If the recorded information reveals an incident that contains personal information about an individual, and the public body uses this information to make a decision that directly affects the individual, s. 31 of the Act requires the recorded information to be retained for one year after the decision is made.)

(d) A public body should retain and store storage devices required for evidentiary purposes according to standard procedures until law enforcement authorities request them. A storage device release form should be completed before any storage device is disclosed to appropriate authorities. The form should indicate who took the device, under what authority, when this occurred, and if it will be returned or destroyed after use.

(e) An individual who is the subject of surveillance has a right to request access to his or her recorded personal information under s. 5 of the Act. Access in full or in part may be refused on one of the grounds set out in Division 2 of Part 2 of the Act. However, if that information can reasonably be severed from a record, an applicant has the right of access to the remainder of the record. Public body policies and procedures should be designed to accommodate this right to seek access.

(f) A public body must securely dispose of old storage devices. Physically breaking open a videotape cassette, audiotape, or computer disk is not sufficient. The storage media should be shredded, burned or magnetically erased.

4.5 Audit Procedures

Public bodies should ensure employers and contractors are aware of, and implement, the following audit procedures:

(a) All surveillance equipment operators must be aware that their operations are subject to audit and that they may be called upon to justify their surveillance interest in any given individual.

(b) A public body should appoint a review officer to audit the use and security of surveillance equipment, including monitors and storage devices. The reviews should be done periodically at irregular intervals. The results of each review should be documented in detail and any concerns should be addressed promptly and effectively.

APPENDIX D

Office of the Information and Privacy Commissioner for British Columbia

OPC Guidelines for the Use of Video Surveillance of Public Places by Police and Law Enforcement Authorities

March 2006

Over the past ten years, digital cameras have shrunk in cost and size, and have proliferated across the country. Networking these cameras used to be a significant expense, but now thanks to the Internet, wireless hubs, and progress in digital streaming and image compression, transmission adds little expense or technical challenges.

As a result, and partly in response to a growing perception that video surveillance increases our security, video surveillance of public spaces is increasing rapidly, by public sector authorities, private sector parties, and property owners.

Video surveillance of public places nonetheless presents a challenge to privacy, to freedom of movement and freedom of association, all rights we take for granted in Canada. This is especially true when the surveillance is conducted by police or other law enforcement authorities.

Widespread Use by Law Enforcement

The use of video surveillance to detect, deter and prosecute crime has increased significantly over the last few years – in Canada and abroad. Police and law enforcement authorities increasingly view it as a legitimate tool to combat crime and ward off criminal activity – including terrorism. Recent events have heightened the interest of public authorities in deploying video-surveillance in public places. It is widespread in the United Kingdom and increasingly used by law enforcement and anti-terrorism authorities in the U.S. and Canada, particularly since September 2001.

Here at home, police and public security agencies monitor public parks and streets. Some cities have put in place video surveillance systems for specific festival periods. The Royal Canadian Mounted Police (RCMP) use cameras to monitor high-security areas such as Parliament Hill. Cameras are used to survey Canada-US border crossings. They are very extensively used in airports, and port authorities are becoming increasingly interested in using video cameras to monitor their facilities.

A Challenge to Privacy

Video surveillance of public places subjects everyone to scrutiny, regardless of whether they have done anything to arouse suspicion. At the very least it circumscribes, if it does not eradicate outright, the expectation of privacy and anonymity that we have as we go about our daily business.

The medium's very nature allows law enforcement to observe and monitor the movements of a large number of persons, the vast number of whom are law-abiding citizens, where there are no reasonable grounds to be capturing a record of their activities. When video surveillance was done with tapes, where an operator had to watch each event to make a judgement about an individual, the volume of work kept misuse down to a minimum. Now we have facial recognition systems and pattern recognition software that can massage the vast stream of images, so the actual use of the data increases, even if it is not by human operators. The likelihood of images being retained for further data mining increases simply because the workload is now potentially manageable. The risk of systematized observations of groups or persons now exists, simply because it is technically feasible. On top of all this, fear of terrorism and street crime has driven the numbers of cameras up, as public officials seek to assuage the fears of citizens and gain control of the uncontrollable.

Proliferation of video-surveillance raises a concern that inferences will be drawn about people, that the data will be used for trivial or discriminatory purposes. People are well aware of the presence of cameras, in fact there is a brisk trade in fake cameras because they are promoted as being as effective as real ones in deterring bad behaviour. For these reasons, there is good reason to believe that video surveillance of public places by the police or other law enforcement authorities has a chilling effect on behaviour – and by extension on rights and freedoms.

The Need for Guidelines

Given the widespread use by police of video surveillance in public spaces, and its potentially chilling effect on privacy, the Office of the Privacy Commissioner of Canada (OPC) offers these guidelines to help define and circumscribe the use of this medium. The guidelines below set out principles for evaluating the need for resorting to video surveillance and for ensuring that, if it is conducted, it is done in a way that minimizes the impact on privacy.

These guidelines were developed as a result of the work of a discussion group established jointly by the Office of the Privacy Commissioner of Canada and the RCMP with other stakeholders, following an investigation into the use of video surveillance in Kelowna which started in 2001.

Notwithstanding discussions between the OPC and the RCMP, nothing in these guidelines should be considered to interfere with or fetter the discretion of the RCMP to carry out its responsibilities as it deems fit, or the discretion of the Office of the Privacy Commissioner of Canada to carry out its responsibilities, especially with respect to any complaint filed by an individual under the Privacy Act or the Personal Information Protection and Electronic Documents Act (PIPEDA).

In the conduct of these discussions, we reviewed the extent of use of video surveillance in Canada and abroad, the circumstances that gave rise to this use, the way in which video surveillance has been conducted, and an assessment of the effectiveness of the tool in curbing or investigating crime.

Scope of Application

The guidelines are intended as guidance for overt, general video surveillance by law enforcement agencies – what some police forces refer to as "community cameras" – in places to which the public has largely free and unrestricted access, such as streets or public parks.

They apply to continuous or periodic video recording, observing or monitoring of individuals in open, public spaces, in the absence of particularized suspicion of an individual or individuals.

While the guidelines can be used to promote and protect privacy in other settings, such as police facilities like cell blocks or interview rooms, and more generally could be useful as guidance for other applications of video surveillance technology, their scope remains within the limits of generalized surveillance of public spaces.

These guidelines are not intended to apply to circumstances where targeted video surveillance may be used as a case-specific investigative tool for law enforcement purposes, under statutory authority or the authority of a search warrant.

We anticipate that there will be further technical advances in video-surveillance, and that the appetite for its deployment will continue to grow. Since the OPC started working on these guidelines, there has been continued interest in the use of video surveillance by privacy and data protection authorities, in Canada and abroad. For example, the United Kingdom Home Office published in early 2005 an in-depth study assessing the impact of closed-circuit television systems implemented in a range of contexts. Closer to home, a number of provincial government departments and authorities have published guidelines for the use of video surveillance by public bodies. These include British Columbia, Alberta, Saskatchewan, Nova Scotia, New Brunswick, Newfoundland & Labrador, Ontario, and Quebec in particular which recently completed an extensive consultation on the use of video surveillance cameras in public places by government bodies.

As our knowledge of the efficacy and impact of video surveillance increases and becomes ever more precise, adjustments to how this technology should be controlled will likely need to be made. Indeed, as part of its Contributions Program, the OPC awarded in the fall of 2004 funding to Quebec's l'École nationale d'administration publique (ENAP) for research on the use of video surveillance cameras in public spaces in Canada. We received the ENAP's research report in December 2005 and plan to integrate its findings in future work we undertake on video surveillance.

The Office of the Privacy Commissioner will monitor the guidelines set out in this document to ensure that they continue to reflect needs dictated by the state of the technology and its implementation. In the meantime, we are analyzing the application of PIPEDA to the deployment of video surveillance by the private sector, and plan to publish our findings in this regard in 2006.

Guidelines

Video surveillance should only be deployed to address a real, pressing and substantial problem. The problem to be addressed by video surveillance must be pressing and substantial, of sufficient importance to warrant overriding the right of innocent individuals to be free from surveillance in a public place. Accordingly, concrete evidence of the problem to be addressed is needed. This should include real evidence of risks, dangers, crime rates, etc. Specific and verifiable reports of incidents of crime, public safety concerns or other compelling circumstances are needed, not just anecdotal evidence or speculation.

Video surveillance should be viewed as an exceptional step, only to be taken in the absence of a less privacy-invasive alternative. Less privacy-invasive alternative ways of addressing the identified problem should be chosen unless they are not feasible or significantly less effective.

The impact of the proposed video surveillance on privacy should be assessed before it is undertaken. A Privacy Impact Assessment of the proposed video surveillance should be conducted to determine the actual or potential kind and degree of interference with privacy that will result, and the ways in which adverse effects will be mitigated.

Public consultation should precede any decision to introduce video surveillance. Public consultation should be conducted with relevant stakeholders, including representatives of communities that will be affected. "Community" should be understood broadly; it should be recognized that a particular geographic area may have several distinct communities, and one community should not be presumed to speak for the others.

The video surveillance must be consistent with applicable laws. Video surveillance must be conducted in accordance with all applicable laws, including overarching laws such as the Canadian Charter of Rights and Freedoms and Quebec's Charter of Human Rights and Freedoms.

The video surveillance system should be tailored to minimize the impact on privacy. The surveillance system should be designed and operated so that the privacy intrusion it creates is no greater than absolutely necessary to achieve the system's goals. For example, limited use of video surveillance (e.g., for limited periods of day, public festivals, peak periods) should be preferred to always-on surveillance if it will achieve substantially the same result.

The public should be advised that they will be under surveillance. The public should be informed with clearly written signs at the perimeter of surveillance areas, which advise that the area is or may be under surveillance, and indicate who is responsible for the surveillance, including who is responsible for compliance with privacy principles, and who can be contacted to answer questions or provide information about the system.

Fair information practices should be respected in collection, use, disclosure, retention and destruction of personal information. The information collected through video surveillance should be minimal; its use should be restricted, its disclosure controlled, its retention limited, and its destruction assured. If a camera is manned, the recording function should only be turned on in the event of an observed or suspected infraction. If a camera records continuously, the recordings should be conserved for a limited time only, according to a retention schedule, unless they have captured a suspected infraction or are relevant to a criminal act that has been reported to the police. Information collected through video surveillance should not be used for any purpose other than the purpose that the police force or public authority has explicitly stated in the policy referred to in 14 below. Any release or disclosure of recordings should be documented.

Excessive or unnecessary intrusions on privacy should be discouraged. Surveillance cameras should not be aimed at or into areas where people have a heightened expectation of privacy: for example, windows of buildings, showers, washrooms, change rooms, etc. If cameras are adjustable by an operator, reasonable steps should be taken to ensure that they cannot be adjusted or manipulated to capture images in areas that are not intended to be under surveillance.

System operators should be privacy-sensitive. The operators of surveillance systems, including operators hired on contract, should be fully aware of the purposes of the system, and fully trained in rules protecting privacy.

Security of the equipment and images should be assured. Access to the system's controls and reception equipment, and to the images it captures, should be limited to persons authorized in writing under the policy referred to in 14 below. Recordings should be securely held, and access within the organization limited to a need-to-know basis.

The right of individuals to have access to their personal information should be respected. People whose images are recorded should be able to request access to their recorded personal information. Under many privacy statutes, they have a right of access. Severing the personal information in a recording (including technological blurring or blocking of the identities of others) may be necessary to allow individual access. Policies and procedures should be designed to accommodate these requests.

The video surveillance system should be subject to independent audit and evaluation. The system's operations should be subject to frequent audit, and its effectiveness should be evaluated regularly to identify unintended negative effects. Audit and evaluation should be conducted by persons or organizations independent of the management and direction of the video surveillance system. Audits should ensure compliance with the policy governing the system, including ensuring that only pertinent information is collected, that the system is used only for its intended purpose, and that privacy protections in the system are respected. Evaluation should take special note of the reasons for undertaking surveillance in the first place, as determined in the initial statement of the problem and the public consultation, and determine whether video surveillance has in fact addressed the problems identified at those stages. Evaluation may indicate that a video surveillance system should be terminated, either because the problem that justified it in the first place is no longer significant, or because the surveillance has proven ineffective in addressing the problem. Evaluation should take into account the views of different groups in the community (or different communities) affected by the surveillance. Results of audits and evaluations should be made publicly available.

The use of video surveillance should be governed by an explicit policy. A comprehensive written policy governing the use of the surveillance equipment should be developed. The policy should clearly set out:

- the rationale and purpose of the system
- the location and field of vision of equipment
- the rationale and purpose of the specific locations of equipment and fields of vision selected
- which personnel are authorized to operate the system
- the times when surveillance will be in effect
- whether and when recording will take place
- the place where signals from the equipment will be received and monitored, and
- the fair information principles applying to recordings, including

  - security
  - use
  - disclosure
  - retention and destruction
  - rights of individual access to personal information captured, and
  - rights to challenge compliance

The policy should identify a person accountable for privacy compliance and privacy rights associated with the system. The policy should require officers, employees and contractors to adhere to it, and provide sanctions if they do not. It should provide a process to be followed in the event of inadvertent privacy and security breaches. Finally, it should provide procedures for individuals to challenge compliance with the policy.

The public should have a right to know about the video surveillance system that has been adopted. Police forces and public authorities should recognize that individuals will want information about video surveillance systems. They may seek to know, for example, who has authorized the recording, whether and why their images have been recorded, what the images are used for, who has access to them, and how long they are retained. Police forces and public authorities should be prepared to provide this information.

Source: Guidelines for the Use of Video Surveillance of Public Places by Police and Law Enforcement Authorities, Office of the Information and Privacy Commissioner of Canada (2006). Reproduced with permission.

APPENDIX E

Rules for Use of Surveillance Cameras with Recording in Public Places by Public Bodies

June 2004

Table of Contents

Presentation

Camera surveillance of public places is a growing phenomenon in Québec, as the development of new technology facilitates access to this mode of surveillance. The growing sense of insecurity in modern societies has also rendered us more tolerant to the presence of cameras in public places. This tolerance, like the technology, has developed gradually.

However, the very concept of surveillance implies methods of population control associated with regimes remote from our democratic culture. On the contrary, the freedoms of citizens to circulate and assemble peacefully, and everyone's rights to privacy and personal freedom, recognized in our fundamental laws, give reason to believe that observation of the behaviour of individuals is still an act derogatory to our fundamental democratic values. With valid reason, therefore, camera surveillance has become a matter of concern for the Commission d'accès à l'information. The component of its mandate concerning protection of personal information is specifically intended to ensure that the collection, processing and retention of personal information respect the privacy of citizens in the face of the State's growing powers.

Aware of its responsibilities, the Commission d'accès à l'information has decided to issue rules for use of camera surveillance with recording. These rules provide public bodies with a common analytical framework. Their purpose is to guide decision-making by public bodies by offering them an approach that will allow them to find a fair balance among protection of personal information, privacy and security. These guidelines should be completed by a policy drafted in accordance with the Commission's current general rules.

Scope of Application

The following rules apply to camera surveillance of public places by public bodies.

Public bodies are those defined in sections 3 to 7 of the Act respecting access to documents held by public bodies and the protection of personal information. For example, they include municipalities (including their police departments), school institutions, educational institutions and transit authorities.

The public character of the place is due to its accessibility to the entire community. Streets, public parks, playgrounds, public transit systems, and common areas of educational institutions and hospitals will certainly be classified as "public places," to cite only these examples.

Similarly, it is understood that the rules do not cover surveillance of employee work areas or hospital rooms, because these places are not community spaces generally accessible to the public. Rather, by definition, they are spaces where the individual reasonably expects more privacy and solitude than in public spaces as such. The intended use of a place is therefore also a relevant indicator for recognizing a public space.

Likewise, these rules do not apply to surveillance used as an investigative method focusing on a specific individual or suspects.

In short, the following rules concern and govern the general observation of citizens by public bodies.

Justification

The use of camera surveillance represents a form of intrusion by government authorities into citizens' lives. This intrusion, which absorbs the image and behaviour of individuals, is an infringement of the right to privacy. This fundamental fact shall remain a concern of government agents that is reflected on their decision to resort to camera surveillance.

One of the essential bases of the Act respecting access to documents held by public bodies and the protection of personal information is to contain and limit the power of public bodies to collect personal information on citizens. This component is the concrete reflection of the right to privacy enshrined in Section 5 of the Québec Charter of Human Rights and Freedoms.

For the purposes of the Access Act, camera surveillance shall produce documents that are recovered and stored in any form. This does not mean that surveillance without recording, used as the extension of human surveillance by technical means, does not pose any problem with regard to respect for fundamental rights.

Once camera surveillance has the effect of collecting personal information on any medium regarding identifiable individuals, public bodies shall meet the criterion of necessity set out in Section 64 of the Access Act ("No person may, on behalf of a public body, collect nominative information if it is not necessary for the carrying out of the attributions of the body or the implementation of a program under its management").

In each case, the institutions shall be able to establish that the objective pursued by the use of camera surveillance is important enough to justify the collection of personal information. Then the institution shall adjust the scope of this method to ensure that the means deployed are proportional to the objective it is seeking.

Rules of Use

Factors to Consider before Opting for Camera Surveillance

1 Camera surveillance shall be necessary to achieve a specified purpose.

   It may not be used generally as a public security mechanism. The problem to be solved shall be identified, recurring and circumscribed.

2 The objective sought by the use of camera surveillance shall be serious and important.

   The prevention of minor offences or the occurrence of occasional problems cannot justify an invasion of individual privacy. Camera surveillance should not turn out to be an easy solution. In particular, the places targeted must be recognized as a source of criminal activity.

3 A report shall be produced concerning the concrete risks and real dangers presented by a situation regarding public order and the security of persons, places or property.

   This report should particularly deal with the following points:

   • the specific, serious and concordant events that have occurred;
   • clear identification of the problem to be solved;
   • the concrete and real public security requirements at stake;
   • the places targeted for camera surveillance and their relation to the grounds invoked;
   • the important, clear and precise objectives that have been identified.

4 Alternative solutions less prejudicial to privacy should have been considered or tested and have proved difficult to apply or implement or are ineffective.

   Depending on the problem to be solved and the places concerned, other solutions should have been tested or studied, particularly:

- the presence of security guards;
- foot patrols in key locations;
- the involvement of street workers;
- accompaniment to the car on request;
- better lighting of the zone to be protected (streets, parks, corridors, etc.);
- reinforcement of access doors;
- installation of protective grilles and alarm systems or marking of objects related to an alarm system;
- intervention by surveillance personnel;
- formation of a vigilance committee.

5 The real impact of camera surveillance shall be measured.

An analysis of the risks for protection of privacy has been completed.

The advantages and disadvantages of the measure shall be weighed, as well as its potentially perverse or undesirable effects, such as shifting criminal activity to another location. The effectiveness of the measure to correct the situation shall be conclusive.

6 The public body shall ensure the legitimacy of its objectives so that the purpose of camera surveillance cannot be diverted or distorted.

For example, camera surveillance shall not serve:

- to categorize or rank groups of people;
- to establish distinctions based on racial, religious, political or union affiliation or the sexual behaviour of individuals;
- to study human behaviour in order to exercise control over these persons.

7 The purpose of camera surveillance shall be transparent and explicit.

The populations concerned shall be consulted and involved before the decision is made.

The use of camera surveillance shall have been approved by the accountable authorities of the public body.

8 Camera surveillance shall be considered in conjunction with at least one of the factors set out in Rule 4 or its equivalent.

Rules Concerning Collection of Information

9 The public body shall designate from the outset a person responsible for the collection, retention and communication of data collected by means of camera surveillance.

At every step, this person shall ensure that these rules are observed.

10 Camera surveillance shall be adjusted as needed and adapted to the situation. The public body shall set limits for its use.

The periods of surveillance and eventually of recording, the area covered and the manner in which the operation will be conducted shall be designed to minimize the effects of camera surveillance and preserve the public's privacy as much as possible.

11 Camera surveillance shall be used only during critical events and for limited periods.

The use of cameras and recording shall be limited to specific times of day and periods of the year corresponding to the peak periods when crimes usually occur. For example, if it is established that offences are perpetrated on weekends, during the evening or at night, or during public holidays or specific events, camera surveillance shall not extend beyond these periods.

12 Only the necessary recordings shall be made.

When a person can permanently view the image captured by a camera, this person shall expect to have reasonable grounds to believe that an offence will be committed to start recording.

If nobody can view the screens continuously, the tape recordings shall be destroyed once they are no longer necessary.

13 The arrangement of the cameras and the type of technology used shall minimize the effects of camera surveillance on people's privacy.

The cameras shall not be directed at private locations, such as a home, building windows, shower rooms, toilet stalls or locker rooms. For this purpose, the new information technology of masking locations shall be adopted to avoid shooting private places or places not concerned by the camera surveillance operation.

The angles of vision, the type of cameras, and the zoom or stop image function shall be evaluated according to the ends sought and the appropriate means of achieving these ends. The same principle applies for use of equipment connected to an alarm or response centre.

14 The persons operating the devices shall be well aware of the rules intended to protect privacy.

The persons shall have received the appropriate training and know the limits imposed by the Act regarding protection of privacy before working as operators. The same principle applies for third parties, i.e. those not directly under the body's authority, in particular those involved by contract in camera surveillance.

15 The public concerned by this surveillance shall be informed by any appropriate notice.

Notices shall announce unequivocally that the place is the object of camera surveillance with recording.

These notices shall:

• be placed in visible locations, at a reasonable distance from the place under surveillance and have the format required by the spatial

context;
- mention the object of the camera surveillance and the name of the person responsible.

Rules Concerning Management of Information

16 The equipment used for the recording or recordings shall be protected.

The material recorded shall be the object of precise retention rules to protect the confidentiality of the data.

Security measures shall be implemented to restrict access to the viewing station and recordings to the persons expressly authorized for this purpose.

A limited number of authorized persons may have access to the premises accommodating the equipment and view the recordings.

17 Use of the recordings shall be limited.

Subject to the exceptions prescribed in the Access Act, the recordings shall not be disclosed to third parties. In this regard, the interconnection of surveillance systems, whether by Internet or otherwise, constitutes disclosure to a third party.

The recordings shall not be the object of associations of images or biometric data, particularly by means of automatic image consultation or facial recognition software.

The recordings shall not be matched, linked or shared with other files, nor serve to constitute data banks.

18 The recording media shall be taken into account in the retention schedule.

The recording media shall be numbered and dated for each site that has been the object of surveillance.

Apart from judicial requirements and police or administrative investigations, the recordings are erased or destroyed as soon as their retention is no longer necessary.

19 A person is entitled to access to the information concerning him.

This person is entitled to access to the recordings made in accordance with the Access Act.

The Decision to Resort to Camera Surveillance Shall Be Reviewed Periodically

20 The public body shall periodically review (at least on an annual basis) the necessity of its decisions regarding camera surveillance.

The following aspects shall be considered for this purpose:
- the initial grounds still exist;
- the expected results are achieved. Otherwise, the public body must question the actual effects of the process;

- the conditions of use are still adequate and adapted to the situation;
- the appropriateness of the type of cameras used and their number;
- a more appropriate alternative compatible with the right to privacy cannot now be envisioned;
- if applicable, the number of hours of recording per day and the recording periods during the week or the year.

Adoption of Policy on Use of Camera Surveillance

The public bodies should adopt a policy on use of camera surveillance with recording in public places in the light of these rules.

In particular, this policy should define the public consultation mechanism before proceeding to use camera surveillance.

Source: Authorization to reproduce granted by Les Publications du Québec.

Notes

Chapter 1: Introduction

1 The cities or towns that have investigated and rejected streetscape monitoring programs include Nanaimo, Victoria, and Penticton, British Columbia; Lethbridge, St. Albert, and Medicine Hat, Alberta; Guelph, Cardinal, and Barrie, Ontario; Saskatoon and Fort Qu'Appelle, Saskatchewan; and Selkirk and Dauphin, Manitoba.

2 The federal government of Canada and the provincial governments of Ontario and British Columbia have made three significant investments in public-area CCTV surveillance. First, following the 7/7 terrorist attacks, in November 2006 the federal government invested $37 million as part of a cost-sharing program to increase public transit security. Among the provisions set out in the funding package was the expansion of CCTV surveillance on public buses and trains. The funding, part of an $80 million surveillance network initiative, was directed toward intensifying transit security in six major cities (Ottawa-Gatineau, Toronto, Calgary, Edmonton, Vancouver, and Montreal). Second, the Toronto Police Service received funding from the Ontario government's Ministry of Community Safety and Correctional Services. In 2006, the ministry granted up to $2 million for the Toronto Police Service to pilot a streetscape CCTV surveillance program. Third, in 2008, the solicitor general of British Columbia earmarked $1 million to fund streetscape surveillance in the cities of Kelowna, Surrey, Williams Lake, and Vancouver (see Chapter 8). Branches of the Ontario government also granted a total of $100,000 to fund an audit of streetscape monitoring in the city of Sudbury (see Chapter 4) and to provide startup funds in the city of Brockville (see Chapter 9). And in 2005, Transport Canada commissioned a study of public opinions about surveillance in the public transit system.

3 See http://www.priv.gc.ca/.

4 In 2001, the Personal Information Protection and Electronic Documents Act (PIPEDA) was introduced; it applies to the collection, use, or disclosure of personal information in connection with the operation of federal works, undertakings, or businesses and to the disclosure of personal information outside a province for consideration. In 2002, PIPEDA was expanded to cover the health sector. In 2004, organizations collecting personal information through commercial activity fell under PIPEDA, save in provinces that had similar privacy laws (i.e., Quebec, Alberta, British Columbia, and Ontario). The act applies to all collections, uses, or disclosures of personal information in the course of commercial activity, either within or outside a province.

5 See http://www.ipc.on.ca/ for the Ontario OIPC's updated guidelines; http://www.oipc.bc.ca/ for the BC OIPC guidleines; and http://www.cai.gouv.qc.ca/ for the Quebec Commission d'accès à l'information guidelines.

6 Privacy pragmatism is an orientation to privacy advocacy that balances the needs and desires of surveillance advocates with the interests of minimizing privacy invasion. In the context of streetscape CCTV surveillance in Canada, pragmatism has involved encouraging proponents of public-area and streetscape CCTV systems to comply voluntarily

with a set of principles designed to minimize the impact of video surveillance on privacy infringement.

7 Flaherty's report (published in March 1998) briefly outlines eight guidelines that public bodies should review before considering the use of video surveillance: written policy; camera location, operation, and control; operational times; protection of information and disclosure; public awareness of cameras; audits; use of information collected; and access to personal information. Cavoukian's report (published in September 1998) focuses on covert surveillance and presents eleven privacy considerations for institutions considering the use of video surveillance: definitions of personal information, as conceptualized in the Freedom of Information and Protection of Personal Privacy Act and the Municipal Freedom of Information and Protection of Personal Privacy Act; needs assessment, including authority of data collection; collective agreements (i.e., data-sharing agreements); access to personal information; provisions set out in section 8 of the Canadian Charter of Rights and Freedoms; advice of legal council; notice provisions; protection of confidentiality; use and retention protocols; circumstances leading to videotape use; and auditing.

8 The study spanned six years, with the major data-gathering activities taking place between 2005 and 2008. The project was supported by a Social Sciences and Humanities Research Council of Canada (SSHRC) Standard Research Grant. The project was also supported by an internal SSHRC grant at the University of Victoria (2004-5) and a SSHRC-funded postdoctoral fellowship on the Surveillance Project at Queen's University (2003-4).

9 Over parts of the six-year investigation, the research team was composed of Josh Greenberg, Carleton University, and a set of research assistants at Carleton University, Queen's University, and the University of Victoria that conducted interviews, performed document analyses, investigated the scope of monitoring programs, and analyzed media stories.

10 The questionnaire was submitted as the initial phase of Walby's (2005b) investigation.

11 In the beginning of each empirically driven chapter (i.e., Chapters 3-9), the interviewees directly informing data analyses and the enactment of the social history of monitoring initatives are listed to avoid repetitive citations in the text.

Chapter 2: Establishing Streetscape Monitoring Programs

1 The arguments in the first portion of this section are adapted from Hier et al. (2007).

Chapter 3: Monitoring Programs in French Canada

1 This chapter focuses strongly on Sherbrooke because it was the centre of the earliest and some of the most important privacy protection intervention in Canada.

2 Rules for Use of Surveillance Cameras with Recording in Public Places by Public Bodies was introduced in 2004 (see Appendix E).

3 Information presented in this section of the chapter is based in part on interviews with Steven Webkins, deputy directeur général, City of Drummondville (4 May 2007; 14 February 2008); Gilles Troie, City of Drummondville (4 May 2008); Claude Proulx, directeur général, City of Drummondville (4 May 2007); G. Séguin, City of Drummondville (5 May 2007); and Thérèse Cajole, City of Drummondville (15 May 2007).

4 The information in this section of the chapter is based in part on interviews with Johanne Mercier, Sherbrooke Police Services (22 February 2007); Constable Martin Carrier, Sherbrooke Police Services (25 January 2007); Pierre-Hugues Boisvenu, Murdered or Missing Persons' Families' Association (2 January 2007); and Josée Anctil, CALACS Estrie, a sexual assault prevention and awareness organization (28 January 2007, 28 April 2008).

5 The four phases represent overlapping developments in video surveillance in Sherbrooke. They should be constructed as analytical more than empirical.

6 See http://www.iijcan.org/.

7 The King Street Bridge camera was installed primarily to monitor river levels in the spring.

8 Section 3 of the Access Act defines public bodies thus:

> The Government, the Conseil exécutif, the Conseil du Trésor, the government departments and agencies, municipal and school bodies and the health services and social services institutions are public bodies ... The Lieutenant-Governor, the National Assembly, agencies whose members are appointed by the Assembly and every person

designated by the Assembly to an office under its jurisdiction, together with the personnel under its supervision, are classed as public bodies ... Exception: The courts within the meaning of the Courts of Justice Act (chapter T-16) are not public bodies (1982, c. 30, s. 3; 1982, c. 62, s. 143; 1992, c. 21, s. 375).

See http://www2.publicationsduquebec.gouv.qc.ca/.

9   He also founded the Murdered or Missing Persons' Families' Association, and he published *Survivre à l'innommable: Et reprendre le pouvoir sur la vie* (2008).

10 Statistics Canada identified Sherbrooke as the safest city in Canada in 2000, but the police defended their use of cameras to police nightlife and the notorious bar flush.

11 After the second phase of the pilot project, the CAI periodically sent on-site inspectors to oversee the monitoring system. The inspectors voiced concerns about the ability of camera operators to see through windows.

12 The 2007 summer monitoring intervals cost the city $32,538 in equipment and labour, excluding administration of the program by salaried staff (Mercier and Racine 2008).

13 Information in this section of the chapter is based in part on interviews with Pierre Caron, City of Gatineau deputy police chief (21 May 2008); Claude Millette, one-time member of the Comité du renouveau de la Promenade du Portage (23 April 2008); Claude Bonhomme, one-time member of the Comité du renouveau de la Promenade du Portage (27 August 2008); and Danni Belisle, City of Hull lawyer (27 April 2008).

14 The Temperance Act was passed in Ontario in 1916. It led to the immediate closure of establishments serving alcohol. Beer and wine were sold in hotels by 1934, but alcohol was not sold in other establishments until 1946. After 1927, the Liquor Control Board of Ontario also maintained strict control over alcohol consumption, particularly consumption patterns of Natives, women, and known drunks (see Thompson 2009).

15 The drinking age in Quebec was eighteen; in Ontario, it was nineteen.

16 At one point, city council attempted to introduce a special booze tax to cover the costs of policing and vandalism. Council also tried to impose special taxes on bars in the late 1980s and early 1990s. And in 1984, it approved zoning changes that limited opportunities to open new bars along the Promenade and on Saint Joseph Boulevard.

17 The zero-tolerance policy was also criticized for excessive levels of harassment, racism, over-policing, and privacy violations (see Upton 1992). In the days following the introduction of zero tolerance, for example, Hull police shot a dog on a crowded street around 1 a.m. After approaching the dog's owner and requesting him to put a leash on the dog, the owner released the dog. Police arrested the man, prompting the dog to bark and growl. The dog was shot thirteen times.

18 The start-up money was taken out of the match-funded revitalization project.

19 The impact of closing time harmonization was felt in Ottawa. In the period spanning 1995-98, the number of bars in the Byward Market increased from twenty-three to thirty-five. Yet the spatial layout of the market was different than it was in Hull. The legal drinking age in Ontario remained at 19, and Ottawa supported a far more efficient public transit system (Brosseau and Cellard 2003). For these reasons, Ottawa did not become a transplanted Hull.

20 The information presented in this section of the chapter is based in part on interviews with Hélène Martel, community organizer, Centre de santé et des services sociaux de Manicouagan (Health and Social Services Centre of Manicouagan) (8 August 2007), and François Corriveau, city clerk, Ville de Baie-Comeau (17 November 2008).

21 Crime analyses in the city are conducted in eight city blocks.

22 The city purchased two cameras, two monitors, and two mini-computers for approximately $20,000. It also covered the ongoing costs of administration.

23 Manicouagan is a regional county municipality located on the north shore of the St. Lawrence River in eastern Quebec.

24 Centrealarme retained the recorded images for twenty-four hours before it replaced them with new images. The city did not post signs informing the public that the area was under video surveillance, and no consultation was held with city partners associated with the social service sector (e.g., social workers, youth services workers) or the schools in the area under surveillance.

25 Although Bilodeau consulted representatives beyond the formal CCTV surveillance advocacy network, he also questioned why social services representatives had not been quicker to respond to the shift in drug use and the concomitant spike in crime. Social services workers, he argued, could have responded more independently to drug-use problems. Bilodeau speculated that, if social services workers had been more proactive, there would be grounds to adopt a more critical position on the use of the CCTV surveillance camera.

26 Social services representatives informed Bilodeau that youth loitering had shifted from the alleyway in question to the courtyard bordering the yard of Pavillion Richelieu beyond Saint-Coeur-de-Marie School and to the Trudel schoolyard and the skate park. Bilodeau observed this on his visit to Baie-Comeau. The SQ failed to provide requested crime statistics for 2002 to examine better what the shift meant for criminality in the city.

27 One reason why the CAI chose to ignore this recommendation was that the 2003 public hearings were coming up.

Chapter 4: Sudbury's Lions Eye in the Sky

1 The information in this chapter is based in part on interviews with Alex McCauley, former Sudbury police chief (17 April 2006); Jan Moore, communications officer, Sudbury Police Service (24 April 2006); Maureen Luoma, executive director, Sudbury Metro Centre (25 April 2006); Lucy Derro, administrator, Christ the King Centre (seniors' independent living) (24 April 2006); Mike Lawson, Northern Voice and Video (24 April 2006); Carole Pilon, housing support/youth worker, Sudbury Action Centre for Youth (25 April 2006); John Rutherford, owner of Black Cat (a downtown bookstore) (26 April 2006); Sharon Baiden, Sudbury Police Service (26 April 2006; 17 May 2006); Richard Deypuk, Sudbury Police Service (26 April 2006); Tom Walton, Lions Eye in the Sky Video Monitoring Advisory Committee (18 May 2006); and Marlene Gorman, executive director, Sudbury Action Centre for Youth (9 June 2006).

2 These oversights are significant: Sudbury is a bilingual city with a little less than 30 percent of the population reporting French as a primary language (Statistics Canada 2001).

3 The stipulations presented in *Guidelines* are influenced by the MFIPPA and FIPPA, but they focus more clearly on video surveillance practices. Cavoukian's (1998) position paper more directly engages with MFIPPA and FIPPA and abstracts the general principles to video surveillance practices.

4 The Metro Centre (Sudbury's downtown business improvement association) launched the Downtown Action Agenda in November 1995. The agenda called for urgent proactive measures to help revitalize the core. The same year the Sudbury city councillor for the downtown area filed an appeal with the Ontario Municipal Board; he complained that planning and development trends in the city had caused a migration of businesses from the downtown area. This migration, he argued, left empty offices and stores, and it contributed to a disintegration of community relations in the area (Carmichael 1995b). Indeed, the *Sudbury Star* articulated concerns about the downtown area in a set of articles under the title of "What's Ailing Downtown?" The series concentrated on the perception of high crime and the closure of businesses in the core (Carmichael 1995a; Gordon 1995).

5 Managers of downtown banks had approached police to raise concerns about panhandling around automated teller machines. There are four banks in the downtown area.

6 McCauley was inspired by Glasgow's City Watch program, which became operational in November 1994. City Watch, a streetscape CCTV surveillance system composed of thirty-two civilian-monitored cameras distributed across the city centre, originated with the Glasgow Development Agency's efforts to promote economic development by addressing real or perceived criminal activity (Fyfe and Bannister 1996). A partnership between the Glasgow Development Agency and the Strathclyde Regional Council led to around-the-clock monitoring of the city's main business, commercial, cultural, and tourist areas.

7 In 1995, the images from the underpass cameras were apparently used to identify a murder suspect (Brazeau 1995).

8 The existence of an actual written proposal could not be confirmed. Chief McCauley speculates that there must have been something written down, but he has no recollection of any specific document. Data-gathering activities with the Greater Sudbury Police Service and the Metro Centre failed to uncover a written proposal.

9   One of the most significant infrastructural factors that enabled video surveillance monitoring in Sudbury was Bell Canada's deregulation in the early 1990s. In 1996, Sudbury Hydro, in collaboration with Cisco Systems, AT&T Canada, and a variety of public and private sector partners, utilized existing electric infrastructure in the city to overlay fifty-two kilometres of fibre optic cables and a broadband asynchronous transfer mode network. The availability of fibre optic cables in the city made possible the transmission of video surveillance camera images at low cost.

10 The project ended up costing police $3,600 for cable rentals from Northern Cable Holdings.

11 Since its inception in 1997, the composition of the committee has remained stable, save for periods in which the committee was unable to fill all the positions. Representatives from the Lions Club joined the committee in 1998, and a student representative position was added in 2007. After 1997, the members of the committee accepted applications from members of the community. The committee favoured applicants with a clear interest in the downtown area.

12 The cameras were linked to a monitoring network that included interior and exterior cameras on the newly established police headquarters. The police station was moved to Tom Davies Square at 200 Brady Street after a bomb was placed against the west wall of the former police station on Larch Street. The bomb was detonated on 15 December 1996 at approximately 1:45 a.m. (Pender 1996).

13 The Police Services Board estimated start-up costs of $52,300 in camera equipment and $3,600 for cabling (Greater Sudbury Police Service 2005). By the end of November, the LVMAC had raised $48,000 from the Lions Club, $10,000 from the Metro Centre, and $7,500 from insurance companies. The total cost of three cameras and equipment was $66,500. Northern Video donated switching equipment, software, and installation and training costs to maintain the system.

14 For example, representatives of the Toronto Police Service visited Sudbury to attend an LVMAC meeting and examine the system. Members of the LVMAC were subsequently invited to present in Toronto. Mike Shea of the Hamilton Police Services also visited Sudbury in 2003 (see Chapter 7).

15 Another advantage of using social assistance recipients to monitor cameras was that Ontario Works paid the LVMAC (through the Sudbury Police Service) to provide workers with practical work experience. The Sudbury Police Service negotiated an agreement with the Social Services Advisory Board to receive $15,000. The funds were used to subsidize the operating costs of the scheme (Lions Video Monitoring Advisory Committee 1998b). Training workers also further enabled members of the LVMAC to promote the system as a community-service initiative by claiming that they were providing skills and training to people on social assistance. In fact, as a component of the LVMAC's promotional strategy, Ontario Works used the monitoring program in an information video (Lions Video Monitoring Advisory Committee 1998b).

16 In March 1999 the Metro Centre donated $2,800, and in June 1999 the California Company donated $9,000.

17 Camera operators from Ontario Works are not long-term employees, and the lack of full-time monitoring staff results in unmanned cameras at night and on weekends.

18 Two absences in the KPMG report are noteworthy. First, the audit fails to address the issue of recording surveillance images, an issue that was so important in Sherbrooke. In fact, a pattern across Anglo-Canadian privacy advocacy is to encourage responsible handling of recorded images rather than challenge the practice of recording. Second, the audit fails to address privacy protection advocacy that took place in Quebec.

19 In 2005, the camera was decommissioned because Teletech's lease on the parking lot expired.

Chapter 5: Kelowna and the Constitutional Debate about Public-Area Video Surveillance

1   The information in this chapter is based partially on interviews with Karen Cairns, communications manager, City of Kelowna (25 August 2005); Ron Born, city manager, City of Kelowna (30 August 2005); Bill McKinnon, Kelowna RCMP (18 August 2005); Doug

Brecknell, Kelowna RCMP (18 August 2005); Barry Clark, Kelowna City Council (19 August 2005); Clint McKenzie, Downtown Kelowna Association (30 August 2005); Reg Burgess, Kelowna RCMP (30 August 2005); Walter Gray, former mayor of Kelowna (30 August 2005); Joe Gordon, lawyer in the City of Kelowna (29 August 2005); Wade Jenson, lawyer in the City of Kelowna (29 August 2005); Selena Stearns, executive director, Kelowna Drop-In Centre (31 August 2005); Randy Benson, executive director, Gospel Mission, City of Kelowna (31 August 2005); Sharon Sheppard, former city councillor and current mayor, City of Kelowna (31 August 2005); Don Harrison, Kelowna RCMP (7 September 2005); Jim Porter, Trojan Security, City of Kelowna (31 August 2005); Terisa Eichler, youth worker, City of Kelowna (30 August 2005); Bruce Phillips, one-time information and privacy commissioner of Canada (10 February 2006); and David Loukidelis, information and privacy commissioner of British Columbia (24 August 2005).

2 In 1997 and 1998, the RCMP received a number of complaints from merchants about drug dealing in Kerry Park and the negative effects that it had on commercial tourist activity in the area.

3 See census figures at http://www12.statcan.ca/.

4 The population of Kelowna was estimated at 89,500 in 1996 and 96,000 in 2001. Nearly 20 percent of the population is over sixty-five years of age.

5 As the number of retirees and tourists close to the waterfront continued to grow in the context of urban sprawl in the early 1990s, a number of strip malls appeared along Highway 97. The highway runs through the Okanagan Valley and is the main thoroughfare connecting downtown Kelowna to the perimeter and to other regions of the Okanagan. Acceleration of commercial development along Highway 97 in Kelowna increasingly pulled commercial activity away from the downtown core.

6 Members of the public were not informed that the area was under video surveillance. No signs were posted, and no public meetings were held.

7 In August 1999, Craig Jones, president of the BCCLA, wrote to the RCMP in Kelowna to argue that cameras fail to achieve safety objectives and that they do not warrant the infringement of personal privacy.

8 The interior of Kasugai Garden is visible from the planning department in city hall. Employees at city hall reported seeing what appeared to be drug dealing in the park.

9 As Lett (2007) explains, among city officials, transients are understood as out-of-town types who take advantage of Kelowna's warm weather and seasonal labour opportunities at surrounding farms.

10 Loukidelis sent a letter to the City of Kelowna on 9 February 2000 to express concerns about using video surveillance cameras in public areas. The letter was in response to a complaint laid against the camera in Kerry Park.

11 On 29 June 2001, Mayor Gray responded to Loukidelis, stating that the cameras comply with the requirements set out by the OPC. Gray informed Loukidelis that Commissioner Phillips had found no fault with the monitoring systems in Kelowna (City of Kelowna n.d.).

12 Released by the OPC.

13 The section states that "no personal information shall be collected by a government institution unless it relates directly to an operating program or activity of the institution." According to the Privacy Act, personal information refers to "information about an identifiable individual that is recorded in any form."

14 The cameras were set up to demonstrate the capabilities of CCTV surveillance for marketing purposes.

15 Radwanski's office also investigated a PIPEDA complaint laid by an employee of a company that supplied a railway company. The complainant charged that the railway had not instituted appropriate security measures to safeguard his personal information against unauthorized use; that the company had inappropriately collected his personal information via video surveillance without consent; and that the company had disclosed to his employer, without his consent, that he had filed a complaint with the OPC – a complaint that led to his termination (Office of the Information and Privacy Commissioner of Canada 2002). In 2003, a similar case was investigated concerning Toronto's CP Rail using digital video surveillance cameras throughout its rail yard (Office of the Information and Privacy Commissioner of Canada 2003a).

16   Released by the OPC.
17   After the letter was sent to Minister MacAulay, the Department of Justice started to examine Commissioner Radwanski's approach to privacy advocacy (compared to that of Commissioner Phillips), his dealings with the media, his relationship with federal departments, and the "vigorous debate and controversy" generated by his findings pertaining to anti-terrorism legislation after 9/11 and to passenger information gathering, storage, and sharing by Air Canada (Department of Justice n.d.a).
18   *R. v. Wong*, 60 C.C.C. (3d) 460, [1990] 3 S.C.R. 36, 1 C.R. (4th), PN 2004-87.
19   Canadian Charter of Rights and Freedoms, s. 8.
20   Similar speeches were delivered in Vancouver (Radwanski 2002b), Hamilton (Radwanski 2002c), and Toronto (Radwanski 2002d) – all cities contemplating video surveillance systems – from February to May 2002.
21   Part of Radwanski's justification for filing the suit concerned the fact that other police forces, including those in Edmonton, Halifax, Toronto, Vancouver, and Calgary, had expressed interest in public-area streetscape video surveillance.
22   For instance, in his 2000-1 annual report to Parliament, Radwanski issued an urgent warning about post-9/11 security measures. He reiterated his concerns when Bill C-17 (the Public Safety Act) was proposed.
23   The interim commissioner dealt with complaints about CCTV surveillance cameras capturing images of a publicly accessible boardwalk area in Nanaimo, British Columbia. See http://www.privcom.gc.ca/.
24   Interviews with study participants across the country revealed a constant theme of ridiculing Radwanski as untrustworthy and radically left.
25   The NCPB was involved, as well as the Community, Contract, and Aboriginal Policing Services, because both agencies had developed basic operational manuals on community cameras.
26   Two funded investigations stemmed from this initiative: Christian Boudreau and Monica Tremblay's (2006) *L'utilisation des caméras de surveillance dans les lieux à accès public au Canada* and David Lyon's Surveillance Camera Awareness Network study (see Chapter 10).
27   Despite claims that the RCMP would publicly disclose the results of the study, repeated efforts by members of the research team never confirmed that the evaluation had been conducted.
28   The analyst charged with reviewing the proposed guidelines was given a single business day to report on issues/concerns to the RCMP as well as to identify differences between the federal guidelines and the guidelines listed on a provincial comparison chart provided by the OPC. In the analysis, the analyst notes the inappropriateness of the CCAPS making recommendations to the RCMP and the inadequate time allocation to perform the task (Community, Contract and Aboriginal Policing Services 2004).
29   In 2002, the city started to include a question on video surveillance in its annual residents' survey. The question read, "Do you agree with the RCMP's use of community safety cameras as a crime prevention tool?"
30   Signs notifying the public about the Queensway camera were moved to City Park and the surrounding Leon-Abbott area.
31   Translink Vancouver staff recommended installing cameras in the parkade based on their experiences administering more than 700 cameras.

Chapter 6: London's Downtown Camera Project
1   Information presented in this chapter is based in part on interviews with Amanda Alvaro, one-time member of Friends Against Senseless Endings and co-chair of the Coordinating Committee for Community Safety (12 April 2006); Steve Goodine, sergeant of community services, London Police Service (26 April 2006); David Tennant, the Hampton Group and former co-chair of the Coordinating Committee for Community Safety (27 April 2006); Marie DeCicco, mayor, City of London (27 April 2006); David O'Brien, manager of corporate security, City of London (27 April 2006; 3 April 2009); and Sandy Levin, former city councillor, City of London (27 April 2006).

2 Sudbury's LVMAC sent promotional and operational materials to Goodine as well as the five-minute promotional video (see Chapter 4). A brief overview of monitoring in Glasgow is provided in Chapter 4. The monitoring program in Ipswich entailed seventy-two cameras used to monitor a variety of public spaces.

3 Both men, unknown to one another, were taken to the London Health Sciences Centre. Goldie-Ryder was placed on life support until he died on 19 January. Beebe survived the attack.

4 Within a month's time, signs appeared in downtown bars warning patrons that knives were not permitted. Bar owners were also supplied with information (from the police) about their rights and responsibilities under the Liquor Licence Act, the Trespass to Property Act, and the Criminal Code of Canada.

5 The meeting was held a week after another knife attack in downtown London on 3 February (Howe 1999).

6 Williamson was a young father engaged to be married when he was randomly stabbed to death in 1995 on a downtown London street corner. He was killed outside a downtown bar while he waited for his father to pick him up after an evening of drinking.

7 The Legislative Subcommittee made recommendations to the LPSB on 25 March 1999. The recommendations were approved.

8 The Educational Subcommittee's awareness and educational strategies were based on similar strategies adopted by Mothers Against Drunk Driving (MADD). They sought to induce measurable changes in young people's perceptions of wearing and carrying knives, in a manner similar to how MADD changed attitudes about drinking and driving.

9 The campaign entailed distributing nearly 6,000 gold ribbons to churches, schools, community centres, et cetera in late February 1999. The purpose was to symbolize and raise awareness of knife-related violence.

10 A few months before Tennant publicized funding commitments primarily from London-area businesses, London Hydro agreed to cover half of the cost of installing new lighting fixtures in the core (approximately $900,000). In the fall of 1999, FASE also requested $100,000 through the National Crime Prevention Bureau Grant Program.

11 Letter from David Tennant to Mayor Anne Marie DeCicco, 16 March 2000; released by the City of London's manager of records and information services.

12 "CCTV Question," e-mail from Sandy Levin to Al Gramolini, 30 January 1999 (response on 31 January 1999); released by the City of London's manager of records and information services and by Councillor Levin.

13 Other stakeholders identified are the CCCS (with a mandate to raise start-up funds for the system), the City of London (with a mandate to research liability and privacy matters), London Hydro (with a mandate to manage technical operations), and the LPS (with a mandate to work in an advisory capacity with the DSCAC).

14 Section 2(3) of MFIPPA defines bodies comprising municipal institutions as appointed or chosen by or under the authority of the council of the municipality (R.S.O. 1990, c. M.56, s. 2(3); 2002, c. 17, Sched. F, table).

15 "Downtown Surveillance Camera System," memorandum to Chairs and Members, Community and Protective Services Committee, from Jeff Malpass, Deputy City Manager, 27 March 2000; released by City of London's manager of records and information services.

16 Letter from David Tennant and Mandy Alvaro, Co-Chairs, Coordinating Committee for Community Safety, to Anne Marie DeCicco, 16 March 2000; released by the City of London's manager of records and information services.

17 Letter from Police Chief Gramolini to Councillor Ab Chahbar, Chair of the CPSC, 30 March 2000; released by the City of London's manager of records and information services.

18 On the day the council met, Deborah Goldie-Ryder authored an editorial in the *London Free Press* (see Goldie-Ryder 2000). She argued that, if every person in London allocated $1.06 of their annual tax dollars, the expense of the cameras would be covered.

19 Mirtech proposed two systems to the city: one based on fibre optics, and the other based on wireless transmission. The wireless system was selected because of excessive costs associated with laying fibre optic cables. As the system was being planned, Steve Goodine

and David O'Brien visited the Toronto Police Service headquarters on 17 December 2001 to present on streetscape CCTV surveillance. Letter from Staff Superintendent Operational Support, Toronto Police Service, to Mayor Anne Marie DeCicco, 28 January 2002; released by the City of London's manager of records and information services.

20 "Request for Proposals 00-47, Monitored Surveillance Camera Program," Community and Protective Services Committee, 21 March 2001; released by the City of London's manager of records and information services.

21 The Bank of Nova Scotia, where Goldie-Ryder's mother worked, pledged $24,000. Another six donors (the Hampton Group, the *London Free Press*, Ceeps and Barney's, Aboutown Transportation, the London Police Service Board, and the University of Western Ontario board of governors) pledged $12,500. An anonymous donation of $50,000 was also received.

22 Letter from Brian Beamish, Ontario OIPC, to Cathie Best, FOI Co-ordinator, Corporation of the City of London, 10 August 2001; released by the City of London's manager of records and information services.

23 Letter from Margery Sherritt, Chair, CPSC, to Bob Blackwell, Legal Services, City of London, 26 November 2001; released by the City of London's manager of records and information services.

24 Letter from Arthur Horrell, President, Neighbourhood Watch London, to Board of Control, City of London, c/o Guy Hallman, City Clerk, 25 July 2002; released by the City of London's manager of records and information services.

25 Letter from Ann Cavoukian, Information and Privacy Commissioner of Ontario, to Michelle Smibert, FOI Co-ordinator, City of London, 26 September 2002; released by the City of London's manager of records and information services.

26 London Police Service, "Public Needs Survey."

27 E-mail "RE: Information Report on CCTV Project" from Sandy Levin to Fred Tranquilli and David O'Brien, 9 February 2003; released by the City of London's manager of records and information services.

28 As of 8 December 2005, the CCCS had reimbursed the city $188,500.

Chapter 7: The Expansion of Streetscape Monitoring Programs

1 The information in this section of the chapter is based partially on interviews with Mike Shea, Hamilton Police Service (14 June 2006); John Petz, Hamilton Police Service (14 June 2006); Ken Weatherill, Hamilton Police Service (1 June 2006); Mary Pocius, executive director, International Village Business Improvement Association, City of Hamilton (14 June 2006); Kathy Drewit, executive director, Hamilton Downtown Business Improvement Association (1 June 2006); Bernie Morelli, previous chair of Hamilton-Wentworth Police Services Board (1 June 2006); Pat Saunders, citizen-volunteer, community activist, and one-time chair of Hamilton-Wentworth Police Services Board (14 June 2006); and Matt Jelly, local activist, City of Hamilton (14 June 2006).

2 Surrey operated thirty-one live-monitored CCTV surveillance cameras in 1998.

3 Especially visible to members of the IVBIA was the rise of drug activity in the core. The IVBIA is located on the south side of King Street East, and for years adjacent to its location stood the Sandbar Tavern. The tavern was notorious for drug dealing, prostitution, and violence until the IVBIA had the establishment's liquor licence revoked in 1999. After a woman's body was found in the apartments above what became Big Lisa's in 2001, the drinking establishment on the street level was closed indefinitely.

4 Tim Fletcher of the HPS had produced *Video Monitoring Proposal: City of Hamilton Downtown Core* by July 1998 (Hamilton Police Service 2000, 66).

5 In 2004, Superintendent John Petz assumed responsibility for the project, and in 2005 responsibility was transferred to Staff Sergeant Ken Weatherill. The project is currently co-ordinated by Inspector Scott Rastin.

6 The response to Radwanski's talk was presented in the form of "Issues/Concerns of Mr. Radwanski versus the Position of the HPS." It cited twenty-three arguments made by Radwanski and defended the HPS endorsement of streetscape CCTV surveillance based primarily on data from Sudbury, disproportionally high crime rates in Beat 672, and the

community basis of the project. It also noted Radwanski's scare-mongering tactics pertaining to function creep, police integrity, and public-area CCTV surveillance as the thin edge of the wedge.

7 The HPS also posted general information on its website, including the point-by-point response to Commissioner Radwanski's presentation at McMaster University.

8 The Evaluation Committee was composed of eight members: David Blanchard (developer and member of HDBIA), Mary Pocius (IVBIA), Gord Thompson (downtown business owner), Janet Manners (downtown business community), Max Reimer (manager of Theatre Aquarius, a popular downtown theatre), Scott Gilbey (Neighbourhood Watch), Ron Marini (city director of downtown renewal), and Michael Shea (HPS).

9 Professor Henry Giroux of McMaster University was readily available. Outside the city, a surveillance expert such as David Lyon (Queen's University) or representatives of the OIPC and the Canadian Civil Liberties Association could have been invited to address issues of displacement, effectiveness, legality, cost, and privacy.

10 The reaction resembled the response of Sudbury's LVMAC to students' responses to a public survey about CCTV surveillance in 2004 (see Chapter 4).

11 Unlike some other cities examined here, Hamilton's core does not face challenges posed by a post-2 a.m. bar flush.

12 Five-year maintenance costs facing the city were estimated at $189,329 when the pilot project was launched in 2004.

13 Area 6703 lies between Main Street and the Canadian National line below Barton Street on the south and north and between Wellington and Bay Streets on the east and west. On King Street between Ferguson and James, where the cameras are mounted, is a small portion of Area 6703. The HPS technology would not allow for isolated analyses of the area covered by the cameras (approximately 10 percent of Area 6703). However, the HPS did have data on calls for service in the camera area. The latter showed a decrease in all calls for service, save for controlled drug and substance act criminal behaviours. "Anecdotally," he wrote, "it is felt that the core portion covered by the cameras would have even better statistics than the whole of 6703" (Hamilton Police Services Board 2005, 2).

14 On 8 December 2004, local activist Matt Jelly presented a five-minute video to city council. The video was designed to raise a number of concerns about the speed and scope of the consultation process and to encourage the HPS to target those who would be most affected by monitoring practices for interactive consultation. The video specifically lamented the overemphasis on consulting with seniors at First Place.

15 The information in this section of the chapter is partially informed by interviews with Tristan Jentzel, one-time member of the City Centre Security Enhancement Resource Team (19 August 2005, 13 June 2006); Alan Halberstadt, one-time city councillor and member of the City Centre Security Enhancement Resource Team (18 August 2005, 13 June 2006); Doug Schmidt, reporter, the *Windsor Star* (24 August 2005); Judith Veresuk, executive director, City Centre Business Association (19 August 2005); Patrick Brode, legal counsel, City of Windsor (14 September 2005); Glen McCourt, Elite Protection Security Specialists (18 August 2006); Bruno Ierullo, Chief Administrative Office, City of Windsor (12 June 2006); and Joyce Zuk, city councillor, City of Windsor (13 June 2006).

16 In 2006, Casino Windsor's name was changed to Caesars Windsor. The name change was accompanied by major expansion to attract American tourists.

17 Prior to the proliferation of kiddie bars in the late 1990s, Windsor attracted cross-border drinkers to venues in the downtown area. Students from the University of Windsor and St. Clair College also frequent Detroit's bars and nightclubs.

18 Also prominent in crime control debate in Windsor was the 24 March 2003 murder of twenty-two-year-old Brian Bolyantu, who was shot in the head and chest at approximately 1:30 a.m. while he waited for friends outside a nightclub on Pelissier Street.

19 CCSERT was composed of members of the CCBA, Casino Windsor, some city councillors, the WPS, and downtown residents.

20 The initiative to install CCTV surveillance cameras in the core was gaining momentum prior to the Bellmio report. For example, Sherry McCourt of Elite Protection Specialists appeared before city council to extend an invitation to the mayor, members of council,

Police Chief Stannard, members of the CCRTF, and the local media to a "live-monitoring session" on 24 October 2003 (City of Windsor 2003).

21 Contract between Elite Protection Specialists and Larry Horwitz, City Centre Business Association, "Re: Pelissier Street Remote Video Monitoring Demonstration," 16 March 2004; released by the City of Windsor freedom of information and privacy co-ordinator.

22 As of July 2009, Elite Security reported ten cameras in the system: four on Ouelette and Wyandotte (three static cameras and one pan-tilt model), four on Ouelette and Park (three static cameras and one pan-tilt model), and two on Maiden Lane and Pelissier (Pelissier North and Pelissier South). Live monitoring takes place from midnight to 5 a.m. on Friday through Sunday; images are recorded the rest of the week.

Chapter 8: Thwarted Efforts to Establish Streetscape Monitoring Programs

1 The information in this section of the chapter is based in part on interviews with the information and privacy commissioner of British Columbia, David Loukidelis (24 August 2005); Micheal Vonn and Murray Mollard, British Columbia Civil Liberties Association (10 August 2005); Bruce Phillips, previous information and privacy commissioner of Canada (10 February 2006); Kim Kerr, executive director of the Downtown Eastside Residents Association (11 August 2005); Ann Livingstone, executive director of Vancouver Area Network of Drug Users (22 August 2005); David Jones, director of Crime Prevention Services, Downtown Business Improvement Association of Vancouver (22 August 2005); Judy McGuire, executive director of the Downtown Eastside Youth Activities Society (22 August 2005); David Cunningham, organizer, Anti-Poverty Committee, City of Vancouver (26 August 2005); Kathy Kwan, executive director, Strathcona Business Improvement Association (26 August 2005); Sharon Kravitz, previous employee, Carnegie Centre (7 September 2005); Phillip Owen, previous mayor of Vancouver (3 April 2006); and Doug MacPherson, Carnegie Centre (3 April 2006). The VPD is the only police service in Canada that refused repeated requests for interviews. The VPD is also the only public institution that failed to honour repeated requests for information after formal access to information requests were submitted.

2 The population of metro or Greater Vancouver is over 2 million people.

3 Grant Fredericks was one of two members of the VPD's Video Forensic Unit. From at least 1994 to 2000, the two-person unit was responsible for analyzing video images for the VPD.

4 The proposal entailed volunteer camera monitors who would listen to police radio transmissions to make decisions about where to focus cameras. When radio signals were quiet, volunteer monitors would scan the areas under surveillance in the DTES for suspicious activities.

5 On 5 November 1998, city council approved an initiative to establish businesses along Hastings Street. Part of this initiative was to address the pervasiveness of single resident/room occupancy. By 2000, new development projects started to appear at the edges of the DTES.

6 The National Crime Prevention Program is part of the government of Canada's framework to help enhance the safety and security of Canadians. The program entails partnerships with volunteers, academics, governments, foundations, and community organizations to develop ways to prevent crime. The joint application entailed a multi-faceted DTES intervention strategy, including the conversion of single-room occupancies, immunizations, drug treatment programs, five new community policing offices, and forty new beat cops.

7 The final application (the Vancouver Agreement) was a joint-funding initiative between the City of Vancouver, the Coalition for Crime Prevention and Drug Treatment, and the VPD. The co-applicants were awarded $5 million of the $6.25 million requested over a five-year period. The CCTV initiative was introduced at the same time that forty new officers were assigned to the DTES.

8 The VPD subsequently apologized to the Carnegie Centre for the "open-air drug market" reference.

9 The Carnegie Centre is a community centre for residents of the DTES.

10 Pharmanet is British Columbia's province-wide network that links pharmacies to a central database. Pharmanet contains information on drug dispensing and prescriptions, and it is available to a range of medical practitioners, including emergency departments, community pharmacies, and the College of Pharmacists of British Columbia.

11 In April 2000, Fredericks left the VPD to take a job with an American technology company.

12 The portable camera system is owned by the City of Vancouver. It is used for purposes of crowd control and traffic management during major events in the city. The system was first used in December 1999 during Prime Minister Jean Chrétien's visit to the Hyatt Regency Hotel.

13 The riot at the Hyatt entailed CCTV surveillance of protesters during Chrétien's visit. The violent protest, which led to an inquiry, was motivated by excessive use of police force authorized by the Prime Minister's Office (PMO) during the Asia-Pacific Economic Cooperation (APEC) Summit on 25 November 1997. Among other things, the 1999 protesters were motivated by information that the PMO had attempted to move the protest zone out of view of visiting world leaders. These claims were linked to the use of VPD CCTV surveillance camera images during the 1994 Stanley Cup riots.

14 "Vancouver Police Department – Proposed Video Surveillance – Freedom of Information and Protection of Privacy Act (FIPPA) – OIPC FILE F06-28759," letter from David Loukidelis, Information and Privacy Commissioner of British Columbia, to Police Chief Jamie Graham, 12 May 2006; released by the Office of the Information and Privacy Commissioner of Canada.

15 "Re: Public Consultation on Video Surveillance Proposal," letter from Richard Rosenberg to the Vancouver Police Board, 25 May 2006; released by the Office of the Information and Privacy Commissioner of Canada.

16 RCMP, "Briefing Note on Interdepartmental Meeting: RCMP Video Surveillance Plan for Vancouver 2010 Olympics," 22 February 2005; released by the Office of the Information and Privacy Commissioner of Canada.

17 Information in this section of the chapter is based partially on interviews with Linda Eyre, Brockville City Council (22 August 2005); Bob Huskinson, Brockville City Council (19 and 25 August 2005); Rob Hunter, Brockville Business Improvement Association (19 August 2005); Barry Raison, editor, *Recorder and Times* (28 November 2005); Doug Coward, city editor, *Recorder and Times* (24 November 2005); David Taylor, *Recorder and Times* (21 November 2001); and Barry King, Brockville police chief (27 June 2005).

18 Walby's study was based partially on the early findings of the present study.

19 The information in this portion of the chapter is based partially on interviews with Ron Rawlings, detective constable, Peterborough-Lakefield Community Police (30 May 2005); Walter Johnstone, executive director, Downtown Peterborough Business Improvement Association (30 May 2006); Sylvia Sutherland, mayor, City of Peterborough (30 May 2005); Roy Brady and Jane Burns, Stop the Camera Coalition (31 May 2005); Linda Slavin, political activist, City of Peterborough (31 May 2005); Paul Rex, councillor, City of Peterborough (31 May 2005); Bill Juby, councillor, City of Peterborough (30 May 2005); Terry Guill, councillor, City of Peterborough (30 May 2005); and Lance Sherke, central area facilitator, City of Peterborough (31 May 2005).

20 In 2002, the OIPC reviewed monitoring systems in Peterborough, Thessalon, London, Sudbury, and Sturgeon Falls.

21 In a four-block area of downtown Peterborough, six large drinking establishments offer seating capacity of 3,000. Johnstone used the Internet to investigate monitoring programs in London, Hamilton, Sudbury, and Kelowna as well as in the United Kingdom.

22 See http://www.stopthecameras.tripod.com/.

Chapter 9: Thunder Bay's Eye on the Street

1 The information presented in this chapter is based partially on interviews with Bonnie Nistico, deputy city clerk, City of Thunder Bay (4 June 2006); Bo Huk, chair of Eye on the Street Steering Committee and member of the Simpson Street BIA (3 June 2006); Robert Quinn, north downtown business owner, Thunder Bay (4 June 2006); Robert Tuchenhagen,

councillor for McKellar Ward (5 June 2006); David Glover, Heart of the Harbour BIA (5 June 2006); Rob Martyn, network engineering planner for TBayTel (5 June 2006); Alex Grant, manager of Thunder Bay Transit (6 June 2006); Barb Stacey, manager of Central Support for Transportation and Works, City of Thunder Bay (6 June 2006); and Kathy O'Brien, City of Thunder Bay MFIPPA co-ordinator (6 June 2006).

2 Until it was launched in November 2005, Thunder Bay's streetscape CCTV system was known as the Eye in the Sky – named after Sudbury's program. The name of the program was changed based on a recommendation from the City of Thunder Bay's Department of Communications; the Eye in the Sky was perceived to convey Big Brother connotations.

3 Approximately 10,000 full-time students attend Lakehead University and Confederation College of Applied Arts and Sciences.

4 The new inter-city area is demarcated by the intersections of Memorial Avenue and Fort William Road (the two main roads that link Fort William and Port Arthur) with Main Street and Central Avenue, roughly midway between the two traditional downtown cores.

5 It is important that an ad hoc Implementation Committee was formed in 2000, because standard council rules stipulate that policy proposals, if defeated once in a council vote, cannot be proposed again. The committee policy proposals are exempt from this restriction.

6 Based on estimates provided by the BIA coalition, the actual cost of implementing the sixteen-camera system was projected to be between $189,000 and $220,000, excluding upgraded cameras in the transit terminal system, and between $254,000 and $290,000, including upgraded transit cameras. Annual operations costs were estimated at $21,000. Council directed the Implementation Committee to explore ways to raise funds to cover the shortfall based on Sudbury's LVMAC fundraising efforts.

7 TBayTel is Canada's largest independent telecommunications company.

8 The locations in the south core included Victoria Avenue at May Street, Victoria Avenue at Archibald Street, an electrical pole on North Brodie Street, Simpson Street at Victoria Avenue, Syndicate Avenue at Donald Street, and Charry's Corner traffic lights at Simpson Street. The locations in the north core included Red River Road at Cumberland Street, Red River Road at Court Street, and Court Street at Park Avenue. Three additional cameras were planned for the north transit terminal at North Water Street, and four cameras were planned for the south transit terminal located north of Victoriaville Mall.

9 To address *Guidelines* and relevant sections of the MFIPPA, the mayor's office allocated a staff member – a graduate student at Lakehead University who had carried out research on downtown Thunder Bay – to aid the Implementation Committee in creating a Code of Practice. The student developed a draft code based on stipulations set out in *Guidelines*, in the MFIPPA, and in existing codes of practice and other policy documents collected from Sudbury and London.

10 The proposed locations correspond almost exactly to the final locations of the cameras, with two exceptions: the camera at Court and Park was originally intended to be housed on a government building, but the relevant federal authorities produced an agreement for usage that posed complications for the ETSSC. The ETSCC decided to locate the cameras on an alternative building in the vicinity. The Red River and Cumberland camera was originally supposed to be mounted on a building owned by a local lawyer, but securing permission was difficult. The camera's installation was delayed until 2006, when an alternative location was found at 215 Red River Road.

11 Further capital costs of $19,000 were incurred in 2007 to replace the video monitoring recorders to improve performance. To date, the city has absorbed the costs as well as all capital costs not covered by the original funding.

12 A ten-dollar annual payment is allocated to business owners to compensate for hosting the cameras. This is one of the stipulations of the Wall Owners Agreement: a legal document designed to ensure access to camera sites for installation and maintenance of cameras. The agreement has a term of ten years, in which time a building owner may terminate the agreement only for the purpose of building demolition.

13 Stacey served as program director until May 2009.

14 The final Code of Practice stipulates that the memorandum of understanding was a measure to avoid individual police officers having to go through a public access-to-information procedure every time they wanted to request footage for police purposes.

15 The Steering Committee decided that the specific hours of live monitoring should be kept secret to prevent criminals from taking advantage of times when the cameras are not manned. Therefore, details about the times when the cameras are monitored – rather than simply recorded – are unavailable.

16 Four downtown areas (coded ESZ – Eye on the Street Zones) within the range of CCTV cameras were the subject of the study: ESZ112 (Red River, Cumberland, and Court cameras), ESZ404 (Brodie, Victoria, Archibald, Donald, and Syndicate cameras), ESZ410 (Simpson and Rowland cameras), and ESZ413 (Simpson and Victoria cameras).

17 The surveys featured identical questions about crime, safety, and CCTV cameras – worded differently to reflect the fact that, in 2005, expectations of CCTV cameras were assessed rather than experiences with CCTV cameras in 2006.

18 This question was not asked in 2005.

Chapter 10: Panoptic Dreams: Arguments, Implications, and Recommendations

1 In 1998, three non-specific pieces of legislation were introduced that significantly influenced the CCTV policy environment: the Data Protection Act, Human Rights Act, and Crime and Disorder Act. The legislation is non-specific because it is not exclusively designed to address CCTV surveillance. The Crime and Disorder Act was especially significant in shaping the regulation of CCTV surveillance because it institutionalized the requirement for responsible authorities to enter into community safety partnerships to address crime and disorder.

2 On 12 February 1993, Jamie Bulger was abducted from the New Strand Shopping Centre in Bootle, Liverpool. Bulger's abductors, two boys aged ten years, tortured, beat, and murdered him and left his body on a train track. The abduction was captured on video surveillance cameras in the shopping centre, and the images, set in the context of the murder, contributed to the realignment of British law-and-order politics as well as public conduct interventions.

3 These patterns and processes are currently under investigation in several Canadian cities in a project funded by the Social Sciences and Humanities Research Council of Canada (Administering Public-Area Streetscape CCTV Surveillance Monitoring Programs in Canada, sole investigator, Sean Hier).

Appendix A

1 Interviews informing part of Appendix A were conducted with dozens of city representatives, police, government representatives, and members of the privacy policy sector. These data will be reported more fully at a later date.

2 Canadian news media have reported on several Ontario cities that have initiated efforts to establish monitoring programs. For example, Midland considered cameras to address concerns with vandalism, and Niagara Falls is considering cameras to address concerns with prostitution.

3 TAVIS is led by the Toronto Police Service, and partners include Toronto Community Housing and City of Toronto departments such as Parks, Forestry, and Recreation; Public Health; Social Development; Finance and Administration; and Partnerships.

4 Frankford, ten kilometres from Trenton, falls under the same municipality of Quinte West.

5 The Winnipeg Police Service maintains a website dedicated to communicating the progress of the CCTV scheme at http://www.winnipeg.ca/police/cctv/.

6 See ibid. for a map of the camera locations compared with crime hot spots.

7 See http://www.bcprogressboard.com/.

8 The funds were initially designated for Kelowna, Vancouver, and Surrey only.

Appendix B

1 See Jeffrey Rosen, The Naked Crowd: Reclaiming Security and Freedom in an Anxious Age (Toronto: Random House, 2004), page 123. Also, see generally The Naked Crowd, Chapter Three, "The Silver Bullet."

2 See Wireless Communication Technologies: Video Surveillance Systems (Fact Sheet) available on the Office of the Information and Privacy Commissioner of Ontario's website (www.ipc.on.ca).

3 Note, our Office has held that under the Personal Health Information Protection Act, a record is created when a camera and transmitter capture an image, and encode and wirelessly transmit that image, even if a physical artifact is not created such as a videotape or CD containing the image. See Order HO-005 available on the Office of the Information and Privacy Commissioner of Ontario's website (www.ipc.on.ca).

4 Cash Converters Canada Inc. v. Oshawa (City) [2007] O.J. No. 2613, at 40.

5 This document is available at http://www.accessandprivacy.gov.on.ca/english/pub/screeningtool.html

6 A privacy breach occurs when personal information is collected, retained, used or disclosed in ways that are not in accordance with the provisions of the Acts. See publications available on the Office of the Information and Privacy Commissioner of Ontario's website (www.ipc.on.ca) such as the Breach Notification Assessment Tool, and What to do if a privacy breach occurs: Guidelines for government organizations.

References

Ali, S. Harris. 2003. "Disaster and the Political Economy of Recycling: Toxic Fire in an Industrial City." *Social Problems* 49, 2: 129-49.

Aubry, Jack. 1987. "Hull Bars Offering Free Shuttle Service." *Ottawa Citizen,* 7 August, C1.

Austin, J. 2003. "Why Criminology Is Irrelevant." *Criminology and Public Policy* 2, 3: 557-64.

Ball, Kristie, and Frank Webster, eds. 2003. *The Intensification of Surveillance: Crime, Terrorism and Warfare.* London: Pluto Press.

Bell, Jocelyn. 2002. "Public Views Wanted on Street Cameras." *Hamilton Spectator,* 21 May, A3.

Bellmio, Peter. 2003. *Site Visit Report: Assessment of Social and Physical Conditions in Windsor's City Centre.* Windsor: City of Windsor.

Bennett, Colin. 1997. "Arguments for the Standardization of Privacy Protection Policy: Canadian Initiatives and American and International Responses." *Government Information Quarterly* 14, 4: 351-62.

–. 2003. "The Privacy Commissioner of Canada: Multiple Roles, Diverse Expectations, and Structural Dilemmas." *Canadian Public Administration* 46, 2: 218-42.

Bennett, Colin, and Robin Bayley. 2005. "Video Surveillance and Privacy Protection Law in Canada." In *Reasonable Expectations of Privacy? Eleven Country Reports on Camera Surveillance and Workplace Surveillance,* ed. Sjaak Nouwt, Berend R. de Vries, and Corien Prins, 61-90. The Hague: T.M.C. Asser Press.

Bennett, Colin, and Charles Raab. 2006. *The Governance of Privacy.* Cambridge, MA: MIT Press.

Berton, P. 1999. "Stats Show Downtown as Safe as Rest of City." *London Free Press,* 19 January, A1.

Bilodeau, Laurent. 2002. *Final Inquiry Report into the Installation of a Surveillance Camera in the City of Baie-Comeau.* File 02 09 62. Québec: Commission d'accès à l'information.

Blondin, Stephanie. 2002. "National Framework: Policy Considerations." Ottawa: Office of the Information and Privacy Commissioner of Canada. Released by the Office of the Information and Privacy Commissioner of Canada.

Boisvenu, Pierre-Hugues. 2008. *Survivre à l'innommable: Et reprendre le pouvoir sur la vie.* Montréal: Éditions de l'Homme.

Boudreau, Christian, and Monica Tremblay. 2005. *L'utilisation des cameras de surveillance dans les lieux à accès public au Canada.* Étude présentée au Commissariat à la protection de la vie privée du Canada. Ottawa: Office of the Privacy Commissioner of Canada.

Brazeau, David. 1995. "Police Seek Possible Witnesses to Murder." *Sudbury Star,* 17 August, A1.

Brien, Tony. 2006. *Analysis of Crime in Downtown Sherbrooke, 2000-2004.* Sherbrooke: Sherbooke Police Service.

British Columbia Civil Liberties Association. 1999. "Video Surveillance in Public Places." Vancouver: British Columbia Civil Liberties Association.

Brockville Police Service. 1999. *Safe Streets Program: CCTV Surveillance of the Downtown Core*. Brockville: Brockville Police Service.

Brode, Patrick. 2004. *Video Surveillance Cameras in the Downtown Area*. File No. 18-81-04, 19 November. Windsor: City of Windsor.

Brosseau, Marc, et André Cellard. 2003. "Un sièclede boires et de déboires: Hull aux prises avec son histoire et sa géographie." *Cahiers de géographie du Québec* 47: 7-34.

Brown, M., and D. Yasvinski. 1999. "Victim Dies from Stab Wound." *The Gazette* [London, ON], 20 January, A1.

Buell, Peter. 2008. *Video Surveillance in Downtown Brockville*. Brockville: Brockville Police Service.

Burawoy, Michael. 2004. "For Public Sociology." *American Review of Sociology* 70, 1: 4-25.

Burman, John, and Joan Walters. 2002. "Cameras to Monitor City." *Hamilton Spectator*, 9 January, A01.

Canadian Broadcasting Corporation. 1992. "Electric Eyes on the Streets." 16 June.

Carmichael, H. 1995a. "What's Wrong with the Downtown?" *Sudbury Star*, 20 March, A5.

–. 1995b. "Councillor Aims to Prove Core Is Dying." *Sudbury Star*, 20 March, A1.

Carnegie Community Action Project. 1999. *Closed-Circuit Television Surveillance of Public Space in Vancouver*. Vancouver: Carnegie Centre.

Carson, T., I. Johnston, J. Mangat, and J. Tupper. 2004. "You Are Being Watched! Navigating Citizenship within the Controlled Spaces of a Public High School." Paper presented at the Canadian Society for the Study of Education Annual Conference, Winnipeg, June.

Cavoukian, Ann. 1998. *Video Surveillance: The Privacy Implications*. IPC Practices 10. Toronto: Information and Privacy Commissioner of Ontario.

Chancer, Lynn, and Charles McLaughlin. 2007. "Public Criminologies: Diverse Perspectives on Academia and Policy." *Theoretical Criminology* 11, 2: 155-73.

City Centre Security Enhancement Resource Team. 2005a. "Downtown Surveillance Camera Sub Committee Update." City Centre Security Enhancement Resource Team Meeting Minutes, Windsor, 14 April.

–. 2005b. "June 9, 2005 Minutes – City Centre Security Enhancement Resource Team." Memo from Chief Administrative Officer to Mayor Francis and Members of City Council, Windsor, 17 June.

City of Kelowna. 1999. *Community Profile*. Kelowna: City of Kelowna, Department of Planning and Development Services.

–. 2005. "Video Surveillance at Queensway to Be Revisited." News release, 18 August. Kelowna: City of Kelowna.

–. N.d. *Community Safety Camera Guidelines*. Kelowna: City of Kelowna.

City of London. 2000. "Chairs and Members, Community and Protective Services Committee: Downtown Camera Surveillance System." Meeting Minutes, London, 3 April. Released by the City of London's Manager of Records and Information Services.

–. 2001a. "Measuring the Success of the Monitored Surveillance Camera Project." London: Community and Protective Services Committee, 12 March. Released by the City of London's Manager of Records and Information Services.

–. 2001b. "Video Surveillance Cameras." Community and Protective Services Committee, Meeting Minutes, London, 30 July. Released by the City of London's Manager of Records and Information Services.

–. 2002. "The Downtown Monitored Surveillance Camera Program." Community and Protective Services Committee, Meeting Minutes, London, 29 July. Released by the City of London's Manager of Records and Information Services.

–. 2004a. "Annual Evaluation Report of the Downtown Monitored Surveillance Camera Project." Community and Protective Services Committee, Meeting Minutes, London, 23 February. Released by the City of London's Manager of Records and Information Services.

–. 2004b. "Update on the Downtown Monitored Surveillance Camera Project." Community and Protective Services Committee, Meeting Minutes, London, 12 October. Released by the City of London's Manager of Records and Information Services.

–. 2005. "Annual Evaluation Report of the Downtown Monitored Surveillance Camera Project." Community and Protective Services Committee, Meeting Minutes, London, 21 March. Released by the City of London's Manager of Records and Information Services.

City of London Steering Management Group. 2001. *Downtown Surveillance CCTV Camera Program: Steering Management Group Terms of Reference.* London: City of London.

City of Thunder Bay. 2001. City Council Meeting Minutes, Meeting No. 31, 23 April.

City of Vancouver. 1998a. "Administrative Report: National Crime Prevention Program Funding Application – 'Building a Future Together – The Downtown Eastside Revitalization Program.'" Vancouver: City of Vancouver.

–. 1998b. *A Program of Strategic Actions for the Downtown Eastside.* Vancouver: City of Vancouver.

–. 2001a. "Downtown Eastside Community Monitoring Report" (6th report). Vancouver: City of Vancouver, Planning Department.

City of Windsor. 1994. *Windsor City Centre Revitalization and Design Study: Final Report.* Windsor: City of Windsor.

–. 2003. "Council Minutes." Windsor, 30 January.

–. 2004. *City Centre Interim Land-Use Study.* Windsor: City of Windsor.

–. 2006. "Council Minutes." Windsor, 16 January.

Coleman, R. 2003a. "Images from a Neoliberal City: The State, Surveillance, and Social Control." *Critical Criminology* 12: 21-42.

–. 2003b. "Researching the Emergent City States: Articulating the Proper Objects of Power and CCTV." In *Researching the Crimes of the Powerful: Scrutinising States and Corporations,* ed. S. Tombs and D. Whyte, 88-104. New York: Peter Lang.

–. 2005. "Surveillance in the City: Primary Definition and Urban Spatial Order." *Crime, Media, and Culture* 1, 2: 131-48.

–. 2006. "Confronting the Hegemony of Vision: State, Space, and Urban Crime Prevention." In *Expanding the Criminological Imagination: Critical Readings in Criminology,* ed. A. Barton et al., 38-64. Cullompton, UK: Willan.

Coleman, R., and J. Sim. 2000. "'You'll Never Walk Alone': CCTV Surveillance, Order, and Neo-Liberal Rule in Liverpool City Centre." *British Journal of Sociology* 51, 4: 623-39.

Commission d'accès à l'information. 2001-2. *Annual Report, 2001-2.* Montreal: Commission d'accès à l'information.

–. 2003. "Surveillance Cameras: For a Reasonable Balance between Privacy and Security." Montreal: Commission d'accès à l'information.

Community Contract and Aboriginal Policing Services. 2004. "Analysis of Video Surveillance Guidelines Proposed by the Office of the Information and Privacy Commissioner of Canada." Operational Policy Section. Released by the Office of the Information and Privacy Commissioner of Canada.

Coordinating Committee for Community Safety. 1999a. "Legislative Recommendations." London: City of London. 25 March.

–. 1999b. "Police/Public Interaction Subcommittee: Report and Recommendations." London: City of London. 29 April.

–. 1999c. "Educational Recommendations." London: City of London. 14 June.

Corporation of the City of London. 2001. *Code of Practice for the Operation of a Closed Circuit Television System for Downtown Surveillance in the City of London.* London: Corporation of the City of London.

Coward, Doug. 1998. "Invading Our Spaces." *Recorder and Times* [Brockville], 3 November, A6.

Davis, M. 1990. *The City of Quartz: Excavating the Future in Los Angeles.* New York: Vintage.

Department of Justice. N.d.a. "Memorandum for the Minister." MLU2002-004643. Released by the Office of the Information and Privacy Commissioner of Canada.

–. N.d.b. "Memorandum for the Minister: Kelowna Camera Case: Challenge to Privacy Commissioner's Standing." Released by the Office of the Information and Privacy Commissioner of Canada.

Ditton, Jason. 1999. *The Effect of Closed Circuit Television Cameras on Recorded Crime Rates and Public Concern about Crime in Glasgow.* The Scottish Office Central Research Unit Main Findings No. 30, 4. Glasgow, Scotland: The Scottish Office Central Research Unit.

–. 2002. "Crime and the City: Public Attitudes to CCTV in Glasgow." *British Journal of Criminology* 40: 692-709.

Ditton, Jason, and E. Short. 1999. "'Yes It Works, No, It Doesn't': Comparing the Effects of Open-Street CCTV Surveillance in Two Adjacent Scottish Towns." In *Surveillance of Public Space*, ed. K. Painter and N. Tilley, 201-23. Monsey, NY: Criminal Justice Press.

Dubois, Nancy, et Johanne Mercier. 2005. *Projet de videosurveillance 2005*. Sherbrooke: Ville de Sherbrooke Police.

Flaherty, David. 1998. *Video Surveillance by Public Bodies: An Investigation Report*. Investigation P98-012. Victoria: Information and Privacy Commissioner of British Columbia.

Foucault, Michel. 1979. *Discipline and Punish: The Birth of the Modern Prison*. London: Peregrine.

–. 1982. "The Subject and Power." In *Michel Foucault: Beyond Structuralism and Hermeneutics*, by Hubert Dreyfus and Paul Rabinow, 208-30. Chicago: University of Chicago Press.

Fredericks, Grant. 1999. *CCTV: A Community Policing Option for the Downtown Eastside*. Vancouver: Vancouver Police Department.

–. 2001. *Neighbourhood Safety Watch: Closed Circuit TV – A Safer Community Option for the Downtown Eastside, Strathcona, Chinatown, and Gastown Area*. Vancouver: Vancouver Police Department.

Fussey, Peter. 2007. "New Labour and New Surveillance: Theoretical and Political Ramifications of CCTV Implementation in the UK." *Surveillance and Society* 2, 2-3: 251-69.

Fyfe, N., and J. Bannister. 1996. "City Watching: Closed Circuit Television Surveillance in Public Spaces." *Area* 28, 1: 37-46.

–. 1998. "The 'Eyes upon the Street': Closed Circuit Television Surveillance and the City." In *Images of the Street: Planning, Identity, and Control in Public Space*, ed. N. Fyfe, 254-67. London: Routledge.

Garland, D. 2001. *The Culture of Control*. Chicago: University of Chicago Press.

Gazso, Amber, and Kevin Haggerty. 2009. "Public Opinion about Surveillance in Post-9/11 Alberta: Trading Privacy for Security?" In *Anti-Terrorism: Security and Insecurity after 9/11*, ed. Sandra Magnusson, 141-59. Halifax: Fernwood.

Gill, M., and A. Spriggs. 2005. *Assessing the Impact of CCTV*. Home Office Research Study Number 292. London, UK: Home Office.

Gill, Martin. 2003. *CCTV*. Leicester, UK: Perpetuity.

Goldie-Ryder, Deborah. 2000. "He Didn't Die for Nothing." *London Free Press*, 17 June, F2.

Goodine, Steve. 1999. *Monitored Surveillance Program: Feasibility Study*. London, ON: London Police Service.

Goold, B. 2004. *CCTV and Policing*. Oxford: University of Oxford Press.

Gordon, K. 1995. "What's Ailing Downtown?" *Sudbury Star*, 20 March, A1.

Greater Sudbury Police Service. 2001. "Video Surveillance System, Business Plan." 5 April. Released by the Greater Sudbury Police Service.

Greater Sudbury Police Services Board. 2005. "Lions Eye in the Sky." PowerPoint Presentation, Sudbury, 11 April. Released by the Greater Sudbury Police Service.

Greenberg, Josh, and Sean P. Hier. 2009. "CCTV Surveillance and the Poverty of Media Discourse: A Content Analysis of Canadian Newspaper Coverage." *Canadian Journal of Communication* 34, 3: 461-86.

Groombridge, Nic. 2008. "Stars of CCTV? How the Home Office Wasted Millions – A Radical 'Treasury/Audit Commission' View." *Surveillance and Society* 5, 1: 73-80.

Guildford Borough Council. 1996. *Safer Guildford: A Partnership Approach*. Guildford, UK: Guildford Borough Council.

Haggerty, Kevin. 2004. "Displaced Expertise: Three Constraints on the Policy Relevance of Criminological Thought." *Theoretical Criminology* 8, 2: 211-31.

–. 2006. "Tearing Down the Walls: On Demolishing the Panopticon." In *Theorizing Surveillance: The Panopticon and Beyond*, ed. D. Lyon, 23-45. Devon, UK: Willan Publishing.

Haggerty, Kevin, and Richard Ericson. 1997. *Policing the Risk Society*. Toronto: University of Toronto Press.

Haggerty, Kevin, Laura Huey, and Richard Ericson. 2008. "The Politics of Sight/Site: Locating Cameras in Vancouver's Public Space." *Sociology of Law, Crime, and Deviance* 10, 1: 35-55.

Hall, Dave. 2003. "Bars Face Levy for Police." *Windsor Star,* 24 January, A4.

Hall, Stuart. 1988. *The Hard Road to Renewal.* London: Verso.

Hamilton Police Service. 2000. *Challenging Our Patrol Priorities into the Next Century – C.O.P.P. 2000.* Hamilton: Hamilton Police Service.

Hamilton Police Services Board. 2002a. "Closed Circuit Television (CCTV) Community Consultation Proposal – PSB #02-033." 18 March. Hamilton: Hamilton-Wentworth Police Services Board.

–. 2002b. "Closed Circuit Television (CCTV) Community Consultation Update – PSB #02-033A." 8 November. Hamilton: Hamilton-Wentworth Police Services Board.

–. 2005. "CCTV Program – 1st Year in Review (PSB 02-033c)." 9 September. Hamilton: Hamilton-Wentworth Police Services Board.

–. 2006. "CCTV Program (PSB 02-033e)." 23 October. Hamilton: Hamilton-Wentworth Police Services Board.

Hamilton Spectator. 2002."Video Monitoring Deserves Public Input; Safety: Goal Acceptable, Process Flawed." Editorial. *Hamilton Spectator,* 10 January, A10.

Hay, Colin. 1994. "Mobilization through Interpellation: James Bulger, Juvenile Crime, and the Construction of Moral Panic." *Social Legal Studies* 4, 2: 197-223.

Hays, Scott P. 1996. "Patterns of Reinvention: The Nature of Evolution during Policy Diffusion." *Policy Studies Journal* 24, 4: 551-66.

Hier, Sean P. 2004. "Risky Spaces and Dangerous Faces: Surveillance, Social Disorder, and CCTV." *Social and Legal Studies* 13, 4: 541-54.

Hier, Sean P., J. Greenberg, K. Walby, and D. Lett. 2007. "Media, Communication, and the Establishment of Public Camera Surveillance in Canada." *Media, Culture, and Society* 29, 5: 727-51.

Hier, Sean P., K. Walby, and J. Greenberg. 2006. "Supplementing the Panoptic Paradigm: Surveillance, Moral Governance, and CCTV." In *Theorizing Surveillance: the Panopticon and Beyond,* ed. D. Lyon, 228-42. Devon, UK: Willan Publishing.

Howe, Brendan. 1999. "Argument Ends in Stabbing." *The Gazette* [London, ON], 4 February, 2.

Information and Privacy Commissioner of Ontario. 2001. *Guidelines for the Use of Surveillance Cameras in Public Places.* Toronto: Information and Privacy Commissioner of Ontario.

–. 2004. *Privacy Review: Video Surveillance Programs in Peterborough.* Toronto: Information and Privacy Commissioner of Ontario.

Innes, Martin. 2001. "Control Creep." *Sociological Research Online* 6, 3. www.socresonline.org.

–. 2004. "Signal Crimes and Signal Disorders: Notes on Deviance as Communicative Action." *British Journal of Sociology* 55, 3: 335-55.

Jessop, Bob. 2004. "Critical Semiotic Analysis and Cultural Political Economy." *Critical Discourse Studies* 1, 2: 159-74.

Jiggins, Michael. 2008. "Councillor Says She's Heard Mostly Favourable Response on Video Surveillance." *Recorder and Times* [Brockville], 19 August, A3.

Jones, Marshall. 2002. "Spy Camera Helps Stop Vicious Beating." *Capital News* [Kelowna], 19 July 2002, A3.

Kanashiro, Marta Mourao. 2008. "Surveillance Cameras in Brazil: Exclusion, Mobility Regulation, and the New Meaning of Security." *Surveillance and Society* 5, 3: 270-89.

King, Barry. 1999. *Safe Streets Program: CCTV Surveillance of the Downtown Core* report. Brockville, ON: Brockville Police Service.

Knight, Graham. 1998. "Hegemony, the Media, and New Right Politics: Ontario in the Late 1990s." *Critical Sociology* 24, 1-2: 105-29.

L'Express. 2007. "Insécurité et malpropreté: Des citoyens ont peur d'emprunter le tunnel sous la voie ferrée." *L'Express* [Drummondville], 5 September. http://www.journalexpress.ca/.

Labréque, Alice. 1992. *Final Investigation Report: La Ligue des Droits et Libertés v. La Ville de Sherbrooke.* File 91 07 84. Québec: Commission d'accès à l'information.

La Forest, Gérard. 2002. "Re: Opinion – Video Surveillance." Letter to Information and Privacy Commissioner of Canada George Radwanski, 5 April.

Laporte, Michel. 2004. *Consultation publique: L'utilisation de cameras de surveillance par des organismes publics dans les lieux publics.* Québec: Commission d'accès à l'information.

Legault, Rita. 2003. "Sherbrooke Police Object to Policing by Civilians." *La Tribune* [Sherbrooke], 26 June, 4.

–. 2005. "Big Brother Is Watching and Taping Downtown." *La Tribune* [Sherbrooke], 21 June, 1.

Leman-Langlois, Stéphane. 2003. "The Myopic Panopticon: The Social Consequences of Policing through the Lens." *Policing and Society* 13, 1: 44-58.

Lett, Dan. 2007. "Bringing into Focus the Experience of Public-Area CCTV Surveillance." MA thesis, University of Victoria.

Lions Club. 2002. "Fact Sheet." Sudbury: Lions Club. Released by the Greater Sudbury Police Service and Sudbury Metro Centre.

Lions Eye in the Sky. 1997. "Statistics and Facts." Sudbury: Lions Eye in the Sky. Released by the Greater Sudbury Police Service and Sudbury Metro Centre.

Lions Video Monitoring Advisory Committee. 1998a. Committee Minutes. Sudbury, 5 June.

–. 1998b. Committee Minutes. Sudbury, 4 September.

–. 1998c. Committee Minutes. Sudbury, 4 December.

–. 2000. Committee Minutes. Sudbury, 15 December.

–. 2001. Committee Minutes. Sudbury, 16 February.

–. 2002. Committee Minutes. Sudbury, 11 January.

Lippert, Randy. 2007. "Open-Street CCTV Canadian Style." *Criminal Justice Matters* 68, 1: 31-32.

–. 2008. "Urban Revitalization, Security, and Knowledge Transfer: The Case of Broken Windows and Kiddie Bars." *Canadian Journal of Law and Society* 22, 2: 29-53.

–. 2009. "Signs of the Surveillant Assemblage: Privacy Regulation, Urban CCTV and Governmentality." *Social and Legal Studies* 18, 4: 505-22.

London Police Service. 1999. *Downtown Crime Study.* London, ON: Crime Analysis Unit.

Mackay, David. 2003. "Multiple Targets: The Reasons to Support Town-Centre CCTV Systems." *Crime Prevention and Community Safety* 5, 1: 39-48.

Maclean, Victoria. 1998. "There's a Better Way to Keep Downtown Safe." *Recorder and Times* [Brockville], 18 November, A3.

Madanipour, Ali. 2003. *Public and Private Spaces of the City.* New York: Routledge.

Maguire, Mike. 1999. "Restraining Big Brother? The Regulation of Surveillance in England and Wales." In *Surveillance, Closed-Circuit Television, and Social Control,* ed. Clive Norris, Gary Armstrong, and Jade Moran, 229-39. Aldershot, UK: Ashgate.

Management Team. 2001. *Corporate Report 2001.126.* Thunder Bay: Management Team.

–. 2003a. *Corporate Report 2003.246.* Thunder Bay: Management Team.

–. 2003b. *Corporate Report 2003.371.* Thunder Bay: Management Team.

Manning, Peter. 1992. "Information Technology and the Police." In *Modern Policing,* ed. M. Tonry and N. Morris, 349-98. Chicago: University of Chicago Press.

Matchett, Alan. 2003. *CCTV for Security Professionals.* Burlington, MA: Butterworth-Heineman/Elsevier.

Mather, George. 1998. "Cop Better than Camera." *Recorder and Times* [Brockville], 4 December, A7.

Mathews, Roger. 2009. "Beyond 'So What?' Criminology: Rediscovering Realism." *Theoretical Criminology* 13, 3: 341-62.

McCahill, M. 2002. *The Surveillance Web: The Rise of CCTV in an English City.* Cullompton, UK: Willan Publishing.

Mennie, James. 1997. "MUC Police Reject Plan for Cameras on Main Street: Sherbrooke Program Hailed." *The Gazette* [London, ON], 24 January, A5.

Mercier, Johanne, et Michel Racine. 2008. *Rapport de videosurveillance 2007.* Sherbrooke: Ville de Sherbrooke Police.

Metheson, D. 1986. *Report to the Attorney General by the Police Commission on the Use of Video Equipment by Police Forces in British Columbia.* Victoria: British Columbia Attorney General.

Morse, Paul. 2002. "Video Camera Public Hearings Find Opposition to Proposal." *Hamilton Spectator,* 6 April, A03.

Nicholson-Crotty, Sean. 2009. "The Politics of Diffusion: Public Policy in the American States." *Journal of Politics* 71, 1: 192-205.

Norris, C., and G. Armstrong. 1999. *The Maximum Surveillance Society: The Rise of CCTV.* Oxford: Berg.

Norris, Clive, Mike McCahill, and David Wood. 2004. "The Growth of CCTV: A Global Perspective on the International Diffusion of Video Surveillance in Publicly Accessible Space." *Surveillance and Society* 2, 2-3: 110-35.

O'Connor, Naoibh. 2001. "Carnegie Assoc. Casts Doubts on Surveillance Camera Report." *Vancouver Courier,* 3 October, A3.

Office of the Information and Privacy Commissioner of Canada. 2001. *Annual Report.* Ottawa: Office of the Information and Privacy Commissioner of Canada.

–. 2002. *Case Summary #107 2002.* http://www.priv.gc.ca/.

–. 2003a. *Case Summary #114 2003.* http://www.priv.gc.ca/.

–. 2003b. "Memorandum: Terms of Reference: Task Force on Video Surveillance." From Raymond D'Aoust, 12 December. Released by the Office of the Information and Privacy Commissioner of Canada.

–. 2004a. Letter from Commissioner G. Zaccardelli to Jennifer Stoddart, 29 July. Released by the Office of the Information and Privacy Commissioner of Canada.

–. 2004b. *Proposed Project on Video Surveillance.* From Brian K. Stewart, 22 March. Released by the Office of the Information and Privacy Commissioner of Canada.

Parnaby, Patrick, and C. Victoria Reed. 2009. "Natural Surveillance and the Effects of Being Seen." In *Surveillance: Power, Problems, and Politics,* ed. Sean P. Hier and Josh Greenberg, 87-100. Vancouver: UBC Press.

Peesker, Saira. 2004a. "Few Answers at Camera Meeting." *Peterborough Examiner,* 17 June, B2.

–. 2004b. "Camera Debate Refused." *Peterborough Examiner,* 23 April, B1.

Pender, Terry. 1996. "Bomb Blast Rips into Police Headquarters." *Sudbury Star,* 16 December, A1.

Peterborough Examiner. 2005. "Do You Know When You're Being Watched?" Editorial. *Peterborough Examiner,* 22 January, B1.

Phillips, Andrew. 1998. "Are City Residents Ready for Big Brother?" *Recorder and Times* [Brockville], 29 October, A3.

Poloni, Oscar. 2000. *Evaluation of the Lions Eye in the Sky Video Monitoring Project.* http://www.police.sudbury.on.ca/.

Radwanski, George. 2001. Letter to Southam News, 17 July. Ottawa: Office of the Information and Privacy Commissioner of Canada.

–. 2002a. Speech to the Kelowna Chamber of Commerce, 6 February. Ottawa: Office of the Information and Privacy Commissioner of Canada.

–. 2002b. "Watching You: Privacy Rights and Video Surveillance." Speech to the BC Branch of the Canadian Bar Association, Vancouver, 7 February. Ottawa: Office of the Information and Privacy Commissioner of Canada.

–. 2002c. "Watching You: Privacy Rights and Video Surveillance." Speech at McMaster University, Hamilton, 13 February. Ottawa: Office of the Information and Privacy Commissioner of Canada.

–. 2002d. "Video Surveillance in Public Places." Speech to the Ontario Bar Association, Toronto, 27 May. Ottawa: Office of the Information and Privacy Commissioner of Canada.

Recorder and Times. 1998. "Surveillance Cameras." Letter to the Editor. *Recorder and Times* [Brockville], 4 December, A7.

–. 1999a. "Cameras Should Be Last Resort." Editorial. *Recorder and Times* [Brockville], 16 January, A6.

–. 1999b. "Debate's Far from Over." Editorial. *Recorder and Times* [Brockville], 23 January, A6.

–. 1999c. "It's Time to Get Back on Track." *Recorder and Times* [Brockville], 26 January, A6.

Reeve, Alan. 1998. "The Panopticisation of Shopping: CCTV and Leisure Consumption." In *Surveillance, Closed Circuit Television, and Social Control,* ed. C. Norris, J. Moran, and G. Armstrong, 69-87. Aldershot, UK: Ashgate.

Rhodes, R.A.W. 1996. "The New Governance: Governing without Government." *Political Studies* 44: 652-67.

Rogers, Everett. 1995. *Diffusion of Innovation*. 4th ed. New York: Free Press.

–. 2003. *Diffusion of Innovation*. 5th ed. New York: Free Press.

Rose, Nicholas, and Peter Miller. 1992. "Political Power beyond the State: Problematics of Government." *British Journal of Sociology* 43, 2: 173-205.

Royal Canadian Mounted Police. 2001. "CCTV Q&A." Released by Kelowna RCMP.

–. 2003. "Assessment." RCMP Memorandum, 17 September. Released by the Office of the Information and Privacy Commissioner of Canada.

–. 2005. "Talking Points Pre-Meeting with OPC." 22 March. Released by the Office of the Information and Privacy Commissioner of Canada.

Schmidt, Doug. 2003. "Street Cameras Opposed: Too Intrusive, Most Argue." *Windsor Star,* 26 February, A3.

Sheller, Mimi, and John Urry. 2003. "Mobile Transformations of 'Public' and 'Private' Life." *Theory, Culture, and Society* 20, 3: 107-25.

Sherk, Lance. 2004. *Peterborough Downtown Business Improvement Area Proposal for Security Cameras in Downtown Area*. Staff Report PLPD04-085. Peterborough: City of Peterborough.

Sim, Jane, and Paula Schuck. 1999. "Bar Introduces Metal Detectors in Knife Crackdown." *London Free Press,* 21 January, A3.

Simon, Jonathan. 2007. *Governing through Crime*. Oxford: Oxford University Press.

Sorensen, Chris. 2001. "Surveillance Cameras Would Cut Crime: Expert: The Devices Could Cut Crime in Area by up to 5%, Advocate Says." *Vancouver Sun,* 31 July, B1.

Statistics Canada. 2001. "2001 Community Profile: Sudbury, Ontario." Ottawa: Statistics Canada.

Stewart, Brian. 2002. "Baie-Comeau Surveillance Cameras." RDIMS#39386 v2, 27 December. Ottawa: Office of the Information and Privacy Commissioner of Canada. Released by the Office of the Information and Privacy Commissioner of Canada.

–. 2004. "Proposed Project on Video Surveillance." 22 March. Ottawa: Office of the Information and Privacy Commissioner of Canada. Released by the Office of the Information and Privacy Commissioner of Canada.

Stop the Cameras Coalition. 2004. "Submission to City Council" [Peterborough]. 12 October.

Strang, David, and John W. Meyer. 1993. "Institutional Conditions for Diffusion." *Theory and Society* 22, 2: 487-511.

Sudbury Metro Centre. 1996. "Downtown CCTV Committee Minutes." Sudbury, 13 November.

Sudbury Star. 1996. "Police Chief Should Heed Orwell's Warning." Letter to the Editor. *Sudbury Star,* 19 November, A5.

Surveillance Camera Awareness Network. 2009. *A Report on Surveillance Cameras in Canada: Part 1*. Kingston: The Surveillance Project, Queen's University.

The Surveillance Project. 2008. "The Globalization of Personal Data Project: An International Survey on Privacy and Surveillance." Kingston, The Surveillance Project, Queen's University.

Taylor, David. 1999. "We Don't Need Video Surveillance." *Recorder and Times* [Brockville], 15 January, A6.

Thompson, Scott. 2009. "A Kind of Prohibition: Targets of the Liquor Control Board of Ontario's Interdiction List, 1953-1955." In *Surveillance: Power, Problems, and Politics,* ed. Sean P. Hier and Josh Greenberg, 59-84. Vancouver: UBC Press.

Transport Canada. 2005. *Exploring Canadians' Attitudes on Issues Related to National Security*. Project #T8053-050201/001/CY. Ottawa: EKOS. Released by the Department of Justice.

Transportation and Works. 2005a. *Corporate Report 2005.082*. Thunder Bay: City of Thunder Bay.

–. 2005b. *Corporate Report 2005.178*. Thunder Bay: City of Thunder Bay.

–. 2008. *Corporate Report 2008.004*. Thunder Bay: City of Thunder Bay.

Upton, Sean. 1992. "Does Zero Tolerance Go Too Far? No-Nonsense Approach of Hull Police Can Embarrass Officers and Bystanders." *Ottawa Citizen,* 30 November, C1.

Vancouver Police Board. 2000. "Minutes of Regular Meeting." Vancouver, 29 June.
–. 2005. "Closed Circuit TV (CCTV) – Update and Recommendation." Submission from Axel Hovbrender, Inspector, Commanding District Four, to Vancouver Police Board, 9 May. Board Report No. 0539.
–. 2006. "CCTV Project Plan." Vancouver Police Board Minutes, 13 December.
Video Monitoring Advisory Committee. 1997. "Committee Minutes." Sudbury, 26 August.
Walby, Kevin. 2005a. "Open-Street Camera Surveillance and Governance in Canada." *Canadian Journal of Criminology and Criminal Justice* 47, 4: 655-83.
–. 2005b. "The Rise of Open-Street CCTV Surveillance in Canada." MA thesis, University of Victoria.
–. 2005c. "How Closed-Circuit Television Surveillance Organizes the Social: An Institutional Ethnography." *Canadian Journal of Sociology* 30, 2: 189-215.
–. 2006. "Little England: The Rise of Open-Street Closed-Circuit Television Surveillance in Canada." *Surveillance and Society* 4, 1-2: 29-51.
–. 2009. "Police Surveillance of Male-with-Male Public Sex in Ontario, 1983-94." In *Surveillance: Power, Problems, and Politics,* ed. Sean P. Hier and Josh Greenberg, 46-58. Vancouver: UBC Press.
Walker, Jack. 1969. "The Diffusion of Innovations among the American States." *American Political Science Review* 63, 3: 880-99.
Walters, William. 2009. "Anti-Policy and Anti-Politics: Critical Reflections on Certain Schemes to Govern Bad Things." *Cultural Studies* 11, 5: 267-88.
Waples, Sam, and Martin Gill. 2006. "Effectiveness of Redeployable CCTV." *Crime Prevention and Community Safety* 8, 1: 1-16.
Weatherill, Ken. 2006. "Closed Circuit Television Forum: Community Forum." PowerPoint presentation. Released by the Hamilton Police Service.
Webster, William R. 1996. "Closed Circuit Television and Governance: The Eve of a Surveillance Age." *Information Infrastructure and Policy* 5, 4: 253-63.
–. 2004. "The Diffusion, Regulation, and Governance of Closed-Circuit Television in the UK." *Surveillance and Society* 2, 2-3: 230-50.
–. 2009. "CCTV Policy in the UK: Reconsidering the Evidence Base." *Surveillance and Society* 6, 1: 10-22.
Welsh, Brandon C., and David P. Farrington. 2003. "Effects of Closed-Circuit Television on Crime." *Annals of the American Academy of Political and Social Science* 587, 1: 110-35.
–. 2004a. "Evidence-Based Crime Prevention: The Effectiveness of CCTV." *Crime Prevention and Community Safety* 6, 2: 21-33.
–. 2004b. "Surveillance for Crime Prevention in Public Space: Results and Policy Choices in Britain and America." *Criminology and Public Policy* 3, 3: 497-525.
–. 2005. "Evidence-Based Crime Prevention: Conclusions and Directions for a Safer Society." *Canadian Journal of Criminology and Criminal Justice* 47, 2: 337-54.
Williams, K., and C. Johnstone. 2000. "The Politics of the Selective Gaze: Closed Circuit Television and the Policing of Public Space." *Law and Social Change* 34, 2: 183-210.
Zajac, Ronald. 2003. "Downtown Got through a Tough Year: Businesses Faced Many Challenges from King St. Work to Fewer Tourists." *Recorder and Times* [Brockville], 25 November, A3.

Index